ACCA

Applied Skills

Taxation (TX – UK) FA 2024

Exam Practice Kit

For exams in June 2025, September 2025, December 2025 and March 2026

Nineteenth edition 2024

ISBN 9781 0355 2561 4

Previous ISBN 9781 0355 1326 0

eISBN 9781 0355 2568 3

British Library Cataloguing-in-Publication Data

A catalogue record for this book is available from the British Library

Published by

BPP Learning Media Ltd
BPP House, Aldine Place
142–144 Uxbridge Road
London W12 8AA

learningmedia.bpp.com

> Your learning materials are printed on paper obtained from traceable sustainable sources.

All rights reserved. No part of this publication may be reproduced, stored in a retrieval system or transmitted in any form or by any means, graphic, electronic or mechanical including photocopying, recording or otherwise, without the prior written permission of the publisher.

The contents of these learning materials are intended as a guide and not professional advice. Although every effort has been made to ensure that the contents of this book are correct at the time of going to press, BPP makes no warranty that the information in this book is accurate or complete and accept no liability for any loss or damage suffered by any person acting or refraining from acting as a result of the material in these learning materials.

© BPP Learning Media Ltd 2025

A note about copyright

Breach of copyright is a form of theft. Without the express permission of BPP you are breaching copyright if you:

- Photocopy our materials
- Print our digital materials in order to share them with or forward them to a third party or use them in any way other than in connection with your BPP studies
- Distribute our digital materials online (including sharing them with third parties and uploading them to websites)

Please note that eBooks are sold on a single user licence basis.

NO AI TRAINING. Unless otherwise agreed in writing, the use of BPP material for the purpose of AI training is not permitted. Any use of this material to "train" generative artificial intelligence (AI) technologies is prohibited, as is providing archived or cached data sets containing such material to another person or entity.

Contents

Finding questions

Question index	iv
Topic index	x
About this BPP Exam Practice Kit	xii
The exam	xiii
Passing the TX – UK exam	xv
Essential skills areas to be successful in Taxation (TX – UK)	xvii
Exam success skills	xxi

Questions and answers

Questions	3
Answers	159

Exam Practice

Mock exam 1 (September 2016 (amended to FA 2024))

Questions	365
Answers	381

Mock exam 2 (ACCA Specimen exam (updated to FA 2024))

Questions	401
Answers	417

Mock exam 3 (December 2016 (amended to FA 2024))

Questions	443
Answers	461

Mock exam 4 (Section C from March/June 2024)

Questions	481
Answers	499

Tax Tables	517
Additional CBE Mock Exam	525

Question index

The headings in this checklist/index indicate the main topics of questions, but questions may cover several different topics. Questions set under the old F6 Taxation (TX – UK) exam format are included in this Kit because their style and content are similar to those that may appear in the Taxation (TX – UK) exams from 1 September 2016.

Some of these questions have been amended to reflect the new exam format and this is shown by (amended) in the title of the question.

	Marks	Time allocation (mins)	Page number Questions	Page number Answers
Part A: The UK tax system and its administration				
Section A				
1-10 OTQ bank – The UK tax system and its administration 1	20	36	3	159
11-20 OTQ bank – The UK tax system and its administration 2	20	36	6	161
21-25 OTQ bank – The UK tax system and its administration 3	10	18	9	163
Section B				
26-30 OT case – Domingo and Fargo (June 2009) (amended)	10	18	11	165
31-35 OT case – Ernest (June 2010) (amended)	10	18	12	165
36-40 OT case – Thai Curry Ltd	10	18	13	166
Section C				
41 John	10	18	16	168
42 Sugar plc	10	18	16	169
Part B: Income tax and NIC liabilities				
Section A				
43-52 OTQ bank – Income tax and NIC liabilities 1	20	36	17	171
53-62 OTQ bank – Income tax and NIC liabilities 2	20	36	19	174
63-72 OTQ bank – Income tax and NIC liabilities 3	20	36	23	177
73-77 OTQ bank – Income tax and NIC liabilities 4	10	18	25	180
Section B				
78-82 OT case – Ann, Basil and Chloe (December 2008) (amended)	10	18	27	181

	Marks	Time allocation (mins)	Page number Questions	Page number Answers
83-87 OT case – Rosie and Sam (December 2012) (amended)	10	18	28	182
88-92 OT case – Chi (June 2014) (amended)	10	18	30	183
Section C				
93 Kagan (September/December 2019)	10	18	32	186
94 Michael and Sean (June 2012) (amended)	10	18	34	189
95 Paul and Palu Ltd (March/June 2021) (amended)	10	18	35	190
96 Lucy	10	18	35	192
97 Poppy (March/June 2022)	15	27	36	194
98 Kazuo (Mar/Jun 2023)	10	18	37	195
99 Joe (December 2010) (amended)	15	27	38	195
100 Esme (September/December 2023)	15	27	38	197
101 Hannah and Gregor (Mar/Jun 2023, amended)	15	27	39	200
102 Alfred and Amaia (March/June 2021) (amended)	15	27	40	201
103 John (June 2013) (amended)	15	27	41	204
104 Wai (June 2015) (amended)	15	27	43	207
105 Samson and Delilah (September/December 2015) (amended)	15	27	44	210
106 Petula (March/June 2017)	15	27	45	213
107 Dill (September/December 2017) (amended)	15	27	46	216
108 Danh (March/June 2018)	15	27	47	219
109 Martin (September/December 2018)	15	27	48	222
110 Tonie (March/June 2019)	15	27	50	225
111 Alicia (September/December 2022)	10	18	51	227
112 Dom (September/December 2022)	15	27	52	229

Part C: Chargeable gains for individuals

Section A

	Marks	Time allocation (mins)	Page number Questions	Page number Answers
113-122 OTQ bank – Chargeable gains for individuals 1	20	18	53	231
123-132 OTQ bank – Chargeable gains for individuals 2	20	36	56	234

Section B

	Marks	Time allocation (mins)	Page number Questions	Page number Answers
133-137 OT case – Aloi, Bon and Dinah (June 2011) (amended)	10	18	59	238
138-142 OT case – Ginger, Innocent and Nigel (June 2013) (amended)	10	18	61	239
143-147 OT case – Jerome (March/June 2016) (amended)	10	18	62	240
148-152 OT case – Hali and Goma (March/June 2019)	10	18	64	241
153-157 OT Case – Lily (March/June 2021)	10	18	65	243
Section C				
158 Jorge (December 2011) (amended)	10	18	68	246
159 Winston (June 2012) (amended)	10	18	68	248
160 Mick (June 2014) (amended)	10	18	69	250
161 Ruby (September/December 2015) (amended)	10	18	70	252
Part D: Inheritance tax				
Section A				
162-166 OTQ bank – Inheritance tax 1	10	18	71	255
167-176 OTQ bank – Inheritance tax 2	20	36	72	256
Section B				
177-181 OT case – Dianne (September/December 2023)	10	18	77	260
182-186 OT case – Rishi and Nagina (March/June 2022) (amended)	10	18	78	261
187-191 OT case – Zoe and Luke (June 2015) (amended)	10	18	80	263
192-196 OT case – Marcus (September/December 2015) (amended)	10	18	82	264
197-201 OT case – Lebna and Lulu (March/June 2019)	10	18	83	266
Section C				
202 Pere and Phil (June 2013) (amended)	10	18	86	268
203 Afiya (December 2013) (amended)	10	18	86	270
204 Kendra (June 2014) (amended)	10	18	87	272
205 James (March/June 2016)	10	18	87	273
206 Dembe (March/June 2019)	10	18	88	275

	Marks	Time allocation (mins)	Page number Questions	Page number Answers
Part E: Corporation tax liabilities				
Section A				
207-216 OTQ bank – Corporation tax liabilities 1	20	36	90	278
217-226 OTQ bank – Corporation tax liabilities 2	20	36	93	281
Section B				
227-231 OT case – Luna Ltd (June 2015) (amended)	10	18	97	284
232-236 OT case – Tay Ltd	10	18	98	285
237-241 OT case – Hyde plc group	10	18	99	287
Section C				
242 Problematic Ltd (June 2010) (amended)	10	18	102	289
243 Volatile Ltd (December 2009) (amended)	10	18	102	290
244 Maison Ltd (September/December 2019)	15	27	103	292
245 Black Ltd (December 2011) and Gastron Ltd (June 2009) (amended)	10	18	105	295
246 Crumble Ltd (September/December 2022)	15	27	105	297
247 Hopi Ltd (March/June 2018)	10	18	108	299
248 Kat (September/December 2018)	10	18	108	301
249 Venus Ltd (March/June 2023) (Mar/Jun 2023)	15	27	109	304
250 Mooncake Ltd (March/June 2021 amended)	15	27	111	308
251 Maximum Ltd (September/December 2023)	15	27	112	310
252 Lucky Ltd (September/December 2015) (amended)	15	27	114	313
253 Jump Ltd (March/June 2016)	15	27	115	315
254 Online Ltd (March/June 2017)	15	27	117	317
255 Last-Orders Ltd (September/December 2017)	15	27	118	320
256 Solo Ltd (March/June 2018)	15	27	120	323
257 Ash Ltd, Beech Ltd and Cedar Ltd (September/December 2018)	15	27	122	327

Introduction **vii**

	Marks	Time allocation (mins)	Page number Questions	Page number Answers
258 Aoede Ltd, Bianca Ltd and Charon Ltd (March/June 2019)	15	27	124	330
259 Mixture Ltd (March/June 2022)	15	27	125	333
Part F: Value added tax				
Section A				
260-264 OTQ bank – Value added tax 1	10	18	127	336
265-274 OTQ bank – Value added tax 2	20	36	129	337
Section B				
275-279 OT case – Anne (June 2009) (amended)	10	18	133	340
280-284 OT case – Auy and Bim (June 2010) (amended)	10	18	134	342
285-289 OT case – Mabel (March/June 2023)	10	18	136	342
290-294 OT case – Starfish Ltd (December 2011) (amended)	10	18	137	343
295-299 OT case – Greenzone Ltd (June 2013)	10	18	139	344
300-304 OT case – Long Ltd group (B) (June 2014) (amended)	10	18	140	346
305-309 OT case – Zim (June 2015) (amended)	10	18	142	348
310-314 OT case – Smart Ltd (September/December 2015) (amended)	10	18	144	349
315-319 OT case – Thidar (March/June 2019)	10	18	146	350
Section C				
320 Jogger Ltd (B) (December 2008) (amended)	10	18	149	352
321 Flick (June 2012) (amended)	10	18	149	353
322 Richard (December 2013) (amended)	10	18	150	354
323 Clueless Ltd (December 2012) (amended)	10	18	150	355
324 Garfield (March/June 2016)	10	18	151	356
325 Zhi (March/June 2017)	10	18	153	358
Mock Exams				
Mock exam 1 (September 2016 (amended to FA 2024))			365	381

	Marks	Time allocation (mins)	Page number Questions	Page number Answers
Mock exam 2 (ACCA Specimen exam (updated to FA 2024))			401	417
Mock exam 3 (December 2016 (amended to FA 2024))			443	461
Mock exam 4 (March/June 2024 (Section C from [Month] [Year]))			481	499

Topic index

Listed below are the key Taxation (TX – UK) syllabus topics and the numbers of the questions of this Kit (excluding the Mock exams) covering those topics.

If you need to concentrate your practice and revision on certain topics, or if you want to attempt all available questions that refer to a particular subject, you will find this index useful.

Syllabus topic	Question numbers	Course Book chapter
UK tax system	31–35, 41, 112	1, 17, 23
Computing taxable income and the income tax liability	78–82, 88–92, 93, 95, 96, 97, 102, 103, 104, 105, 106, 107, 108, 109, 110, 111, 112, 247, 325	2, 4
Employment income	96, 97, 98, 99, 100, 101, 103, 104, 105, 106, 107, 109, 110, 325	3, 4
Pensions	78–82, 83–87, 93, 103, 106, 107	5
Property income for individuals	102, 103, 108, 109, 110, 248	6
Computing trading income for individuals	88–92, 96, 108, 109	7, 8, 9
Trading losses for individuals	94, 97, 102, 107, 108	10
Partnerships	97, 106, 108, 109	11
National insurance contributions	88–92, 95, 96, 98, 111, 112, 247, 252, 325	12
Computing chargeable gains for individuals	83–87, 133–137, 138–142, 148–152, 158, 159, 160, 161, 248	13
Chargeable gains for individuals: Chattels and PPR exemption	143–147, 158	14
Chargeable gains for individuals: Business reliefs	133–137, 138–142, 143–147, 148–152, 160, 161, 325	15
Chargeable gains for individuals: Shares and securities	138–142, 160, 161	16
Self-assessment and payment of tax by individuals	26–30, 31–35, 41, 109, 133–137, 325	17
Inheritance tax	162–206	18
Computing taxable total profits (including property income and capital allowances for companies) and the corporation tax liability	95, 244, 246, 247, 248, 249, 250, 251, 252, 253, 255, 256, 257, 258, 259	8, 19
Chargeable gains for companies	227–231, 232–236, 242, 244, 248, 254, 255, 256, 257, 258	20

Syllabus topic	Question numbers	Course Book chapter
Losses for companies	243, 246, 250, 250, 251, 254, 256, 257, 258	21
Groups of companies	237–241, 245, 251, 253, 255	22
Self-assessment and payment of tax by companies	36–40, 42, 254	23
Value added tax	260–325	24, 25

 Videos can be viewed online by accessing your ebook version on VitalSource.

About this BPP Exam Practice Kit

TX – UK exam questions in this Kit have been grouped according to the section of the syllabus to which they mainly relate. There are also four mock exams which provide you the opportunity to refine your knowledge and skills as part of your final exam preparations.

As an ACCA Content Partner, BPP Learning Media gives you the opportunity to use the revision materials created by BPP's expert team of Subject Matter Experts who have years of experience authoring professional qualification content. The Subject Matter Experts ensure the content covers the depth and breadth of the syllabus and provides excellent support for your revision.

BPP Learning Media do everything possible to ensure the material is accurate and up to date when sending to print. In the event that any errors are found after the print date, they are uploaded to the following website: learningmedia.bpp.com/pages/errata.

Selecting questions

We provide signposts to help you plan your revision.

- A full question index
- A topic index listing all the questions that cover key topics, so that you can locate the questions that provide practice on these topics, and see the different ways in which they might be examined

Attempting mock exams

There are four mock exams that provide practice at coping with the pressures of the exam day. We strongly recommend that you attempt them under exam conditions.

Mock exam 1 is the September 2016 exam, Mock exam 2 is the Specimen exam, Mock exam 3 is the December 2016 exam and Mock exam 4 (Section C) is the March/June 2024 exam.

Question practice

This is the most important thing to do if you want to get through. Many of the most up-to-date exam questions are in this Kit. Practise doing them under timed conditions, then go through the answers and go back to the Course Book for any topic you are really having trouble with. Come back to a question a week later and try it again – you will be surprised at how much better you are getting. Be very ruthless with yourself at this stage – you have to do the question in the time, without looking at the answer. This will really sharpen your wits and make the exam experience less worrying. Just keep doing this and you will get better at doing questions and you will really find out what you know and what you don't know.

Practising as many exam-style questions as possible in the ACCA CBE practice platform will be the key to passing this exam. You must do questions under timed conditions and ensure you produce full answers to the discussion parts as well as doing the calculations.

Also ensure that you attempt all mock exams under exam conditions.

ACCA have launched a free on-demand resource designed to mirror the live exam experience helping you to become more familiar with the exam format. You can access the platform via the Study Support Resources section of the ACCA website navigating to the CBE question practice section and logging in with your myACCA credentials.

 Videos can be viewed online by accessing your ebook version on VitalSource.

The exam

Approach to examining the syllabus

- There is no choice in this exam, all questions have to be answered. You must therefore study the **entire syllabus**, there are no short-cuts.
- The first section of the exam consists of 15 **objective test questions**, worth two marks each. These will inevitably cover a **wide range of the syllabus**.
- The second section of the exam consists of three scenarios each being tested with five **objective test questions**, worth two marks each. You must make sure you **understand the scenario** before attempting the related questions.
- The third section of the exam consists of **three constructed response questions**, one 10-mark question and two 15-mark questions.
- Practising longer questions set in the third section of the exam under **timed conditions** is essential. BPP's **Exam Practice Kit** contains 10-mark and 15-mark questions on all areas of the syllabus. Answer all parts of the question. Even if you cannot do all of the calculation elements, you will still be able to gain marks in the discussion parts.
- **Answer selectively** – the examining team will expect you to consider carefully what is relevant and significant enough to include in your answer. Do not include unnecessary information.
- Keep an eye out for **articles** as the **examining team** will use **Student Accountant** to communicate with students. Tax rates, allowances and information on certain reliefs will be given in the exam. You should familiarise yourself with the information provided so that you know how to find it quickly in the exam.

Computer-based exams

All ACCA papers are computer-based examinations (CBEs). The CBE exams for Applied Knowledge modules can be taken at any time; these are referred to as 'exams on demand.' The Applied Skills and Strategic Professional exams can be sat in September, December, March and June of each year; these are referred to as 'exams on sitting.' Financial Management is an 'exam on sitting.' Computer-based examinations must be taken at an ACCA CBE Licensed Centre.

The exam is formatted as follows.

Section	Style of question type	Description	Proportion of exam (%)
A	Objective test (OT)	15 questions × 2 marks	30
B	Objective test (OT) case	3 questions × 10 marks Each question will contain 5 subparts each worth 2 marks	30
C	Constructed Response (Long questions)	1 question × 10 marks 2 questions × 15 marks	40
Total			100

The TX exam pass mark is 50%. The exam is three hours in duration and the timings of the questions are based on this time allocation. Prior to the start of each exam there will be time allocated for students to be informed of the exam instructions.

Section A and B questions will be selected from the entire syllabus. The responses to each question or subpart in the case of OT cases are marked automatically as either correct or incorrect by computer.

The 10-mark Section C question can come from any part of the syllabus. The 15-mark Section C questions will mainly focus on the following syllabus areas, but a minority of marks can be drawn from any other area of the syllabus:

- Income tax (syllabus area B)
- Corporation tax (syllabus area E)

The responses to these questions are human marked.

Remote invigilated exams

In certain geographical areas, it may be possible for you to take your exam remotely. This option, which is subject to strict conditions, can offer increased flexibility and convenience under certain circumstances. Further guidance, including the detailed requirements and conditions for taking the exam by this method, is contained on ACCA's website at:

accaglobal.com/an/en/student/exam-entry-and-administration/about-our-exams/remote-exams/remote-session-exams.html

Passing the TX – UK exam

learningmedia.bpp.com/catalog?pagename=ACCA_Syllabus_Changes

accaglobal.com/gb/en/student/exam-support-resources/fundamentals-exams-study-resources/f6/syllabus-study-guide.html

Revising TX – UK

All questions are compulsory so you must revise the **whole** syllabus. Since the exam includes 15 objective test questions in Section A and 15 objective test questions in Section B, you should expect questions to cover a large part of the syllabus. Selective revision **will limit** the number of questions you can answer and hence reduce your chances of passing. It is better to go into the exam knowing a reasonable amount about most of the syllabus rather than concentrating on a few topics to the exclusion of the rest.

At BPP Learning Media we realise that you need more than just questions and model answers to get the most from your question practice.

- Our Top tips included for certain questions provide essential advice on tackling questions, presenting answers and the key points that answers need to include.
- We show you how you can pick up easy marks on some questions, as we know that picking up all readily available marks often can make the difference between passing and failing.
- We include marking guides to show you what the examining team rewards.
- We include comments from the examining team to show you where students struggled or performed well in the actual exam.
- We refer to the FA 2024 Course Book (for exams in June 2025, September 2025, December 2025 and March 2026) for detailed coverage of the topics covered in questions.

Using feedback obtained from the ACCA examining team review:

- We look at the dos and don'ts of revising for, and taking, ACCA exams.
- We focus on Taxation (TX – UK); we discuss revising the syllabus, what to do (and what not to do) in the exam, how to approach different types of question and ways of obtaining easy marks.

accaglobal.com/gb/en/student/exam-support-resources/fundamentals-exams-study-resources/f6/examiners-reports1.html

Displaying the right qualities

- You will be required to identify the requirements of objective test questions quickly, so that you can make your answers confidently within the available time.
- In constructed response questions you will be required to carry out calculations, with clear workings and a logical structure. If your numbers are not perfect, you will not necessarily lose too many marks so long as your method is correct and you have stated any assumptions you have made.
- You will also be expected to apply your tax knowledge to the facts of each particular question and also to identify the compliance issues for your client.
- You may also be required to describe rules and conditions, so take care to practise the descriptive elements of the answers.

Avoiding weaknesses

- There is no choice in this exam, all questions have to be answered. You must therefore study the entire syllabus, there are no short-cuts.
- Ability to answer objective test questions and cases improves with practice. Try to get as much practice with these questions as you can.
- The constructed response questions will be based on simple scenarios and answers must be focused and specific to the requirement of the question.
- Answer all parts of the constructed response questions. Even if you cannot do all the calculation elements, you will still be able to gain marks in the descriptive parts.

Gaining the easy marks

Easy marks in this exam tend to fall into three categories.

Objective test questions (OTQs)

Some OTQs are easier than others. Answer those that you feel fairly confident about as quickly as you can. Come back later to those you find more difficult. This could be a way of making use of the time in the examination most efficiently and effectively. Some OTQs will not involve calculations. Make sure that you understand the wording of 'written' OTQs before selecting your answer.

Calculations in Section C questions

There will always be basic marks available for straightforward tasks such as putting easy figures into proformas, for example putting the cost figure for an addition into a capital allowances proforma. Do not miss out on these easy marks by not learning your proformas properly.

Discussions in Section C questions

A constructed response question may separate descriptive requirements from calculations, so that you do not need to do the calculations first in order to answer the descriptive parts. This means that you should be able to gain marks from the descriptive parts without having to complete the calculations.

Descriptive requirements may focus on administrative, or compliance, details such as filing deadlines and tax payment dates. Make your points concisely, bearing in mind that one mark usually equates to one point to be made.

Read the question carefully and more than once, to ensure you are actually answering the specific requirements. Don't write about matters which are not specifically required – even if these are technically correct, you will not gain any marks and will waste valuable time.

Tackling objective test case questions

First, read the whole case scenario. Highlight any specific instructions or assumptions, such as 'Ignore the annual exempt amount' in a capital gains tax question. Then skim through the requirements of the five questions. If you are sitting your exam in-centre, you can make notes on the on-screen scratchpad available to you in the exam. If you are sitting your exam via remote invigilation only the on-screen scratchpad can be used. You can familiarise yourself with the on-screen scratchpad by testing it on the Practice Platform.

The questions are independent of each other and can be answered in any order. Some of the OTQs will be easier than others. For example, you may be asked to identify the filing date for a tax return and the penalty for late filing. Answer these OTQs quickly.

Other OTQs will be more difficult and/or complex. There are two types of OTQ that may take you longer to answer.

The first more time-consuming OTQ will involve doing a computation. For example, you may be asked to calculate the personal allowance available to a taxpayer whose adjusted net income exceeds £100,000. You will probably need to use a quick pro-forma to answer a computational question like this.

If the OTQ is a multiple-choice question, remember that the wrong answers will usually involve common errors, so don't assume that because you have the same answer as one of the options that your answer is necessarily correct! Double check to make sure you haven't made any silly mistakes, such as deducting the whole of the excess of adjusted net income over the £100,000 threshold (instead of half of it) when working out the restriction for the personal allowance. If you haven't got the same answer as any of the options, rework your computation, thinking carefully about what errors you could have made. If you still haven't got one of the options, choose the one which is nearest to your answer.

The second more time-consuming OTQ is one where you are asked to consider a number of statements and identify which one (or more) of them is correct. Make sure that you read each statement at least twice before making your selection. Be careful to follow the requirements of the OTQ exactly, for example if you are asked to identify TWO correct statements.

Essential skills areas to be successful in Taxation (TX – UK)

We think there are three areas you should develop in order to achieve exam success in TX:

(a) Knowledge application
(b) Specific ATX skills
(c) Exam success skills

These are shown in the diagram below.

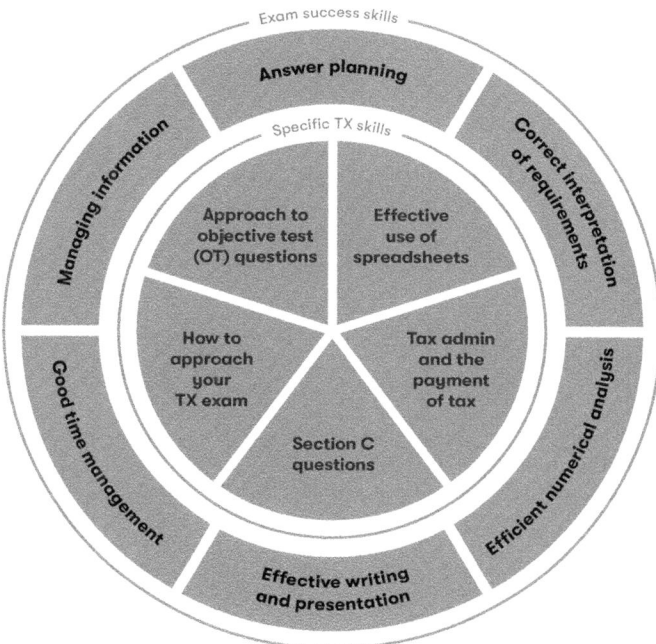

Specific TX – UK skills

These are the skills specific to TX – UK that we think you need to develop in order to pass the exam.

In the BPP TX – UK Course Book, there are five **Skills checkpoints** which define each skill and show how it is applied in answering a question. A brief summary of each skill is given below.

Skill 1: Approach to objective test (OT) questions

Section A of the exam will include 15 OT questions worth two marks each. Section B of the exam will include three OT cases, worth 10 marks each. Each OT case contains a group of five OT questions based around a single scenario. 60% of your TX exam is therefore made up of OT questions. It is essential that you have a good approach to answering these questions. OT questions are auto-marked; your workings will therefore not be considered; you have to answer the whole question correctly to earn their two marks.

A step-by-step technique for tackling OT questions is outlined below:

> **General guidance for approaching OT questions**
>
> **STEP 1: Answer the questions you know first.**
>
> If you're having difficulty answering a question, move on and come back to tackle it once you've answered all the questions you know.
>
> It is often quicker to answer discursive style OT questions first, leaving more time for calculations.

> **General guidance for approaching OT questions**
>
> **STEP 2: Answer all questions.**
>
> There is no penalty for an incorrect answer in ACCA exams; there is nothing to be gained by leaving an OT question unanswered. If you are stuck on a question, as a last resort, it is worth selecting the option you consider most likely to be correct and moving on. Make a note of the question using the flag functionality, so if you have time after you have answered the rest of the questions, you can revisit it.

> **Guidance for answering specific OT questions**
>
> **STEP 3: Read the requirement first!**
>
> The requirement will be stated in bold text in the exam. Identify what you are being asked to do, any technical knowledge required and **what type of OT question** you are dealing with. Look for key words in the requirement such as "which **TWO** of the following," "which of the following is **NOT**"

> **Guidance for answering specific OT questions**
>
> **STEP 4: Apply your technical knowledge to the data presented in the question.**
>
> Take your time working through questions, and make sure to read through each answer option with care. OT questions are designed so that each answer option is plausible. Work through each response option and eliminate those you know are incorrect.

Skills checkpoint 1 in the BPP TX – UK Course Book covers this technique in detail through application of an OT case question.

 Videos can be viewed online by accessing your ebook version on VitalSource.

Skill 2: Effective use of spreadsheets

It is very likely that you will be required to use the spreadsheet response option in the constructed workspace for Section C questions. It is imperative that you know how to use the spreadsheet functions to prepare accurate and easy to follow calculations.

The key steps are outlined below:

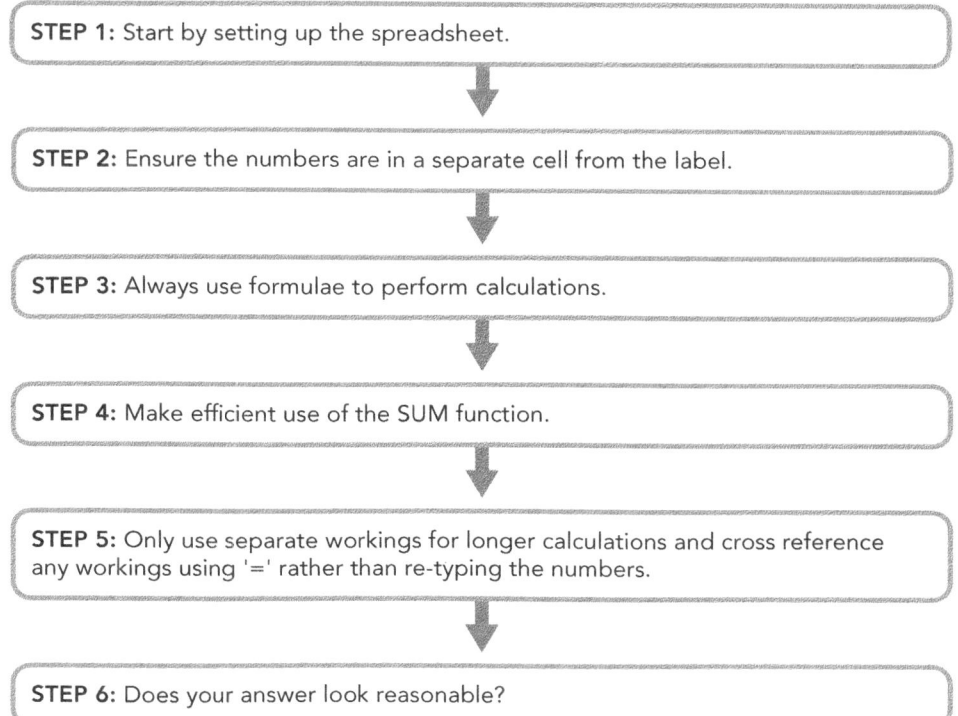

STEP 1: Start by setting up the spreadsheet.

STEP 2: Ensure the numbers are in a separate cell from the label.

STEP 3: Always use formulae to perform calculations.

STEP 4: Make efficient use of the SUM function.

STEP 5: Only use separate workings for longer calculations and cross reference any workings using '=' rather than re-typing the numbers.

STEP 6: Does your answer look reasonable?

Skills checkpoint 2 in the BPP TX – UK Course Book covers this technique in detail through application to a question.

Videos can be viewed online by accessing your ebook version on VitalSource.

Skill 3: The UK tax system and its administration

You must study the whole syllabus in order to pass the TX exam but having the administration knowledge at your fingertips will give you extra time in the exam to answer the more difficult questions.

This Skills checkpoint gives you a list of quickfire questions to help you learn the basic information.

Videos can be viewed online by accessing your ebook version on VitalSource.

Skill 4: Section C questions

Section C questions contain one 10-mark question and two 15-mark questions. One 15-mark question will focus on income tax and the other one will focus on corporation tax. This means that you know roughly what to expect and you can use proformas where relevant to help with the long calculations. Discursive elements will be relatively short. 10-mark questions often cover more than one tax and are designed to act as a bridge question between TX and the higher-level exam, ATX.

A step-by-step technique for attempting these questions is outlined below:

> **STEP 1:** Read the requirements first and read them carefully.

> **STEP 2:** Learn and use the proformas where relevant.

> **STEP 3:** Input easy numbers from the question directly into your proforma.

> **STEP 4:** Always use formulae to perform basic calculations.

> **STEP 5:** Show longer workings separately.

Skills checkpoint 4 in the BPP TX – UK Course Book covers this technique in detail through application to a question.

> Videos can be viewed online by accessing your ebook version on VitalSource.

Skill 5: How to approach your TX exam

You can answer your TX exam in whatever order you prefer. It is important that you adopt a strategy that works best for you. We would suggest that you decide on your preferred approach and practice it by doing a timed mock exam before your real exam.

A suggested approach to tackling your TX exam is outlined below.

Complete Section A first – allocated time 54 minutes

Tackle any easier OT questions first. Often discursive style questions can be answered quickly, saving more time for calculations. Do not leave any questions unanswered. Even if you are unsure make a reasoned guess.

Complete Section B next – allocated time 54 minutes

You will have 18 mins of exam time to allocate to each of the three OT case questions in Section B. Use the same approach to OT questions as discussed for Section A.

There will normally be discursive and numerical questions within each case. Again, it is better to tackle the discursive type questions first and make a reasoned guess for any questions you are unsure on.

Finally, complete Section C – allocated time 72 minutes

Start with the question you feel most confident with.

Skills checkpoint 5 covers this technique in more detail.

> Videos can be viewed online by accessing your ebook version on VitalSource.

Exam success skills

Passing the TX exam requires more than applying syllabus knowledge and demonstrating the specific TX skills; it also requires the development of excellent exam technique through question practice.

We consider the following six skills to be vital for exam success. The Skills checkpoints show how each of these skills can be applied in the exam.

Exam success skill 1

Managing information

Questions in the exam will present you with a lot of information. The skill is how you handle this information to make the best use of your time. The key is determining how you will approach the exam and then actively reading the questions.

Advice on developing: Managing information

Approach

The exam is three hours long. There is no designated 'reading' time at the start of the exam, however, one approach that can work well is to start the exam by spending 10–15 minutes carefully reading through all of the questions to familiarise yourself with the exam.

Once you feel familiar with the exam, consider the order in which you will attempt the questions; always attempt them in your order of preference. For example, you may want to leave to last the question you consider to be the most difficult.

If you do take this approach, remember to adjust the time available for each question appropriately – see Exam success skill 6: Good time management.

If you find that this approach doesn't work for you, don't worry – you can develop your own technique.

Active reading

You must take an active approach to reading each question. Focus on the requirement first, underlining/highlighting key verbs such as 'prepare,' 'comment,' 'explain,' 'discuss,' to ensure you answer the question properly. Then read the rest of the question, underlining/highlighting and annotating important and relevant information, and making notes of any relevant technical information you think you will need.

Exam success skill 2

Correct interpretation of the requirements

The active verb used often dictates the approach that written answers should take (eg 'explain,' 'discuss,' 'evaluate'). It is important you identify and use the verb to define your approach. The **correct interpretation of the requirements** skill means correctly producing only what is being asked for by a requirement. Anything not required will not earn marks.

Advice on developing: Correct interpretation of the requirements

This skill can be developed by analysing question requirements and applying this process:

Step 1 Read the requirement

Firstly, read the requirement a couple of times slowly and carefully and highlight the active verbs. Use the active verbs to define what you plan to do. Make sure you identify any sub-requirements and any topics which you are specifically told you do not need to cover in your answer. Also note the number of marks available for each requirement or sub-requirement, as this will indicate the time available and hence the level of depth required in your answer.

Step 2   **Read the rest of the question**

By reading the requirement first, you will have an idea of what you are looking out for as you read through the scenario. This is a great time saver and means you don't end up having to read the whole question in full twice. You should do this in an active way – see Exam success skill 1: Managing Information.

Step 3   **Read the requirement again**

Read the requirement again to remind yourself of the exact wording before starting your answer. This will capture any misinterpretation of the requirements or any missed requirements entirely. This should become a habit in your approach and, with repeated practice, you will find the focus, relevance and depth of your answer plan will improve.

Exam success skill 3

Answer planning: Priorities, structure and logic

This skill requires the planning of the key aspects of an answer which accurately and completely responds to the requirement.

Advice on developing: Answer planning: Priorities, structure and logic

Everyone will have a preferred style for an answer plan. For example, it may be a mind map, bullet-pointed lists or simply making some notes. Choose the approach that you feel most comfortable with, or, if you are not sure, try out different approaches for different questions until you have found your preferred style.

For 10-mark Section C questions, it can be useful to draw up a separate answer plan in the format of your choosing (eg a mind map or bullet-pointed lists). You will want to remind yourself of key facts from the scenario to avoid having to re-read the question – you should at the very least make a few notes including vital information such as the following key factors:

- Nature of the taxpayer: is it an individual or a company?
- For individuals: their age, any family relationships, their residence and domicile status, whether they're a basic, higher or additional rate taxpayer, and whether they've used their CGT annual exempt amount/IHT exemptions
- For companies: their ownership structure and group relationships
- Relevant dates: the year end(s) of businesses, dates of actual or proposed transactions, the date that a business started, dates of gifts (or death!) for IHT

Exam success skill 4

Efficient numerical analysis

This skill aims to maximise the marks awarded by making clear to the marker the process of arriving at your answer. This is achieved by laying out an answer such that, even if you make a few errors, you can still score subsequent marks for follow-on calculations. It is vital that you do not lose marks purely because the marker cannot follow what you have done.

Advice on developing: Efficient numerical analysis

This skill can be developed by applying the following process:

Step 1   **Use a standard proforma working where relevant**

If answers can be laid out in a standard proforma then always plan to do so. This will help the marker to understand your working and allocate the marks easily. It will also help you to work through the figures in a methodical and time-efficient way.

Step 2   **Show your workings**

Keep your workings as clear and simple as possible and ensure they are cross-referenced to the main part of your answer.

Step 3 Keep moving!

It is important to remember that, in an exam situation, it is difficult to get every number 100% correct. The key is therefore ensuring you do not spend too long on any single calculation. If you are struggling with a solution then make a sensible assumption, state it and move on.

Exam success skill 5

Effective writing and presentation

Written answers should be presented so that the marker can clearly see the points you are making, presented in the format specified in the question. The skill is to provide efficient written answers with sufficient breadth of points that answer the question, in the right depth, in the time available.

Advice on developing: Effective writing and presentation

Step 1 Use headings

Using the headings and sub-headings from your answer plan will give your answer structure, order and logic. This will ensure your answer links back to the requirement and is clearly signposted, making it easier for the marker to understand the different points you are making. Underlining your headings will also help the marker.

Step 2 Write your answer in short, but full, sentences

Use short, punchy sentences with the aim that every sentence should say something different and generate marks. Write in full sentences, ensuring your style is professional.

Step 3 Do your calculations first and explanation second

Questions sometimes ask for an explanation with supporting calculations. The best approach is to prepare the calculation first then add the explanation. Performing the calculation first should enable you to explain what you have done.

Exam success skill 6

Good time management

This skill means planning your time across all the requirements so that all tasks have been attempted at the end of the three hours available and actively checking on time during your exam. This is so that you can flex your approach and prioritise requirements which, in your judgement, will generate the maximum marks in the available time remaining.

Advice on developing: Good time management

The exam is three hours long, which translates to 1.8 minutes per mark. At the beginning of a question, work out the amount of time you should be spending on each requirement. If you take the approach of spending 10–15 minutes reading and planning at the start of the exam, adjust the time allocated to each question accordingly.

Keep an eye on the clock

Aim to attempt all requirements but be ready to be ruthless and move on if your answer is not going as planned. The challenge for many is sticking to planned timings. Be aware this is difficult to achieve in the early stages of your studies and be ready to let this skill develop over time.

Questions

> **Part A: The UK tax system and its administration**
>
> Part A covers the UK tax system and its administration, the subject of Chapters 1, 17 and 23 of the BPP Course Book for Taxation (TX – UK).

Section A

OTQ bank – The UK tax system and its administration 1

(36 mins)

1 Which TWO of the following statements are true about inheritance tax?
- ☐ It is an indirect tax.
- ☐ It is a progressive tax.
- ☐ It is an environmental tax.
- ☐ It is a redistributive tax.

(2 marks)

2 Bod Ltd's employees are all paid on the last day of the calendar month. The PAYE information for September 2024 was not filed with HM Revenue and Customs (HMRC), using the real time information (RTI) software, until 7 November 2024. This was the second late submission during the tax year 2024/25.

Indicate the latest date by which Bod Ltd should have filed the PAYE information for September 2024, and whether or not a penalty will have been charged.

	Date	Penalty alternative
○	30 September 2024	Penalty not charged
○	30 September 2024	Penalty charged
○	22 October 2024	Penalty not charged
○	22 October 2024	Penalty charged

(2 marks)

3   Which TWO of the following have legal force?
    ☐ Revenue and Customs Brief
    ☐ A Statutory Instrument
    ☐ An Act of Parliament
    ☐ An Extra Statutory Concession   (2 marks)

4   Fare plc wishes to appeal against the assessment of £10,000,000 of corporation tax by HM Revenue & Customs (HMRC).

    By whom is Fare plc's appeal most likely to be heard?
    ○ By the First Tier Tribunal
    ○ By the Upper Tribunal
    ○ By the Supreme Court
    ○ By the Court of Appeal   (2 marks)

5   Daren made a chargeable gain of £50,000 on the sale of a painting on 30 June 2024. This was Daren's only disposal in the tax year 2024/25. He had previously paid his income tax through deduction at source so has not had to submit a self-assessment tax return.

    By what date must Daren notify HM Revenue & Customs (HMRC) of his chargeability to capital gains tax in relation to the gain made on 30 June 2024 and by what date must he pay the capital gains tax liability?

Notification	Payment
○ 31 January 2026	31 January 2026
○ 5 October 2025	31 January 2026
○ 5 October 2025	31 July 2026
○ 31 January 2026	31 July 2026

    (2 marks)

6   Mammoth Ltd commenced trading on 1 January 2025. The company's profits have been:

Period	£
Year ended 31 December 2025	524,000
Year ended 31 December 2026	867,000
Year ended 31 December 2027	912,000

    Throughout all of these periods, Mammoth Ltd had one associated company.

    What is the first year for which Mammoth Ltd will be required to pay its corporation tax liability by quarterly instalments?
    ○ Year ended 31 December 2026
    ○ None of the years ended 31 December 2025, 2026 or 2027
    ○ Year ended 31 December 2027
    ○ Year ended 31 December 2025   (2 marks)

7   Taxes can be capital taxes or revenue taxes, although some taxes are neither type of tax.

Identify, by clicking on the relevant boxes in the table below, the correct classification for the following three taxes.

Value added tax	NEITHER TYPE	CAPITAL TAX	REVENUE TAX
Inheritance tax	NEITHER TYPE	CAPITAL TAX	REVENUE TAX
National insurance contributions	NEITHER TYPE	CAPITAL TAX	REVENUE TAX

(2 marks)

8   In the year ended 31 March 2025, Luck Ltd had taxable total profits of £400,000 and received the following dividends:

	£
From unconnected companies	5,200
From a company in which Luck Ltd has an 80% shareholding	4,300
From a company in which Luck Ltd has a 45% shareholding	1,400

What is the value of Luck Ltd's profits for the year ended 31 March 2025 for the purposes of determining whether it should pay corporation tax in instalments?

Pull down list
- £405,200
- £405,700
- £406,600
- £410,900

(2 marks)

9   Hassan filed his self-assessment tax return for the tax year 2022/23 on 31 August 2024. The return showed a tax liability of £6,200, which Hassan paid in full on 31 August 2024.

Which THREE of the following penalties could Hassan be charged in respect of the late filing of his self-assessment tax return?   *(March/June 2022)*

☐ £100 fixed penalty
☐ £900 of daily penalties
☐ £200 fixed penalty
☐ £310 tax geared penalty
☐ £620 tax geared penalty
☐ £2,120 of daily penalties

(2 marks)

10   Ruby was required to make payments on account of £5,000 in total towards her tax liability for the tax year 2024/25.

She paid both payments on account, of £2,500 each, on 1 July 2025.

After completing her self-assessment tax return for the tax year 2024/25, Ruby calculates that her tax liability for that year is £7,000.

Ruby pays her balancing payment of £2,000 on 31 January 2026.

How much late payment interest will Ruby have to pay in relation to her tax liability for the tax year 2024/25?   *(March/June 2023)*

- ○ £81
- ○ £388
- ○ £194
- ○ £543

(2 marks)

(Total = 20 marks)

OTQ bank – The UK tax system and its administration 2
(36 mins)

11   HM Revenue & Customs (HMRC) issued Lenny with a notice to file his self-assessment tax return for the tax year 2024/25 on 30 April 2025. Lenny submitted the return online on 15 March 2026.

Match the due date for submission of the online return and the date by which HMRC will have to notify Lenny of a compliance check into this return.

| 31 October 2025 |
| 31 January 2026 |
| 15 March 2027 |
| 30 April 2027 |

| Submission |
| Notification |

(2 marks)

12 Gareth's tax payable for 2023/24 and 2024/25 is as follows:

	2023/24 £	2024/25 £
Income tax	10,000	12,500
Class 4 NIC	2,000	2,500
Capital gains tax	1,000	2,000

Gareth always pays the correct amount of tax on each due date.

What is the amount payable by Gareth to HM Revenue & Customs (HMRC) on 31 January 2026 in respect of the tax year 2024/25?

[▼]

Pull down list
- £3,000
- £4,000
- £4,500
- £5,000

(2 marks)

---

13 For the year to 31 March 2025 Key Ltd, which is not a large company, had a corporation tax liability of £22,400. It paid £10,000 of this liability on 1 December 2025 and the remaining £12,400 on 1 February 2026.

What is the interest payable by Key Ltd on late paid tax?

£ [ ]   (2 marks)

---

14 Tom is employed and also has some self-employment income.

Tom's income tax liability and class 4 national insurance contributions (NICs) for the tax year 2024/25 totalled £39,000, of which £5,000 was deducted via PAYE.

Tom's income tax liability and class 4 NICs for the tax year 2025/26 will total £51,000, of which £6,000 will be deducted via PAYE.

What will be the amount of each of Tom's payments on account for the tax year 2025/26?   *(September/December 2022)*

£ [ ]   (2 marks)

---

15 More Ltd prepares accounts to 30 September each year. It was given notice by HM Revenue & Customs (HMRC) to submit its corporation tax return for the year to 30 September 2024 on 30 November 2024. The return was submitted on 1 December 2025. This was the first late return for the company.

What is the maximum penalty payable by More Ltd as a result of its late submission?

£ [ ]   (2 marks)

16 Mick has already realised a capital gain on the disposal of Asset 1 but is proposing to pretend that the disposal date actually falls into next tax year.

Mick is also planning to dispose of Asset 2 but is proposing to delay the actual sale until after 5 April.

In relation to which disposal(s) is Mick committing tax evasion?

○ Both disposals
○ Neither disposal
○ Asset 1 only
○ Asset 2 only

(2 marks)

---

17 Quinn will not make the balancing payment in respect of her tax liability for the tax year 2023/24 until 17 October 2025.

What is the total percentage penalty which Quinn will be charged by HM Revenue & Customs (HMRC) in respect of the late balancing payment for the tax year 2023/24?

[▼]

Pull down list

- 10%
- 15%
- 30%
- 5%

(2 marks)

---

18 Dennis has made a deliberate error in his self-assessment tax return for the tax year 2024/25.

What is the time limit for HM Revenue & Customs (HMRC) to issue a discovery assessment? *(June 2018)*

○ 5 April 2026
○ 5 April 2029
○ 5 April 2031
○ 5 April 2045

(2 marks)

---

19 Daljit received a notice from HM Revenue & Customs (HMRC) to submit his self-assessment tax return for the tax year 2024/25. He did not submit the return by the due date.

What can HMRC do to collect any tax owing in respect of Daljit's unfiled return?

(March 2017)

[▼]

Pull down list

- Make a determination
- Offer an internal review
- Raise a discovery assessment
- Start a compliance check enquiry into the return

(2 marks)

20 Based on her income tax liability of £15,600 for the tax year 2023/24, Sarah was liable to make two payments on account for the tax year 2024/25 of £7,800 each. In May 2025, Sarah made a claim to reduce her second payment on account to £6,000. This reduced payment was made on 30 September 2025. Sarah's actual income tax liability for the tax year 2024/25 was £16,000, and she paid the full balance outstanding on 31 January 2026.

How much interest is payable by Sarah to HM Revenue & Customs (HMRC) in respect of her second payment on account for the tax year 2024/25? *(March 2017)*

○ £148
○ £101
○ £70
○ £78 (2 marks)

(Total = 20 marks)

OTQ bank – The UK tax system and its administration 3
(18 mins)

21 Little Fence Ltd has made up accounts for the 15-month period ended 31 March 2025.

By which date(s) must Little Fence Ltd file its corporation tax self-assessment tax return(s) for the 15-month period ended 31 March 2025? *(September 2017)*

○ The return for the year ended 31 December 2024 must be filed by 31 October 2025. The return for the period ended 31 March 2025 must be filed by 31 December 2025.

○ One return for the 15-month period ended 31 March 2025 must be filed by 31 March 2026.

○ The return for the year ended 31 December 2024 must be filed by 31 December 2025. The return for the period ended 31 March 2025 must be filed by 31 March 2026.

○ The returns for the year ended 31 December 2024 and the period ended 31 March 2025 must both be filed by 31 March 2026. (2 marks)

22 Dayfis Ltd was incorporated on 1 October 2024. The company started to trade on 1 December 2024 and made up its first accounts for the period to 30 June 2025.

By which date must Dayfis Ltd notify HM Revenue & Customs (HMRC) of its first accounting period? *(September 2017)*

○ 1 December 2024
○ 1 January 2025
○ 1 March 2025
○ 30 June 2026 (2 marks)

23 Dee Ltd has been late in filing its last two self-assessment corporation tax returns. The company's self-assessment corporation tax return for the year ended 31 December 2024 shows corporation tax due of £7,000.

If Dee Ltd files its self-assessment tax return for the year ended 31 December 2024 on 31 August 2026, what amount of penalty will be charged by HM Revenue & Customs (HMRC)? *(December 2017)*

- ○ £1,200
- ○ £700
- ○ £1,000
- ○ £1,700 *(2 marks)*

24 Phillip did not file his self-assessment tax return for the tax year 2023/24 until 31 March 2025. This was two months after the 31 January 2025 due date.

What is the latest date that HM Revenue and Customs (HMRC) can begin a compliance check enquiry into Phillip's self-assessment tax return for the tax year 2023/24? *(March/June 2024)*

- ○ 31 January 2026
- ○ 30 April 2026
- ○ 31 July 2026
- ○ 31 March 2026 *(2 marks)*

25 Certain individuals are required to complete a self-assessment tax return.

The taxpayer must sign a declaration that the information given on the tax return and any supplementary pages is correct and complete to the best of the taxpayer's knowledge.

Which of the following statements is FALSE? *(March 2018)*

- ○ The tax return comprises a main return form, together with supplementary pages for particular sources of income.
- ○ Partnerships must file a separate return and account for each partner's tax through this return.
- ○ If HM Revenue & Customs (HMRC) calculates the tax for the taxpayer, it merely does so based on the information provided and does not judge the accuracy of it.
- ○ An employee who only has employment income, with the tax collected under PAYE, is not required to complete a tax return. *(2 marks)*

(Total = 10 marks)

Section B

OT case – Domingo and Fargo (June 2009) (amended)   (18 mins)

Domingo and Fargo are brothers. In the tax year 2024/25, Domingo is employed and Fargo is self-employed. Fargo is required to make a balancing payment of £1,800 in respect of his income tax liability for the tax year 2024/25 and payments on account for the tax year 2025/26.

For the tax year 2024/25 Domingo wants to file a paper self-assessment tax return. Fargo wants to file his tax return online. Both notices to file returns were issued by HM Revenue & Customs (HMRC) to Domingo and Fargo on 1 July 2025.

26   What are the latest dates for Domingo and Fargo to submit their respective self-assessment tax returns for the tax year 2024/25 given their stated filing preferences?

Domingo	Fargo
○ 31 October 2025	31 October 2025
○ 31 October 2025	31 January 2026
○ 31 January 2026	31 October 2025
○ 31 January 2026	31 January 2026

(2 marks)

27   How long must Domingo and Fargo retain the records used in preparing their respective tax returns for the tax year 2024/25?

Domingo	Fargo
○ 31 January 2031	31 January 2026
○ 31 January 2031	31 January 2028
○ 31 January 2027	31 January 2027
○ 31 January 2027	31 January 2031

(2 marks)

28   What is the maximum penalty that may be imposed on Domingo and Fargo for not retaining their records for the required period?

○ £100
○ £500
○ £1,500
○ £3,000

(2 marks)

29 What are the dates by which Fargo should make the balancing payment for the tax year 2024/25 and the first payment on account for the tax year 2025/26, and the second payment on account for the tax year 2025/26?

Balancing payment 2024/25 and first POA 2025/26	Second POA 2025/26
○ 31 July 2025	31 July 2026
○ 31 July 2025	31 January 2027
○ 31 January 2026	31 July 2026
○ 31 January 2026	31 January 2027

(2 marks)

30 What is the interest payable and the maximum penalty payable if Fargo makes the balancing payment for the tax year 2024/25 exactly four months late?

○ Interest £47, penalty £90
○ Interest £140, penalty £90
○ Interest £47, penalty £180
○ Interest £140, penalty £180

(2 marks)

(Total = 10 marks)

OT case – Ernest (June 2010) (amended)   (18 mins)

You should assume that today's date is 30 June 2025.

You are a trainee Chartered Certified Accountant and your firm is dealing with the tax affairs of Ernest.

Ernest's self-assessment tax return for the tax year 2023/24 was submitted to HM Revenue & Customs (HMRC) on 15 May 2024 and Ernest paid the resulting income tax liability by the due date. However, you have just discovered that during the tax year 2023/24 Ernest disposed of a freehold non-residential property, the details of which were omitted from his self-assessment tax return. The capital gains tax liability in respect of this disposal is £18,000 and this amount has not been paid.

Ernest has suggested that since HMRC's right to make a compliance check enquiry into his self-assessment tax return for the tax year 2023/24 expired on 15 May 2025, no disclosure should be made to HMRC of the capital gain.

31 Identify, by clicking on the relevant boxes in the table below, whether each of the following statements concerning tax evasion and tax avoidance is true or false.

Tax evasion is illegal.	TRUE	FALSE
Both tax evasion and tax avoidance are illegal.	TRUE	FALSE
Tax avoidance is legal but may fail if challenged in the courts by HMRC.	TRUE	FALSE
Tax evasion always involves providing HM Revenue & Customs with false information.	TRUE	FALSE

(2 marks)

32 Which TWO of the following statements are correct about how your firm should deal with the suggestion from Ernest that no disclosure is made to HMRC of his capital gain?
- ☐ Ernest should be advised to disclose details of the capital gain to HMRC.
- ☐ If Ernest does not disclose the gain, your firm can still continue to act for him.
- ☐ If your firm ceases to act for Ernest, it must disclose this to HMRC and provide detailed reasons why it has ceased to act.
- ☐ If Ernest does not disclose the gain to HMRC, your firm would be obliged to report under the money laundering regulations.

(2 marks)

33 What is the maximum penalty that could be imposed on Ernest for the error by omission in his tax return, assuming that it is considered to be deliberate but not concealed?
- ○ £18,000
- ○ £12,600
- ○ £9,000
- ○ £5,400

(2 marks)

34 Assuming that HMRC discovers the capital gain and Ernest then makes a disclosure of it, what is the minimum penalty that could be imposed on Ernest for the error if it is considered to be deliberate but not concealed?

[▼]

Pull down list
- £0
- £2,700
- £6,300
- £9,000

(2 marks)

35 If Ernest pays the capital gains tax liability on 31 July 2025, what is the interest that will be charged on this late payment?

£ [   ]

(2 marks)

(Total = 10 marks)

OT case – Thai Curry Ltd   (18 mins)

Thai Curry Ltd prepares accounts for the year ended 31 March 2025 and has taxable total profits of £171,705, resulting in a corporation tax liability of £32,624.

Thai Curry Ltd has previously always submitted its corporation tax returns on time and had a corporation tax liability for the year to 31 March 2024 of £22,000.

The company is in dispute with HM Revenue & Customs (HMRC) in relation to its corporation tax return for the year ended 31 March 2024 and has been offered an internal review of the case.

The case is likely to be allocated to either the complex track or the standard track if it instead chooses to go to a formal appeal.

36 What is the date by which Thai Curry Ltd's self-assessment corporation tax return for the year ended 31 March 2025 should be submitted?

- ○ 31 December 2025
- ○ 31 January 2026
- ○ 31 March 2026
- ○ 31 July 2026

(2 marks)

37 What is the total amount of late filing penalties that will be charged on Thai Curry Ltd if it submits its return for the year ended 31 March 2025 and pays the corporation tax due eight months late?

[▼]

Pull down list
- £3,262
- £3,462
- £6,525
- £6,725

(2 marks)

38 How should Thai Curry Ltd's corporation tax liability for the year ended 31 March 2025 be paid?

- ○ £32,624 on 1 January 2026
- ○ £11,000 on 31 January 2025 and 31 July 2025, £10,624 on 31 January 2026
- ○ £8,156 on 14 October 2024, 14 January 2025, 14 April 2025 and 14 July 2025
- ○ £5,500 on 14 October 2024, 14 January 2025 and 14 April 2025, £16,124 on 14 July 2025

(2 marks)

39 Which TWO of the following statements are correct about the internal review procedure?

- ☐ An internal review is a less costly and more effective way to resolve disputes informally than a formal appeal.
- ☐ The review is carried out by the HMRC officer who has previously dealt with the case.
- ☐ HMRC must usually carry out the review within 45 days.
- ☐ After the review conclusion is notified, the company cannot make a further appeal.

(2 marks)

40 Match what body is initially likely to hear Thai Curry Ltd's appeal if it does not take up the offer of an internal review.

| First tier | | Complex track |
| Upper tier | | Standard track |

(2 marks)

(Total = 10 marks)

Section C

41 John (18 mins)

(a) You should assume today's date is 30 November 2025.

John is a new client whom you met today. On 6 April 2024, he commenced in self-employment and prepared his first set of accounts to 5 April 2025. John had not previously filed a self-assessment tax return and has not received any communication from HM Revenue & Customs (HMRC) about his tax affairs. As this will be his first self-assessment tax return, John is also concerned that HMRC might carry out a compliance check.

Required

(i) Advise John of the latest date by which he should have notified HMRC of his chargeability to income tax for the tax year 2024/25 and the maximum and minimum penalties for late notification if he immediately notifies HMRC of his chargeability and is deemed to have been careless. **(3 marks)**

(ii) State the period during which HMRC will have to notify John if it intends to carry out a compliance check in respect of his self-assessment tax return for the tax year 2024/25, and the possible reasons why such a check would be made.

Note. You should assume for part (ii) that John will file his tax return by the due date. **(3 marks)**

(b) The UK Government uses tax policies to encourage certain types of activity.

Briefly explain how the UK Government's tax policies encourage:

(i) Individuals to save **(1 mark)**

(ii) Individuals to support charities **(1 mark)**

(iii) Entrepreneurs to build their own businesses and to invest in plant and machinery **(2 marks)**

(Total = 10 marks)

42 Sugar plc (18 mins)

Sugar plc has been in business for many years. It owns 45% of the ordinary shares of Honey plc and 75% of the ordinary shares of Molasses plc. Molasses plc owns 70% of the ordinary shares of Treacle plc. This structure has existed for many years.

In the year to 31 March 2025, Sugar plc had taxable total profits of £470,000. It also received dividends of £50,000 from Honey plc. In the year to 31 March 2026, Sugar plc will have taxable total profits of £600,000. It will not receive any dividends in that year.

Required

(a) Define what is meant by an associated company and explain which companies are associated companies of Sugar plc. **(3 marks)**

(b) Explain whether or not Sugar plc is a large company for the purposes of payment of corporation tax for the years ended 31 March 2025 and 31 March 2026. **(3 marks)**

(c) Assuming that Sugar plc is a large company in both years but was not a large company for any previous year, calculate Sugar plc's corporation tax liabilities for the years ended 31 March 2025 and 31 March 2026 and explain when these will be paid. **(4 marks)**

(Total = 10 marks)

Part B: Income tax and NIC liabilities

Part B covers income tax and NIC liabilities, the subject of Chapters 2 to 12 of the BPP Course Book for Taxation (TX – UK).

Section A

OTQ bank – Income tax and NIC liabilities 1 (36 mins)

43 Hana was UK resident in the tax year 2023/24. He worked full-time in Egypt throughout the tax year 2024/25.

   What is the maximum number of days which Hana can spend in the UK and be treated as automatically not resident in the UK for the tax year 2024/25? *(March 2019)*

   ○ 15
   ○ 45
   ○ 90
   ○ 182
   (2 marks)

44 Which TWO of the following types of income are exempt from income tax?
   ☐ Interest on an NS&I Investment account
   ☐ Premium bond prizes
   ☐ Interest on UK government stocks ('gilts')
   ☐ Dividends on shares held in an Individual Savings Account
   (2 marks)

45 In the tax year 2024/25, Claudio has taxable income (after deduction of his personal allowance) consisting of £3,000 of non-savings income and £12,500 of savings income.

   What is Claudio's income tax liability for the tax year 2024/25?

   ○ £2,500
   ○ £2,900
   ○ £2,700
   ○ £3,100
   (2 marks)

46 Mike and Delia are a married couple. In the tax year 2024/25, Mike has taxable non-savings income (after deducting his personal allowance) of £13,500.

   Delia has no income in the tax year 2024/25. Delia has made an election in relation to her personal allowance for the tax year 2024/25.

   What is Mike's income tax liability for the tax year 2024/25?

   ○ £186
   ○ £2,448
   ○ £1,440
   ○ £2,700
   (2 marks)

47 John is employed by Zebra plc. He was provided with a computer for private use on 6 November 2023.

The market value of the computer when first provided to an employee for private use was £3,600 and the computer had a market value of £2,000 when first provided to John for private use. Zebra plc gave the computer to John on 5 April 2025 when it had a market value of £1,000.

What are the total taxable benefits for John in respect of the computer for the tax year 2024/25?

○ £2,880
○ £3,300
○ £1,720
○ £1,833

(2 marks)

---

48 In the tax year 2024/25, Susie receives employment income of £170,000. She made a gross gift aid donation of £10,000 in January 2025.

What is Susie's income tax liability for the tax year 2024/25?

○ £60,703
○ £62,703
○ £60,203
○ £54,547

(2 marks)

---

49 Petunia is a single parent with a two-year old son. She receives child benefit of £1,331 in the tax year 2024/25. Petunia has net income of £67,000 in 2024/25 and she made gross personal pension contributions of £2,000 during 2024/25.

What is Petunia's child benefit income tax charge for the tax year 2024/25?

○ £1,331
○ £532
○ £333
○ £466

(2 marks)

---

50 Judith works for Sabre Ltd for an annual salary of £18,000. On 30 September 2024, she received a bonus of £4,000 in respect of Sabre Ltd's trading results for the year ended 31 March 2024. She expects to receive a bonus of £4,800 on 30 September 2025 in respect of Sabre Ltd's results for the year ended 31 March 2025. Judith also received £500 from a customer on 1 December 2024 as a gratuity for good service.

What is Judith's employment income for the tax year 2024/25?

○ £22,000
○ £22,800
○ £22,500
○ £23,300

(2 marks)

51 Which TWO of the following are qualifying travel expenses?
- ☐ Travel from employer's office to visit a client
- ☐ Travel from home to a workplace to which an employee has been seconded for 36 months
- ☐ Travel from home to a permanent place of work
- ☐ Travel from home to visit a trade fair relevant to the employer's business 100 miles away from permanent place of work

(2 marks)

52 Since 2020, Sergey has lived in job-related accommodation provided by his employer for Sergey's personal security. He has an annual gross salary of £60,000 for the tax year 2024/25.

Throughout the tax year 2024/25, Sergey's employer paid for heating, cleaning and lighting the accommodation at a cost of £7,000. His employer also provided Sergey with furniture on 6 April 2024 at a cost of £10,000.

What is the amount assessable on Sergey in the tax year 2024/25 in relation to the furniture, heating, cleaning and lighting costs? *(March 2018)*

- ○ £6,000
- ○ £9,000
- ○ £7,000
- ○ £8,000

(2 marks)

(Total = 20 marks)

OTQ bank – Income tax and NIC liabilities 2 (36 mins)

53 Marion bought £20,000 (nominal value) 5% UK Government Loan Stock on 1 July 2024. Interest is payable on 30 June and 31 December each year. Marion sold the loan stock to Gerald on 31 October 2024 including interest.

Match the amounts of savings income taxable on Marion and Gerald in respect of the loan stock for the tax year 2024/25.

| £0 |
| £333 |
| £500 |
| £167 |

| | Marion |
| | Gerald |

(2 marks)

54 Trevor is employed by Cress plc. He is provided with a car available for private use for the tax year 2024/25. The car has CO_2 emissions of 102 g/km and a list price of £20,000 although Cress plc actually paid £18,000 for the car as the result of a dealer discount.

The car has a diesel engine which does not meet the RDE2 standard. No private fuel is provided.

What is Trevor's taxable car benefit for the tax year 2024/25?

○ £4,500
○ £5,220
○ £5,000
○ £5,800

(2 marks)

55 Troy is a sole trader who had trading income of £80,000 in the tax year 2023/24 and £100,000 in the tax year 2024/25. He has no other income. He joined a personal pension scheme on 6 April 2023 and made gross contributions of £25,000 in 2023/24. This was the first pension provision that Troy had made.

What gross amount can Troy contribute to his personal pension scheme in March 2025 without incurring an annual allowance charge?

[▼]

Pull down list

- £175,000
- £45,000
- £60,000
- £95,000

(2 marks)

56 Luke rents out a room in his own residence throughout 2024/25. The rent is £150 a week. Luke's expenses of the letting are £20 per week, none of which is loan interest on the property.

What is the amount of property business income taxable on Luke for 2024/25 if he makes any relevant election?

○ £6,760
○ £0
○ £7,800
○ £300

(2 marks)

57 Susie rents out a furnished house. The house does not qualify as a furnished holiday letting. The furnishings include a new sofa which was bought in the tax year 2024/25 to replace an old one which was disposed of at the same time. The old sofa cost £3,000 in 2017 and was disposed of in January 2025 for proceeds of £200. The new sofa was bought in January 2025 for £5,500 and was larger than the old one. If Susie had bought a newer sofa of the same model as the old one, it would have cost £4,000.

What deduction against property business income can Susie claim for the cost of the sofa bought in 2024/25?

- ○ £5,500
- ○ £3,800
- ○ £5,300
- ○ £4,000

(2 marks)

58 Amrul bought a house on 1 September 2024 and immediately let it out on a quarterly tenancy with rent of £900 being payable in advance on 1 September, 1 December, 1 March and 1 June each year. The tenant also paid a security deposit of £500. The tenant was still in the property on 5 April 2025.

Amrul paid a buildings insurance premium of £150 on 1 September 2024 for a 12-month period from that date.

Amrul drove 178 miles in his own car in relation to the letting during the period 1 September 2024 to 5 April 2025. He wishes to use approved mileage allowances to calculate his motoring expenses.

What is Amrul's property business income for the tax year 2024/25?

Pull down list
- £1,932
- £2,470
- £2,505
- £2,970

(2 marks)

59 Harry is a sole trader. He prepares accounts under the accruals basis for the year ended 5 April 2025, and has deducted the following items of expenditure in the statement of profit or loss:

	£
Depreciation	3,000
Accountancy fees for preparing accounts	1,000
Entertainment of:	
– Staff (party at £300 per person for 6 employees)	1,800
– Customers	2,400

How much should be added back to Harry's net profit to arrive at his adjusted taxable profit?

£ ☐

(2 marks)

60 Rose is a sole trader who prepares accounts to 5 April each year using the cash basis of accounting. Her results for the period of account to 5 April 2025 show the following:

	£
Cash sales	41,000
Invoice sales	4,000
Cash expenses	20,200

The figure for invoice sales includes an invoice for £1,500 which was paid on 10 April 2025. In addition to the cash expenses of £20,200, Rose incurred motoring expenses of £2,800 for driving 8,000 miles of which 6,500 miles were for business purposes. Rose wishes to use approved mileage allowances for motoring.

What is Rose's taxable trading income for the tax year 2024/25?

£ ⬜ (2 marks)

---

61 Olive is self-employed, preparing her accounts to 5 April each year. She claims capital allowances on a car used in her business. The car has a CO_2 emission rate of 145 grams per kilometre, with 40% of Olive's mileage for private purposes. The car had a tax written down value of £12,000 at 6 April 2024. Olive sold the car for £6,000 on 1 November 2024.

What amount of capital allowances can Olive claim in respect of the car for the tax year 2024/25? (June 2019)

- ○ £3,600
- ○ £648
- ○ £2,400
- ○ £216

(2 marks)

---

62 Ella started in business as a sole trader on 6 November 2024 and prepared her first set of accounts to 5 April 2025 under the accruals basis. On 6 December 2024, she acquired plant at a cost of £430,000.

What are the maximum capital allowances that Ella can claim for the period of account to 5 April 2025?

⬇

Pull down list
- £339,133
- £417,667
- £419,067
- £430,000

(2 marks)

(Total = 20 marks)

OTQ bank – Income tax and NIC liabilities 3 (36 mins)

63 Humphrey is a sole trader who has been trading for a number of years.

Humphrey incurred a trading loss in the tax year 2024/25. He wishes to make a claim to offset this loss against his total income of the tax year 2023/24.

What is the deadline for Humphrey to claim this relief? *(December 2018)*

○ 31 January 2026
○ 31 January 2027
○ 5 April 2028
○ 5 April 2029

(2 marks)

---

64 Peter and Jane have been in partnership for many years preparing accounts to 31 March each year and sharing profits equally. On 1 May 2024, they changed their profit-sharing agreement so that Peter was entitled to a salary of £9,000 each year and the remaining profits were then split two parts to Peter and three parts to Jane. The partnership made a trading profit of £96,000 in the year to 31 March 2025.

What is Peter's taxable trading profit for the tax year 2024/25?

£ [   ]

(2 marks)

---

65 Shona started in business on 1 January 2025 as a sole trader and prepared her first set of accounts for the 14 weeks to 5 April 2025. Her assessable profit for 2024/25 was £13,500.

What are Shona's total national insurance contributions for the tax year 2024/25?

£ [   ]

(2 marks)

---

66 Raj is self-employed and his trading profit for the tax year 2024/25 is £52,000. Raj also had property income of £5,200 from furnished holiday accommodation for this tax year.

What are Raj's class 4 national insurance contributions for the tax year 2024/25?
(September/December 2023)

○ £2,297
○ £3,155
○ £3,051
○ £2,401

(2 marks)

67   Mina's salary for the tax year 2024/25 was £68,000.

Mina's employer provided her with a loan throughout the tax year 2024/25, and this resulted in a taxable benefit of £1,500.

During the tax year 2024/25, Mina contributed £3,000 into her employer's occupational pension scheme. Her employer contributed a further £7,000 into the scheme on Mina's behalf.

What were Mina's earnings for the purpose of calculating the class 1 national insurance contributions payable for the tax year 2024/25? *(March/June 2024)*

○ £68,000
○ £69,500
○ £72,000
○ £65,000   (2 marks)

---

68   Katya is provided with a hybrid-electric company car from 1 July 2024 to 31 December 2024. The car has a list price of £26,000 with CO_2 emissions of 35 g/km and an electric range of 39 miles.

What is Katya's car benefit for 2024/25?

£ _____   (2 marks)

---

69   Elsa is employed by Bee Ltd. During the tax year 2024/25, Bee Ltd provided Elsa with the following benefits:

- A private gym membership
- A contribution of £1,800 into Elsa's private pension scheme

Elsa had use of the private gym membership throughout the tax year. The normal membership fee is £1,000, but Bee Ltd negotiated a discount and paid £900 for it.

What amount of class 1A national insurance contributions (NICs) are payable by Bee Ltd in respect of Elsa for the tax year 2024/25? *(September 2019)*

○ £124
○ £138
○ £373
○ £386   (2 marks)

---

70   Johan is provided with an electric company car throughout the tax year 2024/25. The car has a list price of £30,000 with zero CO_2 emissions. Johan made a capital contribution of £5,550.

What is Johan's car benefit for 2024/25?

£ _____   (2 marks)

71 Niamhe has adjusted income for the tax year 2024/25 of £330,000.

During the year, she made personal pension scheme contributions of £100,000 (gross).

Niamhe has no brought forward unused annual allowances.

What is the amount of annual allowance charge to be added to Niamhe's taxable income for the tax year 2024/25? *(December 2019)*

○ £75,000

○ £60,000

○ £90,000

○ £25,000

(2 marks)

72 Dane and Zara are a married couple.

They jointly own a residential property which is let to tenants. In the tax year 2024/25 the property business income from the property is £20,000. Dane owns 25% of the property and Zara owns the other 75%. No election has been made in relation to the ownership of the property.

Zara earns employment income of £85,000 and Dane receives £2,213 of child benefit in the tax year 2024/25. Dane has no other income.

Which TWO of the following statements are true in relation to Zara's income tax liability for the tax year 2024/25? *(March 2020)*

☐ Zara's taxable income is £82,430.

☐ Zara can reduce her income tax liability by claiming the transferable personal allowance (the 'marriage allowance').

☐ It would be beneficial to Zara if the couple were to make a joint election to HM Revenue and Customs (HMRC) specifying their actual ownership share in the residential property.

☐ A child benefit charge of £2,213 will be added to Zara's income tax liability.

(2 marks)

(Total = 20 marks)

OTQ bank – Income tax and NIC liabilities 4 (18 mins)

73 Identify, by clicking on the relevant boxes in the table below, whether each of the following statements about assessable profit is true or false.

Statement		
For tax year 2024/25 to 2027/28, profit subject to class 4 national insurance will include any transitional profit.	TRUE	FALSE
A period of account ending on 5 April requires apportionment to calculate assessable profit.	TRUE	FALSE
Transition profits are included as a separate entry in the income tax computation.	TRUE	FALSE
If accounts are not finalised on time, estimated profit figures are used for the later part of the profit apportionment.	TRUE	FALSE

(2 marks)

74   Alessia has trading profit of £106,000 and transitional profit of £9,000 in 2024/25.
      What is Alessia's tax liability for 2024/25?
      £ 34,632   (2 marks)

75   Lamine prepares accounts to 31 May each year. In the year ended 31 May 2024, his tax-adjusted profits are £63,800 and, in the year ended 31 May 2025, his tax-adjusted profits are estimated to be £70,400.
      What profits will Lamine be assessed on for 2024/25?
      £ 69,300   (2 marks)

76   Leah started trading on 1 February 2025 and prepares accounts for the period ended 31 December 2025 which show a profit of £82,500.
      What are Leah's assessable profits for 2024/25?
      £ 15,000   (2 marks)

77   Yulia ceased trading on 30 November 2024 and trading profits for the year ended 30 November 2024 were £45,000.
      What are Yulia's assessable profits for 2024/25?
      £ 30,000   (2 marks)

(Total = 10 marks)

Section B

OT case – Ann, Basil and Chloe (December 2008) (amended)
(18 mins)

Ann

Ann is self-employed. Her taxable income for the tax year 2024/25 was £76,000 which was all trading income. Ann made contributions of £49,000 (gross) into a personal pension scheme between September 2024 and March 2025. This was the second year that she had been a member of a pension scheme and she had an unused annual allowance of £20,000 brought forward from 2023/24.

Basil

Basil is employed. During the tax year 2024/25 Basil had taxable income of £310,000 which was all employment income. Basil made contributions of £50,000 (gross) into a personal pension scheme during the tax year 2024/25. This was the first year that he had been a member of a pension scheme. In future, his employer may contribute to Basil's personal pension scheme.

Chloe

Chloe lets out an unfurnished property. For the tax year 2024/25, her taxable income was £16,630 which was all property business income. Chloe made contributions of £8,200 (gross) into a personal pension scheme during the tax year 2024/25. This was the first year that she had been a member of a pension scheme. Chloe does not have any interest payable on her buy-to-let property.

78 Which TWO of the following statements about relevant earnings are correct?

☐ Individuals can always make gross pension contributions of £3,600 in 2024/25 even if they do not have any relevant earnings in that tax year.

☐ Relevant earnings relate both to contributions to personal pension schemes and to occupational pension schemes.

☐ If an individual makes pension contributions less than relevant earnings in a tax year, the excess can be carried forward for three years and used to cover pension contributions.

☐ Relevant earnings do not include income from furnished holiday lettings.

(2 marks)

79 Identify, by clicking on the relevant boxes in the table below, whether each of the following statements about the annual allowance is true or false.

Employer contributions do not count towards the annual allowance.	TRUE	FALSE
The annual allowance can be carried forward for three years to the extent that it is unused in the tax year.	TRUE	FALSE
The annual allowance is available even if the individual is not a member of a pension scheme in a tax year and so can be carried forward.	TRUE	FALSE
If tax-relievable pension contributions exceed the annual allowance, there is a charge to income tax.	TRUE	FALSE

(2 marks)

80 What is Ann's income tax liability for the tax year 2024/25?

£ ☐ (2 marks)

81 What is Basil's annual allowance charge for the tax year 2024/25?

£ ☐ (2 marks)

82 What is Chloe's tax relief on her pension contribution for the tax year 2024/25?
- ○ £0
- ○ £1,640
- ○ £900
- ○ £720

(2 marks)

(Total = 10 marks)

OT case – Rosie and Sam (December 2012) (amended) (18 mins)

You should assume that today's date is 15 February 2025.

Rosie

Rosie has recently been promoted to managing director at Hornburg plc. During the tax year 2024/25, Rosie will be paid gross director's remuneration of £260,000 and she has received dividend income of £500,000. She had income of £130,000 in 2021/22, 2022/23 and 2023/24.

She has made the following gross personal pension contributions:

Tax year	Pension contribution £
2022/23	26,000
2023/24	Nil

Rosie has been a member of a pension scheme since the tax year 2022/23 and Hornburg plc makes an employer's contribution of £10,000 per year.

Sam

In September 2022, Sam invested £7,000 in a flexible cash ISA. In May 2024, he invested a further £6,000 in that cash ISA. He withdrew £5,000 from the cash ISA in October 2024. Sam is now considering investing more cash into the cash ISA before 5 April 2025. He also invested £4,000 in premium bonds and government securities ('gilts') in the tax year 2024/25.

83 What is the total pension scheme annual allowance that Rosie has available for the tax year 2024/25?
- ○ £104,000
- ○ £64,000
- ○ £154,000
- ○ £84,000

(2 marks)

84 Use ONE of the following to complete the sentence below:

If Rosie makes pension contributions in excess of her available annual allowances, there will be a charge to income tax at [▼] % on the excess contributions.

Pull down list
- 20
- 25
- 45
- 55

(2 marks)

85 What are the tax consequences for Rosie if she takes pension benefits under flexible access drawdown?

	Lump sum	Rest of pension fund
○	Up to 10% of fund can be taken tax free	Taxable as pension income when received
○	Up to 10% of fund can be taken as tax-free lump sum	5% of fund taxable as pension income each year whether or not received
○	Up to 25% of fund can be taken as tax-free lump sum	5% of fund taxable as pension income each year whether or not received
○	Up to 25% of fund can be taken as tax-free lump sum	Taxable as pension income when received

(2 marks)

86 What is the maximum amount that Sam can invest into the cash ISA for the tax year 2024/25 in addition to his investments already made?

[▼]

Pull down list
- £12,000
- £14,000
- £15,000
- £19,000

(2 marks)

87 Match the income tax and capital gains tax treatments of Sam's investments in premium bonds and government securities.

| Exempt from income tax, chargeable to capital gains tax |
| Chargeable to income tax and capital gains tax |
| Exempt from both income tax and capital gains tax |
| Chargeable to income tax, exempt from capital gains tax |

| Premium bonds |
| Government securities |

(2 marks)

(Total = 10 marks)

OT case – Chi (June 2014) (amended)   (18 mins)

Chi commenced self-employment on 6 April 2024, and for the year ended 5 April 2025 her trading profit using the accruals basis was £53,000, calculated as follows:

	Note	£	£
Revenue	1		72,500
Expenses			
Motor expenses	2	4,400	
Other expenses	3	8,200	
Capital allowances	4	6,900	
			(19,500)
Trading profit			53,000

Notes.

1   **Revenue**

The revenue figure of £72,500 includes receivables of £1,600 which were owed as at 5 April 2025.

2   **Motor expenses**

The total motor expenses for the year ended 5 April 2025 were £5,500, of which 20% was for private journeys. This proportion has been disallowed in calculating the trading profit. During the year ended 5 April 2025, Chi drove 13,200 business miles.

3 **Other expenses**

The other expenses figure of £8,200 includes payables of £900 owed as at 5 April 2025.

4 **Capital allowances**

Capital allowances consist of an annual investment allowance claim of £4,020 in respect of office equipment purchased on 6 April 2024, and a writing down allowance of £2,880 claimed in respect of Chi's car. The car had cost £20,000 on 6 April 2024.

88 Based on the trading profit of £53,000 for the year ended 5 April 2025, what is Chi's income tax liability for the tax year 2024/25?

£ ☐ (2 marks)

89 Based on the trading profit of £53,000 for the year ended 5 April 2025, what are the Class 4 national insurance contributions payable by Chi for the tax year 2024/25?

£ ☐ (2 marks)

90 Which TWO of the following statements about the cash basis of assessment are correct?
- ☐ The trader must prepare accounts to 5 April each year.
- ☐ The trader can deduct capital expenditure on plant and machinery (other than cars) as business expenses rather than using capital allowances.
- ☐ Under the cash basis, a trader can create a specific bad debt provision.
- ☐ Under the cash basis, legal fees relating to a short lease on land are disallowable.

(2 marks)

91 If Chi uses the cash basis and claims approved mileage allowances, what is the amount of motor expenses (Note 2) which are allowable?
- ○ £4,400
- ○ £5,300
- ○ £5,940
- ○ £8,180

(2 marks)

92 If Chi uses the cash basis, what is the amount of revenue which is chargeable (Note 1) and the other expenses (Note 3) which are allowable for the year ended 5 April 2025?
- ○ Revenue £72,500, other expenses £8,200
- ○ Revenue £70,900, other expenses £8,200
- ○ Revenue £72,500, other expenses £7,300
- ○ Revenue £70,900, other expenses £7,300

(2 marks)

(Total = 10 marks)

Section C

93 Kagan (September/December 2019) (18 mins)

You should assume that today's date is 4 April 2024.

On 2 April 2024, Kagan inherited some quoted ordinary shares valued at £510,000 following the death of his aunt. Kagan is unsure whether to retain the shares or sell some of them in order to make some alternative investments.

Kagan is aged 61 and is an additional rate taxpayer. Prior to the inheritance, his taxable income, consisting entirely of employment income, for the tax year 2024/25 would have been £400,000. The income tax liability on this income for the tax year 2024/25 would have been £165,000.

Prior to receiving the inheritance, Kagan's chargeable estate for inheritance tax (IHT) purposes was valued at £1,700,000. IHT of £550,000 would be payable were he to die in the near future.

Retain the inherited shares

If Kagan simply retains the inherited shares, then he will receive dividend income of £13,800 during the tax year 2024/25. This is in addition to his employment income of £400,000.

Sell some inherited shares and make four alternative investments

Kagan is considering selling some of his inherited shares (for which there has only been a minimal increase in value since he inherited them) to fund the following four investments, all of which will be made at the start of the tax year 2024/25:

(1) Kagan will make a gross personal pension contribution of £100,000. Kagan is a member of a pension scheme but has not made any contributions in recent years because his income has been substantially lower than it is for the tax year 2024/25. Kagan will immediately withdraw £25,000 of the pension fund tax free. This is the permitted 25% tax-free lump sum. However, no pension will be taken during the tax year 2024/25.

(2) Kagan will invest £50,000 in premium bonds. The expected amount of premium bond prizes which will be received during the tax year 2024/25 is £700.

(3) Kagan will invest the maximum permitted amount of £20,000 in a cash individual savings account (ISA). This ISA will pay interest of £400 during the tax year 2024/25.

(4) Kagan will purchase a freehold property for £295,000 (including all costs of purchase). The property will be let out unfurnished, with Kagan receiving property income of £9,600 during the tax year 2024/25.

After making these four investments, Kagan will be left with £65,000 of inherited shares, on which he will receive dividend income of £450 during the tax year 2024/25. He will also have his employment income of £400,000.

Kagan will not make any other disposals during the tax year 2024/25.

Required

(a) Calculate Kagan's revised income tax liability for the tax year 2024/25 if he retains the inherited shares. **(1 mark)**

(b) Answer the following questions:

(i) Explain why little or no capital gains tax (CGT) will be payable if Kagan sells some of his inherited shares. **(1 mark)**

(ii) Calculate Kagan's revised income tax liability for the tax year 2024/25 if he sells some of his inherited shares and makes the four alternative investments.

Notes.

1 For this part, you are expected to produce a full income tax computation.

2 You should indicate by use of zero (0) any items which are not taxable. **(6 marks)**

(c) For each of the four alternative investments (pension contribution, premium bonds, ISA and freehold property), state whether the investment will reduce Kagan's potential IHT liability compared to him retaining the inherited shares.

Note. For this part of the question, no computations are required. **(2 marks)**

(Total = 10 marks)

94 Michael and Sean (June 2012) (amended) (18 mins)

You are a trainee Chartered Certified Accountant and your manager has asked for your help regarding two taxpayers who have both made trading losses.

Michael

Michael commenced in self-employment on 1 July 2024, preparing accounts to 5 April. His results for the first two periods of trading resulted in profits and losses as follows:

Tax year	Assessable trading profits/(loss)
	£
2024/25	(26,230)
2025/26	9,665 (estimated)

For the tax years 2020/21 to 2022/23, Michael had the following income from employment:

	£
2020/21	45,100
2021/22	20,365
2022/23	57,095

Michael did not have any income during the period 6 April 2023 to 30 June 2024.

Sean

Sean has been in self-employment since 2012 but ceased trading on 31 March 2025. He has always prepared accounts to 31 March. His results for the final five years of trading were:

	£
2020/21 – Trading profit	21,300
2021/22 – Trading profit	14,400
2022/23 – Trading profit	18,900
2023/24 – Trading profit	3,700
2024/25 – Trading loss	(26,700)

For each of the tax years 2020/21 to 2024/25, Sean has property business profits of £12,600.

Required

For each of the two taxpayers, Michael and Sean, identify the loss relief claims that are available to them, and explain which of the available claims would be the most beneficial.

Notes.

1. You should clearly state the amount of any reliefs claimed and the rates of income tax saved. However, you are not expected to calculate any income tax liabilities.
2. Assume that the tax rates and allowances for the tax year 2024/25 apply throughout.
3. The following mark allocation is provided as guidance for this requirement:

Michael, 4½ marks	Sean, 5½ marks

(Total = 10 marks)

95 Paul and Palu Ltd (March/June 2021) (amended)   (18 mins)

You should assume that today's date is 15 March 2024.

Paul is the managing director of, and 100% shareholder in, Palu Ltd. For the year ended 5 April 2025, Palu Ltd's tax adjusted trading profit, before taking account of director's remuneration, is forecast to be £275,000.

Paul intends to extract all of Palu Ltd's profits (after allowing for corporation tax). This will be achieved by paying himself gross director's remuneration of £8,000 and dividends of £200,250.

Paul wants to know if it would be beneficial to cease trading via Palu Ltd on 5 April 2024, and instead run his business from 6 April 2024 onwards as a sole trader. His tax adjusted trading profit for the year ended 5 April 2025 would remain unchanged at £275,000.

Paul will not have any other income for the tax year 2024/25.

Required

Determine whether or not there will be an overall saving of tax and national insurance contributions (NICs) for the year ended 5 April 2025 if Palu Ltd's business is instead run by Paul as a sole trader from 6 April 2024.

Notes.

1. You are expected to calculate the income tax payable by Paul, any NICs payable by Paul and Palu Ltd, and the corporation tax liability of Palu Ltd for the year ended 5 April 2025 assuming that he continues to run the business via the company.
2. You should then compare this total amount with the income tax and NICs payable by Paul assuming that he runs the business as a sole trader.
3. You should assume that the rate of corporation tax remains unchanged.

(Total = 10 marks)

96 Lucy   (18 mins)

Assume that it is 1 March 2024.

Lucy is considering two work arrangements. She will start her chosen arrangement on 6 April 2024 and will continue with that arrangement for the whole of the tax year 2024/25.

Employment with Red plc

Lucy has been offered employment with Red plc.

She would be paid a salary of £36,000 and would be required to work at Red plc's offices. Lucy would travel from home to Red plc's offices by train and would buy an annual season ticket costing £1,500.

Self-employment

Lucy would work for clients at their offices and receive fees of £36,000 from her clients in the year to 5 April 2025. Lucy would travel to client offices in her own car. Her business mileage would be 4,600 miles during the year and she estimates this would cost 40p per mile.

Lucy would prepare accounts to 5 April 2025 and use the cash basis with approved mileage allowances.

Required

Determine which of the work arrangements would result in Lucy having a higher amount of disposable income after deducting income tax, national insurance contributions and travel costs.

Note. You need to calculate the income tax and NIC liability for Lucy for each arrangement and calculate her disposable income in each case, taking into account her travel costs.

(Total = 10 marks)

97 Poppy (March/June 2022) (27 mins)

Poppy is employed by Zune plc and she is also a member of a partnership.

The following information is available:

Employment

(1) During the tax year 2024/25, Poppy was paid a gross annual salary of £65,000 in respect of her employment with Zune plc.

(2) During the period from 1 August 2024 to 5 April 2025, Zune plc provided Poppy with a diesel car which has a list price of £21,800. The car cost Zune plc £20,600, and it has an official CO_2 emission rate of 70 grams per kilometre.

The car does not meet the real driving emissions 2 (RDE2) standard. Poppy was not provided with any fuel for private use.

(3) Throughout the tax year 2024/25, Zune plc provided Poppy with two mobile telephones. The telephones had each cost £480 when purchased by the company in March 2024.

(4) All of the taxable benefits provided by Zune plc to Poppy are payrolled.

Partnership

(1) Poppy has been in partnership with Rose and Teasel since 6 April 2015, but Teasel resigned as a partner on 6 July 2024. The partners have always shared profits equally.

(2) For the year ended 5 April 2025, the partnership had a tax adjusted trading loss of £19,500. This figure is before taking account of capital allowances.

(3) The only item of plant and machinery owned by the partnership is a car with a CO_2 emission rate of 90 grams per kilometre. The car was used by Poppy and 70% of the mileage was for private journeys.

The written down value of the car as at 6 April 2024 was £8,400. The car was sold on 31 July 2024 for £5,400 and was not replaced.

UK Government securities (gilts)

On 1 January 2025, Poppy purchased, for £50,000, gilts with a nominal value of £40,000.

The gilts paid interest at the rate of 3%, with interest paid half-yearly on 30 June and 31 December based on the nominal value.

Poppy sold the gilts on 31 March 2025 for £50,300 (including accrued interest).

Balancing payment for tax year 2023/24

Poppy filed her self-assessment tax return for the tax year 2023/24 by the filing date but did not make the balancing payment of £2,600 until 31 August 2025.

She was not required to make any payments on account.

Required

(a) Assuming that Poppy claims loss relief against her total income for the tax year 2024/25, calculate her taxable income for this tax year. **(10 marks)**

(b) Explain how Poppy's income tax liability in respect of her taxable benefits for the tax year 2024/25 will have been collected, and if any forms containing details of these benefits will have been reported to HM Revenue and Customs (HMRC). **(2 marks)**

(c) Advise Poppy of the interest and penalties that will be charged by HM Revenue and Customs (HMRC) as a consequence of her not making the balancing payment for the tax year 2023/24 until 31 August 2025. **(3 marks)**

(Total = 15 marks)

98 Kazuo (Mar/Jun 2023) (18 mins)

You should assume that today's date is 25 March 2024 and the tax rates and allowances for the tax year 2024/25 apply throughout.

Kazuo is currently employed at a gross annual salary of £200,000. Kazuo will continue to earn the same salary until he retires on 5 April 2028, at which point his income will reduce to gross annual pension income of £55,000. This means that Kazuo is currently an additional rate taxpayer but will only be a higher rate taxpayer from when he retires on 5 April 2028.

Kazuo will undertake £40,000 of work on a freelance basis during the year ended 5 April 2025. To carry out this work, Kazuo will form a new limited company, Zaoku Ltd, of which he will be an employee. This freelance work will not involve any expenditure and will last for just one year, from 6 April 2024 to 5 April 2025. Zaoku Ltd will prepare accounts for the year ended 5 April 2025.

Kazuo is looking at three alternative ways of extracting the profits of Zaoku Ltd:

Alternative 1

After allowing for corporation tax, Kazuo will withdraw the entire net of tax profits as dividends during the tax year 2024/25.

Alternative 2

Zaoku Ltd will pay Kazuo gross directors' remuneration of £8,000 and Zaoku Ltd will make a pension contribution of £32,000 into a company occupational pension scheme on Kazuo's behalf during the tax year 2024/25. Kazuo has sufficient unused pension annual allowances so that a pension contribution of this amount will not result in an annual allowance charge.

Alternative 3

Kazuo will not withdraw any amounts during the tax year 2024/25. Instead, the net of tax profits will be left undrawn in Zaoku Ltd until the tax year 2028/29 when Kazuo has retired. He will then withdraw the entire net of tax amount as dividends in the tax year 2028/29.

Kazuo does not have any other income.

Required

(a) Assuming that Kazuo withdraws the entire net of tax profits of Zaoku Ltd as dividends (Alternative 1) during the tax year 2024/25:

 (i) Calculate the corporation tax liability of Zaoku Ltd for the year ended 5 April 2025; and **(1 mark)**

 (ii) Calculate the income tax payable by Kazuo in respect of his dividend income. **(2 marks)**

(b) Assuming that Zaoku Ltd will pay Kazuo gross directors' remuneration of £8,000 and Zaoku Ltd will make a pension contribution of £32,000 into a company occupational pension scheme on Kazuo's behalf (Alternative 2) during the tax year 2024/25:

 (i) Explain the corporation tax, income tax and national insurance contributions (NICs) implications of Alternative 2; and **(3 marks)**

 (ii) Calculate the tax saving of Alternative 2 compared with 1 (entirely as dividends).

 Notes.

 1 You are not expected to explain the tax implications of ultimately receiving a pension from the pension scheme.

 2 Zaoku Ltd is not entitled to the NICs annual employment allowance. **(1 mark)**

(c) Calculate the tax saving in respect of Kazuo's dividend income and Zaoku Ltd's corporation tax liability if Kazuo withdraws the entire net of tax profits of Zaoku Ltd as dividends during the tax year 2028/29 (Alternative 3) when Kazuo has retired, rather than during the tax year 2024/25 (Alternative 1). **(3 marks)**

(Total = 10 marks)

99 Joe (December 2010) (amended) (27 mins)

On 31 December 2024, Joe resigned as an employee of Firstly plc, and on 1 January 2025 commenced employment with Secondly plc. The following information is available for the tax year 2024/25:

Employment with Firstly plc

(1) From 6 April 2024 to 31 December 2024, Joe was paid a salary of £6,360 per month. In addition to his salary, Joe was paid a bonus of £12,000 on 12 May 2024. He had become entitled to this bonus on 22 March 2024.

(2) Joe contributed 6% of his monthly gross salary of £6,360 into Firstly plc's occupational pension scheme. Firstly, plc contributed 3%.

(3) On 1 May 2024, Firstly plc provided Joe with an interest-free loan of £120,000 so that he could purchase a holiday cottage. Joe repaid £50,000 of the loan on 31 July 2024 and repaid the balance of the loan of £70,000 when he ceased employment with Firstly plc on 31 December 2024.

(4) During the period from 6 April 2024 to 31 December 2024, Joe was provided with a company van that he used as his only vehicle. The van had emissions of 40 g/km CO_2.

(5) Firstly plc provided Joe with a home entertainment system for his personal use costing £4,400 on 6 April 2024. The company gave the home entertainment system to Joe for free when he left the company on 31 December 2024, although its market value at that time was £3,860.

Employment with Secondly plc

(1) From 1 January 2025 to 5 April 2025, Joe was paid a salary of £6,565 per month. He worked one day a week at home and the remainder at Secondly plc's offices.

(2) During the period 1 January 2025 to 5 April 2025, Joe contributed a total of £3,000 (gross) into a personal pension scheme.

(3) From 1 January 2025 to 5 April 2025, Secondly plc provided Joe with living accommodation. The property has an annual value of £10,400 and is rented by Secondly plc at a cost of £2,250 per month. On 1 January 2025, Secondly plc purchased furniture for the property at a cost of £16,320.

(4) From 1 January 2025 to 5 April 2025, Secondly plc paid Joe £15 per month to cover additional household costs incurred when he worked at home.

Required

Calculate Joe's employment income for the tax year 2024/25.

(Total = 15 marks)

100 Esme (September/December 2023) (27 mins)

Esme is employed by HHK plc. The following information is available for the tax year 2024/25:

Employment

(1) HHK plc paid Esme a gross annual salary of £45,000.

(2) During the tax year 2024/25, Esme received a bonus of £19,000 on 10 April 2024 and another bonus of £22,000 on 22 March 2025. Esme was contractually entitled to receive these bonuses on 31 March 2024 and 31 March 2025 respectively.

(3) During the period 6 April to 30 November 2024, Esme was provided with a petrol company car. The car has a list price of £42,000 and an official CO_2 emissions rate of 178 grams per kilometre. Esme was not provided with any fuel for private journeys.

(4) On 1 December 2024, Esme purchased her own car for £20,000. During the period 1 December 2024 to 5 April 2025, Esme drove a total of 23,000 miles, of which 12,000 were for business journeys. HHK plc reimbursed Esme £5,760 for the business journeys.

(5) Esme contributed 4% of her gross annual salary of £45,000 into HHK plc's occupational pension scheme. HHK plc contributed a further 2% into the pension scheme on Esme's behalf.

Other information

(1) During the tax year 2024/25, Esme received dividend income of £4,500 from quoted shares. Esme is considering transferring these shares to her husband, Andy.

(2) During the tax year 2024/25, Esme made a charitable donation of £5,000 (net) under the gift aid scheme.

Esme's husband

Esme is married to Andy. Andy's only income in the tax year 2024/25 is dividend income of £8,500.

Both Esme and Andy's income is expected to remain the same for the foreseeable future.

Required

(a) Calculate Esme's income tax liability for the tax year 2024/25.

Note. You should indicate by the use of zero (0) any items which are not taxable or deductible. **(10 marks)**

(b) Explain how a married couple can reduce their income tax liabilities for the tax year 2024/25 by claiming the transferable amount of personal allowance (the marriage allowance), and state why such a claim is not possible for Esme and Andy. **(3 marks)**

(c) Explain how both Esme's income tax liability and Andy's income tax liability for the tax year 2025/26 would be affected if they were to transfer all of the quoted shares currently held by Esme to Andy.

Notes.

1. You are not expected to recalculate all of Esme's income tax liability.
2. You should assume that income tax rates and allowances remain unchanged. **(2 marks)**

(Total = 15 marks)

101 Hannah and Gregor (Mar/Jun 2023, amended) (27 mins)

Hannah

On 1 January 2025, Hannah commenced employment with Lomly Ltd.

The following information is available in respect of the tax year 2024/25:

Employment

On 1 January 2025, Hannah commenced employment with Lomly Ltd earning a gross annual salary of £125,000. Lomly Ltd also provides Hannah with the following benefits:

Living accommodation

On 1 January 2025, Hannah moved into a property owned by Lomly Ltd which does not qualify as job-related accommodation. The property has an annual value of £16,000. The property was purchased by Lomly Ltd on 1 September 2022 for £250,000 and its market value on 1 January 2025 was £280,000.

Beneficial loan

Lomly Ltd provided Hannah with an interest-free loan of £60,000 on 1 January 2025. She has repaid £2,500 at the end of each month starting on 31 January 2025. The taxable benefit in respect of this loan is calculated using the average method.

Travel and expenses

During the period 1 January to 5 April 2025, Hannah used her private car to travel 6,000 business miles. She was reimbursed by Lomly Ltd at a rate of 50 pence per mile.

Hannah also paid £450 out of her own bank account for hotel rooms which she stayed in during business trips. Lomly Ltd reimbursed her for these expenses on 20 March 2025.

Gregor

Gregor has been self-employed since 6 April 2006. He has the following income and chargeable gains for the tax years 2023/24 and 2024/25:

	2023/24	2024/25
	£	£
Trading profit/(loss)	14,700	(68,800)
Property business profit/(loss)	4,600	(2,300)
Building society interest (gross)	1,300	900
Chargeable gain/(loss)	(2,900)	17,400

Required

(a) Calculate the employment income of Hannah for the tax year 2024/25.

 Note. You should indicate by the use of zero (0) any items which are not taxable or deductible. **(8 marks)**

(b) Explain how the tax treatment of the property provided to Hannah would differ if it qualified as job-related accommodation. **(1 mark)**

(c) On the assumption that Gregor relieves his trading loss of £68,800 as early as possible, calculate the amount of trading loss carried forward to the tax year 2025/26. You should assume that tax allowances for the tax year 2024/25 apply throughout. **(6 marks)**

(Total = 15 marks)

102 Alfred and Amaia (March/June 2021) (amended)   (27 mins)

Alfred and Amaia are a married couple.

Alfred

Alfred commenced trading as a sole trader on 1 September 2024. He prepared his first set of accounts under the accruals basis for the seven-month period ended 31 March 2025, and his draft tax adjusted trading profit before capital allowances was £63,000. The draft tax adjusted trading profit is **before** adjusting for any deductions arising from the following:

(1) £5,000 incurred during January and February 2024 on a marketing campaign for his business

(2) A premium of £30,000 paid on 1 September 2024 to acquire a ten-year lease on a workshop used for trade purposes

(3) Cost of a golf day on 31 March 2025 for a group of Alfred's largest clients totalling £1,000

(4) Expenditure of £116,000 on 1 September 2024 for plant and equipment

(5) The purchase of a car on 15 December 2024 for £24,000

 The car has a CO_2 emissions rate of 24 grams per kilometre and is used by Alfred's employee.

Amaia

Amaia is employed by Argole Ltd and her remuneration package comprises:

(1) A gross annual salary of £80,000

(2) From 1 January 2025, Argole Ltd provided Amaia with a petrol-powered company car. The car had a list price of £25,000, although Argole Ltd received a discount and only paid £23,500. The car has a CO_2 emissions rate of 52 grams per kilometre. Argole Ltd did not provide any fuel for Amaia's private use.

(3) Since 6 April 2022, Argole Ltd has provided Amaia with living accommodation which qualifies as job-related accommodation. The annual value of the property is £23,000 and Argole Ltd pays rent of £2,500 per month.

Argole Ltd deducted income tax under PAYE of £19,240 from Amaia's salary during the tax year 2024/25. Since 6 April 2022, Amaia has let out her own house unfurnished at a rent of £1,200 per month. Amaia received 13 months' rent during the tax year 2024/25.

Amaia has a mortgage which she took out to acquire the house and, in the tax year 2024/25, she made mortgage payments of £6,000, including interest of £2,600. On 1 December 2023, Amaia paid an insurance premium of £800 for the house in respect of the year ended 31 December 2024. Then, on 1 December 2024, she paid an insurance premium of £1,250 for the year ended 31 December 2025.

Required

(a) Calculate Alfred's revised tax adjusted trading profit or loss for the seven-month period ended 31 March 2025.

   Notes.

   1 Your computation should commence with the draft tax adjusted trading profit of £63,000 and list all of the items referred to in the notes, indicating with the use of zero (0) any items which do not require adjustment.

   2 You should assume Alfred claims the maximum amount of capital allowances. **(6 marks)**

(b) Calculate the income tax payable by Amaia for the tax year 2024/25.

   Note. Your computation should list all of the items referred to in the scenario, indicating with the use of zero (0) any items which are not taxable. **(9 marks)**

   (Total = 15 marks)

103 John (June 2013) (amended) (27 mins)

John is employed by Surf plc. The following information is available for the tax year 2024/25:

(1) During the tax year 2024/25, John was promoted and paid gross remuneration of £338,318. In each of the tax years 2021/22, 2022/23 and 2023/24, his adjusted income was below £150,000.

(2) During the tax year 2024/25, John contributed £18,000 into Surf plc's occupational pension scheme. The company contributed a further £12,000 on his behalf. Both John and Surf plc have made exactly the same contributions for the previous five tax years.

(3) During 2021 Surf plc provided John with a loan which was used to purchase a yacht. The amount of loan outstanding at 6 April 2024 was £84,000. John repaid £12,000 of the loan on 31 July 2024, and then repaid a further £12,000 on 31 December 2024. He paid loan interest of £90 to Surf plc during the tax year 2024/25. The taxable benefit in respect of this loan is calculated using the average method.

(4) During the tax year 2024/25, John made personal pension contributions up to the maximum amount of available annual allowances, including any unused amounts brought forward from previous years. These contributions were in addition to the contributions he made to Surf plc's occupational pension scheme (see note (2)). John has not made any personal pension contributions in previous tax years.

(5) John owns a holiday cottage which is let out as a furnished holiday letting, although the letting does not qualify as a trade under the furnished holiday letting rules. The property business profit for the year ended 5 April 2025 was £14,855 before taking into account interest and £1,875 paid to a letting agent. John paid loan interest of £7,500 for the year in respect of a loan to buy this property.

Required

(a) Calculate John's income tax liability for the tax year 2024/25. **(12 marks)**

(b) State THREE tax advantages of a rental property qualifying as a trade under the furnished holiday letting rules. **(3 marks)**

(Total = 15 marks)

104 Wai (June 2015) (amended) (27 mins)

Wai is employed as a sales manager by Qaz plc, and the following information is available in respect of the tax year 2024/25:

(1) During the tax year 2024/25, Wai was paid a gross monthly salary of £10,200.

(2) In addition to her salary, Wai has been paid the following bonuses:

Amount	Date of payment	Date of entitlement	In respect of the six-month period ended
£4,600	25 April 2024	31 March 2024	31 December 2023
£8,100	20 August 2024	3 July 2024	30 June 2024
£2,900	3 May 2025	15 April 2025	31 December 2024

(3) During the period 6 April to 31 August 2024, Wai used her private car for both private and business journeys. She was reimbursed by Qaz plc at the rate of 55p per mile for the following mileage:

	Miles
Normal daily travel between home and Qaz plc's offices	2,420
Travel between home and the premises of Qaz plc's clients (none of the clients' premises were located near the offices of Qaz plc)	8,580
Travel between home and a temporary workplace (the assignment was for ten weeks)	2,860
Total mileage reimbursed by Qaz plc	13,860

(4) During the period 1 September 2024 to 5 April 2025, Qaz plc provided Wai with a new diesel-powered car which meets the RDE2 standard. The car has a list price of £10,013 and an official CO_2 emission rate of 86 grams per kilometre. Qaz plc does not provide Wai with any fuel for private journeys.

(5) During January 2025, Wai spent ten nights overseas on company business. Qaz plc paid Wai a daily allowance of £10 to cover the cost of personal incidental expenses, such as telephone calls to her family.

(6) Throughout the tax year 2024/25, Qaz plc allowed Wai the use of two mobile telephones. The telephones had each cost £400 when purchased by the company in March 2024.

(7) Throughout the tax year 2024/25, Qaz plc provided Wai with living accommodation. The company had purchased the property on 1 June 2021 for £142,000, and it has been provided to Wai since 1 February 2023. Improvements costing £24,200 were made to the property during October 2021, and further improvements costing £9,800 were made during August 2024. The annual value of the property is £4,828.

Qaz plc does not payroll employee benefits.

Required

(a) Calculate Wai's taxable income for the tax year 2024/25. **(12 marks)**

(b) Briefly outline the information to be included in PAYE forms P60 and P11D, and state the dates by which they should have been provided to Wai for the tax year 2024/25.

Note. Your answer should be confined to the details which are relevant to Wai, although no figures are required. **(3 marks)**

(Total = 15 marks)

105 Samson and Delilah (September/December 2015) (amended) (27 mins)

Samson and Delilah are a married couple. They are both employed by Rope plc, and Delilah is also a partner in a partnership. The following information is available in respect of the tax year 2024/25:

Samson

During the tax year 2024/25, Samson was paid a gross annual salary of £112,000 in respect of his employment with Rope plc.

Delilah

(1) During the tax year 2024/25, Delilah was paid a gross annual salary of £184,000 in respect of her employment with Rope plc.

(2) Throughout the tax year 2024/25, Rope plc provided Delilah with a petrol powered car which has a list price of £67,200, and an official CO_2 emission rate of 147 grams per kilometre. Rope plc does not provide Delilah with any fuel for private journeys. Delilah was unable to drive her car for a period during the tax year 2024/25 because of a skiing accident, and during this period Rope plc provided her with a chauffeur at a total cost of £9,400.

(3) Rope plc provided all its employees with a hamper of groceries costing £42 each in December 2024.

(4) Delilah spent £70 in July 2024 on travelling by train to visit a customer of Rope plc. This amount was reimbursed by Rope plc in August 2024.

(5) During the tax year 2024/25, Delilah donated £250 (gross) per month to charity under the payroll deduction scheme operated by Rope plc.

(6) Delilah has been in partnership with Esther and Felix for a number of years. The partnership's tax adjusted trading profit for the year ended 31 December 2024 was £93,600. Esther is paid an annual salary of £8,000, with the balance of profits being shared 40% to Delilah, 30% to Esther and 30% to Felix.

(7) During the tax year 2024/25, Delilah paid interest of £6,200 (gross) on a personal loan taken out to purchase her share in the partnership.

(8) During the tax year 2024/25, Delilah made charitable gift aid donations totalling £4,864 (net).

Joint income – building society deposit account

Samson and Delilah have savings in a building society deposit account which is in their joint names. During the tax year 2024/25, they received building society interest totalling £9,600 from this joint account.

Required

(a) Calculate Samson and Delilah's respective income tax liabilities for the tax year 2024/25.

Note. The following mark allocation is provided as guidance for this requirement:

Samson (4 marks)

Delilah (9 marks) **(13 marks)**

(b) Calculate Samson's income tax saving for the tax year 2024/25 if the building society deposit account had been in Delilah's sole name instead of in joint names for the entire year.

(2 marks)

(Total = 15 marks)

106 Petula (March/June 2017) (27 mins)

Petula has been employed as a sales manager by Downtown plc since 6 April 2015. The following information is available in respect of the tax year 2024/25:

(1) During the tax year 2024/25, Petula was paid a gross annual salary of £300,000.

(2) In addition to her salary, Petula has been paid the following bonuses by Downtown plc:

Amount	Date of payment	Date of entitlement	In respect of the six-month period ended
£21,200	30 April 2024	1 April 2024	31 December 2023
£18,600	31 October 2024	1 October 2024	30 June 2024
£22,400	30 April 2025	1 April 2025	31 December 2024

(3) During the tax year 2024/25, Petula used her private car for both private and business journeys. The total mileage driven by Petula throughout the tax year was 26,000 miles, with all of this mileage reimbursed by Downtown plc at the rate of 60p per mile. However, only 21,000 miles were in the performance of Petula's duties for Downtown plc.

(4) Petula pays an annual professional subscription of £630 which is relevant to her employment with Downtown plc. Petula also pays an annual subscription membership fee of £1,840 to a golf club which she uses to entertain Downtown plc's clients. Downtown plc does not reimburse Petula for either of these costs.

(5) During the tax year 2024/25, Petula paid interest of £140 on a personal loan taken out on 6 April 2024 to purchase a computer for sole use in her employment with Downtown plc.

(6) Each tax year since 6 April 2017 (including the tax year 2024/25), Downtown plc has contributed £25,000 into the company's occupational pension scheme on Petula's behalf. Petula has never personally made any pension contributions. Petula's adjusted income for 2021/22, 2022/23 and 2023/24 was below £240,000 (and therefore below the pension income limits).

(7) Petula owns a freehold house which was let out furnished throughout the tax year 2024/25. The total amount of rent received during the tax year was £12,000.

During August 2024, Petula purchased a new washer-dryer for the property at a cost of £730. This was a replacement for an old washing machine which was scrapped, with nil proceeds. The cost of a similar washing machine would have been £420.

During November 2024, Petula purchased a new dishwasher for the property at a cost of £580. The property did not previously have a dishwasher.

The other expenditure on the property paid in the tax year 2024/25 amounted to £1,640, none of which is loan interest, and all of this is allowable.

(8) During the tax year 2024/25, Petula rented out one furnished room of her main residence. During the year, she received rent of £8,900 and incurred allowable expenditure of £2,890 in respect of the room. Petula always uses the most favourable basis as regards the tax treatment of the furnished room.

(9) On 1 July 2024, Petula purchased £250,000 (nominal value) of gilts paying interest at the rate of 3% for £300,000. Interest is paid half-yearly on 30 June and 31 December based on the nominal value. Petula sold the gilts on 31 October 2024 for £302,500 (including accrued interest).

Required

(a) Calculate Petula's taxable income for the tax year 2024/25.

   Note. Your computation should list all of the items referred to in notes (1) to (9), indicating with the use of zero (0) any items which are not taxable or deductible. **(12 marks)**

(b) Advise Petula of the total amount of her unused pension annual allowances which are available to carry forward to the tax year 2025/26. **(3 marks)**

(Total = 15 marks)

107 Dill (September/December 2017) (amended) (27 mins)

Up to and including the tax year 2022/23, Dill was always resident in the United Kingdom (UK), being in the UK for more than 300 days each tax year. She was also resident in the UK for the tax year 2024/25. However, during the tax year 2023/24, Dill was overseas for 305 days, spending just 60 days in the UK. Dill has a house in the UK and stayed there on the 60 days which she spent in the UK. She also has a house overseas. For the tax year 2023/24, Dill did not have any close family in the UK, did not do any work in the UK and was not treated as working full-time overseas.

On 6 April 2024, Dill returned to the UK and commenced employment with Herb plc as the IT manager. She also set up a small technology business which she ran on a self-employed basis, but this business failed and Dill ceased self-employment on 5 April 2025. The following information is available for the tax year 2024/25:

Employment

(1) During the tax year 2024/25, Dill was paid a gross annual salary of £430,000.

(2) In addition to her salary, Dill has been paid the following bonuses by Herb plc:

Amount	Date of payment	Date of entitlement	In respect of the four-month period
£16,200	31 December 2024	1 November 2024	31 July 2024
£29,100	30 April 2025	1 March 2025	30 November 2024

(3) Throughout the tax year 2024/25, Dill had the use of Herb plc's company gym which is only open to employees of the company. The cost to Herb plc of providing this benefit was £780.

(4) Throughout the tax year 2024/25, Herb plc provided Dill with a home entertainment system for her personal use. The home entertainment system cost Herb plc £5,900 on 6 April 2024.

(5) During the tax year 2024/25, Dill's three-year-old son was provided with a place at Herb plc's workplace nursery. The total cost to the company of providing this nursery place was £7,200 (240 days at £30 per day).

(6) On 1 June 2024, Herb plc provided Dill with an interest-free loan of £96,000 which she used to renovate her main residence. No loan repayments were made before 5 April 2025.

(7) On 25 January 2025, Herb plc paid a health club membership fee of £990 for the benefit of Dill.

(8) During the tax year 2024/25, Dill used her private car for both private and business journeys. The total mileage driven by Dill throughout the tax year was 16,000 miles, with all of this mileage reimbursed by Herb plc at the rate of 25p per mile. However, only 14,500 miles were in the performance of Dill's duties for Herb plc.

(9) During the tax year 2024/25, Dill paid an annual professional subscription of £560 which is relevant to her employment with Herb plc. She also paid an annual membership fee of £1,620 to a golf club which she uses to entertain Herb plc's suppliers. Herb plc did not reimburse Dill for either of these costs.

(10) During the tax year 2024/25, Dill contributed the maximum possible tax relievable amount into Herb plc's occupational pension scheme. The company did not make any contributions on her behalf. Dill has never previously been a member of a pension scheme.

Self-employment

For the tax year 2024/25, Dill's self-employed business made a tax adjusted trading loss of £58,000. Dill will claim relief for this loss against her total income for the tax year 2024/25.

Other information

(1) On 1 November 2024, Dill received a premium bond prize of £1,000.

(2) On 28 February 2025, Dill received interest of £1,840 on the maturity of savings certificates from NS&I (National Savings and Investments).

Required

(a) Explain why Dill was treated as not resident in the United Kingdom for the tax year 2023/24.

(3 marks)

(b) Calculate Dill's taxable income for the tax year 2024/25.

Note. You should indicate by the use of zero (0) any items which are not taxable or deductible.

(12 marks)

(Total = 15 marks)

108 Danh (March/June 2018) (27 mins)

Up to and including the tax year 2021/22, Danh was always automatically treated as not resident in the UK, spending fewer than 46 days in the UK each year. Danh knows that for the tax year 2024/25, he will automatically be treated as resident in the UK, but is unsure of his residence status for the tax years 2022/23 and 2023/24.

For these two tax years, Danh was neither automatically not resident in the UK nor automatically resident. For both of these tax years, Danh spent 100 days in the UK, with the remainder of each tax year spent in the same overseas country. Throughout both tax years, Danh had a property in the UK and stayed there on the 100 days which he spent in the UK. Danh also did substantive work in the UK during both tax years. He does not have any close family in the UK.

On 6 August 2024, Danh commenced self-employment as a sole trader, preparing accounts under the accruals basis. In addition, on 6 September 2024, Danh joined an existing partnership run by Ebele and Fai. The following information is available for the tax year 2024/25.

Self-employment

(1) Danh's statement of profit or loss for the eight-month period ended 5 April 2025 is:

	Note	£
Income		96,400
Expenses		
Depreciation		(2,300)
Motor expenses	2	(3,300)
Professional fees	3	(1,800)
Other expenses (all allowable)		(18,800)
Net profit		70,200

(2) During the eight-month period ended 5 April 2025, Danh drove a total of 12,000 miles, of which 4,000 were for private journeys.

(3) The figure for professional fees consists of £340 for accountancy and £1,460 for legal fees in connection with the grant of a new five-year lease for business premises.

(4) Danh runs his business using one of the six rooms in his private house as an office. The total running costs of the house for the eight-month period ended 5 April 2025 were £4,200. No deduction has been made for using the office in calculating the net profit of £70,200.

(5) The only item of plant and machinery owned by Danh is his car. This was purchased on 6 August 2024 for £14,800 and has a CO_2 emission rate of 40 grams per kilometre.

Partnership loss

(1) For the year ended 5 April 2025, the partnership made a tax-adjusted trading loss of £12,600. Until 5 September 2024, profits and losses were shared 60% to Ebele and 40% to Fai. Since 6 September 2024, they were shared 20% to Danh, 50% to Ebele and 30% to Fai.

(2) Danh will claim to relieve his share of the partnership's loss against his total income for the tax year 2024/25.

(3) During the tax year 2024/25, Danh paid interest of £875 (gross) on a personal loan taken out to purchase his share in the partnership.

Property income

(1) On 6 April 2024, Danh purchased a freehold house which was then let out. The total amount of rent received during the tax year 2024/25 was £14,400.

(2) Danh partly financed the purchase of the property with a repayment mortgage, paying mortgage interest of £10,000 during the tax year 2024/25.

(3) The other expenditure on the property for the tax year 2024/25 amounted to £3,980, and this is all allowable.

Required

(a) Explain whether Danh was treated as resident or not resident in the UK for each of the tax years 2022/23 and 2023/24. **(3 marks)**

(b) Calculate Danh's income tax liability for the tax year 2024/25.

Note. When calculating Danh's trading profit from self-employment for the eight-month period ended 5 April 2025, your computation should commence with the net profit figure of £70,200, indicating by the use of zero (0) any items which do not require adjustment.

(12 marks)

(Total = 15 marks)

109 Martin (September/December 2018) (27 mins)

Martin is employed by Global plc and he is also a member of a partnership. The following information is available in respect of the tax year 2024/25.

Employment

(1) During the tax year 2024/25, Martin was paid a gross annual salary of £144,000 in respect of his employment with Global plc.

(2) In addition to his salary, Martin was paid the following bonuses by Global plc:

Amount	In respect of the six-month period ended	Date of payment	Date of entitlement
£18,200	29 February 2024	31 March 2024	20 March 2024
£21,400	31 August 2024	31 August 2024	20 September 2024
£13,700	28 February 2025	30 April 2025	20 March 2025

48 Taxation (TX – UK) FA 2024

(3) During the tax year 2024/25, Global plc provided Martin with these petrol-powered cars:

Period provided	List price	CO_2 emission date
6 April to 31 December 2024	£18,450	57 grams per kilometre
1 January to 5 April 2025	£24,905	72 grams per kilometre

Martin was not provided with any fuel for private use.

(4) On 6 April 2024, Global plc provided Martin with an interest free loan of £8,000 which he used to purchase a motor bike. No loan repayments were made during the year.

(5) Throughout the tax year 2024/25, Global plc allowed Martin private use of a home entertainment system owned by the company. The home entertainment system cost Global plc £7,400 on 6 April 2024.

(6) During the tax year 2024/25, Martin donated a total of £1,000 (gross) to charity under the payroll deduction scheme operated by Global plc.

(7) Martin paid an annual professional subscription of £560 which is relevant to his employment with Global plc. Martin also paid an annual membership fee of £1,240 to a health club which he used to entertain Global plc's clients. Global plc did not reimburse Martin for either.

Partnership

(1) Martin has been in partnership with Norma and Oprah since 1 April 2010. The partnership's trading profit for the year ended 31 March 2025 was £54,600.

(2) Until 31 December 2024, profits were shared 40% to Martin, 30% to Norma and 30% to Oprah. Since 1 January 2025, profits have been shared equally.

Other income

(1) During the tax year 2024/25, Martin rented out one furnished room of his main residence, receiving rent of £9,200 for the year. No additional expenditure was incurred as a result of the letting.

(2) During the tax year 2024/25, Martin received dividends of £440.

(3) On 30 November 2024, Martin received interest of £1,330 on the maturity of savings certificates from NS&I (National Savings and Investments).

Self-assessment tax return

Martin always files his self-assessment tax return online on 26 December, so his tax return for the tax year 2024/25 will be filed on 26 December 2025.

Because more than 80% of Martin's tax liability is paid under PAYE, he is not required to make self-assessment payments on account.

Required

(a) Calculate Martin's taxable income for the tax year 2024/25.

Note. You should indicate by the use of zero (0) any items which are not taxable or deductible.
(11 marks)

(b) (i) Advise Martin of the deadline for making an amendment to his self-assessment tax return for the tax year 2024/25, and state how HM Revenue and Customs (HMRC) will calculate interest if such an amendment results in additional tax becoming payable.
(2 marks)

(ii) State the latest date by which HMRC will have to notify Martin if they intend to carry out a compliance check in respect of his self-assessment tax return for the tax year 2024/25, and (assuming the check is not made on a completely random basis) the possible reasons why such a check would be made.
(2 marks)

(Total = 15 marks)

110 Tonie (March/June 2019) (27 mins)

Up to and including the tax year 2022/23, Tonie was resident in the UK for tax purposes, spending more than 300 days in the UK each year. Tonie understands that for the tax year 2024/25, she will again automatically be treated as resident in the UK, but is unsure of her residence status for the tax year 2023/24. For this tax year, Tonie was neither automatically resident in the UK nor automatically not resident. Throughout the tax year 2023/24, Tonie was travelling around the world and did not stay in any one country for longer than 30 days, although she did spend a total of 50 days in the UK. Tonie has a house in the UK, but it was let out throughout the tax year 2023/24. She is single, has no children, and stayed with a friend on the 50 days which she spent in the UK. Tonie did not do any substantive work in the UK during the 2023/24.

The following information is available for the tax year 2024/25:

Employment

On 6 April 2024, Tonie, who is a software developer, accepted a one-year contract to maintain websites for Droid plc. Droid plc treated the contract as one of employment, with the payments to Tonie being subject to PAYE. However, Tonie thought that, because she was working from home, her employment status should instead have been one of self-employment.

(1) For the term of the contract, from 6 April 2024 to 5 April 2025, Tonie was paid a fixed gross amount of £6,200 a month. During the term of the contract, Tonie was not permitted to work for any other clients. She was required to do the work personally, not being permitted to sub-contract the work to anyone else.

(2) During the term of the contract, Tonie worked from home, but had to attend weekly meetings at Droid plc's offices to receive instructions regarding the work to be performed during the following week. During the period 6 April 2024 to 5 April 2025, Tonie used her private car for business visits to Droid plc's clients. She drove 2,300 miles, for which Droid plc paid an allowance of 60 pence per mile.

(3) During the term of the contract, Tonie leased computer equipment at a cost of £180 a month. This was used 100% for business purposes.

Property income

(1) Tonie owns a freehold house which is let out (this is not a furnished holiday letting). The total amount of rent received during the tax year 2024/25 was £10,080.

(2) Tonie partly financed the purchase of the property with a repayment mortgage, paying mortgage interest of £8,400 during the tax year 2024/25.

(3) During May 2024, Tonie purchased a new washer-dryer for the property at a cost of £640. This was a replacement for an old washing machine which was scrapped, with nil proceeds. The cost of a similar washing machine would have been £380.

(4) During November 2024, Tonie purchased a new dishwasher for the property at a cost of £560. The property did not previously have a dishwasher.

(5) The other expenditure on the property for the tax year 2024/25 amounted to £3,210, and this is all allowable.

(6) During the tax year 2024/25, Tonie rented out one furnished room of her main residence. During the year, she received rent of £8,580 and incurred allowable expenditure of £870 in respect of the room. Tonie always uses the most favourable basis as regards the tax treatment of the furnished room.

Other income

(1) On 1 July 2024, Tonie inherited £100,000 (nominal value) of gilts paying interest at the rate of 3%. The inheritance was valued at £120,000. Interest is paid half-yearly on 30 June and 31 December based on the nominal value. Tonie sold the gilts on 30 November 2024 for £121,250 (including accrued interest).

(2) On 31 January 2025, Tonie received a premium bond prize of £100.

(3) On 31 March 2025, Tonie received interest of £520 on the maturity of savings certificates from NS&I (National Savings and Investments).

Required

(a) Explain why Tonie was treated as not resident in the UK for the tax year 2023/24. **(2 marks)**

(b) List FOUR factors which are indicators of Tonie being treated as employed in relation to her contract with Droid plc rather than as self-employed.

Note. You should confine your answer to the information given in the question. **(2 marks)**

(c) On the basis that Tonie is treated as employed in relation to her contract with Droid plc, calculate her taxable income for the tax year 2024/25.

Note. You should indicate by the use of zero (0) any items which are not taxable or deductible. **(11 marks)**

(Total = 15 marks)

111 Alicia (September/December 2022) (18 mins)

You should assume that today's date is 28 March 2024.

Alicia is employed by Tusk Ltd, and is currently paid a gross annual salary of £60,000. She is therefore a higher rate taxpayer. Alicia does not have any other income.

Tusk Ltd has offered Alicia the choice of either being provided with a company car or alternatively receiving a salary increase and also being paid a mileage allowance for using her private car for business journeys.

Regardless of which alternative is chosen, Alicia's new remuneration package will take effect from 6 April 2024 and will apply throughout the tax year 2024/25.

Company car alternative

The car will be petrol-powered with a list price of £22,400. It will have an official CO_2 emissions rate of 51 grams per kilometre.

Tusk Ltd will not provide Alicia with any fuel for private journeys.

Under this alternative, Alicia will not run a private car.

Salary and mileage allowance alternative

Alicia will receive an annual gross salary increase of £10,000.

Tusk Ltd will also pay Alicia a mileage allowance of 45p per mile when she uses her private car for business journeys. Alicia will drive 8,000 miles in the performance of her duties for Tusk Ltd during the tax year 2024/25.

Alicia's annual car running costs will be £6,200 higher if she uses her own car for both business and private journeys compared to using a company car.

Required

(a) Advise Alicia of the income tax and national insurance contribution implications for the tax year 2024/25 if she is provided with a company car.

Note. Your answer should be supported by appropriate calculations. As Alicia is a higher rate tax payer you can use a working at the margin approach. However, a full computation approach is equally acceptable. You are not expected to consider any implications for Tusk Ltd. **(3 marks)**

(b) Advise Alicia of the income tax and national insurance contribution implications for the tax year 2024/25 if she receives a gross salary increase of £10,000 and is also paid a mileage allowance.

Note. Your answer should be supported by appropriate calculations. As Alicia is a higher rate tax payer you can use a working at the margin approach. However, a full computation approach is equally acceptable. You are not expected to consider any implications for Tusk Ltd. **(3 marks)**

(c) Advise Alicia as to which of the two alternative remuneration packages is the most beneficial to her, clearly showing the details from the scenario in your workings. **(4 marks)**

(Total = 10 marks)

112 Dom (September/December 2022) (27 mins)

On 31 July 2024, Dom left his employment with Abacus Ltd where he had worked since 2022. Dom started a new employment with Brass Ltd on 1 August 2024. The following information is available in respect of Dom's employments in the tax year 2024/25.

Employment with Abacus Ltd

(1) Dom was paid a gross annual salary of £64,800 when employed by Abacus Ltd.

(2) On 15 May 2024 Abacus Ltd gave Dom a briefcase costing £100 as a reward for passing a professional exam.

(3) During the tax year 2024/25, Dom drove 900 miles on Abacus Ltd company business using his private car. Abacus Ltd reimbursed him for this mileage at a rate of 35 pence per mile.

Employment with Brass Ltd

(1) Dom was paid a gross annual salary of £76,800 once employed by Brass Ltd.

(2) On 1 September 2024 he was provided with a new diesel-powered company car. The car has a list price of £25,200 and an official CO_2 emission rate of 117 grams per kilometre. The car does not meet the real driving emissions 2 (RDE2) standard.

(3) Dom was provided with fuel for private use in respect of this car from 1 September 2024 to 5 April 2025.

(4) Brass Ltd has a workplace nursery on its premises which is available to all employees, and Dom's child took up a place there on 1 January 2025. Dom does not pay anything in respect of this nursery place although the nursery fees payable by members of the public for any available places are £700 per month.

(5) During the tax year 2024/25, Dom paid £300 to renew his membership of a professional body. This professional membership is a requirement of his employment by Brass Ltd.

Other income

(1) During the tax year 2024/25, Dom received savings income of £700 and dividend income of £1,500.

(2) During the tax year 2024/25, Dom made a charitable gift aid donation of £240 (net).

Required

(a) Calculate Dom's income tax liability for the tax year 2024/25.

Note. Your computation should include all of the items referred to in the notes, indicating by the use of zero (0) any items which are not taxable or not deductible. **(12 marks)**

(b) Calculate the total amount of employee class 1 national insurance contributions that Dom will suffer in respect of the tax year 2024/25. **(2 marks)**

(c) State which PAYE form Abacus Ltd will have provided to Dom when his employment with the company ceased, and what Dom will have been required to do with this form. **(1 mark)**

(Total = 15 marks)

Part C: Chargeable gains for individuals

Part C covers chargeable gains for individuals, the subject of Chapters 13 to 16 of the BPP Course Book for Taxation (TX – UK).

Section A

OTQ bank – Chargeable gains for individuals 1 (18 mins)

113 Which of the following gifts made by an individual is exempt from capital gains tax?
(March 2019)

- ○ Gift of a motor boat valued at £10,000 (cost £5,000) to their aunt
- ○ Gift of unquoted shares in a UK company valued at £2,500 (cost £1,800) to their brother
- ○ Gift of antique jewellery valued at £6,800 (cost £3,200) to their sister
- ○ Gift of a sculpture valued at £3,000 (cost £10,000) to their nephew (2 marks)

114 Daniel has had a 30% share in a manufacturing partnership since 2016. He intends to dispose of his entire interest in the partnership in the tax year 2024/25 by selling it to his son for less than its market value.

Daniel has also been a director and 10% shareholder in an unquoted investment (nontrading) company since 2012. He has decided to gift his shares to his daughter in the tax year 2024/25.

Which of the following statements is true? *(September/December 2023)*

- ○ Gift holdover relief is available on the disposal of the interest in the partnership but not on the shares.
- ○ Gift holdover relief is available on the disposal of the shares but not the interest in the partnership.
- ○ Gift holdover relief is available on both disposals.
- ○ Gift holdover relief is available on neither disposal. (2 marks)

115 Trudy sold a house in November 2024. She had never lived in the house.

Her chargeable gain on the sale was £17,000.

Trudy has taxable income of £25,620 in the tax year 2024/25.

The house does not qualify for business asset disposal relief.

What is Trudy's capital gains tax liability for the tax year 2024/25 assuming that she has no other disposals in that year?

- ○ £2,635
- ○ £3,360
- ○ £3,355
- ○ £1,592 (2 marks)

116   Clive purchased a ten-hectare plot of land in May 2011 for £80,000.

In January 2025, Clive sold three of the hectares for £36,000 with expenses of sale amounting to £1,000.

The market value of the remaining seven hectares of land in January 2025 was £90,000.

What is Clive's chargeable gain on the disposal of the three hectares of land in the tax year 2024/25?

[▼]

Pull down list
- £11,000
- £12,143
- £12,600
- £13,143

(2 marks)

---

117   James has the following gains and losses arising from disposals of chargeable assets:

Tax year	2022/23	2023/24	2024/25
	£	£	£
Gains	2,000	4,000	5,600
Losses	(14,000)	(2,000)	(2,000)

The allowable loss carried forward to 2025/26 will be:
- ○ £0
- ○ £2,000
- ○ £11,400
- ○ £100

(2 marks)

---

118   In the tax year 2024/25, Tomaz has taxable income of £14,000 and realises a chargeable gain of £24,000 on the disposal of a painting and a gain of £45,000 on the disposal of a house which he used to let out to tenants.

What is Tomaz's capital gains tax liability for 2024/25?

£ [   ]

(2 marks)

---

119   Ellen purchased an antique vase for £1,500. In October 2024, she sold the vase for £7,000.

What is Ellen's chargeable gain on the sale of the vase?
- ○ £0
- ○ £1,000
- ○ £1,667
- ○ £5,500

(2 marks)

120 Franny has taxable income of £30,000 for the year. She also makes chargeable gains of £20,000 on the disposal of some shares and £10,500 on the disposal of some residential property. She has a capital loss of £3,000.

Identify, by clicking on the relevant boxes in the table below, whether each of the following statements is true or false.

The best use of the annual exempt amount is against the residential property gain first.	TRUE	FALSE
Any unused basic rate band should be used against the gain on disposal of the shares before the gain on the disposal of the residential property.	TRUE	FALSE
For disposal of the residential property, a payment on account must be made.	TRUE	FALSE
Any capital losses should be deducted from the gain on disposal of the shares in preference to the gain on residential property.	TRUE	FALSE

(2 marks)

121 **Which TWO of the following statements about allowable capital losses for an individual are true?** *(September/December 2020)*

☐ The annual exempt amount is deducted before any brought forward capital losses are utilised against current year gains.

☐ Current year capital losses remaining after offset against current year chargeable gains can always be offset against current year income.

☐ The annual exempt amount is deducted before any current year capital losses are utilised against current year gains.

☐ Excess current year capital losses are carried forward indefinitely until future chargeable gains arise.

(2 marks)

122 Naomi realised a chargeable gain of £20,700 in the tax year 2024/25. The gain related to the disposal of a residential property held for investment purposes and did not qualify for business asset disposal relief. In the tax year 2024/25, Naomi had taxable income of £29,500 and she contributed £2,000 (net) into her personal pension scheme.

What is Naomi's capital gains tax liability for the tax year 2024/25?
(September/December 2021)

○ £3,606
○ £4,326
○ £3,756
○ £4,476

(2 marks)

(Total = 20 marks)

OTQ bank – Chargeable gains for individuals 2   (36 mins)

123 Harold bought a painting for £8,500. In December 2024, he sold the painting for £5,000.

What is Harold's allowable loss on the sale of the painting?

£ [2,500]   (2 marks)

---

124 Angela purchased a house and lived in it for three years. The house was then unoccupied for five years because Angela was seconded to an overseas office. She then lived in the house for two years. Angela then went to live with her sister and the house was unoccupied for four years. Angela then lived in the house for the last year of ownership.

How many years of Angela's 15-year period of ownership of the house will be exempt for the purposes of private residence relief?

[▼]

Pull down list
- 11 years
- 14 years
- 14½ years
- 15 years

(2 marks)

---

125 Sascha owned a factory which had always been used in her business. She sold the factory on 14 May 2024 and realised a gain of £60,000. On 12 August 2024, she purchased a 20-year lease on a warehouse using all the proceeds from the sale of the factory. A claim for relief for replacement of business assets was made. The warehouse will continue to be used in Sascha's trade until it is sold on 14 October 2034.

When will the deferred gain of £60,000 become chargeable to capital gains tax?

12 August 2024   14 May 2034   12 August 2034   14 October 2034

- ○ 12 August 2024
- ○ 14 May 2034
- ○ 12 August 2034
- ○ 14 October 2034

(2 marks)

---

126 Louise has two chargeable gains from the disposal of shares in the tax year 2024/25:
- £8,000 – claim made for business asset disposal relief
- £4,800 – claim not made for business asset disposal relief

Louise has taxable income of £38,000 in the tax year 2024/25.

What is Louise's capital gains tax liability for the tax year 2024/25?

£ [   ]   (2 marks)

---

56   Taxation (TX – UK) FA 2024

127 Neil bought 1,000 shares in Garden plc for £1,500 in October 2004. In November 2006, there was a 1 for 2 bonus issue when the shares had a market value of £2.40 each. In July 2011, there was a 3 for 1 rights issue when the shares had a market value of £3 but were offered to existing shareholders for £2.70 each. Neil took up his full entitlement to shares under the rights issue. Neil sold all of his shares in Garden plc in February 2025.

What is the cost of the shares sold in February 2025?

£ ☐ (2 marks)

128 Lotte purchased a freehold warehouse on 24 November 2016 for £52,000. On 30 June 2024, the warehouse was destroyed in a fire.

On 28 August 2024, Lotte received insurance proceeds of £71,000. She spent £64,000 of the proceeds on a replacement warehouse on 29 January 2025.

Assuming that, as far as possible, Lotte claims to defer any chargeable gains arising in the tax year 2024/25, calculate the carried forward base cost of the new warehouse purchased on 29 January 2025? *(September/December 2022)*

○ £45,000
○ £52,000
○ £57,000
○ £64,000 (2 marks)

129 On 31 March 2025, Jessica sold a copyright for £28,800. The copyright had been purchased on 1 April 2019 for £21,000 when it had an unexpired life of 15 years.

What is Jessica's chargeable gain in respect of the disposal of the copyright?

○ £0
○ £20,400
○ £16,200
○ £7,800 (2 marks)

130 For the tax year 2024/25, Nog has a chargeable gain of £15,100 and a capital loss of £10,000. She has unused capital losses of £6,100 brought forward from the tax year 2023/24.

What amount of capital losses can Nog carry forward to the tax year 2025/26?

£ ☐ (2 marks)

131 Brian had the following income and chargeable gains for the tax year 2024/25:

	£
Employment income	43,000
Chargeable gain from the sale of an antique vase	8,700

What is Brian's capital gains tax liability for the tax year 2024/25?
(September/December 2022)

○ £1,013
○ £1,740
○ £570
○ £1,140

(2 marks)

---

132 Larry is a sole trader who made a disposal of a factory on 31 July 2024.

Match the earliest date and the latest date that Larry can make an acquisition of a new qualifying business asset and claim replacement of business asset (rollover) relief.

- 1 August 2021
- 31 July 2025
- 1 August 2023
- 31 July 2027

Earliest date: 1 August 2023
Latest date: 31 July 2027

(2 marks)

(Total = 20 marks)

Section B

OT case – Aloi, Bon and Dinah (June 2011) (amended)   (18 mins)

On 15 October 2024 Alphabet Ltd, an unquoted trading company, was taken over by XYZ plc. Prior to the takeover Alphabet Ltd's share capital consisted of 100,000 £1 ordinary shares, and under the terms of the takeover the shareholders received for each £1 ordinary share in Alphabet Ltd either cash of £6 per share or one £1 ordinary share in XYZ plc worth £6.50. The following information is available regarding three of the shareholders of Alphabet Ltd:

Aloi

Aloi has been the managing director of Alphabet Ltd since the company's incorporation on 1 January 2012, and she accepted XYZ plc's cash alternative of £6 per share in respect of her shareholding of 60,000 £1 ordinary shares in Alphabet Ltd. Aloi had originally subscribed for 50,000 shares in Alphabet Ltd on 1 January 2012 at their par value and purchased a further 10,000 shares on 20 May 2013 for £18,600.

On 6 February 2025, Aloi sold an investment non-residential property, and this disposal resulted in a chargeable gain against which her annual exempt amount will be set.

For the tax year 2024/25, Aloi has taxable income of £60,000. All her income tax has previously been collected under PAYE, so she has not received a notice to file a return for the tax year 2024/25 and so is required to give notice of her chargeability to capital gains tax to HMRC.

Bon

Bon has been the sales director of Alphabet Ltd since 1 February 2024, having not previously been an employee of the company, although she had been a shareholder since 1 March 2022. She accepted XYZ plc's share alternative of one £1 ordinary share for each of her 25,000 £1 ordinary shares in Alphabet Ltd. Bon had purchased her shareholding on 1 March 2022 for £92,200.

On 4 March 2025 Bon made a gift of 10,000 of her £1 ordinary shares in XYZ plc to her brother. On that date the shares were quoted on the stock exchange at £7.10 – £7.14. Gift holdover relief is not available in respect of this disposal.

Dinah

Dinah has been an employee of Alphabet Ltd since 1 May 2022. She accepted XYZ plc's share alternative of one £1 ordinary share for each of her 3,000 £1 ordinary shares in Alphabet Ltd. Dinah had purchased her shareholding on 20 June 2021 for £4,800.

On 13 November 2024, Dinah sold 1,000 of her £1 ordinary shares in XYZ plc for £6,600.

Dinah died on 5 April 2025, and her remaining 2,000 £1 ordinary shares in XYZ plc were inherited by her daughter. On that date these shares were valued at £16,000.

For the tax year 2024/25, Dinah had taxable income of £12,000.

133 Which TWO of the following statements are correct about Bon and Dinah's entitlement to business asset disposal relief in relation to their shares in Alphabet Ltd if they had accepted the cash alternative on the takeover by XYZ plc?

☐ Alphabet Ltd was not Bon's personal company for the requisite time before disposal.
☐ Bon was not an officer or employee of Alphabet Ltd for the requisite time before disposal.
☐ Dinah was not an officer or employee of Alphabet Ltd for the requisite time before disposal.
☐ Alphabet Ltd was not Dinah's personal company for the requisite time before disposal.

(2 marks)

---

134 What is Aloi's capital gains tax liability on the disposal of her shares in Alphabet Ltd assuming that the gain qualifies for business asset disposal relief?

○ £31,000
○ £52,452
○ £29,140
○ £81,592

(2 marks)

---

135 Match the latest dates by which Aloi must:

(1) Give notice of her chargeability to capital gains tax for the tax year 2024/25 to HMRC

(2) Pay her capital gains liability for the tax year 2024/25 in order to avoid interest and penalties

| 5 October 2025 |
| 31 January 2026 |
| 31 December 2025 |
| 31 July 2026 |

Notification

Payment

(2 marks)

---

136 What is the chargeable gain arising on Bon's gift of her shares in XYZ plc to her brother?

○ £34,320
○ £6,200
○ £34,220
○ £61,200

(2 marks)

137 What is Dinah's capital gains tax liability for the tax year 2024/25?

○ £610
○ £0
○ £900
○ £1,090 (2 marks)

(Total = 10 marks)

OT case – Ginger, Innocent and Nigel (June 2013) (amended) (18 mins)

You should assume that today's date is 1 March 2025.

Ginger

Ginger has a holding of 10,000 £1 ordinary shares in Nutmeg Ltd, an unquoted trading company, which she had purchased on 13 February 2005 for £2.40 per share.

The current market value of the shares is £6.40 per share, but Ginger intends to sell some of the holding to her daughter at £4.00 per share during March 2025. Ginger and her daughter will elect to use gift holdover relief to hold over any gain.

For the tax year 2024/25, Ginger will not make any other disposals, and has therefore not utilised her annual exempt amount. She has a loss brought forward from 2023/24 of £(10,100).

Innocent and Nigel

Innocent and Nigel, a married couple, both have shareholdings in Cinnamon Ltd, an unquoted trading company with a share capital of 100,000 £1 ordinary shares.

Innocent has been the managing director of Cinnamon Ltd since the company's incorporation on 1 July 2008, and she currently holds 20,000 shares (with matching voting rights) in the company. These shares were subscribed for on 1 July 2008 at their par value.

Nigel has never been an employee or a director of Cinnamon Ltd, and he currently holds 3,000 shares (with matching voting rights) in the company. These shares were purchased on 23 April 2012 for £46,200.

Either Innocent or Nigel will sell 2,000 of their shares in Cinnamon Ltd during March 2025 for £65,000 but are not sure which of them should make the disposal.

For the tax year 2024/25, both Innocent and Nigel have already made disposals which will fully utilise their annual exempt amounts, and they will each have taxable income of £80,000.

138 What is the chargeable gain per share that Ginger will make on her disposal of shares in Nutmeg Ltd to her daughter?

○ £4.00
○ £1.60
○ £2.40
○ £0 (2 marks)

139 If the chargeable gain per share on Ginger's disposal of shares in Nutmeg Ltd had been £1.54 per share, what would be the maximum number of shares that Ginger could have sold to her daughter without incurring a charge to capital gains tax?

- ○ 2,046
- ○ 7,207
- ○ 8,506
- ○ 3,275

(2 marks)

140 Which TWO of the following statements about business asset disposal relief are correct?
- ☐ Business asset disposal relief is only available on shareholdings owned by a director.
- ☐ There is a lifetime limit of £1,000,000 for business asset disposal relief.
- ☐ Business asset disposal relief is only available on shareholdings if they are held in a trading company.
- ☐ The conditions for business asset disposal relief in relation to a shareholding must be satisfied for five years before the disposal.

(2 marks)

141 What would Innocent's capital gains tax liability be if she sold her shares in Cinnamon Ltd during March 2025?

£ _____ (2 marks)

142 What would Nigel's capital gains tax liability be if he sold his shares in Cinnamon Ltd during March 2025?

£ _____ (2 marks)

(Total = 10 marks)

OT case – Jerome (March/June 2016) (amended) (18 mins)

Jerome made the following disposals of assets to family members during the tax year 2024/25:

(1) On 28 May 2024, Jerome sold a house to his wife for £140,000. The value of the house at that date was £187,000. Jerome's uncle had purchased it on 14 July 1995 for £45,900. The uncle died on 12 June 2005, and it was inherited by Jerome. On that date, the house was valued at £112,800. Jerome has never occupied the house as his main residence.

(2) On 24 June 2024, Jerome made a gift of his entire 12% holding of 12,000 £1 ordinary shares in Reward Ltd, an unquoted trading company, to his son. The market value of the shares on that date was £98,400. The shares had been purchased on 15 March 2006 for £39,000. On 24 June 2024, the market value of Reward Ltd's chargeable assets was £540,000, of which £460,000 was in respect of chargeable business assets. Jerome and his son will elect to use gift holdover relief to hold over the gain on this gift of a business asset.

(3) On 7 November 2024, Jerome made a gift of an antique bracelet valued at £12,200 to his granddaughter. The antique bracelet had been purchased on 1 September 2001 for £2,100.

(4) On 29 January 2025, Jerome made a gift of nine hectares of land valued at £78,400 to his brother. He had originally purchased ten hectares of land on 3 November 2005 for £37,800. The market value of the unsold hectare of land as at 29 January 2025 was £33,600. The land has never been used for business purposes.

143 What is the base cost of the house for capital gains tax purposes for Jerome's wife?
   ○ £45,900
   ○ £187,000
   ○ £112,800
   ○ £140,000
   (2 marks)

144 What is the amount of gift holdover relief that can be claimed on the gift of the Reward Ltd shares?

   £ [   ]   (2 marks)

145 Match the latest date for submission of the election for gift holdover relief on the gift of the Reward Ltd shares and person(s) who must make the election.

   | 31 January 2026 | | Latest date for election |
   | 5 April 2029 | | Person(s) making election |
   | Jerome |
   | Jerome and his son |

   (2 marks)

146 What is the amount of the chargeable gain on the disposal of the antique bracelet?

   [▼]

   Pull down list
   - £10,000
   - £10,100
   - £10,333
   - £3,900

   (2 marks)

147 What is the amount of the chargeable gain on the disposal of the nine hectares of land?
   ○ £66,200
   ○ £40,600
   ○ £44,380
   ○ £51,940
   (2 marks)

(Total = 10 marks)

OT case – Hali and Goma (March/June 2019) (18 mins)

You should assume that the tax allowances for the tax year 2024/25 applied in previous tax years.

Hali and Goma are a married couple.

Capital losses brought forward

Hali had capital losses of £39,300 for the tax year 2022/23. He had chargeable gains of £7,000 for the tax year 2023/24.

Goma had capital losses of £9,100 and chargeable gains of £6,900 for the tax year 2023/24. She did not have any capital losses for the tax year 2022/23.

Ordinary shares in Lima Ltd

On 24 July 2024, Hali sold 5,000 £1 ordinary shares in Lima Ltd, for £4.95 per share. Lima Ltd's shares have recently been selling for £5.30 per share, but Hali sold them at the lower price because he needed a quick sale.

Goma had originally subscribed for 30,000 ordinary shares in Lima Ltd at their par value of £1 per share on 28 July 2008. On 18 August 2017, she gave 8,000 ordinary shares to Hali. On that date, the market value for 8,000 shares was £23,200.

Hali and Goma will both dispose of their remaining shareholdings in Lima Ltd during the tax year 2025/26. However, they are unsure as to whether these disposals will qualify for business asset disposal relief.

Antique table

On 11 October 2024, an antique table owned by Hali was destroyed in a fire. The table had been purchased on 3 June 2010 for £44,000. Hali received insurance proceeds of £62,000 on 12 December 2024, and on 6 January 2025, he purchased a replacement antique table for £63,600. Hali will make a claim to roll over the gain arising from the receipt of the insurance proceeds.

Disposals by Goma during the tax year 2024/25

Goma disposed of the following assets during the tax year 2024/25, all of which resulted in gains:

(1) Qualifying corporate bonds sold for £38,300

(2) A car (suitable for private use) sold for £11,600

(3) An antique vase sold for £6,200

(4) A copyright (with an unexpired life of eight years when purchased) sold for £5,400

(5) Quoted shares held within an individual savings account (ISA) sold for £24,700

148 **What amount of unused capital losses do Hali and Goma have brought forward to the tax year 2024/25?**

Option	Hali	Goma
	£	£
1	32,300	13,000
2	32,300	2,200
3	35,300	13,000
4	35,300	2,200

(2 marks)

149 What cost figure and what value per share (disposal value) will be used in calculating the chargeable gain on Hali's sale of 5,000 ordinary shares in Lima Ltd?

Option	Cost figure £	Value per share £
○ 1	5,000	4.95
○ 2	14,500	4.95
○ 3	14,500	5.30
○ 4	5,000	5.30

(2 marks)

150 In deciding whether Hali and Goma's future disposals of their shareholdings in Lima Ltd will qualify for business asset disposal relief, which of the following statements is correct?

○ Hali and Goma must be directors of Lima Ltd.
○ Lima Ltd must be a trading company.
○ Hali and Goma must have shareholdings of at least 10% each in Lima Ltd.
○ The qualifying conditions must be met for a period of three years prior to the date of disposal.

(2 marks)

151 What is the base cost of Hali's replacement antique table for capital gains tax (CGT) purposes?

○ £62,000
○ £63,600
○ £45,600
○ £44,000

(2 marks)

152 How many of the five assets disposed of by Goma during the tax year 2024/25 are exempt assets for the purposes of capital gains tax (CGT)?

○ Three
○ Five
○ Two
○ Four

(2 marks)

(Total = 10 marks)

OT Case – Lily (March/June 2021) (18 mins)

Lily disposed of various assets during the tax year 2024/25, resulting in chargeable gains.

Lily's disposals included the following:

A copyright sold on 30 June 2024

The copyright had been purchased on 1 July 2021 for £22,000 when it had an unexpired life of 15 years.

Four hectares of land sold on 12 August 2024

Lily had originally purchased six hectares of land on 30 May 2008 for £84,000. The four hectares of land were sold for £140,000, and the market value of the unsold two hectares of land at the time of sale was £60,000. Prior to the disposal, Lily spent £14,400 clearing and levelling the four hectares of land that were sold.

A house sold on 31 December 2024

The house had been purchased on 1 January 2011, and throughout the 168 months of ownership had been occupied by Lily as follows (periods shown chronologically):

	Months
Occupied	32
Unoccupied – travelling overseas	36
Unoccupied – required to work elsewhere in the UK	60
Occupied	20
Unoccupied – travelling overseas	20
	168

Throughout the period 1 January 2011 to 31 December 2024, Lily did not have any other main residence.

Cash received following takeover of Moon plc by Sun plc on 22 February 2025

Lily had originally purchased her £1 ordinary shares in Moon plc on 18 July 2011 for £27,280. Under the terms of the takeover, Lily received total cash of £19,800 and 22,000 £1 ordinary shares in Sun plc. Immediately after the takeover, Sun plc's £1 ordinary shares were quoted at £2.20.

Lily's sister

Lily's sister has chargeable gains for the year 2024/25 of £44,200 which qualify for business asset disposal relief and £98,100 of chargeable gains relating to the disposal of a residential property which is not her main residence.

Lily's sister does not have any taxable income for the tax year 2024/25.

153 **What cost figure will have been used in calculating the chargeable gain on the disposal of Lily's copyright?**

　　○ £22,000
　　○ £17,600
　　○ £4,400
　　○ £19,067

(2 marks)

154 **What are the total deductions which will have been allowed in calculating the chargeable gain on the disposal of Lily's four hectares of land?**

　　○ £68,880
　　○ £73,200
　　○ £70,400
　　○ £58,800

(2 marks)

155 What is the total period of occupation (both actual and deemed) for the purposes of calculating the private residence relief on the disposal of Lily's house?
- ○ 145 months
- ○ 157 months
- ○ 168 months
- ○ 136 months (2 marks)

156 What is Lily's chargeable gain in respect of the cash received following the takeover of Moon plc by Sun plc?
- ○ £11,880
- ○ £6,878
- ○ £19,800
- ○ £8,640 (2 marks)

157 What is Lily's sister's capital gains tax liability for the tax year 2024/25?
- ○ £27,964
- ○ £24,982
- ○ £27,664
- ○ £27,244 (2 marks)

(Total = 10 marks)

Section C

158 Jorge (December 2011) (amended) (18 mins)

Jorge disposed of the following assets during the tax year 2024/25:

(1) On 30 June 2024 Jorge sold a house for £308,000. The house had been purchased on 1 January 2007 for £93,000. On 10 June 2013, Jorge had incurred legal fees of £5,000 in relation to a boundary dispute with his neighbour. Throughout the 210 months of ownership the house had been occupied by Jorge as follows:

	Months
Occupied	34
Unoccupied – Travelling overseas	18
Unoccupied – Required to work overseas by his employer	24
Occupied	11
Unoccupied – Required to work elsewhere in the UK by his employer	30
Unoccupied – Travelling overseas	22
Unoccupied – Required to work elsewhere in the UK by his employer	26
Occupied	17
Unoccupied – Required to work overseas by his employer	12
Unoccupied – Travelling overseas	13
Unoccupied – Lived with sister	2
	210

Jorge let the house out during all of the periods when he did not occupy it personally. Throughout the period 1 January 2007 to 30 June 2024 Jorge did not have any other main residence.

(2) On 30 September 2024, Jorge sold a copyright for £80,300. The copyright had been purchased on 1 October 2022 for £70,000 when it had an unexpired life of ten years.

(3) On 6 October 2024, Jorge sold a painting for £5,400. The painting had been purchased on 18 May 2013 for £2,200.

(4) On 29 October 2024, Jorge sold a car for £10,700. The car had been purchased on 21 December 2016 for £14,600.

Jorge has capital losses brought forward of £25,000.

Required

Calculate Jorge's taxable gains for the tax year 2024/25.

(Total = 10 marks)

159 Winston (June 2012) (amended) (18 mins)

(a) On 19 May 2024, Winston disposed of a painting, and this resulted in a chargeable gain of £38,260. For the tax year 2024/25, Winston has taxable income of £25,100 after the deduction of the personal allowance.

Winston is considering the sale of a business that he has run as a sole trader since 1 July 2009.

The business will be sold for £260,000, and this figure, along with the respective cost of each asset, is made up as follows:

	Sale proceeds	Cost
	£	£
Freehold shop	140,000	80,000
Freehold warehouse	88,000	102,000
Net current assets	32,000	32,000
	260,000	

The freehold warehouse has never been used by Winston for business purposes.

Required

(i) Assuming that Winston does not sell his sole trader business, calculate his capital gains tax liability for the tax year 2024/25. **(3 marks)**

(ii) Calculate Winston's capital gains tax liability for the tax year 2024/25 if he sold his sole trader business on 25 March 2025. **(4 marks)**

(b) On 3 December 2024, Renaldo sold two hectares of land at auction for gross proceeds of £92,000. The auctioneers' commission was 5% of the sale price.

Renaldo's wife's father had originally purchased three hectares of land on 4 August 2002 for £19,500. He died on 17 June 2009, and the land was inherited by Renaldo's wife. On that date, the three hectares of land were valued at £28,600.

Renaldo's wife transferred the land to Renaldo on 14 November 2012. On that date, the three hectares of land were valued at £39,000. The market value of the unsold hectare of land as at 3 December 2024 was £38,000.

Compute Renaldo's chargeable gain in respect of the disposal on 3 December 2024.

(3 marks)

(Total = 10 marks)

160 Mick (June 2014) (amended)   (18 mins)

Mick disposed of the following assets during the tax year 2024/25:

(1) On 19 May 2024, Mick sold a freehold warehouse for £522,000. The warehouse was purchased on 6 August 2003 for £258,000 and was extended at a cost of £99,000 during April 2005. In January 2009, the floor of the warehouse was damaged by flooding and had to be replaced at a cost of £63,000. The warehouse was sold because it was surplus to the business's requirements as a result of Mick purchasing a newly built warehouse during 2023. Both warehouses have always been used for business purposes in a wholesale business run by Mick as a sole trader.

(2) On 24 September 2024, Mick sold 700,000 £1 ordinary shares in Rolling Ltd, an unquoted trading company, for £3,675,000. He had originally purchased 500,000 shares in Rolling Ltd on 2 June 2007 for £960,000. On 1 December 2012, Rolling Ltd made a 3 for 2 bonus issue. Mick has been a director of Rolling Ltd since 1 January 2007.

Required

(a) Assuming that no reliefs are available, calculate the chargeable gain arising from each of Mick's asset disposals during the tax year 2024/25.

Note. You are not required to calculate the taxable gains or the amount of tax payable.

(4 marks)

(b) State which capital gains tax reliefs might be available to Mick in respect of each of his disposals during the tax year 2024/25, and what further information you would require in order to establish if the reliefs are actually available and to establish any restrictions as regards the amount of relief.

Note. For this part of the question, you are not expected to perform any calculations.

(6 marks)

(Total = 10 marks)

161 Ruby (September/December 2015) (amended) (18 mins)

You should assume that today's date is 1 March 2025.

(a) On 27 August 2024, Ruby disposed of a residential investment property and this resulted in a chargeable gain of £37,700.

For the tax year 2024/25, Ruby has taxable income of £23,515.

Required

Calculate Ruby's capital gains tax liability for the tax year 2024/25 if this is her only disposal in that tax year.

(2 marks)

(b) In addition to the disposal already made on 27 August 2024, Ruby is going to make one further disposal during the tax year 2024/25. The disposal will be of either Ruby's holding of £1 ordinary shares in Pola Ltd, or her holding of 50p ordinary shares in Aplo plc.

Shareholding in Pola Ltd

Pola Ltd is an unlisted trading company. The shareholding was subscribed for by Ruby on 14 July 2021 for £23,700 and could be sold for £61,000. Ruby has never been an officer nor an employee of Pola Ltd.

Shareholding in Aplo plc

Aplo plc is a trading company listed on a recognised stock exchange in which Ruby has a shareholding of 40,000 50p ordinary shares. Ruby received the shareholding as a gift from her father on 27 May 2011. On that date, the shares were quoted on the stock exchange at £2.12 – £2.18. The shareholding could be sold for £59,000.

No reliefs are available in respect of this disposal.

Required

Calculate Ruby's revised capital gains tax liability for the tax year 2024/25, if she also disposes of either (1) her shareholding in Pola Ltd; or alternatively (2) her shareholding in Aplo plc.

Note. The following mark allocation is provided as guidance for this requirement:

Pola Ltd (4½ marks)

Aplo plc (3½ marks)

(8 marks)

(Total = 10 marks)

Part D: Inheritance tax

Part D covers inheritance tax, the subject of Chapter 18 of the BPP Course Book for Taxation (TX – UK).

Section A

OTQ bank – Inheritance tax 1 (18 mins)

162 Gillian owned a 70% shareholding in Rose Ltd, an unquoted investment company. On 23 July 2024, she gave a 20% shareholding in Rose Ltd to her son. The values of shareholdings in Rose Ltd on 23 July 2024 were as follows:

	£
100% shareholding	600,000
70% shareholding	350,000
50% shareholding	200,000
20% shareholding	80,000

What is the diminution in value of Gillian's estate as a result of her gift on 23 July 2024?

£ ☐ (2 marks)

163 Joel and Sunita were a married couple. Sunita died in July 2008 and 65% of her nil rate band of £312,000 (2008/09) was unused. Joel died in May 2024. He had made a potentially exempt transfer (after all available exemptions) of £75,000 in August 2020. Joel left his estate to his sister. Any relevant elections were made.

What is the nil rate band available to set against Joel's death estate?

Pull down list
- £325,000
- £452,800
- £461,250
- £536,250

(2 marks)

164 On 7 July 2019, Paul made a gross chargeable transfer (after all exemptions) of £260,000. On 19 December 2024, he gave £190,000 to a trust. Paul agreed to pay any lifetime inheritance tax (IHT) due.

How much IHT will be payable by Paul on the December 2024 transfer of value?

○ £28,250
○ £31,250
○ £29,750
○ £23,800

(2 marks)

165 Donald made the following transactions in the tax year 2024/25:

(1) A gift of £2,000 to his granddaughter on the occasion of her marriage

(2) A sale of a vase to his friend, Alan, for £1,000 which both Donald and Alan believed to be the market value of the vase

The vase was later valued by an auction house as worth £20,000 at the date of the sale.

Ignoring the annual exemption, what is the total value of potentially exempt transfers made by Donald as a result of these gifts?

○ £21,000

○ £0

○ £2,000

○ £19,000

(2 marks)

---

166 Roman died on 1 November 2024. During June 2021, Roman gave an antique vase to his daughter Petra. The transfer value for inheritance tax (IHT) purposes at the date of the gift was £400,000 before any available exemptions. Roman had made no other transfers during his lifetime.

Match the correct amounts from the options below to correctly identify the IHT payable by Petra at the time of the gift in June 2021 and on the death of Roman in November 2024. *(May/June 2023)*

Options		Event
£0		June 2021
£13,800		November 2024
£15,000		
£22,080		
£24,000		
£27,600		

(2 marks)

(Total = 10 marks)

OTQ bank – Inheritance tax 2 (36 mins)

167 Mary made the following gifts in the tax year 2024/25:

(1) £1,000 on the first day of each month for nine months to her grandson to pay university living expenses

Mary used income surplus to her living requirements to make these payments and had made such payments to her grandson throughout his four-year university course.

(2) £100 to her grandnephew on his birthday and a further £250 to the same grandnephew as a Christmas gift

Ignoring the annual exemption, what is the total value of potentially exempt transfers made by Mary as a result of these gifts?

○ £9,350
○ £100
○ £9,000
○ £350

(2 marks)

168 Daniel owned all 1,000 shares in Q Ltd, an unquoted investment company.

On 10 October 2024, Daniel gave 300 of his shares in Q Ltd to his daughter.

The values of the shares on 10 October 2024 were as follows:

% shareholding	Value per share
	£
76–100	150
51–75	120
26–50	90
1–25	30

What is the diminution in value of Daniel's estate as a result of his gift on 10 October 2024?

Pull down list
- £123,000
- £18,000
- £27,000
- £66,000

(2 marks)

169 Ken died on 15 January 2025 leaving a chargeable estate valued at £245,000.

He had made gross chargeable lifetime transfers of £98,000 in October 2017 and £118,000 in June 2021.

How much inheritance tax (IHT) is payable in respect of Ken's chargeable estate of £245,000? *(March/June 2021)*

£ ☐ (2 marks)

170 Rodney died on 13 August 2024.

In his will, he left £200 in cash to each of his five nephews, investments held in ISAs valued at £350,000 to his daughter, and the residue of his estate, which amounted to £520,000, to his wife.

What is the chargeable estate for inheritance tax purposes?

£ ☐ (2 marks)

---

171 Sandeep made a gift of £425,000 to a trust on 10 November 2024. No agreement has been made about who will pay the inheritance tax (IHT) in respect of this gift.

What is the due date for payment of the IHT and who is primarily liable for its payment?
(June 2019)

- ○ The trustees are liable to make the payment by 31 May 2025
- ○ The trustees are liable to make the payment by 30 April 2025
- ○ Sandeep is liable to make the payment by 31 May 2025
- ○ Sandeep is liable to make the payment by 30 April 2025

(2 marks)

---

172 Benjamin died on 30 November 2024 leaving an estate valued at £890,000. Inheritance tax of £276,000 was paid in respect of the estate.

Under the terms of his will, Benjamin left £260,000 to his wife, a specific legacy of £120,000 (free of tax) to his brother, and the residue of the estate to his grandchildren.

What is the amount of inheritance received by Benjamin's grandchildren?

[▼]

Pull down list
- £234,000
- £354,000
- £510,000
- £614,000

(2 marks)

---

173 Heng is a wealthy 45 year old who would like to reduce the potential inheritance tax liability on her estate when she dies.

Which of the following actions will or will not achieve Heng's aim of reducing the potential inheritance tax liability on her estate when she dies?

Changing the terms of her will so that the residue of her estate goes to her grandchildren rather than her children	WILL ACHIEVE	WILL NOT ACHIEVE
Making lifetime gifts to trusts up to the value of the nil rate band every seven years	WILL ACHIEVE	WILL NOT ACHIEVE
Changing the terms of her will so that the residue of her estate goes to her husband rather than her children	WILL ACHIEVE	WILL NOT ACHIEVE
Making lifetime gifts to her grandchildren early in life	WILL ACHIEVE	WILL NOT ACHIEVE

(2 marks)

174 Yuna made a gift of cash into a discretionary trust on 31 July 2020. Yuna died on 1 May 2024.

Inheritance tax (IHT) was payable as a result of this lifetime gift, both during Yuna's lifetime and as a result of her death.

Match the relevant dates to indicate when the IHT liabilities in respect of the cash gift would have become due, both during Yuna's lifetime and as a result of Yuna's death.

(May/June 2024)

| 31 January 2021 |
| 1 November 2024 |
| 30 April 2021 |
| 30 November 2024 |
| 31 January 2022 |
| 30 April 2025 |

In Yuna's lifetime

As a result of Yuna's death

(2 marks)

---

175 Nadia died on 6 December 2024. Her death estate included her main residence which was valued at £360,000 on which there was secured an outstanding repayment mortgage of £140,000. Nadia will leave her entire estate to her three children.

Nadia is a widow. Her husband died in 2009 leaving his entire estate to Nadia.

What amount of residence nil rate band will be available in computing inheritance tax on Nadia's death estate?

○ £175,000
○ £220,000
○ £350,000
○ £360,000

(2 marks)

176 Rachel is aged 85 and in poor health. She is keen to minimise the inheritance tax due on her death estate which is likely to have a value of about £1.2 million. Her will currently leaves her main residence (valued at £300,000) to her brother and the residue of her estate to her son. Rachel has never been married.

Complete the following sentence by matching the correct response in each space.

The inheritance tax liability on Rachel's estate will [(1) ▼] by [(2) ▼] if she leaves her main residence to her son rather than her brother.

Pull down list 1
- Decrease
- Increase

Pull down list 2
- £175,000
- £70,000

(2 marks)

(Total = 20 marks)

Section B

OT case – Dianne (September/December 2023) (18 mins)

You should assume that today's date is 5 March 2024.

Dianne's father died on 14 September 2023. Dianne's mother had died on 28 May 2019.

Cash gifts received from father

Dianne received a cash gift of £84,000 from her father on 4 May 2018, with a further cash gift of £440,000 received on 10 June 2018.

These gifts are stated after taking account of any available exemptions.

Dianne's father did not make any other lifetime gifts.

Father's chargeable estate

For inheritance tax (IHT) purposes, the chargeable estate of Dianne's father is valued at £1,134,000. This is calculated as follows:

	£
Property (main residence)	620,000
Mortgage	(380,000)
	240,000
Other assets	970,000
Debts and funeral expenses	(76,000)
Chargeable estate	1,134,000

The father's estate has been left entirely to Dianne.

When Dianne's mother died, her estate was also left to Dianne. The value of the estate was sufficient to fully utilise all of the mother's nil rate band. The estate did not include a main residence.

Gift made by Dianne

On 1 March 2024, Dianne made a chargeable lifetime transfer of £520,000 to a trust for the benefit of her children. She will pay the IHT arising from this gift.

On 10 June 2023, Dianne had made a chargeable lifetime transfer of £70,000 to a trust for the benefit of her nieces, and a potentially exempt transfer of £30,000 to her sister. Dianne has not made any other lifetime gifts.

The chargeable lifetime transfers of £520,000 and £70,000, and the potentially exempt transfer of £30,000, are after taking account of all available exemptions.

177 As a result of her father's death, Dianne will have to pay how much inheritance tax in respect of the cash gift of £440,000 received on 10 June 2018?

£ ☐   (2 marks)

178 How much inheritance tax will be payable in respect of the chargeable estate of Dianne's father valued at £1,134,000?

- ○ £357,600
- ○ £313,600
- ○ £453,600
- ○ £383,600

(2 marks)

179 Which TWO of the following deductions will have been permitted in calculating the debts and funeral expenses figure of £76,000 in the chargeable estate of Dianne's father?
- ☐ The legal fees of a friend which Dianne's father had verbally promised to pay
- ☐ Capital gains tax payable in respect of the tax year 2022/23
- ☐ Credit card debts
- ☐ An electricity bill which Dianne's father paid on 5 September 2023

(2 marks)

180 Identify, by clicking on the relevant boxes in the table below, the due dates for the inheritance tax (IHT) payable in respect of the lifetime cash gift of £440,000 received by Dianne on 10 June 2018, and the IHT payable in respect of her father's chargeable estate valued at £1,134,000.

Lifetime gift	Chargeable estate
○ 31 March 2024	14 March 2024
○ 31 March 2024	31 March 2024
○ 30 April 2024	14 March 2024
○ 30 April 2024	31 March 2024

(2 marks)

181 What is the amount of lifetime inheritance tax payable by Dianne in respect of the chargeable lifetime transfer of £520,000 which she made to a trust on 1 March 2024?
- ○ £66,250
- ○ £73,750
- ○ £53,000
- ○ £48,750

(2 marks)

(Total = 10 marks)

OT case – Rishi and Nagina (March/June 2022) (amended) (18 mins)

Nagina and Rishi were a married couple. They made three lifetime gifts before Nagina died on 26 June 2024.

Rishi

On 16 April 2018, Rishi made a chargeable lifetime transfer to a trust. The amount of the gift was £355,000 deducting all available exemptions. Rishi agreed to pay any inheritance tax on the gift.

On 10 January 2024, Rishi made a gift of 2,000 £1 ordinary shares in Altion Ltd to his son. Before the transfer, Rishi owned 8,000 shares in Altion Ltd. Altion Ltd has an issued share capital of 10,000 £1 ordinary shares. The value of Altion Ltd's shares on 10 January 2024 were:

Holding	Value per share
1% to 25%	£10
26% to 50%	£14
50% to 75%	£20
75% to 100%	£30

The nil rate band for the tax year 2018/19 was £325,000. These are the only lifetime gifts which Rishi has made.

Nagina

On 11 May 2021, Nagina made a potentially exempt transfer of £350,000 to her grandson as a wedding gift when the grandson got married. This figure is after deducting all available exemptions. The nil rate band for the tax year 2021/22 was £325,000. This is the only lifetime gift made by Nagina.

182 **What was the amount of the gross chargeable transfer in respect of Rishi's chargeable lifetime transfer made to the trust on 16 April 2018?**

£ ☐ (2 marks)

---

183 **For inheritance tax purposes, what was the amount of the transfer of value of Rishi's gift of 2,000 ordinary shares in Altion Ltd?**

- ○ £120,000
- ○ £20,000
- ○ £6,000
- ○ £180,000

(2 marks)

---

184 **What is the total value of the exemptions deducted in calculating the value of the potentially exempt transfer that Nagina made to her grandson on 11 May 2021?**

- ○ £7,000
- ○ £6,000
- ○ £5,500
- ○ £8,500

(2 marks)

---

185 **What is the amount of inheritance tax which will be payable in respect of the potentially exempt transfer made to the grandson on 11 May 2021 as a result of Nagina's death?**

- ○ £8,000
- ○ £10,000
- ○ £140,000
- ○ £112,000

(2 marks)

186 Match the correct tokens from below to identify who is responsible for paying the inheritance tax arising from the potentially exempt transfer made to the grandson on 11 May 2021 as a result of Nagina's death, and when this tax will be payable.

26 December 2024		By whom paid
31 December 2024		Due date
Grandson		
Personal representatives of Nagina's estate		

(2 marks)

(Total = 10 marks)

OT case – Zoe and Luke (June 2015) (amended)   (18 mins)

Zoe and Luke are brother and sister; they died within a few months of each other.

Zoe

Zoe died on 17 February 2025.

She had always used her annual exemption in April each year and had made the following additional gifts during her lifetime:

(1) On 21 March 2018, Zoe made a cash gift of £633,000 to a trust. Zoe paid the inheritance tax (IHT) arising from this gift. The nil rate band for the tax year 2017/18 is £325,000.

(2) On 17 August 2021, Zoe made a further cash gift of £200,000 to the trust. The trustees paid the IHT arising from the gift. The nil rate band for the tax year 2021/22 is £325,000.

Luke

Luke died on 10 October 2024.

He was survived by his two adult children, a son and daughter. Luke's wife had died on 25 July 2008. On 7 March 2023, Luke had made a cash gift of £270,000 to his daughter as a wedding gift. Luke had also paid his son's university tuition fees in each of September 2022, 2023 and 2024, making payments directly to the university.

He was advised that these payments were exempt from inheritance tax under the normal expenditure out of income exemption.

On her death, Luke's wife had left £240,000 to their daughter and the remainder of her estate to Luke. She made no lifetime transfers. The nil rate band for the tax year 2008/09 was £312,000.

187 **Which TWO of these statements about Luke's payment of his son's tuition fees are correct?**

☐ The payments could be exempt without any cash limit under the normal expenditure out of income exemption.

☐ The payments could not be exempt under the normal expenditure out of income exemption because they were paid directly to the university and not to his son.

☐ The payments must have been reported each tax year to HM Revenue & Customs in Luke's income tax return to qualify for the normal expenditure out of income exemption.

☐ The payments must have left Luke with sufficient income to maintain his usual standard of living to qualify for the normal expenditure out of income exemption. **(2 marks)**

188 **What is the amount of the gross chargeable transfer made by Zoe on 21 March 2018?**

○ £702,500
○ £710,000
○ £694,600
○ £756,200 **(2 marks)**

189 **What is the additional IHT which will be payable, as a result of Zoe's death, in respect of the transfer made on 17 August 2021, assuming that the nil rate band has been completely used by the gross chargeable transfer made by Zoe on 21 March 2018?**

[▼]

Pull down list
- £24,000
- £40,000
- £64,000
- £80,000

(2 marks)

190 **What is the value of the potentially exempt transfer made by Luke on 7 March 2023?**

£ [ ] **(2 marks)**

191 **What is the amount of Luke's wife's nil rate band which could be transferred and used in calculating the IHT on Luke's death?**

○ £75,000
○ £72,000
○ £312,000
○ £325,000 **(2 marks)**

(Total = 10 marks)

OT case – Marcus (September/December 2015) (amended)
(18 mins)

Marcus died on 10 March 2025.

He had been married to his wife, Barbara, for many years. He had made the following gifts during his lifetime:

(1) On 14 January 2014, Marcus made a chargeable lifetime transfer of £328,000 to a trust. The trustees paid the lifetime inheritance tax which arose in respect of this gift.

(2) On 3 January 2021, Marcus made a chargeable lifetime transfer to another trust. In addition to the gift, Marcus paid the related lifetime inheritance tax on this gift.

The gross chargeable lifetime transfer amounted to £491,250.

(3) On 17 March 2021, Marcus made a gift (a potentially exempt transfer) of 30,000 £1 ordinary shares in Scarum Ltd, an unquoted investment company, to his daughter.

Before the transfer, Marcus owned all of Scarum Ltd's issued share capital of 100,000 £1 ordinary shares. On 17 March 2021, Scarum Ltd's shares were worth £5 each for a holding of 30%, £9 each for a holding of 70%, and £12 each for a holding of 100%.

(4) On 29 June 2022, Marcus gave a plot of land worth £100,000 to Barbara. Marcus had bought the land in 2008 for £80,000.

The nil rate band for the tax years 2013/14 and 2020/21 was £325,000.

Under the terms of his will, Marcus left his entire estate to Barbara.

Barbara has not made any gifts during her lifetime. She is intending to remarry.

Ignore the inheritance tax annual exemption.

192 What was the amount of the lifetime inheritance tax paid by the trustees (if any) as a result of the gift made on 14 January 2014?

£ ☐ (2 marks)

193 What was the amount of the lifetime inheritance tax paid by Marcus as a result of the gift made on 3 January 2021?

- ○ £122,812
- ○ £33,250
- ○ £98,250
- ○ £41,562

(2 marks)

194 What was the amount of the taper relief deductible from the additional inheritance tax due as a result of the death of Marcus on the gift made on 3 January 2021?

☐ ▼

Pull down list
- £117,900
- £26,600
- £39,900
- £78,600

(2 marks)

195 **What was the amount of the potentially exempt transfer made by Marcus on 17 March 2021?**
- ○ £360,000
- ○ £270,000
- ○ £150,000
- ○ £570,000

(2 marks)

196 **Which TWO of the following statements about Marcus and Barbara for inheritance tax purposes are correct?**
- ☐ There is no liability for inheritance tax on the transfer of Marcus's estate to Barbara because they are treated together as a single chargeable person for inheritance tax.
- ☐ If Barbara remarries, any unused nil rate band on her death can be transferred to her spouse if they survive her.
- ☐ The gift of the land on 29 June 2022 by Marcus to Barbara is a potentially exempt transfer of £80,000.
- ☐ The transfer of Marcus's estate to Barbara on his death is an exempt transfer.

(2 marks)

(Total = 10 marks)

OT case – Lebna and Lulu (March/June 2019) (18 mins)

You should assume that today's date is 1 March 2025.

Lebna and Lulu were a married couple, but Lulu died on 24 January 2017.

Lulu

Lulu left an estate valued at £210,000 for inheritance tax (IHT) purposes.

The estate did not include a main residence.

Under the terms of her will, Lulu left a specific legacy of £40,000 to her brother, with the residue of the estate to her husband, Lebna.

Lulu had made the following lifetime transfers:

Date	Type of transfer	Amount £
13 February 2009	Chargeable lifetime transfer	50,000
21 June 2015	Potentially exempt transfer	80,000

Both of these transfers are after taking account of all available exemptions.

The nil rate band for the tax year 2016/17 is £325,000.

Lebna's chargeable estate

Lebna has a chargeable estate valued at £980,000. His estate includes a main residence valued at £340,000 on which there is an outstanding interest-only mortgage of £152,000.

Under the terms of his will, Lebna has left his entire estate to his son.

Gift to son on 22 February 2020

On 22 February 2020, Lebna made a gift of 60,000 £1 ordinary shares in Blean Ltd, an unquoted investment company, to his son.

Before the transfer, Lebna owned all of Blean Ltd's share capital of 100,000 ordinary shares.

The market value of Blean Ltd's ordinary shares on 22 February 2020 was as follows:

Holding	Market value per share
40%	£4.20
60%	£6.30
100%	£7.10

Lebna had not made any previous lifetime gifts.

Gifts to friends during October 2024

Lebna made cash gifts of £85, £225, £190 and £490 to various friends during October 2024. The gifts of £85 and £190 were to the same friend.

197 If Lebna were to die today, 1 March 2025, how much of Lulu's nil rate band will the personal representatives of Lebna's estate be able to claim when calculating the IHT payable on his chargeable estate?

○ £155,000
○ £205,000
○ £35,000
○ £285,000

(2 marks)

198 If Lebna were to die today, 1 March 2025, what is the total amount of residence nil rate band which will be available when calculating the IHT payable on his chargeable estate?

○ £175,000
○ £350,000
○ £340,000
○ £188,000

(2 marks)

199 What is the amount of the potentially exempt transfer which Lebna has made to his son on 22 February 2020 (the gift of 60,000 shares in Blean Ltd) after deducting any available exemptions?

○ £542,000
○ £536,000
○ £372,000
○ £378,000

(2 marks)

200 If Lebna were to die today, 1 March 2025, what taper relief percentage reduction would be available when calculating the IHT payable on the potentially exempt transfer which he made to his son on 22 February 2020 (the gift of 60,000 shares in Blean Ltd), and when would this IHT be due?

Option	Taper relief reduction	Due date
1	60%	30 September 2025
2	60%	1 September 2025
3	40%	1 September 2025

Option	Taper relief reduction	Due date
4	40%	30 September 2025

○ Option 1
○ Option 2
○ Option 3
○ Option 4 (2 marks)

201 What amount of the cash gifts made by Lebna to his friends during October 2024 is covered by the small gifts exemption?

○ £500
○ £990
○ £225
○ £275 (2 marks)

(Total = 10 marks)

Section C

202 Pere and Phil (June 2013) (amended) (18 mins)

On 23 August 2018, Pere made a gift of a house valued at £420,000 to his son, Phil. This was a wedding gift when Phil got married. The nil rate band for the tax year 2018/19 is £325,000.

Pere

Pere died on 20 March 2025 at which time his estate was valued at £880,000. Under the terms of his will, Pere divided his estate equally, before inheritance tax, between his wife and his son, Phil. Pere had not made any gifts during his lifetime except for the gift of the house to Phil. Pere did not own a main residence.

Phil

Phil sold the house which he received as a wedding gift from Pere, his father, on 5 April 2025. The following information relates to the property:

	£
Net sale proceeds after costs of disposal	487,400
Cost of new boundary wall around the property (previously no boundary wall)	(5,200)
Cost of replacing the property's chimney	(2,800)

Phil has taxable income (after deduction of the personal allowance) of £14,150 in 2024/25. The house was never occupied by Phil.

Required

(a) Calculate the inheritance tax that will be payable as a result of Pere's death. **(6 marks)**

(b) Calculate Phil's capital gains tax liability for the tax year 2024/25. **(4 marks)**

(Total = 10 marks)

203 Afiya (December 2013) (amended) (18 mins)

Afiya died on 29 November 2024. She had made the following gifts during her lifetime:

(1) On 14 September 2023, Afiya made a gift of 6,500 £1 ordinary shares in Cassava Ltd, an unquoted investment company, to her daughter.

Before the transfer Afiya owned 8,000 shares out of Cassava Ltd's issued share capital of 10,000 £1 ordinary shares. On 14 September 2023, Cassava Ltd's shares were worth £3 each for a holding of 15%, £7 each for a holding of 65%, and £8 each for a holding of 80%.

(2) On 27 January 2024, Afiya made a cash gift of £400,000 to a trust. Afiya paid the inheritance tax arising from this gift.

On 29 November 2024, Afiya's estate was valued at £623,000 including her main residence which was valued at £90,000. Her executors paid funeral expenses of £3,000 on 12 January 2025. Under the terms of her will Afiya left £150,000 cash to her husband, a specific legacy of £40,000 to her sister, and the residue of the estate to her children.

The nil rate band for the tax year 2023/24 is £325,000.

Required

(a) Calculate the inheritance tax which will be payable as a result of Afiya's death. **(9 marks)**

(b) Calculate the amount of the inheritance which will be received by Afiya's children. **(1 mark)**

(Total = 10 marks)

204 Kendra (June 2014) (amended) (18 mins)

You should assume that today's date is 1 January 2025.

Kendra, aged 93, is in poor health with just a few months left to live. She has made no lifetime gifts.

Kendra owns the following assets:

(1) An investment residential property valued at £970,000

The property has never been occupied by Kendra, and if it were disposed of during the tax year 2024/25 the disposal would result in a chargeable gain of £174,000.

(2) Building society deposits of £387,000

(3) Investments in individual savings accounts (ISAs) valued at £39,000 and savings certificates from national savings and investments (NS&I) valued at £17,000

(4) A life assurance policy on her own life

The policy has an open market value of £210,000 and proceeds of £225,000 will be received following Kendra's death.

None of the above valuations are expected to change in the near future. Kendra has income tax outstanding at her death of £12,800. She also has an outstanding unsecured loan of £1,200 which is due to be repaid on her death.

Under the terms of her will, Kendra has left her entire estate to her children.

The nil rate band of Kendra's husband was fully utilised when he died ten years ago.

For the tax year 2024/25, Kendra will pay income tax at the higher rate.

Required

(a) Calculate the inheritance tax which would be payable if Kendra were to die on 31 March 2025. **(5 marks)**

(b) Advise Kendra why it would not be beneficial to make an immediate lifetime gift of the property valued at £970,000 to her children.

Notes.

1. Your answer should take account of both the capital gains tax and the inheritance tax implications of making the gift.
2. For this part of the question, you should ignore the capital gains tax annual exempt amount and inheritance tax annual exemptions. **(3 marks)**

(c) Advise Kendra why it might be beneficial for inheritance tax purposes to change the terms of her will so that part of her estate was instead left to her grandchildren rather than her children. **(2 marks)**

(Total = 10 marks)

205 James (March/June 2016) (18 mins)

James died on 22 January 2025. He had made the following gifts during his lifetime:

(1) On 9 October 2017, a cash gift of £35,000 to a trust

No lifetime inheritance tax was payable in respect of this gift.

(2) On 14 May 2023, a cash gift of £420,000 to his daughter

(3) On 2 August 2023, a gift of a property valued at £260,000 to a trust

No lifetime inheritance tax was payable in respect of this gift because it was covered by the nil rate band. By the time of James's death on 22 January 2025, the property had increased in value to £310,000.

On 22 January 2025, James's estate was valued at £870,000. James did not own a main residence. Under the terms of his will, James left his entire estate to his children.

The nil rate band of James's wife was fully utilised when she died ten years ago.

The nil rate band for the tax years 2017/18 and 2023/24 is £325,000.

Required

(a) Calculate the inheritance tax which will be payable as a result of James's death, and state who will be responsible for paying the tax. **(6 marks)**

(b) Explain why it might have been beneficial for inheritance tax purposes if James had left a portion of his estate to his grandchildren rather than to his children. **(2 marks)**

(c) Explain why it might be advantageous for inheritance tax purposes for a person to make lifetime gifts even when such gifts are made within seven years of death.

Notes.

1 Your answer should include a calculation of James's inheritance tax saving from making the gift of property to the trust on 2 August 2023 rather than retaining the property until his death.

2 You are not expected to consider lifetime exemptions in this part of the question.

(2 marks)

(Total = 10 marks)

206 Dembe (March/June 2019) (18 mins)

You should assume that today's date is 15 February 2025.

You are a trainee chartered certified accountant dealing with the tax affairs of Dembe and her husband Kato.

Personal pension contribution

Dembe is self-employed and her trading profit for the year ended 31 December 2024 is £125,140. She will not have any other income or outgoings for the tax year 2024/25.

Dembe is planning to make a personal pension contribution of £48,000 (net) before 5 April 2025 and would like to know the amount of income tax and national insurance contributions (NICs) which she will save as a result of making the pension contribution.

Sale of residential property

During March 2025, Dembe is going to sell a residential property, and this will result in a chargeable gain of £67,000 if she makes the disposal.

Dembe wants to know whether it would be beneficial to transfer the property to Kato, her husband, as a no gain/no loss transfer prior to it being sold during March 2025. The transfer from Dembe to Kato will cost £2,000 in additional legal fees, and this cost will reduce the chargeable gain to £65,000 if the disposal is made by Kato.

Dembe has already made other disposals during the tax year 2024/25 which have utilised her annual exempt amount. Kato, however, has not yet made any disposals.

Kato's taxable income for the tax year 2024/25 is £21,350.

Inheritance tax

Dembe, who knows nothing about inheritance tax (IHT), is concerned about the amount of IHT which will be payable when she and Kato die. The couple's combined chargeable estate is valued at £950,000 for IHT purposes. The estate includes a main residence valued at £360,000.

Under the terms of their wills, Dembe and Kato have initially left their entire estates to each other. Then when the second of them dies, the total estate of £950,000 will be left to the couple's children.

The couple are not sure whether to change the terms of their wills so that assets worth £325,000 are left to their children when the first of them dies.

Neither Dembe nor Kato have made any lifetime gifts.

Required

(a) Calculate the reduction in Dembe's income tax liability and NICs for the tax year 2024/25 if she makes the personal pension contribution of £48,000 (net) before 5 April 2025.

   Note. You are not expected to prepare full tax computations. **(4 marks)**

(b) Calculate the couple's overall saving for the tax year 2024/25, after taking account of the additional legal fees of £2,000, if the residential property is transferred to Kato and sold by him, rather than the property being sold by Dembe. **(3 marks)**

(c) Calculate the amount of IHT payable, if any, were Dembe and Kato to both die in the near future and explain whether or not it might be beneficial to leave assets worth £325,000 to their children when the first of them dies.

   Note. You should assume that the IHT rates and thresholds remain unchanged. **(3 marks)**

(Total = 10 marks)

Part E: Corporation tax liabilities

Part E covers corporation tax liabilities, the subject of Chapters 19 to 23 of the BPP Course Book for Taxation (TX – UK).

Section A

OTQ bank – Corporation tax liabilities 1 (36 mins)

207 Jet Ltd has deducted some items in its statement of profit or loss for the year ended 31 December 2023.

Identify, by clicking on the relevant boxes in the table below, whether each of the following items of expenditure are or are not allowable for computing Jet Ltd's taxable trading profit.

Legal expenses relating to the acquisition of a new 40-year lease on its factory	ALLOWABLE	NOT ALLOWABLE
Cost of arranging a new bank loan to purchase machinery for trade	ALLOWABLE	NOT ALLOWABLE
Write off of an irrecoverable loan to a former employee	ALLOWABLE	NOT ALLOWABLE
Donation to local charity with mention of Jet Ltd's support in programme for fundraising concert (not a qualifying charitable donation)	ALLOWABLE	NOT ALLOWABLE

(2 marks)

208 Rat Ltd started trading on 1 December 2023 and prepared its first set of accounts to 31 March 2025.

What will Rat Ltd's accounting periods be for the period of account to 31 March 2025?

○ 4 months to 31 March 2024, 12 months to 31 March 2025
○ 4 months to 5 April 2024, nearly 12 months to 31 March 2025
○ 12 months to 30 November 2024, 4 months to 31 March 2025
○ 16 months to 31 March 2025

(2 marks)

209 Xeon Ltd purchases a newly-constructed office building from a developer for £1,875,000 on 1 March 2024 and starts using it on 1 April 2024.

The purchase price includes acquisition costs of £75,000.

Xeon Ltd has a 31 December year end.

What are the maximum SBAs available to Xeon Ltd in the year ended 31 December 2024?

£ ⬚

(2 marks)

210 Kit Ltd was incorporated and started trading on 1 July 2024 and prepared its first set of accounts to 31 December 2024.

During the six-month accounting period to 31 December 2024, it purchased two vehicles:

		£
28 November 2024	Car [1] (CO_2 emissions 126 g/km)	15,400
2 December 2024	Car [2] (CO_2 emissions 41 g/km)	30,400

Car [1] is used 20% for private purposes by a director of Kit Ltd.

What are the capital allowances to which Kit Ltd is entitled for the period to 31 December 2024?

[▼]

Pull down list
- £3,106
- £3,198
- £4,122
- £6,396

(2 marks)

---

211 Eminal Ltd purchased 50,000 shares in Vesterama Ltd for £3.50 a share on 6 June 2002. On 6 June 2024, Eminal Ltd sold 15,000 shares in Vesterama Ltd for £70,000. Eminal Ltd prepares accounts to 31 December each year.

Indexation factor: June 2002 to December 2017 = 0.578

What is Eminal Ltd's chargeable gain or capital loss for the year ended 31 December 2024? *(June 2017)*

- ○ £12,845 loss
- ○ £105,000 loss
- ○ £0
- ○ £17,500 gain

(2 marks)

---

212 Crane plc started trading on 1 January 2024. In the year ended 31 December 2024, the company made an adjusted trading loss of £40,000. In the year ended 31 December 2025, the company will have trading income of £30,000, other taxable income of £6,000 and will make a qualifying charitable donation of £2,700. Crane plc wishes to use carry forward trading loss relief.

What is the most beneficial carry forward trading loss relief claim that Crane plc can make for the year ended 31 December 2025?

£ [   ]

(2 marks)

---

213 Deal Ltd has the following results:

	12 months to 31 March 2024	9 months to 31 December 2024	12 months to 31 December 2025
	£	£	£
Trading profits/(losses)	45,000	40,000	(160,000)

	12 months to 31 March 2024	9 months to 31 December 2024	12 months to 31 December 2025
	£	£	£
Property business profits	18,000	15,500	5,000

The company wishes to claim relief for its loss as early as possible.

What is the unused loss carried forward at 31 December 2025?

£ ☐ (2 marks)

---

214 Bab Ltd has owned 80% of the ordinary share capital of Boon Ltd for many years. The two companies' results for the year ended 31 December 2024 are as follows:

	Bab Ltd	Boon Ltd
	£	£
Trading profit/(loss)	(38,000)	36,000
Chargeable gains	7,000	4,000

What is the maximum amount of current period group relief which Boon Ltd can claim from Bab Ltd for the year ended 31 December 2024? *(June 2018)*

○ £38,000
○ £31,000
○ £36,000
○ £32,000

(2 marks)

---

215 The Daffodil plc group of companies has the following structure:

All companies are resident in the UK except Geranium Inc.

Identify, by clicking on the relevant boxes in the table below, the companies to which Erica Ltd could surrender a trading loss.

Daffodil plc	YES	NO
Geranium Inc	YES	NO
Flora Ltd	YES	NO
Hellebore Ltd	YES	NO

(2 marks)

216 The Pine plc group of companies has the following structure:

All companies are resident in the UK except Lime Inc.

Identify, by clicking on the relevant boxes in the table below, the companies to which Maple Ltd could transfer a capital loss.

Pine plc	YES	NO
Willow Ltd	YES	NO
Juniper Ltd	YES	NO
Lime Inc	YES	NO

(2 marks)

(Total = 20 marks)

OTQ bank – Corporation tax liabilities 2 (36 mins)

217 Flower Ltd is a trading company. Its results for the year ended 31 March 2025 include the following items relating to interest received and paid in the year:

	£
Loan interest receivable:	
Received in the year	35,000
Accrued at 31 March 2025	5,000
Loan interest payable:	
On loan to purchase a fleet of delivery vans	(10,000)
On loan to buy shares in an unrelated trading company	(8,000)

What amount of non-trade loan relationship income will be included in Flower Ltd's calculation of taxable total profits for the year ended 31 March 2025? *(March/June 2023)*

£ ☐ (2 marks)

218 Frazled Ltd has the following results:

	y/e 31 March 2024	y/e 31 March 2025	y/e 31 March 2026	y/e 31 March 2027
	£	£	£	£
Trading profits/(losses)	20,000	(250,000)	130,000	152,000

	y/e 31 March 2024	y/e 31 March 2025	y/e 31 March 2026	y/e 31 March 2027
	£	£	£	£
Interest income	10,000	10,000	10,000	10,000
Qualifying charitable donations	(5,000)	(5,000)	(7,000)	(5,000)

Assuming that the company wishes to claim relief for its loss in the most beneficial manner, what is the loss amount claimed against total profits in y/e 31 March 2026?

£ ☐ (2 marks)

---

219 Eggsausted Ltd has three associated companies.

What is the lower limit for the purposes of calculating corporation tax?

£ ☐ (2 marks)

---

220 Pelicanby Ltd has one associated company and has the following results for the ten-month period ended 31 March 2025:

	£
Trading profits	60,000
Property business income	30,000
Chargeable gains	16,200

What is the corporation tax payable by Pelicanby for the period ended 31 March 2025?

£ ☐ (2 marks)

---

221 Swallowby Ltd had the following results for the year ended 31 March 2025:

	£
Trading profits	190,000
Dividends received from non-group companies	20,000

What is the corporation tax payable by Swallowby for the year ended 31 March 2025?

£ ☐ (2 marks)

222 Xtra Ltd bought 60% of the ordinary share capital of Yak Ltd on 31 October 2023 and 80% of the ordinary share capital of Zeus Ltd on 31 March 2024.

For the year ended 31 December 2024, Xtra Ltd made a trading profit of £240,000 and Yak Ltd made a trading profit of £120,000. Zeus Ltd made a trading loss of £180,000 for the year ended 31 December 2024.

Which TWO of the following statements are correct in respect of the potential group relief claims which can be made for the year ended 31 December 2024?

(September/December 2023)

☐ Xtra Ltd can claim group relief of £135,000 from Zeus Ltd.
☐ Xtra Ltd can claim group relief of £180,000 from Zeus Ltd.
☐ Yak Ltd can claim group relief of £90,000 from Zeus Ltd.
☐ Yak Ltd cannot claim group relief from Zeus Ltd.

(2 marks)

223 Giant Ltd is a large company, and therefore pays its corporation tax by instalments.

For the eight-month period ended 31 August 2024, the company estimated that its corporation tax liability would be £400,000.

What would Giant Ltd's first corporation tax instalment be in respect of the eight-month period ended 31 August 2024, and what is the due date of this instalment?

(December 2019)

○ £100,000 on 14 April 2024
○ £100,000 on 14 July 2024
○ £150,000 on 14 April 2024
○ £150,000 on 14 July 2024

(2 marks)

224 **Which of the following statements relating to disposals made after 31 March 2024 is FALSE?**

○ When plant and machinery on which the 130% super deduction was claimed is sold, the sale proceeds are deducted from the main pool.
○ When plant and machinery on which the 50% first year allowance was claimed is sold, 50% of the sale proceeds are deducted from the special rate pool, with the other 50% brought in as a balancing charge.
○ When plant and machinery on which the 100% first year allowance (full expensing) was claimed is sold, the sale proceeds are brought in as a balancing charge.
○ When plant and machinery on which AIA and the 50% first year allowance were claimed, is sold, the proportion of sales proceeds relating to the AIA and 50% first year allowance must be calculated.

(2 marks)

225 During the year ended 31 March 2025, Hummus Ltd sold the following items for proceeds less than cost:

Date		Proceeds £
1 May 2024	Machinery (130% super deduction was claimed on full cost)	100,000
15 June 2024	Special rate expenditure (50% FYA was claimed on full cost)	160,000

The TWDV of the main pool at 1 April 2024 was £nil and the special rate pool was £50,000.

What is the overall balancing charge for the year ended 31 March 2025?

£ _____ (2 marks)

---

226 During the year ended 31 March 2025, Pepperz Ltd bought second-hand factory equipment for £350,000 and sold the following items for proceeds less than cost:

Date		Proceeds £
1 May 2024	Machinery (130% super deduction was claimed on full cost)	60,000
15 June 2024	Special rate expenditure (50% FYA was claimed on full cost)	140,000

The TWDV of the main pool at 1 April 2024 was £200,000 and the special rate pool was £100,000.

What are the maximum capital allowances available for the year ended 31 March 2025?

£ _____ (2 marks)

(Total = 20 marks)

Section B

OT case – Luna Ltd (June 2015) (amended) (18 mins)

Luna Ltd had the following transactions in shares during the year ended 31 March 2025:

(1) On 29 November 2024, Luna Ltd sold its entire shareholding of £1 ordinary shares in Pluto plc for £53,400. Luna Ltd had originally purchased these shares in Pluto plc on 14 June 2008 for £36,800.

(2) On 30 November 2024, Luna Ltd sold 10,000 of its shares in Neptune plc for £26,000. Luna Ltd had originally purchased 16,000 shares in Neptune plc on 10 May 2010 for £32,000.

(3) On 10 December 2024, Luna Ltd acquired shares under a rights issue in Saturn plc. Luna Ltd had originally purchased 5,000 £1 ordinary shares in Saturn plc for £7,500 in August 2011. There was a 1 for 1 bonus issue in July 2013 when the shares were worth £1.75 each. The December 2024 rights issue was on a 1 for 4 basis and the cost of the rights issue shares was £2.25 per share.

(4) On 12 February 2025, Luna Ltd's shareholding in Asteroid plc was taken over by Comet plc. Luna Ltd had originally purchased 10,000 £1 ordinary shares in Asteroid plc and their indexed cost on 12 February 2025 was £33,000.

Under the terms of the takeover, for each of its £1 ordinary shares in Asteroid plc, Luna Ltd received £6.50 in cash plus one £1 ordinary share in Comet plc. Immediately after the takeover, Comet plc's £1 ordinary shares were quoted at £4.50.

Indexation factors are as follows:

June 2008–December 2017 = 0.283

May 2010–December 2017 = 0.244

227 **Identify, by clicking on the relevant boxes in the table below, whether each of the following statements concerning the indexation allowance is true or false.**

Indexation allowance can reduce a gain to nil but not create a loss.	TRUE	FALSE
Indexation allowance can increase an unindexed loss.	TRUE	FALSE

(2 marks)

228 **What is Luna Ltd's chargeable gain on the sale of Pluto plc shares on 29 November 2024?**

£ ☐ (2 marks)

229 **What is the indexed cost of Luna Ltd's holding in Neptune Ltd immediately after the sale on 30 November 2024?**

○ £12,000
○ £39,808
○ £24,880
○ £14,928

(2 marks)

230   What is the unindexed cost of Luna Ltd's holding in Saturn plc immediately after the rights issue on 10 December 2024?

  ○ £13,125
  ○ £11,875
  ○ £10,313
  ○ £21,875

(2 marks)

231   What is the cost that was used to compute Luna Ltd's chargeable gain on the takeover of Asteroid plc on 12 February 2025?

  £ [   ]

(2 marks)

(Total = 10 marks)

OT case – Tay Ltd   (18 mins)

Tay Ltd prepares accounts to 31 March each year. In the year to 31 March 2025, it had the following events relating to chargeable assets:

(1) Received insurance proceeds of £180,000 in December 2024 as the result of the destruction of a freehold warehouse in a flood in that month. The warehouse originally cost £140,000 and had an indexed cost in December 2024 of £155,000. Tay Ltd purchased a new warehouse for £162,000 in March 2025.

(2) Received shares and cash on the takeover of Grey Ltd. Tay Ltd had acquired 20,000 shares in Grey Ltd. The shares had an indexed cost in September 2024 of £96,000 when Grey Ltd was taken over by Kline plc. On the takeover, Tay Ltd received one £1 ordinary share in Kline plc worth £4 per share and £2 in cash for each one share held in Grey Ltd.

(3) Sold a piece of machinery which it had used in its trade for £9,000 in July 2024. The machinery had an indexed base cost in July 2024 of £3,500. Capital allowances had been claimed on the machinery.

(4) Sold a plot of land, which it had held as an investment, for £45,000 in October 2024. The land had been acquired in June 2007 for £20,000. Tay Ltd had spent £2,000 on draining the land in January 2011. The indexation factor from June 2007 to December 2017 was 0.342, from January 2011 to December 2017 was 0.214.

In the year to 31 March 2026, Tay Ltd will dispose of an investment property which will realise a loss. The company wants to know how this loss can be relieved.

232   What is the base cost of the new warehouse purchased in March 2025, assuming any relevant claim was made?

  ○ £162,000
  ○ £155,000
  ○ £144,000
  ○ £140,000

(2 marks)

233 What was the chargeable gain or allowable loss arising on the takeover of Grey Ltd?
- ○ £8,000 gain
- ○ £24,000 gain
- ○ £16,000 gain
- ○ £(24,000) loss

(2 marks)

234 What was the chargeable gain (if any) arising on the disposal of the machinery?
- ○ £0
- ○ £5,500
- ○ £2,500
- ○ £5,000

(2 marks)

235 What was the chargeable gain arising on the disposal of the plot of land?
- ○ £16,160
- ○ £15,476
- ○ £15,732
- ○ £15,134

(2 marks)

236 Which TWO of the following statements about the use of the capital loss in the year ended 31 March 2026 are correct?

(1) The capital loss can be carried back against chargeable gains made in the year ended 31 March 2025.

(2) The capital loss can be set against chargeable gains made in the year ended 31 March 2026.

(3) The capital loss can be set against total profits in the year ended 31 March 2026.

(4) The capital loss can be carried forward and set against the first available chargeable gains.

- ○ 1 and 2
- ○ 1 and 3
- ○ 2 and 4
- ○ 3 and 4

(2 marks)

(Total = 10 marks)

OT case – Hyde plc group (18 mins)

The Hyde plc group has the following structure:

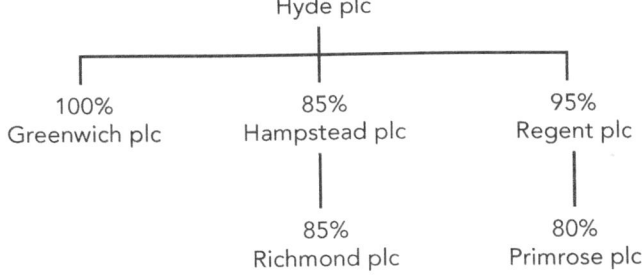

All the group companies prepared accounts to 31 March 2025. However, Greenwich plc intends to change its accounting reference date to 31 December and will prepare accounts to 31 December 2025.

Hyde plc and Greenwich plc are in a group relief group.

In the year ended 31 March 2025, Greenwich plc had the following results:

	£
Trading loss	(68,000)
Capital loss	(4,000)
Interest income	3,000
Qualifying charitable donations	(5,000)

Greenwich plc will surrender the maximum amount possible for the year ended 31 March 2025 to Hyde plc under current period group relief.

In the year ended 31 March 2025, Hyde plc had the following results:

	£
Trading loss	(8,000)
Chargeable gain	48,000
Interest income	12,000
Qualifying charitable donations	(1,500)

Greenwich plc will make a trading loss in the period ended 31 December 2025 and will surrender the maximum amount possible to Hyde plc under current period group relief.

Regent plc and Primrose plc are in a chargeable gains group. In the year to 31 March 2025, Regent plc sold a factory to Primrose plc for £250,000. The market value of the factory at that date was £300,000. Regent plc had acquired the factory for £100,000. The indexation factor between the date of acquisition and December 2017 is 0.200.

237 Identify, by clicking on the relevant boxes in the table below, which of the following companies are also members of the Hyde plc group for group relief purposes.

Hampstead plc	YES	NO
Regent plc	YES	NO
Richmond plc	YES	NO
Primrose plc	YES	NO

(2 marks)

238 What is the maximum amount that Greenwich plc could surrender as current period group relief of the year ended 31 March 2025?

○ £68,000
○ £70,000
○ £73,000
○ £77,000

(2 marks)

239 What are the maximum available taxable total profits of Hyde plc that could be current period group relieved for the year ended 31 March 2025?

Pull down list
- £2,500
- £50,500
- £52,000
- £58,500

(2 marks)

240 Which TWO of the following statements about current period group relief claims between Hyde plc and Greenwich plc are correct?
- ☐ A claim for current period group relief will be ineffective unless Greenwich plc gives a notice of consent.
- ☐ If Hyde plc pays Greenwich plc an amount up to the amount of the loss surrendered, the payment will be deducted from the current period group relief.
- ☐ A claim for current period group relief between Greenwich plc and Hyde plc will be available against the whole of the taxable total profits of Hyde plc for the year to 31 March 2026.
- ☐ The claim for current period group relief would be made on Hyde plc's corporation tax return.

(2 marks)

241 What is base cost of the factory acquired by Primrose plc in the year ended 31 March 2025?
- ○ £100,000
- ○ £120,000
- ○ £250,000
- ○ £300,000

(2 marks)

(Total = 10 marks)

Section C

242 Problematic Ltd (June 2010) (amended) (18 mins)

Problematic Ltd sold the following assets during the year ended 31 March 2025:

(1) On 14 June 2024, 16,000 £1 ordinary shares in Easy plc were sold for £54,400. Problematic Ltd had originally purchased 15,000 shares in Easy plc on 26 June 2005 for £12,600. On 28 September 2008, Easy plc made a 1 for 3 rights issue. Problematic Ltd took up its allocation under the rights issue in full, paying £2.20 for each new share issued. Indexation factors are as follows:

June 2005–September 2008 = 0.136

September 2008–December 2017 = 0.273

(2) On 28 January 2025, a freehold factory was sold for £171,000. The indexed cost of the factory on that date was £127,000. Problematic Ltd has made a claim to hold over the gain on the factory against the cost of a replacement leasehold factory under the rollover relief (replacement of business assets) rules. The leasehold factory has a lease period of 20 years and was purchased on 10 December 2024 for £154,800. The two factory buildings have always been used entirely for business purposes.

Required

(a) Calculate Problematic Ltd's chargeable gains for the year ended 31 March 2025. **(9 marks)**

(b) Advise Problematic Ltd of the carried forward indexed base cost of the leasehold factory.
(1 mark)

(Total = 10 marks)

243 Volatile Ltd (December 2009) (amended) (18 mins)

Volatile Ltd commenced trading on 1 July 2023. The company's results for its first five periods of trading are as follows:

	p/e 31.12.23	y/e 31.12.24	y/e 31.12.25	p/e 30.9.26	y/e 30.9.27
	£	£	£	£	£
Trading profit/(loss)	44,000	(73,800)	86,500	78,700	(186,800)
Property business profit	9,400	6,600	6,500	–	–
Chargeable gain/(loss)	5,100	–	(2,000)	11,700	–
Qualifying charitable donations	(800)	(1,000)	(1,200)	–	–

Required

(a) State the factors that will influence a company's choice of loss relief claims.

Note. You are not expected to consider group relief. **(3 marks)**

(b) Assuming that Volatile Ltd claims relief for its trading losses as early as possible, calculate the company's taxable total profits for the six-month period ended 31 December 2023, each of the years ended 31 December 2024 and 2025 and the nine-month period ended 30 September 2026. Your answer should also clearly identify the amount of any unrelieved trading losses as at 30 September 2027. **(7 marks)**

(Total = 10 marks)

244 Maison Ltd (September/December 2019) (27 mins)

You are a trainee Chartered Certified Accountant dealing with the tax affairs of Maison Ltd.

Your assistant has prepared a partly completed draft corporation tax computation for the year ended 31 March 2025. All of your assistant's workings for the figures provided are correct, but there are four uncompleted sections, all related to property, which your assistant does not know how to deal with.

The assistant's corporation tax computation, along with references to the uncompleted sections (with missing figures indicated by a question mark (?)), is shown below:

Maison Ltd – Corporation tax computation for the year ended 31 March 2025

	Uncompleted section	£
Operating profit		892,900
Non-deductible expenditure		22,340
Deduction for lease premium	1	?
Capital allowances	2	?
Trading profit		?
Property business income	3	?
Loan interest receivable		1,460
Chargeable gains	4	?
Taxable total profits		?
Corporation tax		?

Uncompleted section 1 – Deduction for lease premium

Your assistant has identified that, on 1 January 2025, Maison Ltd acquired a leasehold office building, paying a premium of £44,000 for the grant of a 12-year lease. The office building was used for business purposes by Maison Ltd throughout the period 1 January to 31 March 2025.

Uncompleted section 2 – Capital allowances

Your assistant has correctly calculated that capital allowances of £22,867 are available on the main pool. However, they are unsure of the amount of capital allowance and structures and buildings allowance which are available in respect of the £140,000 spent by Maison Ltd during November 2024 constructing an extension which is adjacent to the company's existing freehold office building. The extension is used by the company's employees as a staff room and was ready for use on 1 December 2024. The total cost of £140,000 is made up of new purchases as follows:

	£
Integral to the building	
Building costs of extension	93,300
Ventilation system	6,700
Heating system	3,900
Not integral to the building	
Furniture and furnishings	33,500
Refrigerator and microwave cooker	2,600
Total cost	140,000

Uncompleted section 3 – Property business income

On 1 July 2024, Maison Ltd purchased a freehold warehouse. The warehouse is currently surplus to requirements, so it was let out from 1 November 2024. However, the warehouse was purchased in a dilapidated state and could not be let until repair work was carried out during August 2024. This fact was represented by a reduced purchase price. Your assistant has listed any income and expenditure that is potentially relevant:

		£
Date received/(paid)		
1 July 2024	Insurance for the period to 31 March 2025	(1,035)
August 2024	Initial repairs	(17,680)
28 September 2024	Advertising for tenants	(780)
1 November 2024	Security deposit of two months' rent	12,200
1 November 2024	Rent for the quarter ended 31 January 2025	18,300
1 February 2025	Rent for the quarter ended 30 April 2025	18,300

Uncompleted section 4 – Chargeable gains

Maison Ltd disposed of two investment properties during August 2024, both resulting in gains. Your assistant has correctly calculated the gains but is unsure of the amount of indexation allowance available. The assistant's workings are as follows:

	Date	1st property	2nd property
		£	£
Disposal proceeds	August 2024	237,000	143,000
Cost	April 2009	(101,000)	(117,000)
Enhancement expenditure	May 2018	(26,200)	0
Gain		109,800	26,000

Indexation factors are:

April 2009 to December 2017   0.315

No rollover relief claim is possible in respect of these gains.

Required

Prepare a completed version of Maison Ltd's corporation tax computation for the year ended 31 March 2025 after dealing with the sections uncompleted by your assistant.

Notes.

1   Your computation should commence with the operating profit figure of £892,900, and you should indicate by the use of zero (0) any items which are not included in your calculation.

2   In calculating the operating profit figure of £892,900, no deduction has been made for the lease premium (uncompleted section 1) or any capital allowances (uncompleted section 2). It also does not include any income or expenditure in relation to property business income (uncompleted section 3) or any chargeable gains in relation to the disposal of the two investment properties (uncompleted section 4).

(Total = 15 marks)

245 Black Ltd (December 2011) and Gastron Ltd (June 2009) (amended) (18 mins)

(a) Black Ltd owns 100% of the ordinary share capital of White Ltd and 80% of the ordinary shares of Grey Ltd. The results of Black Ltd, White Ltd and Grey Ltd for the year ended 31 March 2025 are as follows:

	Black Ltd £	White Ltd £	Grey Ltd £
Trading profit/(loss)	338,900	(351,300)	50,000
Property business profit	21,100	26,700	4,500
Qualifying charitable donations	(4,400)	(5,600)	0

At 1 April 2024, Grey Ltd had brought forward trading losses of £57,500 arising from the year ended 31 March 2024.

Required

Advise Black Ltd as to the maximum amount of group relief that it can set off in the year ended 31 March 2025 if claims are made both from White Ltd in respect of its losses for the year ended 31 March 2025 and from Grey Ltd in respect of its losses for the year ended 31 March 2024.

Note. You are not expected to calculate either company's corporation tax liability. **(5 marks)**

(b) Gastron Ltd is a manufacturing company. In the year to 31 March 2025, Gastron Ltd had taxable total profits of £30,000 and augmented profits of £45,000. The taxable total profits included a chargeable gain of £24,800 on the sale of a 1% shareholding. This figure is after taking account of indexation.

Gastron Ltd owns 100% of the ordinary share capital of Culinary Ltd. On 13 February 2025, Culinary Ltd sold a freehold factory and this resulted in a capital loss of £16,000. For the year ended 31 March 2025 Culinary Ltd made no other disposals and paid corporation tax at the small profits rate.

Required

(i) Explain the group relationship that must exist in order for two or more companies to form a group for chargeable gains purposes. **(2 marks)**

(ii) Explain why it would be beneficial for Gastron Ltd and Culinary Ltd to make a joint election to transfer the whole of the capital gain on Gastron Ltd's disposal of shares to Culinary Ltd. **(3 marks)**

(Total = 10 marks)

246 Crumble Ltd (September/December 2022) (27 mins)

Crumble Ltd has brought forward its accounting reference date to 31 March. Its summarised statement of profit or loss for the nine-month period ended 31 March 2025 is as follows:

	Note	£
Gross profit		261,100
Operating expenses		
– Professional fees	1	(23,900)
– Repairs and renewals	2	(13,100)
– Qualifying charitable donation	3	(3,400)

	Note	£
– Other expenses	4	(408,500)
Operating loss		(187,800)
Other income		
– Property business income	5	7,960
– Profit business income	6	12,800
Finance costs		
– Interest payable	7	(8,750)
Loss before taxation		(175,790)

Notes.

1 **Professional fees**

Professional fees of £23,900 comprise:

	£
Accountancy fees	6,200
Legal fees in connection with varying the terms of Crumble Ltd's loan notes (see note 6)	4,600
Legal fees in connection with the issue of share capital	9,300
Legal fees in connection with the registration of trademarks	3,800
	23,900

The accountancy fees of £6,200 include £2,800 in respect of the additional work arising as a result of a compliance check by HM Revenue and Customs (HMRC) into Crumble Ltd's self-assessment tax return for the year ended 30 June 2023. No additional tax was payable as a result of the compliance check.

2 **Repairs and renewals**

Repairs and renewals of £13,100 comprise:

	£
Constructing a new car park next to the company's business premises (there was previously no car park)	7,300
Repairing the wall of an office building after it was damaged by a lorry	5,800
	13,100

3 Crumble Ltd paid the qualifying charitable donation of £3,400 on 15 March 2025.

4 **Other expenses**

Other expenses of £408,500 comprise:

	£
Removal expenses to the company's new business premises (this was not an expansionary move)	14,400
Fine for infringing health and safety regulations	1,200
Remaining expenses – fully allowable	392,900
	408,500

5 Property business income

Crumble Ltd lets out a warehouse which is surplus to requirements. The building was empty and available for letting from 1 July to 30 November 2024 but was let from 1 December 2024 onwards.

The following income and expenditure was received or incurred during the nine-month period ended 31 March 2025:

Date received/(paid)		£
1 July 2024	Insurance for the year ended 30 June 2025	(840)
1 December 2024	Rent for the six months ended 31 May 2025	6,600
1 December 2024	Security deposit of two months' rent	2,200
		7,960

6 Profit on disposal of shares

On 22 December 2024, Crumble Ltd sold a 1% shareholding in an unconnected company for £25,200. The shareholding had been purchased for £12,400, and its indexed cost on 22 December 2024 was £13,600.

7 Interest payable

The interest payable of £8,750 is in respect of the company's loan notes which were issued on 1 January 2017 and were due for repayment on 31 December 2024.

However, Crumble Ltd has varied the terms of the loan notes so that they are now repayable on 31 December 2029. At the same time, the annual rate of interest payable was reduced from 7% to 4% with effect from 1 January 2025.

Interest of £8,750 was paid on 31 December 2024 in relation to the six-month period ended on that date. Interest for the six-month period ending 30 June 2025 will be £5,000.

The loan notes were issued in order to finance the company's trading activities.

Capital allowances

No capital allowances are available for the nine-month period ended 31 March 2025.

Year ended 30 June 2024

For the year ended 30 June 2024, Crumble Ltd had taxable total profits of £49,000.

Year ended 31 March 2026

Crumble Ltd is expecting to have taxable total profits of £240,000.

Required

(a) Calculate Crumble Ltd's tax adjusted trading loss for the nine-month period ended 31 March 2025.

Notes.

1 Your computation should commence with the operating loss figure of £187,800 and should also list all of the items referred to in notes 1, 2, 3, 4 and 7, indicating by the use of zero (0) any items that do not require adjustment.

2 For this part of the question, the items referred to in notes 5 and 6 are not relevant.

(7 marks)

(b) Before taking account of any possible loss relief claim, calculate Crumble Ltd's taxable total profits for the nine-month period ended 31 March 2025.

Note. For this part of the question, only the items referred to in notes 3, 5 and 6 are relevant.

(4 marks)

(c) (i) State by what date Crumble Ltd must make a claim if it wishes to set its trading loss for the nine-month period ended 31 March 2025 (as calculated in part (a)) against the company's total profits for the year ended 30 June 2024. **(1 mark)**

(ii) State the factors that will influence Crumble Ltd's choice of loss relief claims and the best option from a financial point of view.

Note. You are not expected to consider group relief. **(3 marks)**

(Total = 15 marks)

247 Hopi Ltd (March/June 2018) (18 mins)

You should assume that today's date is 25 March 2025.

Kaya is the managing director of, and 100% shareholder in, Hopi Ltd. Hopi Ltd has no other employees.

For the year ended 5 April 2025, Hopi Ltd's tax adjusted trading profit, after taking account of director's remuneration and employer's class 1 national insurance contributions (NICs), is forecast to be £70,000.

Hopi Ltd has already paid Kaya gross director's remuneration of £30,000 and dividends of £44,000 for the tax year 2024/25. Kaya does not have any other income.

Based on these figures, the tax and NICs for Kaya and Hopi Ltd for the year ended 5 April 2025 will be:

	£
Kaya	
Income tax	13,225
Employee class 1 NICs	1,394
Hopi Ltd	
Employer class 1 NICs	2,884
Corporation tax	7,052

On 31 March 2025 however, Kaya is planning to pay herself a bonus of £25,000.

She is unsure whether to take this as additional director's remuneration (the gross remuneration will be £25,000) or as an additional dividend.

Required

Calculate the revised tax and NICs for Kaya and Hopi Ltd for the year ended 5 April 2025 if, on 31 March 2025, Kaya pays herself the bonus of £25,000 (1) as additional director's remuneration or (2) as an additional dividend.

Note. You are expected to calculate the revised income tax liability and NICs for Kaya and the revised corporation tax liability and NICs for Hopi Ltd under each of options (1) and (2).

(10 marks)

248 Kat (September/December 2018) (18 mins)

You should assume that today's date is 15 March 2024.

On 6 April 2024, Kat will purchase a residential freehold property which she will let out. However, Kat is unsure whether to purchase the property personally or via a limited company. The limited company would be incorporated for the sole purpose of purchasing and letting out the property, and Kat would hold all of the shares in the company.

Regardless of whether the property is purchased personally or via a limited company:

(1) The property will be let throughout the year ended 5 April 2025 at a monthly rent of £2,600 which will be paid when due.

(2) The purchase of the property will be partly financed with a repayment mortgage. Mortgage interest of £12,000 will be paid during the year ended 5 April 2025.

(3) The other expenditure on the property for the year ended 5 April 2025 will amount to £7,600, and this will all be allowable.

(4) Kat will also have employment income of £60,000 for the tax year 2024/25.

If the property is purchased via a limited company, the company's corporation tax liability for the year ended 5 April 2025 will be £2,204 and Kat will withdraw dividends from the company totalling £4,500 during the tax year 2024/25.

Kat will not have any other income for the tax year 2024/25.

Required

(a) Determine if there will be an overall saving of tax for the year ended 5 April 2025 if Kat purchases the property via a limited company rather than purchasing it personally.

Notes.

1 Your answer should include a calculation of Kat's income tax liability if she purchases the property personally and if she purchases it via a limited company.

2 You should ignore national insurance contributions (NICs). **(9 marks)**

(b) Explain the ONE way in which the calculation of a future taxable gain on a property disposal made by the limited company would differ from the calculation of a taxable gain on a disposal made personally by Kat. **(1 mark)**

(Total = 10 marks)

249 Venus Ltd (March/June 2023) (Mar/Jun 2023) (27 mins)

Venus Ltd's summarised statement of profit or loss for the year ended 31 March 2025 is as follows:

	Note	£
Gross profit		521,750
Operating expenses		
Depreciation		(32,046)
Amortisation of leasehold property	1	(4,000)
Other expenses	2	(285,012)
Operating profit		200,692
Income from investments		
Bank interest received	3	18,050
Dividends received	4	34,000
Profit on disposal of shares	5	70,300
Profit before taxation		323,042

Notes.

1 **Leasehold property**

On 1 October 2024, Venus Ltd acquired a leasehold office building for use by the business, paying a premium of £96,000 for the grant of a 12-year lease.

2   **Other expenses**

    Other expenses include the following:

	£
Entertaining UK customers	3,600
Gifts to customers (food hampers costing £30 each)	2,730
Qualifying charitable donations	1,410

3   **Bank interest received**

    The bank interest received during the year ended 31 March 2025 of £18,050 relates to deposits held for non-trading purposes. In addition, on 10 April 2025, £350 of non-trading loan interest was received in relation to the year ended 31 March 2025.

4   **Dividends received**

    During the year ended 31 March 2025, Venus Ltd received dividends of £34,000 from Mars Ltd, an 80% UK subsidiary company.

5   **Profit on disposal of shares**

    The profit on disposal of shares is in respect of a 2% shareholding that was sold on 18 January 2025. The disposal resulted in a chargeable gain of £62,880 after taking account of the indexation allowance.

6   **Plant and machinery**

    On 1 April 2024, the tax written down values of plant and machinery were as follows:

	£
Main pool	8,400
Special rate pool	12,740

    The following purchases took place during the year ended 31 March 2025:

Date	Description	CO_2 emissions	£
10 August 2024	Car (1)	115	22,930
16 November 2024	New delivery van	120	20,800
18 November 2024	Equipment (second hand)	N/A	52,112
12 February 2025	Car (2)	40	26,470

    On 15 March 2025, Venus Ltd sold car (1) that had been purchased on 10 August 2024 for £16,750.

7   **Group relief**

    For the year ended 31 March 2025, Mars Ltd (the 80% UK subsidiary company – see note 4) made a trading loss of £7,635. Venus Ltd has made a group relief claim, for the year ended 31 March 2025, in respect of this loss.

Required

Calculate Venus Ltd's corporation tax liability for the year ended 31 March 2025.

Notes.

1   Your computation should commence with the operating profit figure of £200,692 indicating by the use of zero (0) any items which do not require adjustment.

2   You should assume that the full annual investment allowance is available to Venus Ltd.

(Total = 15 marks)

250 Mooncake Ltd (March/June 2021 amended) (27 mins)

Mooncake Ltd reported an operating loss of £93,820 in its statement of profit or loss for the year ended 31 March 2025 as follows:

	Note	£
Revenue		184,550
Operating expenses		
– Depreciation		(7,230)
– Leasing cost	1	(6,380)
– Other expenses	2	(264,760)
Operating loss		(93,820)

Notes.

1 Leasing costs are as follows:

	£
Lease of office equipment	2,980
Lease of car with CO_2 emissions of 65 grams per kilometre	3,400
	6,380

2 Other expenses are as follows:

	£
Entertaining staff (cost of £160 per head)	4,320
Entertaining overseas customers	8,720
Qualifying charitable donations	1,600
Balance of expenditure (all allowable)	250,120
	264,760

Additional information

Plant and machinery

On 1 April 2024, the tax written down value of the main pool was £43,200.

The following vehicles were sold during the year ended 31 March 2025:

	Date of sale	Proceeds	Original cost
		£	£
Delivery van (130% super deduction was claimed)	12 April 2024	2,124	14,700
Car [1]	13 August 2024	8,400	8,100
Car [2]	9 March 2025	5,300	12,200

The original cost of car [1] had previously been added to the main pool. The original cost of car [2] qualified for a 100% first year allowance.

Property business loss

Mooncake Ltd has a property business loss of £4,400 for the year ended 31 March 2025.

Profit on disposal of shares

Mooncake Ltd made a profit on disposal of shares of £3,700 in respect of a 1% shareholding which was sold on 8 November 2024. This profit on disposal is calculated as disposal proceeds of £34,200 less cost of £30,500. The indexation allowance is £6,700.

Results for the year ended 31 March 2024

Mooncake Ltd's results for the year ended 31 March 2024 were:

	£
Trading profit	138,200
Property business income	23,700
Capital loss	(4,900)
Qualifying charitable donations	(1,400)

Required

(a) State the factors which will influence a company's choice of loss relief claims. **(2 marks)**

(b) Calculate Mooncake Ltd's tax adjusted trading loss for the year ended 31 March 2025.

   Notes.
   1. Your computation should commence with the operating loss figure of £93,820, and should indicate by the use of zero (0) any items which do not require adjustment.
   2. You should assume that the company claims the maximum available capital allowances.

   (7 marks)

(c) Assuming that Mooncake Ltd wishes to claim relief for its losses as early as possible:

   (i) Calculate the company's corporation tax liabilities for each of the years ended 31 March 2024 and 31 March 2025. (Note that Mooncake Ltd has no associated companies and no dividends received.) **(4 marks)**

   (ii) Calculate the amount of unused losses or payments which Mooncake Ltd can carry forward to be utilised in the year ending 31 March 2026.
   (2 marks)

   (Total = 15 marks)

251 Maximum Ltd (September/December 2023) (27 mins)

The following information is available in respect of Maximum Ltd for the year ended 31 March 2025:

Trading profit

The trading profit based on the draft accounts for the year ended 31 March 2025 is £127,200. This figure is before making any adjustments required for:

(1) A premium which was paid on 1 August 2024 to acquire a leasehold office building on an eight-year lease. The amount of premium assessed on the landlord as income was £22,320. The office building was used for business purposes by Maximum Ltd throughout the period 1 August 2024 to 31 March 2025.

(2) Leasing costs of £10,300 which have been deducted in arriving at the profit of £127,200. The leasing costs relate to two cars which have been leased since 1 April 2024. The first car has CO_2 emissions of 40 grams per kilometre and is leased at an annual cost of £6,400. The second car has CO_2 emissions of 120 grams per kilometre and is leased at an annual cost of £3,900.

(3) Employee bonuses of £36,000, which have not been deducted in arriving at the profit of £127,200, all of which relate to the year ended 31 March 2025. Maximum Ltd paid £20,000 of the bonuses on 30 November 2025, with the remainder of £16,000 paid on 15 February 2026. No entitlement to the bonuses arose until the time that they were paid.

Property business income

Maximum Ltd lets out a freehold warehouse which is surplus to requirements. The building was let from 1 April to 31 October 2024 but, although it was available for letting, it was empty from 1 November 2024 to 31 January 2025. Because it was not possible to find new tenants, the warehouse was sold on 31 January 2025 (see chargeable gains).

The following income and expenditure was incurred during the period 1 April 2024 to 31 January 2025:

Date received/(paid)		£
1 January 2024	Rent for the six months ended 30 June 2024	8,400
1 April 2024	Insurance for the year ended 31 March 2025	(1,320)
1 July 2024	Rent for the four months ended 31 October 2024	5,600
31 October 2024	Repaid security deposit of one month's rent	(1,400)
20 January 2025	Advertising for tenants	(720)
31 January 2025	Insurance refund (less an administrative fee)	190

Chargeable gains

Maximum Ltd made two disposals during the year ended 31 March 2025:

(1) On 31 January 2025, Maximum Ltd disposed of a freehold warehouse (see property business income) for £187,000. The disposal resulted in a chargeable gain of £43,300. The warehouse was never used by Maximum Ltd for business purposes.

(2) On 20 February 2025, Maximum Ltd disposed of a freehold factory for £142,000. The disposal resulted in a chargeable gain of £29,100. The factory was used by Maximum Ltd for business purposes.

On 10 December 2024, Maximum Ltd had purchased a new factory for £342,000. This factory is used for business purposes. Maximum Ltd made the maximum possible rollover relief claim against the new factory cost of £342,000.

No rollover relief claim has been, or will be, made in respect of the premium paid for the eight-year lease (see trading profit note (1)).

Donations

During the year ended 31 March 2025, Maximum Ltd made qualifying charitable donations of £2,800 and political donations of £700. Neither of these amounts have been deducted in arriving at the trading profit figure of £127,200.

Subsidiary companies

Maximum Ltd has two subsidiary companies, both of which commenced trading on 1 April 2022. Each company made a trading profit for the year ended 31 March 2025. The following information is available:

Subsidiary	Percentage shareholding	Trading profit
		£
Xim Ltd	85%	21,400
Mum Ltd	65%	13,800

Neither company has any other income or outgoings, with neither making a trading profit for the year ended 31 March 2024.

Brought forward losses

Maximum Ltd has the following brought forward amounts of unused losses from the year ended 31 March 2024:

	£
Trading loss	(288,200)
Property business loss	(3,800)
Capital loss	(4,900)

Required

(a) Before taking account of brought forward losses, apart from any losses which are automatically relieved, calculate Maximum Ltd's taxable total profits for the year ended 31 March 2025.

Note. Your computation should commence with the trading profit based on the draft accounts figure of £127,200, indicating by the use of zero (0) any items that do not require adjustment. **(11 marks)**

(b) On the basis that the maximum possible loss relief and group relief claims are made for the year ended 31 March 2025, calculate the total remaining amount of unused losses which Maximum Ltd can carry forward to the year ended 31 March 2026.

Note. If possible, your loss relief claims should not result in donations becoming unrelieved. **(4 marks)**

(Total = 15 marks)

252 Lucky Ltd (September/December 2015) (amended)   (27 mins)

Lucky Ltd was incorporated on 20 July 2024 and commenced trading on 1 December 2024. The following information is available for the four-month period 1 December 2024 to 31 March 2025:

(1) The operating profit for the four-month period ended 31 March 2025 is £699,266. Advertising expenditure of £4,700 (incurred during September 2024), depreciation of £14,700, and amortisation of £9,000 have been deducted in arriving at this figure.

The amortisation relates to a premium which was paid on 1 December 2024 to acquire a leasehold warehouse on a 12-year lease. The amount of premium assessed on the landlord as income was £46,800. The warehouse was used for business purposes by Lucky Ltd throughout the period ended 31 March 2025.

(2) Lucky Ltd purchased the following new assets during the period 20 July 2024 to 31 March 2025:

		£
19 August 2024	Computer	6,300
22 January 2025	Integral features	291,200
31 January 2025	Office equipment	48,689
17 March 2025	Car	12,800

The integral features of £291,200 are in respect of expenditure on electrical systems, a ventilation system and lifts which are integral to a freehold office building owned by Lucky Ltd.

The car has a CO_2 emission rate of 42 grams per kilometre.

(3) Lucky Ltd made a loan to another company for non-trading purposes on 1 February 2025. Loan interest income of £700 was accrued at 31 March 2025. Lucky Ltd will make a company car available to its chief executive officer. The car will be purchased, rather than leased, and will be made available to the chief executive officer from December 2025 onwards.

Required

(a) State when an accounting period starts for corporation tax purposes. **(2 marks)**

(b) Calculate Lucky Ltd's corporation tax liability for the four-month period ended 31 March 2025.

Note. Your computation should commence with the operating profit of £699,266 and should also indicate by the use of zero (0) any items referred to in the question for which no adjustment is required. **(9 marks)**

(c) Advise Lucky Ltd as to how long it must retain the records used in preparing its self-assessment corporation tax return for the four-month period ended 31 March 2025, and the potential consequences of not retaining the records for the required period. **(2 marks)**

(d) Advise Lucky Ltd on the effects of the company car on its taxable total profits for the year ended 31 March 2026. **(2 marks)**

(Total = 15 marks)

253 Jump Ltd (March/June 2016) (27 mins)

Jump Ltd's summarised statement of profit or loss for the three-month period ended 31 March 2025 is as follows:

	Note	£	£
Revenue			264,900
Operating expenses			
Depreciation		8,100	
Employee costs	1	189,700	
Lease of car	2	1,200	
Professional fees	3	7,800	
Other expenses	4	202,800	
			(409,600)
Loss before taxation			(144,700)

Notes.

1 **Employee costs**

Employee costs are as follows:

	£
Employee training courses	3,400
Employee pension contributions paid	11,600
Cost of annual staff party (for eight employees)	1,500
Balance of expenditure (all allowable)	173,200
	189,700

2 **Lease of car**

The lease is in respect of a car with CO_2 emissions of 59 grams per kilometre.

3 Professional fees

Professional fees are as follows:

	£
Accountancy	2,200
Legal fees in connection with the issue of share capital	3,800
Legal fees in connection with the renewal of a 20-year property lease	1,800
	7,800

4 Other expenses

Other expenses are as follows:

	£
Entertaining UK customers	1,700
Entertaining overseas customers	790
Political donations	800
Balance of expenditure (all allowable)	199,510
	202,800

Additional information

Plant and machinery

On 1 January 2025, the tax written down values of Jump Ltd's plant and machinery were:

	£
Main pool	12,100
Special rate pool	5,700

The following cars were sold during the three-month period ended 31 March 2025:

	Date of sale	Proceeds £	Original cost £
Car [1]	7 January 2025	9,700	9,300
Car [2]	29 March 2025	6,100	13,200

The original cost of car [1] was added to the special rate pool when it was purchased, and the original cost of car [2] was added to the main pool when it was purchased.

Previous results

Jump Ltd's results for its two previous periods of trading are as follows:

	y/e 31 May 2024 £	p/e 31 December 2024 £
Tax adjusted trading profit	78,600	42,400
Bank interest receivable	1,200	0

Group companies

Jump Ltd owns 80% of the ordinary share capital of Hop Ltd and 60% of the ordinary share capital of Skip Ltd.

Hop Ltd commenced trading on 1 August 2024, and for the eight-month period ended 31 March 2025 has taxable total profits of £63,000.

Skip Ltd has been trading for several years and has taxable total profits of £56,000 for the year ended 31 March 2025.

Required

(a) Calculate Jump Ltd's tax adjusted trading loss for the three-month period ended 31 March 2025.

Notes.

1. Your computation should commence with the operating loss figure of £144,700 and should list all of the items referred to in notes (1) to (4), indicating by the use of zero (0) any items which do not require adjustment.

2. You should assume that the company claims the maximum available capital allowances.

(10 marks)

(b) (i) Other than timing of the relief obtained, what is the main factor which will influence Jump Ltd's choice of loss relief or group relief claims? **(1 mark)**

(ii) Advise Jump Ltd as to the maximum amount of its trading loss which can be relieved against its total profits for the year ended 31 May 2024 and the seven-month period ended 31 December 2024. **(2 marks)**

(iii) Advise Jump Ltd as to the maximum amount of its trading loss which can be surrendered as group relief. **(2 marks)**

(Total = 15 marks)

254 Online Ltd (March/June 2017) (27 mins)

The following information is available in respect of Online Ltd for the year ended 31 March 2025:

Operating profit

Online Ltd's operating profit for the year ended 31 March 2025 is £896,700. Depreciation of £21,660 and amortisation of leasehold property of £9,000 (see the leasehold property note below) have been deducted in arriving at this figure.

Leasehold property

On 1 April 2024, Online Ltd acquired a leasehold office building, paying a premium of £90,000 for the grant of a ten-year lease. The office building was used for business purposes by Online Ltd throughout the year ended 31 March 2025.

Plant and machinery

On 1 April 2024, the tax written down values of plant and machinery were as follows:

	£
Main pool	56,700
Special rate pool	13,433

The following transactions took place during the year ended 31 March 2025:

		Costs/(proceeds) £
14 May 2024	Sold a car	(18,100)
18 July 2024	Sold all items included in the special rate pool (no enhanced CA had been claimed)	(9,300)
27 Jan 2025	Purchased a car	13,700

The car sold on 14 May 2024 for £18,100 was originally purchased during the year ended 31 March 2024 for £17,200. This expenditure was added to the main pool.

The car purchased on 27 January 2025 for £13,700 has a CO_2 emission rate of 48 grams per kilometre. The car is used as a pool car by the company's employees.

Qualifying charitable donations

During the year ended 31 March 2025, Online Ltd made qualifying charitable donations of £6,800. These were not included in arriving at the operating profit above.

Disposal of shareholding in Network plc

On 20 March 2025, Online Ltd sold its entire shareholding of £1 ordinary shares in Network plc for £90,600. Online Ltd had originally purchased 40,000 shares (less than a 1% shareholding) in Network plc on 24 June 2010 for £49,300. On 7 October 2013, Online Ltd sold 22,000 of the shares for £62,200.

Indexation factors are as follows:

June 2010 to October 2013	0.124
June 2010 to December 2017	0.241
October 2013 to December 2017	0.104

Brought forward losses

As at 1 April 2024, Online Ltd had the following brought forward amounts of unused losses:

	£
Capital loss	3,104
Property business loss	12,500

Planned acquisition

Online Ltd currently does not have any associated companies. However, Online Ltd is planning to acquire a shareholding in Offline Ltd in the near future which would make it an associated company. Offline Ltd is profitable and will pay regular dividends to Online Ltd.

Required

(a) Calculate Online Ltd's taxable total profits for the year ended 31 March 2025. **(13 marks)**

(b) Briefly explain how the acquisition of Offline Ltd will affect the calculation and payment of Online Ltd's corporation tax liability in future years. **(2 marks)**

(Total = 15 marks)

255 Last-Orders Ltd (September/December 2017) (27 mins)

Last-Orders Ltd ceased trading on 31 January 2025, having traded profitably for the previous ten years. The ordinary share capital of Last-Orders Ltd is owned 80% by Gastro Ltd and 20% by Gourmet Ltd.

Last-Orders Ltd's summarised statement of profit or loss for the ten-month period ended 31 January 2025 is as follows:

	Note	£
Revenue		176,790
Operating expenses		
Depreciation		(9,460)
Employee costs	1	(142,400)
Lease of car	2	(1,600)
Other expenses	3	(299,810)
Operating loss		(276,480)
Other income		
Property business income	4	11,500
Profit on disposal of freehold office building	5	47,400
Loss before taxation		(217,580)

Notes.

1 **Employee costs**

Employee costs are as follows:

	£
Counselling services provided to employees who were made redundant	5,200
Pension contributions paid on behalf of employees	12,200
Employer class 1 national insurance contributions (NICs)	11,890
Employer class 1A NICs payable on benefits provided for employees	1,160
Employee bonuses declared but unpaid – will not be paid during 2025	10,400
Balance of expenditure (all allowable)	101,550
	142,400

2 **Lease of car**

The lease is in respect of a car with CO_2 emissions of 40 grams per kilometre.

3 **Other expenses**

Other expenses are as follows:

	£
Entertaining UK suppliers	1,920
Entertaining overseas suppliers	440
Qualifying charitable donation	800
Balance of expenditure (all allowable)	296,650
	299,810

4 **Property business income**

During the ten-month period ended 31 January 2025, Last-Orders Ltd let out a freehold office building.

Income and expenditure received or incurred during the final 12 months of trading:

Date received/(paid)		£
1 February 2024	Rent for the six months ended 31 July 2024	19,200
1 February 2024	Insurance for the 12 months ended 31 January 2025	(1,800)
1 August 2024	Rent for the six months ended 31 January 2025	19,200
21 November 2024	Repairs following a fire (not covered by insurance)	(7,700)

5 **Property business income**

The office building was sold on 31 January 2025.

The profit has been calculated as disposal proceeds of £126,800 less cost of £79,400. The indexation allowance is £12,900. The office building was never used for business purposes.

Additional information

Plant and machinery – on 1 April 2024, the tax written down value of Last-Orders Ltd's main pool was £24,200. All of the items included in the main pool were sold for £13,600 on 31 January 2025, with none of the items sold for more than their original cost.

Enhanced capital allowances had not been claimed on any of the disposals. Last-Orders Ltd has previously always made up its accounts to 31 March. Both Gastro Ltd and Gourmet Ltd are profitable and make up their accounts to 31 March.

Required

(a) Calculate Last-Orders Ltd's tax adjusted trading loss for the ten-month period ended 31 January 2025.

Notes.

1 Your computation should commence with the operating loss figure of £276,480 and should also list all of the items referred to in notes (1) to (3), indicating by the use of zero (0) any items which do not require adjustment.

2 Assume Last-Orders Ltd claims the maximum amount of capital allowances. **(6 marks)**

(b) Assuming Last-Orders Ltd claims relief for its trading loss against its taxable total profits for the ten-month period ended 31 January 2025, calculate the company's taxable total profits for this period.

Note. Your answer should show the amount of unused trading loss at 31 January 2025.

(5 marks)

(c) Explain the alternative ways in which Last-Orders Ltd's unused trading loss for the ten-month period ended 31 January 2025 could be relieved. **(4 marks)**

(Total = 15 marks)

256 Solo Ltd (March/June 2018) (27 mins)

Solo Ltd's results for the previous two periods of trading are:

	y/e 31 December 2023	3-month p/e 31 March 2024
	£	£
Trading profit	35,900	12,300
Property business income	12,100	4,200
Chargeable gains/(capital losses)	(3,300)	(2,100)
Qualifying charitable donations	(1,200)	(1,600)

The following information is available in respect of the year ended 31 March 2025:

Trading loss

The tax-adjusted trading loss based on the draft statement of profit or loss for the year ended 31 March 2025 is £151,300. This figure is before making any adjustments required for:

(1) A premium which was paid to acquire a leasehold office building on an eight-year lease
(2) Capital allowances

Premium paid to acquire leasehold office building

On 1 April 2024, Solo Ltd acquired a leasehold office building, paying a premium of £20,000 for the grant of an eight-year lease. The office building was used for business purposes by Solo Ltd throughout the year ended 31 March 2025.

Plant and machinery

The tax written down value of the plant and machinery main pool as at 1 April 2024 was £0. During the year ended 31 March 2025, Solo Ltd sold equipment for £4,300. The equipment was originally purchased during the year ended 31 March 2019 for £22,400, with this expenditure qualifying for the 100% annual investment allowance.

Property business income

Solo Ltd lets out a warehouse which is surplus to requirements. The building was empty from 1 April to 31 July 2024 but was let from 1 August 2024 onwards. The following income and expenditure was received or incurred during the year ended 31 March 2025:

Date received/paid

		£
1 April 2024	Insurance for the year ended 31 March 2025	(920)
1 August 2024	Rent for the six months ended 31 January 2025	7,800
1 August 2024	Security deposit equal to two months' rent	2,600
1 March 2025	Rent for the six months ended 31 July 2025	7,800

Disposal of shareholding in Multiple plc

On 12 December 2024, Solo Ltd sold 6,500 £1 ordinary shares in Multiple plc for £31,200. Solo Ltd had originally purchased 20,000 shares (less than a 1% shareholding) in Multiple plc on 18 June 2006 for £27,000 and purchased a further 1,000 shares on 8 December 2024 for £4,600.

Indexation factors are:

June 2006–December 2017   0.401

Required

(a) Calculate Solo Ltd's revised tax-adjusted trading loss for the year ended 31 March 2025.

   Note. You should assume that the company claims the maximum available capital allowances. **(3 marks)**

(b) On the basis that Solo Ltd claims relief for its trading loss against its total profits for the year ended 31 March 2025, prepare a corporation tax computation for this year showing taxable total profits. **(8 marks)**

(c) On the basis that Solo Ltd claims relief for the remainder of its trading loss as early as possible, calculate the company's taxable total profits for the year ended 31 December 2023 and the three-month period ended 31 March 2024. **(4 marks)**

(Total = 15 marks)

257 Ash Ltd, Beech Ltd and Cedar Ltd (September/December 2018) (27 mins)

You are a trainee chartered certified accountant assisting your manager with the tax affairs of three unconnected limited companies, Ash Ltd, Beech Ltd and Cedar Ltd.

Ash Ltd

Ash Ltd was incorporated in the UK on 1 December 2022 and immediately opened a non-interest bearing bank account. The company commenced trading on 1 February 2023, preparing its first accounts for the 14-month period ended 31 March 2024. Accounts were then prepared for the year ended 31 March 2025.

At the date of incorporation, all three of Ash Ltd's directors (who each own one-third of the company's ordinary share capital) were based in the UK. However, on 1 October 2024, two of the directors moved overseas. The directors have always held Ash Ltd's board meetings in the UK and will continue to do so despite two of them moving overseas.

Beech Ltd

Beech Ltd's summarised statement of profit or loss for the year ended 31 March 2025 is as follows:

	Note	£
Gross profit		566,175
Operating expenses		
Depreciation		(14,700)
Gifts and donations	1	(4,975)
Impairment loss	2	(3,700)
Leasing costs	3	(12,600)
Other expenses	4	(217,700)
Finance costs		
Interest payable	5	(7,000)
Profit before taxation		305,500

Notes.

1 **Gifts and donations**

Gifts and donations of £4,975 comprise:

	£
Gifts to customers (pens costing £70 each and displaying Beech Ltd's name)	3,500
Gifts to staff (decorative plaques costing £15 each to celebrate Beech Ltd's ten-year anniversary)	375
Qualifying charitable donations	1,100
	4,975

2 **Impairment loss**

On 31 March 2025, Beech Ltd wrote off an impairment loss of £3,700 relating to a trade debt. This was in respect of an invoice which had been due for payment on 15 October 2024.

3 Leasing costs

The leasing costs of £12,600 are in respect of four car leases which commenced on 1 April 2024. Each of the four leased cars has CO_2 emissions of 60 grams per kilometre.

4 Other expenses

The other expenses of £217,700 include a fine of £6,400 for a breach of data protection law, and legal fees of £5,700 in connection with the renewal of a 15-year property lease. The remaining expenses are all fully allowable.

5 Interest payable

The interest payable of £7,000 is in respect of the company's 4% loan notes which were issued on 1 July 2024. Interest of £6,000 was paid on 31 December 2024, with an accrual of £1,000 provided for at 31 March 2025. The loan notes were issued in order to finance the company's trading activities.

Capital allowances

No capital allowances are available for the year ended 31 March 2025.

Cedar Ltd

Cedar Ltd is a 100% subsidiary company of Timber Ltd. The following information is available in respect of the two companies for the year ended 31 March 2025:

(1) For the year ended 31 March 2025, Cedar Ltd made a trading loss of £19,700.

(2) On 28 December 2024, Cedar Ltd sold its entire shareholding of 25,000 £1 ordinary shares in Forest plc for £6.00 per share. Cedar Ltd had originally purchased 20,000 shares in Forest plc on 1 July 2010 for £24,800. On 20 July 2010, Forest plc made a 1 for 4 rights issue. Cedar Ltd took up its allocation under the rights issue in full, paying £1.15 for each new share issued. The indexation factor from July 2010 to December 2017 is 0.244.

(3) For the year ended 31 March 2025, Timber Ltd made:

	£
Trading loss	20,800
Capital loss	8,800

There is no possibility of Cedar Ltd or Timber Ltd offsetting their trading losses against prior year profits. The group has a policy of utilising losses at the earliest opportunity.

Required

(a) (i) Identify Ash Ltd's accounting periods throughout the period 1 December 2022 to 31 March 2025. **(2 marks)**

   (ii) Explain Ash Ltd's residence status throughout the period 1 December 2022 to 31 March 2025. **(2 marks)**

(b) Calculate Beech Ltd's corporation tax liability for the year ended 31 March 2025.

   Note. Your computation should commence with the profit before taxation figure of £305,500 and should also list all of the items referred to in notes (1) to (5), indicating by the use of zero (0) any items which do not require adjustment. **(6 marks)**

(c) On the basis that all available claims and elections are made, calculate Cedar Ltd's taxable total profits for the year ended 31 March 2025. **(5 marks)**

(Total = 15 marks)

258 Aoede Ltd, Bianca Ltd and Charon Ltd (March/June 2019)

(27 mins)

You are a trainee chartered certified accountant dealing with the tax affairs of three unrelated limited companies, Aoede Ltd, Bianca Ltd and Charon Ltd.

Aoede Ltd

Aoede Ltd commenced trading on 1 April 2023. The company's results are:

	y/e 31 March 2024	y/e 31 March 2025
	£	£
Trading profit/(loss)	(111,300)	67,800
Property business income/(loss)	(26,400)	23,400
Chargeable gains	5,800	16,200
Qualifying charitable donations	(6,000)	(6,600)

Aoede Ltd owns 100% of the ordinary share capital of Moon Ltd. Moon Ltd commenced trading on 1 April 2024 and for the year ended 31 March 2025 made a trading profit of £19,700.

Bianca Ltd

Bianca Ltd commenced trading on 1 April 2024. The company's tax adjusted trading profit based on the statement of profit or loss for the year ended 31 March 2025 is £256,300. This figure is **before** making any adjustments required for:

(1) Advertising expenditure of £5,800 incurred during January 2023 to promote Bianca Ltd's new business

This expenditure has not been deducted in calculating the profit of £256,300.

(2) Leasing costs of £9,300 which have been deducted in arriving at the profit of £256,300

The leasing costs relate to two cars which have been leased since 1 April 2024. The first car has CO_2 emissions of 45 grams per kilometre and is leased at an annual cost of £4,200. The second car has CO_2 emissions of 65 grams per kilometre and is leased at an annual cost of £5,100.

(3) *Capital allowances*

On 1 April 2024, Bianca Ltd purchased four new laptop computers at a discounted cost of £1,000 per laptop. The original cost of each laptop was £1,800, but Bianca Ltd was given a discount because they were damaged.

Bianca Ltd also purchased two second-hand cars on 1 April 2024. Details are:

	Cost	CO_2 emission rate
	£	
Car [1]	12,400	35 grams per kilometre
Car [2]	13,900	120 grams per kilometre

Charon Ltd

During the year ended 31 March 2025, Charon Ltd disposed of two investment properties.

The first property was sold for £368,000 during January 2025. This property was purchased for £147,000 during October 1995 and was extended at a cost of £39,000 during June 2018.

The second property was sold for £167,000 during January 2025. This property was purchased for £172,000 during December 2017.

Indexation factors are:

October 1995–December 2017 0.856

Required

(a) (i) On the basis that Aoede Ltd claims relief for its losses as early as possible, calculate the taxable total profits of Aoede Ltd for the years ended 31 March 2024 and 31 March 2025, and of Moon Ltd for the year ended 31 March 2025. **(5 marks)**

(ii) Explain which aspect of Aoede Ltd's loss relief claim made in part (i) is not beneficial for the company to make. **(1 mark)**

(b) Calculate Bianca Ltd's revised tax adjusted trading profit for the year ended 31 March 2025. **(5 marks)**

(c) Calculate Charon Ltd's chargeable gains and capital losses, if any, for the year ended 31 March 2025. **(4 marks)**

(Total = 15 marks)

259 Mixture Ltd (March/June 2022) (27 mins)

Mixture Ltd is a large company and therefore has to make quarterly instalment payments in respect of its corporation tax liability.

For the year ended 31 March 2025, Mixture Ltd has taxable total profits of £470,000 and dividends from a non-group company of £45,000. The company had the same level of profits for the year ended 31 March 2024. Mixture Ltd has had two associated companies for many years.

Capital expenditure

Mixture Ltd incurred the following capital expenditure during the year ended 31 March 2025:

(1) A new freehold office building was purchased. The purchase price included £22,200 for a staircase linking the two floors of the building, £16,400 for sprinkler equipment and the fire alarm system, £18,700 for doors and windows and £27,100 for the ventilation system.

(2) Machinery was purchased for £76,600. At the same time, a further £9,200 was spent on building alterations which were necessary for the installation of this machinery.

(3) Movable partition walls were purchased for £33,800. Mixture Ltd uses these to divide up its open plan offices, and the partition walls are moved around on a regular basis.

(4) A new decorative wall was constructed around the boundary of Mixture Ltd's business premises at a cost of £44,700.

Property business income

Mixture Ltd lets out a warehouse which is surplus to requirements, although the property was empty between 1 September 2024 and 28 February 2025. The following income and expenditure relates to the year ended 31 March 2025:

Date received/(paid)		£
1 January 2024	Insurance for the year ended 31 December 2024	(1,700)
28 March 2024	Rent for the quarter ended 30 June 2024	7,800
4 July 2024	Rent for July and August 2024	5,200
5 December 2024	Advertising for tenants	(900)
1 January 2025	Insurance for the year ended 31 December 2025	(1,900)
1 March 2025	Premium for the grant of a five-year lease	18,000
1 March 2025	Rent for the quarter ended 31 May 2025	8,400

Required

(a) (i) Explain why Mixture Ltd is classed as a large company for the year ended 31 March 2025. **(2 marks)**

(ii) Calculate Mixture Ltd's corporation tax liability for the year ended 31 March 2025 and explain when this will have been paid.

Note. You should assume that Mixture Ltd's profits accrued evenly throughout the year.
(3 marks)

(b) List the expenditure incurred by Mixture Ltd during the year ended 31 March 2025 which will have qualified as plant and machinery for capital allowance purposes.

Notes.

1 Your answer should indicate by the use of zero (0) any item of expenditure which does not qualify as plant and machinery.

2 You are not expected to calculate the capital allowances or to state the rate of capital allowance available. **(4 marks)**

(c) Explain why a company may wish to make a short-life asset election for capital allowance purposes. **(2 marks)**

(d) Calculate the property business income figure which will have been included in Mixture Ltd's taxable total profits of £470,000 for the year ended 31 March 2025. **(4 marks)**

(Total = 15 marks)

Part F: Value added tax

Part F covers value added tax, the subject of Chapters 24 and 25 of the BPP Course Book for Taxation (TX – UK).

Section A

OTQ bank – Value added tax 1 (18 mins)

260 Jerome is a value added tax (VAT) registered trader who received an order for goods with a 10% deposit on 18 August. The goods were despatched on 26 August and an invoice was sent on 2 September. The balancing 90% of the payment was received on 10 September.

Match the tax points for the deposit and the balancing payment if Jerome does not use the cash accounting scheme.

- 18 August
- 2 September
- 26 August
- 10 September

Deposit

Balancing payment

(2 marks)

---

261 Frances commenced trading on 1 January 2024. An analysis of her taxable supplies for the first year of trading (spread evenly over the quarter) is as follows:

Quarter ended	£
31 March 2024	15,000
30 June 2024	25,000
30 September 2024	30,000
31 December 2024	33,000

Frances notifies HM Revenue and Customs (HMRC) of her liability to compulsorily register for value added tax (VAT) on time.

From what date will Frances be registered for VAT? (March/June 2021)

- ○ 30 December 2024
- ○ 1 January 2025
- ○ 31 January 2025
- ○ 1 February 2025

(2 marks)

262 Light Ltd is registered for value added tax (VAT). On 1 January 2025, Light Ltd purchased a car costing £18,400 (inclusive of VAT) for use by the managing director for business and private purposes. The private use is estimated to be 40%.

The managing director is provided with free petrol for business and private mileage which cost Light Ltd £625 (exclusive of VAT). Light Ltd wishes to use the fuel scale charge: the relevant quarterly VAT inclusive scale charge is £368.

What is Light Ltd's VAT repayment in respect of the car and the fuel for the quarter ended 31 March 2025?

- ○ £51
- ○ £74
- ○ £64
- ○ £43

(2 marks)

263 **Which TWO of the following taxpayers are most likely to benefit financially from voluntary registration for value added tax (VAT)?** (March/June 2023)

- ☐ A business which buys standard rated supplies and sells zero rated goods to members of the public
- ☐ A business which buys zero rated supplies and sells standard rated goods to members of the public
- ☐ A business which buys zero rated supplies and sells zero rated goods to members of the public
- ☐ A business which buys standard rated supplies and sells standard rated goods to other VAT-registered businesses

(2 marks)

264 Mick is a value added tax (VAT) registered trader who prepares quarterly VAT returns to 31 March, 30 June, 30 September and 31 December each year. Mick's accounts are prepared annually to 30 September. Mick made a supply of goods amounting to £6,000 on 22 September 2024 with a due date of payment of 10 October 2024. The customer has defaulted on the payment and Mick has written the debt off in his accounts. He does not use the cash accounting scheme.

Which quarterly VAT return is the earliest in which relief for the impaired debt may be claimed?

- ○ VAT quarter ended 31 December 2024
- ○ VAT quarter ended 31 March 2025
- ○ VAT quarter ended 30 June 2025
- ○ VAT quarter ended 30 September 2025

(2 marks)

(Total = 10 marks)

OTQ bank – Value added tax 2 (36 mins)

265 Olive is a sole trader who is registered for value added tax (VAT). On 10 October 2024, she purchased a car for £12,000 (inclusive of VAT) to use for business and private purposes. The private use is estimated to be 30%. On 1 December 2024, the car was damaged in an accident and the repairs amounted to £2,000 (inclusive of VAT).

What is the input tax Olive can recover in relation to the car for the quarter ended 31 December 2024?

£ ☐ (2 marks)

---

266 Price Ltd incurred the following expenditure (inclusive of value added tax) in the quarter to 31 December:

	£
New car for salesperson (20% private use)	14,040
New van	10,320
Entertaining UK customers	4,200
Entertaining overseas customers	3,600

How much input tax can be recovered by Price Ltd for the quarter to 31 December?

☐ ▼

Pull down list
- £2,320
- £3,020
- £4,192
- £5,360

(2 marks)

---

267 Ben has been in business for three years. Due to an upturn in trade, he applied to register for value added tax (VAT) with effect from 1 October 2024. Prior to registration, he had incurred the following VAT expenditure:

	£
Legal fees on an invoice dated 13 January 2024	500
Accountancy fees on an invoice dated 5 September 2024	30
Inventory of spare parts acquired in past two years and still held on 30 September 2024	240

What is the total pre-registration input tax that Ben can recover in respect of these items?

£ ☐ (2 marks)

268 In the first year of trading to 31 December 2023, Scott's taxable turnover was £5,000 per month. For the first seven months of 2024, his turnover was as follows:

	£
January 2024	8,400
February 2024	8,600
March 2024	8,800
April 2024	9,600
May 2024	15,000
June 2024	10,200
July 2024	10,300

You have advised Scott that he is compulsorily required to be registered for value added tax (VAT).

From what date will Scott be registered for VAT under compulsory registration?
- 30 July 2024
- 1 August 2024
- 30 June 2024
- 1 July 2024

(2 marks)

269 Jack is registered for value added tax (VAT) and has just joined the flat rate scheme. His standard rated sales are £10,000 per month and his standard rated purchases are £7,000 per month. Both of these amounts are exclusive of VAT.

The relevant flat rate percentage for Jack's business is 8%. The percentage reduction for the first year of VAT registration is not available.

What is Jack's monthly VAT liability under the flat rate scheme? *(March/June 2022)*

£ ☐

(2 marks)

270 Charlie, a UK value added tax (VAT) registered trader, made a supply of goods in February 2025 to a customer in France who is VAT registered there.

What rate of VAT will Charlie charge on this sale?
- 0%
- 20%
- 1/6
- 5%

(2 marks)

271 **Which TWO of the following are features of the value added tax (VAT) cash accounting scheme?**
- ☐ Date of payment or receipt determines the VAT period in which the transaction is dealt with
- ☐ Only need to submit an annual VAT return
- ☐ Gives automatic impairment loss relief (bad debt relief)
- ☐ Payments on account of VAT are required throughout the quarter

(2 marks)

130 Taxation (TX – UK) FA 2024

272 Hamza is registered for value added tax (VAT) and calculates his VAT liability using the flat rate scheme.

For the year ended 31 March 2025, Hamza's sales (net of VAT) of standard rated goods were £100,000, with a further £30,000 of zero rated sales. The amount of standard rated purchases (net of VAT) was £15,000.

The relevant flat rate scheme percentage for Hamza's business is 11%.

What was Hamza's VAT liability for the year ended 31 March 2025? *(March/June 2024)*

○ £16,500
○ £14,300
○ £14,520
○ £13,200

(2 marks)

273 Alice is registered for value added tax (VAT) and calculates her VAT liability based on the flat rate scheme. The relevant flat rate percentage for Alice's business is 10%.

For the year ended 31 March 2025, Alice's sales (exclusive of VAT) were:

	£
Standard rated sales	50,000
Zero rated sales	20,000
Exempt sales	5,000

What amount of VAT is payable by Alice to HM Revenue and Customs (HMRC) in respect of the year ended 31 March 2025? *(December 2018)*

○ £8,500
○ £8,000
○ £7,500
○ £6,000

(2 marks)

274 **Match the thresholds for a business to join and to leave the value added tax (VAT) flat rate scheme.**

Tax exclusive annual taxable turnover up to £150,000

Tax inclusive annual taxable turnover up to £150,000

Tax exclusive annual turnover up to £230,000

Tax inclusive annual turnover up to £230,000

	Join scheme
	Leave scheme

(2 marks)

(Total = 20 marks)

Section B

OT case – Anne (June 2009) (amended) (18 mins)

Anne runs a retail clothing shop. She is registered for value added tax (VAT) and is in the process of completing her VAT return for the quarter ended 30 November 2024.

The following information is available (all figures are exclusive of VAT):

(1) Cash sales amounted to £42,000, of which £28,000 was in respect of sales of adult clothing (standard rated) and £14,000 was in respect of sales of children's clothing (zero rated).

(2) Sales invoices totalling £12,000 were issued in respect of credit sales. These sales were all standard rated. Anne states on her invoice that there is a 5% discount for payment within one month of the date of the sales invoice.

90% of the customers pay within this period. The sales figure of £12,000 is stated before any deduction for the 5% discount.

(3) Purchase and expense invoices totalling £19,200 were received from VAT registered suppliers. This figure is made up as follows:

	£
Standard rated purchases and expenses	11,200
Zero rated purchases	6,000
Exempt expenses	2,000
	19,200

Anne pays all of her purchase and expense invoices two months after receiving the invoice.

(4) On 30 November 2024, Anne wrote off two impairment losses that were in respect of standard rated credit sales. The first impairment loss was for £300 and was in respect of a sales invoice due for payment on 15 July 2024. The second impairment loss was for £800 and was in respect of a sales invoice due for payment on 10 April 2024.

Anne does not use the cash accounting scheme, but she is considering using the scheme.

275 **What is the amount of output tax on cash sales payable by Anne for the quarter ended 30 November 2024?**

£ ☐ (2 marks)

276 **What is the amount of output tax on credit sales payable by Anne for the quarter ended 30 November 2024, taking into account impairment loss relief?**

- ○ £2,052
- ○ £2,400
- ○ £2,280
- ○ £2,292

(2 marks)

277 **What is the amount of input tax recoverable by Anne for the quarter ended 30 November 2024?**

£ ☐ (2 marks)

278 Which TWO of the following statements about the cash accounting scheme are correct?
- ☐ Anne will be permitted to join the scheme if her expected taxable turnover for the next 12 months does not exceed £1,350,000.
- ☐ Anne must pay her 90% of the previous year's net VAT liability during the year by means of nine monthly payments commencing at the end of the fourth month of the year.
- ☐ Anne will be permitted to join the scheme if she is up to date with her VAT payments but not necessarily up to date with her VAT returns.
- ☐ If the value of Anne's taxable supplies exceeds £1,600,000 in the 12 months to the end of a VAT period, she must leave the scheme immediately. **(2 marks)**

279 Identify, by clicking on the relevant boxes in the table below, whether each of the following statements are the advantages of Anne using the cash accounting scheme.

Reduced amount of output VAT payable	ADVANTAGE	NOT ADVANTAGE
Automatic impairment loss relief (bad debt relief)	ADVANTAGE	NOT ADVANTAGE
Only one VAT return each year	ADVANTAGE	NOT ADVANTAGE
Output VAT on 10% of credit sales will be accounted for up to 1 month later than at present	ADVANTAGE	NOT ADVANTAGE

(2 marks)

(Total = 10 marks)

OT case – Auy and Bim (June 2010) (amended) (18 mins)

Auy and Bim have been in partnership since 6 April 2006 and have been registered for value added tax (VAT) since that date. In the year ended 5 April 2025, the partnership's summarised statement of profit or loss shows sales revenue of £140,762, which is exclusive of output VAT of £25,600, and expenses of £60,200 which are exclusive of recoverable input VAT of £180 for motor expenses and £140 for other expenses.

The partnership has recently started invoicing for its services on new payment terms, and the partners are concerned about output VAT being accounted for at the appropriate time. The partnership is considering using the flat rate scheme. The relevant flat rate scheme percentage for the partnership's trade is 14%.

280 Which TWO of the following statements about the tax point are correct?
- ☐ The basic tax point for services is the date that services commence.
- ☐ If the VAT invoice is issued within 14 days after the basic tax point and payment has not been received before the basic tax point, the invoice date becomes the tax point.
- ☐ The tax point determines the VAT period in which output tax must be accounted for and credit for input tax will be allowed.
- ☐ If the VAT invoice is issued and payment is received before the basic tax point, the actual tax point is the later of those two dates. **(2 marks)**

281 What is the total amount of VAT paid by the partnership to HM Revenue & Customs for the year ended 5 April 2025?
- ○ £25,600
- ○ £25,420
- ○ £25,280
- ○ £25,460

(2 marks)

282 Which TWO of the following statements about the flat rate scheme are correct?
- ☐ Businesses using the scheme must still issue VAT invoices to their VAT registered customers.
- ☐ Under the scheme, businesses calculate VAT by applying a fixed percentage to their standard rate income only.
- ☐ Businesses using the scheme cannot reclaim any input tax suffered.
- ☐ A 1% reduction off the flat rate percentage can always be made by businesses in the first year that they use the flat rate scheme.

(2 marks)

283 What are the conditions that the partnership must satisfy in order to join and continue to use the VAT flat rate scheme?

	Join	Continue to use
○	Expected taxable turnover (excluding VAT) for the next 12 months does not exceed £230,000.	Until its total turnover (including VAT) for the previous year exceeds £1,350,000
○	Expected taxable turnover (excluding VAT) for the next 12 months does not exceed £150,000.	Until its total turnover (including VAT) for the previous year exceeds £230,000
○	Expected taxable turnover (excluding VAT) for the next 12 months does not exceed £150,000.	Until its total turnover (including VAT) for the previous year exceeds £1,350,000
○	Expected taxable turnover (excluding VAT) for the next 12 months does not exceed £230,000.	Until its total turnover (including VAT) for the previous year exceeds £230,000

(2 marks)

284 What is the amount of VAT that would have been paid to HM Revenue & Customs if the partnership had used the flat rate scheme to calculate the amount of VAT payable for the year ended 5 April 2025?
- ○ £23,291
- ○ £19,707
- ○ £22,971
- ○ £28,152

(2 marks)

(Total = 10 marks)

OT case – Mabel (March/June 2023)   (18 mins)

You should assume today's date is 20 March 2025.

Mabel, a sole trader, is registered for value added tax (VAT) and is in the process of completing her VAT return for the quarter ended 28 February 2025. Mabel does not use the VAT cash accounting scheme.

Outputs

During the quarter ended 28 February 2025, standard rated sales invoices totalling £98,000 (exclusive of VAT) were issued in respect of credit sales. Mabel offers all of her customers a 10% discount for payment within 14 days of the date of the sales invoice, and 60% of customers paid within the 14-day period.

Inputs

During the quarter ended 28 February 2025, standard rated purchase and expense invoices totalling £35,700 were received. This figure includes £690 for entertaining UK customers, £1,200 for entertaining overseas customers, and £900 for mobile telephone calls (of which 20% related to private calls). All of these figures are inclusive of VAT.

Cessation

Mabel wishes to retire and is therefore going to cease trading on 31 March 2025. She will deregister for VAT. Mabel is unsure whether she will sell the assets of her business separately to different purchasers after ceasing to trade, or whether she will sell the entire business as a going concern on 31 March 2025. During the previous three years, Mabel has purchased the following non-current assets:

(1) Computer equipment purchased during July 2022 for £4,100 and sold during November 2024 for £350

(2) A car purchased (for both business and private use) during August 2024 for £9,600 which Mabel still owns

(3) Office equipment purchased during March 2025 for £7,400 which Mabel still owns

All of the non-current asset figures are exclusive of VAT.

285 **What is the amount of output value added tax (VAT) payable by Mabel in respect of her sales for the quarter ended 28 February 2025?**

○ £18,424
○ £17,640
○ £15,353
○ £19,600

(2 marks)

286 **What is the amount of input value added tax (VAT) recoverable by Mabel in respect of her purchases and expenses for the quarter ended 28 February 2025?**

○ £5,920
○ £5,835
○ £5,805
○ £5,605

(2 marks)

287 By what date must Mabel notify HM Revenue and Customs (HMRC) of her ceasing to make taxable supplies, and what is the earliest date from which her business can be deregistered for value added tax (VAT)?

○ Notification: 30 April 2025. Deregistration: 30 April 2025
○ Notification: 30 April 2025. Deregistration: 31 March 2025
○ Notification: 31 March 2025. Deregistration: 31 March 2025
○ Notification: 31 March 2025. Deregistration: 30 April 2025

(2 marks)

288 Assuming that Mabel sells the assets of her business separately to different purchasers, how much output value added tax (VAT) will she have to pay on her final VAT return, in respect of the non-current assets purchased during the three years prior to the cessation of trading?

○ £3,400
○ £2,300
○ £2,230
○ £1,480

(2 marks)

289 What is the advantage for Mabel if she sells her entire business as a going concern for value added tax (VAT) purposes?

○ No output VAT will be payable in respect of the sale of the business
○ The new owner must take over Mabel's VAT registration
○ The new owner must take over Mabel's outstanding VAT liabilities
○ Mabel will not have to prepare a VAT return for the period 1 to 31 March 2025

(2 marks)

(Total = 10 marks)

OT case – Starfish Ltd (December 2011) (amended) (18 mins)

Starfish Ltd, a retailing company, ceased trading on 31 March 2025 and deregistered from value added tax (VAT) on that date.

The following relates to the company's final VAT return for the quarter ended 31 March 2025:

(1) Cash sales revenue amounted to £41,160, of which £38,520 was in respect of standard rated sales and £2,640 was in respect of zero-rated sales.

(2) Sales invoices totalling £2,000 were issued in respect of credit sales revenue. This figure is exclusive of VAT, and the sales were all standard rated. Starfish Ltd states on its invoices that it offers all of its credit sale customers a 4% discount for payment within 14 days of the date of the sales invoice. 60% of the customers paid within this period.

(3) In addition to the above sales revenue, Starfish Ltd sold its remaining inventory on 31 March 2025 for £28,800.

(4) There were no purchases of inventory during the period.

(5) Standard rated expenses amounted to £69,960, of which £4,320 was in respect of entertaining UK customers.

(6) Starfish Ltd wrote off an impairment loss on 31 March 2025 in respect of a sales invoice (exclusive of VAT) that was due for payment on 8 August 2024. Output VAT of £384 was originally paid in respect of this sale.

(7) On 31 March 2025, the company sold all of its machinery for £31,200 and a car for £9,600. The car was used 30% privately by a director of Starfish Ltd.

Unless otherwise stated, all of the above figures are inclusive of VAT where applicable.

Starfish Ltd did not use the cash accounting scheme for VAT.

290 **What is the amount of output tax on credit sales payable by Starfish Ltd for the quarter ended 31 March 2025?**

○ £384

○ £480

○ £390

○ £325

(2 marks)

291 **What is the amount of output tax, other than on credit sales, payable by Starfish Ltd for the quarter ended 31 March 2025?**

○ £16,420

○ £11,620

○ £11,220

○ £10,000

(2 marks)

292 **What is the amount of input tax recoverable by Starfish Ltd for the quarter ended 31 March 2025?**

○ £12,744

○ £11,324

○ £10,940

○ £11,276

(2 marks)

293 Starfish Ltd is 40 days late in paying the VAT for the quarter ended 31 March 2025.

Identify, by clicking on the relevant boxes below, whether the statements are true or false.

It will incur a penalty point for the late payment.	TRUE	FALSE
A fixed late penalty charge of 4% will apply.	TRUE	FALSE
It will incur a daily late penalty charge of 4% for 10 days.	TRUE	FALSE
Late payment interest will be charged at 7.75% for 40 days.	TRUE	FALSE

(2 marks)

294 **Which of the following would be the consequences for VAT if Starfish Ltd had instead sold its entire business as a going concern to a single VAT registered purchaser?**

○ Output VAT would have been due on the sale of the inventory or the sale of the non-current assets but would be payable by the purchaser.

○ No output VAT would have been due on the sale of the inventory but would have been due on the sale of the non-current assets.

○ No output VAT would have been due on the sale of the non-current assets but would have been due on the sale of the inventory.

○ No output VAT would have been due on the sale of the inventory or the sale of the non-current assets. **(2 marks)**

(Total = 10 marks)

OT case – Greenzone Ltd (June 2013) (18 mins)

Greenzone Ltd owns 60% of Are Ltd, 40% of Be Ltd, 90% of Can Ltd and 70% of Doer Inc.

All the companies are UK resident except for Doer Inc which also does not have a fixed establishment in the UK.

The following information is available in respect of Greenzone Ltd's value added tax (VAT) for the quarter ended 31 March 2025:

(1) Output VAT of £38,210 was charged in respect of sales. This figure includes output VAT of £400 on a deposit received on 29 March 2025, which is in respect of a contract that is due to commence on 20 April 2025.

(2) In addition to the above, Greenzone Ltd charged output VAT of £4,330 on sales to Can Ltd. Greenzone Ltd does not have group registration.

(3) The managing director of Greenzone Ltd is provided with free fuel for his company car. The total cost of fuel for the car for the quarter is £500 and 60% of the total mileage is private mileage.

Greenzone Ltd wishes to use the fuel scale charge. The relevant quarterly scale charge is £334. Both these figures are inclusive of VAT.

(4) Input VAT of £12,770 was incurred in respect of expenses (excluding the fuel in (3)). This figure includes the following input VAT:

	£
Entertaining UK customers	210
Entertaining overseas customers	139
Repainting the exterior of the company's office building	1,678
Extending the office building in order to create a new reception area	3,300

295 **What is the amount of output VAT charged on the sales in (1) and (2) for the quarter to 31 March 2025?**

○ £42,540

○ £38,210

○ £42,140

○ £37,810 **(2 marks)**

296 What is the net amount of VAT payable or recoverable for the provision of the fuel for the managing director's company car in (3)?
- ○ £23 payable
- ○ £33 recoverable
- ○ £56 payable
- ○ £27 recoverable

(2 marks)

297 What is the amount of input VAT that can be recovered on the expenses in (4)?

£ ☐ (2 marks)

298 Identify, by clicking on the relevant boxes in the table below, whether the following companies could be registered in a VAT group with Greenzone Ltd.

ARE LTD	YES	NO
BE LTD	YES	NO
DOER INC	YES	NO

(2 marks)

299 Which TWO of the following statements about VAT group registration are correct?
- ☐ Each VAT group must appoint a representative member which accounts for the group's output tax and input tax.
- ☐ Each VAT group must appoint a representative member which is solely liable for paying the group VAT liability.
- ☐ All eligible companies must be part of the group registration.
- ☐ Any supply of goods or services by a member of the group to another member of the group is disregarded for VAT purposes.

(2 marks)

(Total = 10 marks)

OT case – Long Ltd group (B) (June 2014) (amended)   (18 mins)

Long Ltd owns 100% of the ordinary share capital of both Wind Ltd and Road Ltd. Long Ltd and Road Ltd run freight transport businesses, whilst Wind Ltd provides transport related insurance services.

Long Ltd, Wind Ltd and Road Ltd are not registered as a group for value added tax (VAT) purposes, but such a registration is being considered, with Long Ltd being the representative member.

The following VAT information is available for the quarter ended 31 March 2025:

Long Ltd

(1) All of Long Ltd's sales are standard rated for VAT.

(2) Output VAT of £52,640 was charged in respect of sales. This figure includes output VAT of £1,760 on a deposit received on 28 December 2024. The deposit was in respect of a contract which was completed on 6 January 2025, with a sales invoice being issued on 20 January 2025.

(3) In addition to the above, Long Ltd also charged output VAT of £1,940 on sales to Wind Ltd and output VAT of £960 on sales to Road Ltd.

(4) Input VAT of £14,720 was incurred in respect of expenses.

(5) In addition to the above, Long Ltd has discovered that it has not been claiming for the input VAT of £18 which it has paid each month since 1 January 2019 for the hire of a photocopier.

Wind Ltd

(1) All of Wind Ltd's sales are exempt from VAT.

(2) Input VAT of £7,330 was incurred in respect of expenses. This includes input VAT of £1,940 incurred on purchases from Long Ltd.

Road Ltd

(1) All of Road Ltd's sales are zero rated for VAT.

(2) Road Ltd registered for VAT on 1 January 2025 and this is the company's first VAT return.

(3) Input VAT of £3,120 was incurred in respect of expenses. This includes input VAT of £960 incurred on purchases from Long Ltd.

(4) In addition to the above, Road Ltd incurred input VAT in respect of advertising expenditure as follows:

	£
April 2024	640
November 2024	380
	1,020

300 **What is the amount of output tax payable by Long Ltd for the quarter ended 31 March 2025?**

£ _____ (2 marks)

301 **What is the amount of input tax recoverable by Long Ltd for the quarter ended 31 March 2025?**

○ £14,720
○ £14,774
○ £14,882
○ £15,638 (2 marks)

302 **What is the amount of input tax recoverable by Wind Ltd for the quarter ended 31 March 2025?**

£ _____ (2 marks)

303 **What is the amount of input tax recoverable by Road Ltd for the quarter ended 31 March 2025?**

[Pull down list]

Pull down list
- £3,120
- £3,500
- £3,760
- £4,140

(2 marks)

304 **Which TWO of the following statements about the Long Ltd group and VAT group registration are correct?**
- ☐ If Wind Ltd and Road Ltd were both owned by the same individual, they would not be able to be included in a group registration.
- ☐ Supplies of goods or services to Road Ltd from outside the group will be treated as a supply to Long Ltd.
- ☐ Each company in the Long Ltd group must join the VAT group if group registration is applied for.
- ☐ The supplies by Long Ltd to Wind Ltd and Road Ltd would be disregarded for VAT purposes.

(2 marks)

(Total = 10 marks)

OT case – Zim (June 2015) (amended) (18 mins)

Zim has been registered for value added tax (VAT) since 1 April 2007. The following information is available for the year ended 31 March 2025:

(1) Sales invoices totalling £126,000 were issued, of which £115,200 were in respect of standard rated sales and £10,800 were in respect of zero-rated sales. Zim's customers are all members of the general public.

(2) Purchase invoices totalling £49,200 were received, of which £43,200 were in respect of standard rated purchases and £6,000 were in respect of zero-rated purchases.

(3) On 31 March 2025, Zim wrote off two impairment losses which were in respect of standard rated sales.

The first impairment loss was for £780 and was in respect of a sales invoice which had been due for payment on 15 August 2024. The second impairment loss was for £660 and was in respect of a sales invoice which had been due for payment on 15 September 2024.

(4) During the year ended 31 March 2025, Zim spent £2,600 on mobile telephone calls, of which 40% related to private calls.

(5) During the year ended 31 March 2025, Zim spent £1,560 on entertaining customers, of which £240 was in respect of overseas customers.

All of the above figures are inclusive of VAT where applicable.

Zim does not use either the cash accounting scheme or the flat rate scheme. If he did use the flat rate scheme the relevant percentage for his business is 12%.

305 What is the net amount of VAT payable on the sales in (1) and the purchases in (2)?

£ ☐ (2 marks)

306 What is the amount of input VAT which can be recovered on the impairment losses in (3)?
- ○ £0
- ○ £110
- ○ £130
- ○ £240

(2 marks)

307 What is the amount of input VAT which can be recovered on the expenditure on the mobile phone calls in (4) and entertaining customers in (5)?

	Mobile phone	Customers
○	£0	£220
○	£0	£40
○	£260	£220
○	£260	£40

(2 marks)

308 Match the thresholds for Zim to be able to join and to be required to leave the flat rate scheme.

- Taxable turnover excluding VAT not more than £150,000 in next 12 months
- Total turnover including VAT not more than £230,000 in next 12 months
- Taxable turnover including VAT not more than £150,000 in next 12 months
- Total turnover including VAT more than £230,000 in previous 12 months

☐ Join
☐ Leave

(2 marks)

309 How much VAT would Zim have paid in the year to 31 March 2025 if he had been in the flat rate scheme for the whole of that year?

[▼]

Pull down list
- £13,824
- £13,860
- £15,120
- £9,216

(2 marks)

(Total = 10 marks)

OT case – Smart Ltd (September/December 2015) (amended) (18 mins)

Smart Ltd commenced trading on 1 September 2024. Its sales for the first four months were:

2024	£
September	26,000
October	47,000
November	134,000
December	113,000

On 1 November 2024, Smart Ltd signed a contract valued at £91,000 for completion during November 2024. All of the above figures are stated exclusive of value added tax (VAT).

Smart Ltd only supplies services and all of its supplies are standard rated. It allows its customers 60 days' credit when paying for services, and is concerned that some customers will default on the payment of their debts. It pays its purchase invoices as soon as they are received. It does not use the VAT cash accounting or annual accounting scheme. It is concerned about the penalties that could be charged if it makes a careless error in its VAT return resulting in underpaid VAT.

310 **Match the dates from which Smart Ltd was required to register for VAT and by when it was required to notify HM Revenue & Customs (HMRC) of the registration.**

- 1 November 2024
- 30 December 2024
- 30 November 2024
- 31 December 2024

[ ] Register
[ ] Notification

(2 marks)

311 Identify, by clicking on the relevant boxes in the table below, which of the following statements about how and when Smart Ltd will have to submit its quarterly VAT returns and pay any related VAT liability are true or false.

Smart Ltd can file its VAT returns by entering figures manually on HMRC's website.	TRUE	FALSE
Smart Ltd can choose whether to pay the VAT which is due electronically or by cheque.	TRUE	FALSE
The deadline for paying any VAT which is due is one month after the end of each quarter.	TRUE	FALSE
The deadline for filing the VAT return is one month and seven days after the end of each quarter.	TRUE	FALSE

(2 marks)

312 Which TWO of the following statements about the tax point for Smart Ltd's supplies of services are correct?

☐ The basic tax point is the date on which the invoice is issued.

☐ The basic tax point is the date on which services are completed.

☐ If a customer pays for services before the basic tax point, the payment date will be the tax point.

☐ If a customer pays for services after the basic tax point, the payment date will be the tax point.

(2 marks)

313 Which TWO of the following statements are advantages for Smart Ltd to use the VAT cash accounting scheme?

(1) The scheme will provide automatic relief for an impairment loss should a customer default on the payment of a debt.

(2) Only one VAT return will be required each year so there are fewer occasions to trigger a default surcharge.

(3) There will be reduced VAT administration as Smart Ltd will not be required to issue invoices to its customers.

(4) Output VAT will be accounted for 60 days later than at present, as the scheme will result in the tax point becoming the date when payment is received from customers.

○ 1 and 2
○ 2 and 3
○ 1 and 4
○ 2 and 4

(2 marks)

314   What is the maximum amount of penalty that could be charged by HMRC if Smart Ltd makes a careless error in its VAT return resulting in underpaid VAT and the minimum penalty that could be charged as a result of a subsequent prompted disclosure?

Maximum penalty	Minimum penalty for prompted disclosure
○ 70% of the VAT underpaid	15% of the VAT underpaid
○ 70% of the VAT underpaid	0% of the VAT underpaid
○ 30% of the VAT underpaid	15% of the VAT underpaid
○ 30% of the VAT underpaid	0% of the VAT underpaid

(2 marks)

(Total = 10 marks)

OT case – Thidar (March/June 2019) (18 mins)

You should assume that today's date is 25 April 2025.

Thidar commenced trading as a builder on 1 January 2024. She voluntarily registered for value added tax (VAT) on 1 January 2024.

Sales

Thidar's sales for the first 15 months of trading have been:

Month	Standard rated £	Zero rated £	Month	Standard rated £	Zero rated £
1	3,400	0	9	8,800	6,300
2	0	1,900	10	2,900	7,300
3	5,700	2,100	11	0	0
4	6,800	0	12	0	2,600
5	9,500	1,200	13	2,800	900
6	7,900	2,200	14	6,200	1,700
7	0	3,700	15	22,200	3,600
8	12,100	0			

Pre-registration expenditure

Thidar paid for these standard rated services prior to registering for VAT on 1 January 2024:

Date	Cost of service £	Description
10 June 2023	1,800	Advertisement for the building business
8 Dec 2023	300	Advertisement for the building business

Both figures are exclusive of VAT. Thidar paid for the advertisement of £300 by cash, and she does not have any evidence of this transaction (such as a VAT invoice).

VAT return for the quarter ended 30 September 2024

Thidar's VAT return for the quarter ended 30 September 2024 was filed by the submission deadline of 7 November 2024 and the related VAT liability was paid on time. However, on 15

February 2025, Thidar discovered that the amount of VAT paid was understated by £1,200 as a result of incorrectly treating a standard rated sale as zero rated. Given that the underpayment does not exceed £10,000, Thidar is permitted to correct this error on her VAT return for the quarter ended 31 March 2025, and this is what she will do. Thidar will file this VAT return by the submission deadline of 7 May 2025 and pay the related VAT liability (including the underpaid £1,200) on time.

VAT return for the quarter ended 31 March 2025

Thidar is currently completing her VAT return for the quarter ended 31 March 2025 and is unsure as to how much input VAT is non-deductible in respect of two items:

(1) During the quarter ended 31 March 2025, Thidar spent £800 on entertaining UK customers.

(2) During the quarter ended 31 March 2025, Thidar leased a car at a cost of £700. The car is used by Thidar and 75% of the mileage is for private journeys.

Both figures are exclusive of VAT.

315 **In which month did Thidar exceed the VAT threshold for compulsory registration?**
- ○ Month 14
- ○ Month 15
- ○ Month 13
- ○ Not yet exceeded

(2 marks)

316 **What amount of pre-registration input VAT was Thidar able to recover in respect of expenditure incurred prior to registering for VAT on 1 January 2024?**
- ○ £360
- ○ £60
- ○ £420
- ○ £0

(2 marks)

317 For the following:

Option	VAT invoices	Retention
1	Within 14 days	Four years
2	Within 30 days	Six years
3	Within 30 days	Four years
4	Within 14 days	Six years

Within what period must Thidar issue a VAT invoice after making a standard rated supply, and for how long must these VAT invoices then normally be retained by Thidar?
- ○ Option 1
- ○ Option 2
- ○ Option 3
- ○ Option 4

(2 marks)

318 Why will VAT default (or penalty) interest not be charged on Thidar's underpayment of VAT of £1,200 for the quarter ended 30 September 2024?
- ○ Because Thidar corrected the error within 12 months
- ○ Because the error was not deliberate
- ○ Because separate disclosure of the VAT underpayment was not required
- ○ Because Thidar paid the underpayment by the submission deadline of 7 May 2025

(2 marks)

319 For the following:

Option	Entertaining UK customers	Leasing cost
1	£0	£105
2	£160	£105
3	£160	£70
4	£0	£70

For the quarter ended 31 March 2025, what is the amount of non-deductible input VAT in respect of entertaining UK customers and the leasing cost of the car?
- ○ Option 1
- ○ Option 2
- ○ Option 3
- ○ Option 4

(2 marks)

(Total = 10 marks)

Section C

320 Jogger Ltd (B) (December 2008) (amended) (18 mins)

Jogger Ltd is a manufacturing company and has been registered for value added tax (VAT) since 1 April 2014. From that date until 30 June 2023 the company's VAT returns were all submitted on time. Since 1 July 2023 the company's VAT returns have been submitted as follows:

Quarter ended	VAT paid £	Submitted
30 September 2023	42,700	30 days late
31 December 2023	41,200	On time
31 March 2024	38,900	30 days late
30 June 2024	28,300	On time
30 September 2024	49,100	On time
31 December 2024	63,800	On time
31 March 2025	89,100	60 days late

Jogger Ltd always pays any VAT that is due at the same time as the related return is submitted.

Required

(a) State, giving appropriate reasons, the penalty and interest consequences arising from Jogger Ltd's submission of its VAT returns and payment of its VAT, for the quarter ended 30 September 2023 to the quarter ended 31 March 2025 inclusive, at the times stated. **(6 marks)**

(b) Advise Jogger Ltd why it might be beneficial to use the VAT annual accounting scheme, and state the conditions that it will have to satisfy before being permitted to do so. **(4 marks)**

(Total = 10 marks)

321 Flick (June 2012) (amended) (18 mins)

On 1 January 2025, Flick commenced in partnership with Art running a small cinema.

The partnership voluntarily registered for value added tax (VAT) on 1 January 2025, and immediately began using the flat rate scheme to calculate the amount of VAT payable.

The relevant flat rate scheme percentage for the partnership's trade is 12%.

For the quarter ended 31 March 2025, the partnership had standard rated sales of £59,700, and these were all made to members of the general public. For the same period standard rated expenses amounted to £27,300. Both figures are stated inclusive of VAT.

The partnership has two private boxes in its cinema that can be booked on a special basis by privileged customers. Such customers can book the boxes up to two months in advance, at which time they have to pay a 25% deposit.

An invoice is then given to the customer on the day of the screening of the film, with payment of the balance of 75% required within seven days. For VAT purposes, the renting out of the cinema boxes is a supply of services.

Required

(a) Explain whether or not it was beneficial for the partnership to have used the VAT flat rate scheme for the quarter ended 31 March 2025.

Notes.

1 Your answer should be supported by appropriate calculations.

2 You should ignore the 1% reduction from the flat rate that is available during the first year of VAT registration. **(3 marks)**

(b) Explain whether or not it was financially beneficial for the partnership to have voluntarily registered for VAT from 1 January 2025.

Note. Your answer should be supported by appropriate calculations. **(3 marks)**

(c) Advise the partnership as to when it should account for output VAT on the renting out of its private boxes to privileged customers. **(4 marks)**

(Total = 10 marks)

322 Richard (December 2013) (amended) (18 mins)

On 6 April 2024, Richard commenced in self-employment, running a restaurant.

Richard's sales since the commencement of trading have been as follows:

April to July 2024	£10,500 per month
August to November 2024	£17,000 per month
December 2024 to March 2025	£21,500 per month

These figures are stated exclusive of value added tax (VAT). Richard's sales are all standard rated.

As a trainee chartered certified accountant, you have advised Richard in writing that he should be registered for VAT, but he has refused to register because he thinks his net profit is insufficient to cover the additional cost which would be incurred.

Required

(a) Explain from what date Richard was required to be compulsorily registered for VAT and the VAT implications of continuing to trade after this date without registering.

Note. You are not expected to explain the VAT penalties arising from late VAT registration. **(4 marks)**

(b) Briefly explain from an ethical viewpoint the issues you, as a trainee chartered certified accountant, should consider in order for your firm to deal with Richard's refusal to register for VAT. **(2 marks)**

(c) State the circumstances in which a trader can issue a simplified (or less detailed) VAT invoice, when such an invoice should be issued, and FIVE pieces of information which such an invoice must show where the supply is entirely standard rated. **(4 marks)**

(Total = 10 marks)

323 Clueless Ltd (December 2012) (amended) (18 mins)

Clueless Ltd is a manufacturing company. It is registered for value added tax (VAT), but currently does not use any of the special VAT schemes. The company has annual standard rated sales of £1,200,000 and annual standard rated expenses of £550,000. Both these figures are exclusive of VAT and are likely to remain the same for the foreseeable future. Clueless Ltd is up to date with all of its tax returns, including those for corporation tax, PAYE and VAT. It is also up to date with its corporation tax, PAYE and VAT payments. However, the company often incurs considerable overtime costs due to its employees working late in order to meet tax return filing deadlines.

Clueless Ltd pays its expenses on a cash basis and allows customers two months' credit when paying for sales. The company does not have any impairment losses.

Clueless Ltd is planning to purchase some new machinery at a cost of £22,000 (exclusive of VAT). The machinery will be purchased from an overseas supplier. Clueless Ltd is not a regular importer and so is unsure of the VAT treatment for this purchase.

Required

(a) Explain why Clueless Ltd is entitled to use both the VAT cash accounting scheme and the VAT annual accounting scheme, and why it will probably be beneficial for the company to use both schemes. **(6 marks)**

(b) Explain when and how Clueless Ltd will have to account for VAT in respect of the new machinery:

   (i) If they choose not to use postponed accounting

   (ii) If they do choose to use postponed accounting **(4 marks)**

(Total = 10 marks)

324 Garfield (March/June 2016) (18 mins)

Garfield has been registered for valued added tax (VAT) since 1 April 2013. Garfield has previously completed his VAT returns himself, but for the quarter ended 31 March 2025 there are some items for which he is unsure of the correct VAT treatment.

Garfield's partly completed VAT computation for the quarter ended 31 March 2025 is shown below. All of the completed sections of the computation are correct, with the omissions marked as outstanding (O/S).

	Note	£
Output VAT		
Sales (all standard rated)		22,500
Discounted sale	1	O/S
Equipment	2	O/S
Fuel scale charge		414
Input VAT		
Purchases (all standard rated)		(11,200)
Car (purchased on 1 January 2025)		0
Equipment	2	O/S
Impairment losses	3	O/S
Entertaining		
– UK customers		0
– Overseas customers	4	O/S
Motor expenses	5	O/S
VAT payable		O/S

Unless otherwise stated, all of the figures in the following notes are stated exclusive of VAT.

Notes.

1 **Discounted sale**

On 10 February 2025, a sales invoice for £4,300 was issued by Garfield in respect of a standard rated supply. To encourage this previously late paying customer to pay promptly, Garfield offered a 10% discount for payment within 14 days of the date of the sales invoice. The customer paid within the 14-day period.

This invoice has not been taken into account in calculating the output VAT figure of £22,500, and this is the only sale for which Garfield has offered a prompt payment discount.

2 **Equipment**

During the quarter ended 31 March 2025, Garfield acquired some new equipment at a cost of £12,400 from an overseas supplier.

3 **Impairment losses**

On 31 March 2025, Garfield wrote off three impairment losses. Details are as follows:

Amount	Invoice date	Payment due date
£1,400	30 July 2024	29 August 2024
£2,700	12 September 2024	12 October 2024
£1,900	4 October 2024	3 November 2024

4 **Entertainment**

During the quarter ended 31 March 2025, Garfield spent £960 on entertaining overseas customers. This figure is inclusive of VAT.

5 **Motor expenses**

The car purchased on 1 January 2025 is used by Garfield 60% for business mileage.

During the quarter ended 31 March 2025, Garfield spent £1,008 on repairs to the car and £660 on fuel for both his business and private mileage. Both of these figures are inclusive of VAT.

Additional information

Garfield does not use the cash accounting scheme, the annual accounting scheme or the flat rate scheme, but has read that the use of these schemes can be beneficial for small businesses such as his.

Garfield's VAT exclusive annual turnover is currently £450,000, and this is expected to steadily decrease over the coming years.

He pays for most of his purchases and expenses on a cash basis, and allows many of his customers 30 days' credit when paying for sales.

Required

(a) Calculate the amount of value added tax (VAT) payable by Garfield for the quarter ended 31 March 2025. **(7 marks)**

(b) State which VAT schemes Garfield is currently permitted to use, and explain, with supporting reasons, which **ONE** of the available schemes would appear to be the most beneficial for him to use.

Notes.

1 Your answer should be confined to the information given in the question.

2 You are not expected to explain how any of the schemes operate. **(3 marks)**

(Total = 10 marks)

325 Zhi (March/June 2017) (18 mins)

You should assume that today's date is 15 December 2024.

Zhi has been self-employed since 2001, preparing accounts to 31 December. On 1 December 2024, Zhi purchased a new freehold warehouse for £164,000 for use in his business, but this purchase has resulted in Zhi having cash flow problems. He has various tax payments becoming due over the next two months and would like to reduce or postpone these payments as much as possible.

Income tax and national insurance contributions (NICs)

Zhi's income tax liabilities and class 4 NICs for the tax years 2022/23, 2023/24 and 2024/25 are, or are forecast to be:

	2022/23	2023/24	2024/25
	£	£	£
Income tax liability	25,200	27,600	18,000
Class 4 NICs	4,084	4,204	3,724

Zhi has not made any claims to reduce his payments on account.

Capital gains tax (CGT)

Zhi has a CGT liability of £14,600 becoming due for payment on 31 January 2025. This is in respect of a freehold office building which was sold for £210,000 on 10 December 2023, resulting in a chargeable gain of £76,000. The office building had always been used for business purposes by Zhi.

Zhi is a higher rate taxpayer. No claim has been made for rollover relief.

Value added tax (VAT)

Zhi has forecast that he will have to pay VAT of £20,200 on 7 February 2025 to HM Revenue & Customs (HMRC) in respect of the VAT quarter ended 31 December 2024.

On 12 December 2024, Zhi despatched goods relating to an exceptionally large credit sale of standard rated goods of £45,600 (inclusive of VAT). He has not yet issued a sales invoice for this sale.

Because the customer is unlikely to pay until 28 February 2025, Zhi is considering not issuing a sales invoice until 1 February 2025.

PAYE and NICs

Zhi will have to pay PAYE and NICs of £5,724 electronically on 22 January 2025 to HMRC in respect of his two employees for the tax month running from 6 December 2024 to 5 January 2025.

This includes amounts for bonuses which Zhi was planning to pay to his two employees on 1 January 2025 but could delay payment until 10 January 2025. The bonuses are in respect of the year ended 31 December 2024, and they will be treated as being received on whichever is the date of payment.

The first employee has a gross annual salary of £20,000 and is to be paid a bonus of £1,500. The second employee has a gross annual salary of £55,000 and is to be paid a bonus of £5,000.

Required

(a) Calculate the amount by which Zhi can claim to reduce his self-assessment income tax and NICs due for payment on 31 January 2025 without incurring interest or penalties. **(2 marks)**

(b) Calculate the amount by which Zhi's CGT liability due for payment on 31 January 2025 will be reduced if he makes a claim for rollover relief based on the warehouse purchased on 1 December 2024 for £164,000. **(3 marks)**

(c) Explain whether Zhi can reduce the amount of VAT payable on 7 February 2025 by not issuing a sales invoice for the credit sale of £45,600 until 1 February 2025, and, if so, by how much the payment will be reduced. **(2 marks)**

(d) Calculate the amount by which Zhi's PAYE and NICs due on 22 January 2025 will be reduced if he delays the payment of employee bonuses until 10 January 2025, and state when the postponed amount will be payable.

Note. Your calculations should be based on annual income tax and NIC thresholds.

(3 marks)

(Total = 10 marks)

Answers

Part A: The UK tax system and its administration

Section A

OTQ bank – The UK tax system and its administration 1

1 The correct answers are:
- It is a progressive tax.
- It is a redistributive tax.

Inheritance tax is a progressive tax as the amount of tax payable as a proportion of the transfers increases as the transfers get bigger (the amount covered by the nil rate band is charged at 0% and the remainder at 20% or 40%). It is also a redistributive tax as it redistributes wealth.

Inheritance tax is a direct tax and is not an environmental tax.

2 The correct answer is:

Date	Penalty alternative
30 September 2024	Penalty charged

3 The correct answers are:
- A Statutory Instrument
- An Act of Parliament

Statutes (Acts of Parliament) and Statutory Instruments have legal force.

HMRC publications such as Revenue and Customs Briefs and Extra Statutory Concessions do not have legal force.

4 The correct answer is: By the Upper Tribunal

The Upper Tribunal deals with complex cases which either involve an important issue of tax law or a large financial sum.

5 The correct answer is:

Notification	Payment
5 October 2025	31 January 2026

The chargeable gain arises in the tax year 2024/25 and so Daren must notify HMRC of his chargeability within six months from the end of the tax year. The tax liability must be paid by 31 January following the end of the tax year.

6   The correct answer is: Year ended 31 December 2027

The profit threshold for being a large company is £1,500,000/2 = £750,000 since there is one associated company. This threshold is first exceeded in the year ended 31 December 2026 but a company is not required to pay its corporation tax by instalments in the first year that it is large unless its profits exceed £10,000,000, as reduced by associated companies. Mammoth Ltd is also a large company in the year ended 31 December 2027 and so must pay its corporation tax liability by quarterly instalments for that year for the first time.

7   The correct answers are:

Value added tax	**NEITHER TYPE**		
Inheritance tax		**CAPITAL TAX**	
National insurance contributions			**REVENUE TAX**

8   £406,600

	£
Unconnected company	5,200
Group dividend	0
Non-51% group dividend	1,400
Taxable total profits	400,000
Profits	406,600

9   The correct answers are:
- £100 fixed penalty
- £900 of daily penalties
- £310 tax geared penalty

> **ACCA Examining Team's Comments**
>
> The correct three options are – £100 fixed penalty, £900 of daily penalties (90 days at £10 per day because of the failure to file exceeding three months) plus £310 tax geared penalty (being £6,200 at 5% because the failure continued after six months and is greater than £300).
>
> The incorrect choices were:
> - £200 fixed penalty being two lots of £100 late filing;
> - £620 tax geared penalty (being £6,200 at 10%); and
> - £2,120 of daily penalties (being £10 per day for 212 days 1 Feb 2024 to 31 Aug 2024).

10 The correct answer is: £81

> **ACCA Examining Team's Comments**
>
> £81 (2,500 × 7.75% × 5/12)
>
> Ruby's payments on account are due on 31 January 2025 and 31 July 2025 with the balancing payment due on 31 January 2026. Therefore, her first payment on account was late by five months (from 31 January 2025 to 30 June 2025, the day before she paid the tax). The rate of interest on underpaid tax is given to you in the Tax Tables in the exam and is shown there as 7.75%.
>
> The incorrect answers are:
>
> (2,500 + 2,500) × 7.75% = £388
>
> 2,500 × 7.75% = £194
>
> 7,000 × 7.75% = £543

OTQ bank – The UK tax system and its administration 2

11 The correct answers are:

31 January 2026	Submission
30 April 2027	Notification

As the return is filed after the due filing date, the notification must be made by the quarter day following the first anniversary of the actual filing date.

12 £5,000

	£
Income tax £(12,500 – 10,000 payments on account)	2,500
Class 4 NIC £(2,500 – 2,000 payments on account)	500
Capital gains tax	2,000
Amount to pay on 31 January 2026	5,000

The answer £4,500 does not include the NIC. The answer £3,000 excludes the capital gains tax. The answer £4,000 assumes that payments on account are made also for capital gains tax.

13 £ 80

£10,000 is paid by the due date of 1 January 2026. The balance of £12,400 is one month late so the interest on late paid tax is £12,400 × 7.75% × 1/12 = £80.

14   £ 17,000

> **ACCA Examining Team's Comments**
>
> £17,000 ((£39,000 – £5,000)/2 = £17,000). The payments on account for 2025/26 are each based on the income tax and class 4 national insurance not collected through PAYE from the prior year (2024/25) payable in two equal instalments on 31 January in the tax year (31/1/2026) and 31 July after the end of the tax year (31/7/2026). The balancing payment would be due on 31 January after the end of the tax year (31/1/2027).

15   £ 100

There is a £100 penalty for late return which is submitted within three months of the due date (here 12 months after the end of the period to which the return relates).

16   The correct answer is: Asset 1 only

Lying about a disposal date so that a gain is declared a year later amounts to tax evasion, which is illegal. Delaying a disposal until the next tax year is a legitimate example of tax planning.

17   10%

The due date for payment was 31 January 2025. The penalty date is 30 days after the due date for the tax. There is a penalty of 5% of the unpaid tax for failing to pay by the penalty date plus a further penalty of 5% of the unpaid tax as the payment is more than five months after the penalty date but not more than 11 months after the penalty date.

18   The correct answer is: 5 April 2045

> **ACCA Examining Team's Comments**
>
> This was a straightforward administration question, requiring candidates to identify the latest date by which HMRC can raise a discovery assessment where a taxpayer has made a deliberate error in their tax return. Where deliberate error is involved, the time limit for HMRC to raise a discovery assessment is 20 years from the end of the tax year, in this case 5 April 2045.
>
> The majority of candidates selected 5 April 2026, suggesting that they had confused the deadline for a raising a discovery assessment with the deadline for notifying the taxpayer of a compliance check. 5 April 2029 is the basic deadline for issuing a discovery assessment, and 5 April 2031 is the deadline for issuing a discovery assessment where the taxpayer has made a careless error.
>
> Candidates are reminded to devote sufficient attention to tax administration in their revision.

19 Make a determination

If notice has been served on a taxpayer to submit a return but the return is not submitted by the due filing date, an officer of HMRC may make a determination, to the best of their information and belief, of the amounts liable to income tax and CGT and of the tax due, within four years of the end of the relevant tax year.

ACCA Examining Team's Comments

This question tested candidates' knowledge of how HMRC can make a determination of the amount of tax that a taxpayer is liable to. Perhaps not surprisingly, more than 40% of candidates opted for 'start a compliance check enquiry into the return' – possibly because a compliance check was the most well-known of the options. However, the correct answer (a determination) was the second most popular choice. Although this style of question can be answered very quickly, it does not mean that it does not warrant any thought. Realising that a compliance check by its very nature involves a submitted return, could have easily ruled this option out.

20 The correct answer is: £148

ACCA Examining Team's Comments

This question tested candidates' ability to calculate late payment interest where an excessive claim has been made to reduce a payment on account. Answers were spread fairly evenly over the four choices, indicating that many candidates simply made an educated guess. Although not an easy question, taking a careful approach with amounts and dates would probably have achieved the correct answer. The most important point was the £6,000 payment on 30 September 2025, which was two months late. The final payment was made on time. Therefore, £7,800 was late for two months (31 July to 30 September 2025) and £1,800 (£7,800 − £6,000) was late for four months (1 October 2025 to 31 January 2026). The interest at 7.75% is £148, ie (£7,800 × 7.75% × 2/12 = £101) + (£1,800 × 7.75% × 4/12 = £47), making a total of £148. An alternative working would have been £6,000 late for two months (£78) and £1,800 late for six months (£70). This question demonstrates just how much care needs to be taken with dates when calculating interest payable on late tax payments.

OTQ bank – The UK tax system and its administration 3

21 The correct answer is: The returns for the year ended 31 December 2024 and the period ended 31 March 2025 must both be filed by 31 March 2026.

ACCA Examining Team's Comments

This was a straightforward question on filing dates for corporation tax for a long period. The correct answer is the fourth option. Two tax returns are required, one for the year ended 31 December 2024 and one for the period ended 31 March 2025, however both of them have the same filing date and must be filed by 31 March 2026. Most candidates selected the third option, for each return being filed 12 months after the period end, and others selected the first option, using the payment dates rather than filing dates.

22   The correct answer is: 1 March 2025

> **ACCA Examining Team's Comments**
>
> This was another tax administration question on the date which a company must notify HMRC of its first accounting period. A company must notify HMRC of the beginning of its first accounting period within three months. The company was incorporated on 1 October 2024 but did not start to trade until 1 December 2024, and it is the date the company started to trade that is relevant here, so the correct answer is the third option, 1 March 2025. Most candidates chose the second option, being three months after the company was incorporated, with the next most popular answer being the first option, the date that the company started to trade (or two months after the company was incorporated). The fourth option, being 12 months after the first accounts for the period to 30 June 2025, was also selected by more candidates than the correct answer. Tax administration is an important area of the syllabus, so future candidates should ensure they cover this area in their preparation.

23   The correct answer is: £1,700

> **ACCA Examining Team's Comments**
>
> If Dee Ltd files its tax return for the year ended 31 December 2024 on 31 August 2026, this would be eight months late, as it was due on 31 December 2025. As Dee Ltd had already been late filing its last two corporation tax returns, then the correct answer is £1,700, being a fixed penalty of £1,000 and a tax geared penalty of £700 (10% of £7,000). However, most candidates opted for the tax geared penalty of £700.

24   The correct answer is: 30 April 2026

> **ACCA Examining Team's Comments**
>
> The correct answer is 30 April 2026, because the return was filed late and this is the first quarter day after the anniversary of the submission.

25   The correct answer is: Partnerships must file a separate return and account for each partner's tax through this return.

> **ACCA Examining Team's Comments**
>
> The answer which is false is the second option. This is because each partner must include their share of partnership profits on their own personal tax return, not the partnership tax return. The third option was the most commonly chosen. This suggests that candidates' knowledge of tax administration could be improved.

Section B

OT case – Domingo and Fargo (June 2009) (amended)

26 The correct answer is:

Domingo	Fargo
31 October 2025	31 January 2026

27 The correct answer is:

Domingo	Fargo
31 January 2027	31 January 2031

Domingo was not in business during 2024/25, so his records must be retained until one year after 31 January following the tax year, which is 31 January 2027.

Fargo was in business during 2024/25, so all of his records (both business and non-business) must be retained until five years after 31 January following the tax year, which is 31 January 2031.

28 The correct answer is: £3,000

29 The correct answer is:

Balancing payment 2024/25 and first POA 2025/26	Second POA 2025/26
31 January 2026	31 July 2026

30 The correct answer is: Interest £47, penalty £90

Interest £1,800 × 7.75% × 4/12 = £47

The answer £140 is the interest for a whole year.

Penalty £1,800 @ 5% = £90 (balancing payment not more than five months after the penalty date)

OT case – Ernest (June 2010) (amended)

> **Course Book references**
>
> Self-assessment for individuals is covered in Chapter 17. Ethics are covered in Chapter 1.
>
> **Top tips**
>
> If your firm ceases to act for a client, it must notify HMRC that it has ceased to act but not the reasons for doing so.
>
> **Easy marks**
>
> The definitions of tax evasion and tax avoidance should be well known.

31   The correct answers are:

Tax evasion is illegal.	TRUE	
Both tax evasion and tax avoidance are illegal.		FALSE
Tax avoidance is legal but may fail if challenged in the courts by HMRC.	TRUE	
Tax evasion always involves providing HM Revenue & Customs with false information.		FALSE

Tax evasion does not necessarily involve providing HM Revenue & Customs (HMRC) with false information. It could include this situation where Ernest is evading tax by not providing HMRC with information to which it is entitled.

32   The correct answers are:
- Ernest should be advised to disclose details of the capital gain to HMRC.
- If Ernest does not disclose the gain to HMRC, your firm would be obliged to report under the money laundering regulations.

Your firm should also consider ceasing to act for Ernest. If it does cease to act, your firm should notify HMRC that it no longer acts for him although your firm should not provide any reason for this.

33   The correct answer is: £12,600

The maximum penalty for an error which is deliberate but not concealed is 70% of potential lost revenue which is £18,000 × 70% = £12,600.

34   £6,300

The minimum penalty for prompted disclosure of an error which is deliberate but not concealed is 35% of potential lost revenue which is £18,000 × 35% = £6,300.

35   £ 698

The due date for payment was 31 January 2025 so the payment is six months late. The interest payable is therefore £18,000 × 7.75% × 6/12 = £698.

OT case – Thai Curry Ltd

Course Book references
Chapter 23 deals with corporation tax administration. Chapter 17 contains material on the common penalty regime for errors.

Top tips
Remember that some elements of tax administration are the same for both individuals and companies such as penalties for errors. However, you need to watch out for circumstances where they are different such as the penalties for late filing.

Easy marks
Make sure you know due dates for returns and tax payments.

36   The correct answer is: 31 March 2026

The CT return must be submitted one year after the end of the period of account ie by 31 March 2026.

37 £3,462

As the return is more than three months late the fixed penalty is £200. As the return is more than six months late there is also a tax geared penalty of 10% × unpaid tax, ie £32,624 × 10% = £3,262. The total amount of penalties is therefore £(200 + 3,262) = £3,462.

38 The correct answer is: £32,624 on 1 January 2026

As the company is not large (ie its profits do not exceed the profit threshold of £1.5 million) it must pay its corporation tax by nine months and one day after the accounting period, ie by 1 January 2026.

39 The correct answers are:
- An internal review is a less costly and more effective way to resolve disputes informally than a formal appeal.
- HMRC must usually carry out the review within 45 days.

An internal review is a less costly and more effective way to resolve disputes informally than a formal appeal and HMRC must usually carry out the review within 45 days. The internal review will be made by an objective HMRC review officer not previously connected with the case. After the review conclusion is notified, the company has 30 days to appeal to the Tax Tribunal.

40 The correct answers are:

| Upper tier | Complex track |
| First tier | Standard track |

Section C

41 John

> **Course Book references**
>
> Self-assessment for individuals is covered in Chapter 17. The UK tax system is the subject of Chapter 1.
>
> **Top tips**
>
> There are a number of penalties based on potential lost revenue, so you need to be able to explain what this is.
>
> **Easy marks**
>
> There were some easy marks for the date for notification and the date by which the compliance check needed to be started.

Marking guide Marks

			Marks	
(a)	(i)	Date for notification	1	
		Maximum penalty	1	
		Minimum penalty	1	
				3
	(ii)	Compliance check notification date	1	
		Random basis	1	
		Other reasons	1	
				3
(b)	(i)	Saving	1	
				1
	(ii)	Charitable support	1	
				1
	(iii)	Capital gains reliefs	1	
		Plant and machinery	1	
				2
Total				10

(a) (i) **Notification of chargeability**

John should have given notice to HM Revenue & Customs (HMRC) of his chargeability to income tax for 2024/25 by 5 October 2025.

The maximum penalty for careless late notification is 30% of the potential lost revenue (PLR) to HMRC which will be John's tax payable on the return for 2024/25.

However, if John tells HMRC of his failure to notify within 12 months and John has no reason to believe HMRC has discovered, or is about to discover, the error (unprompted disclosure) as appears to be the case here, the penalty can be reduced by HMRC to 0%.

(ii) **Compliance check**

If HMRC intends to carry out a compliance check enquiry into John's 2024/25 tax return, it will have to notify him by the first anniversary of the actual filing date.

HMRC has the right to carry out a compliance check enquiry as regards the completeness and accuracy of any return, and some returns are selected for a compliance check enquiry at random.

Other returns are selected for a particular reason; for example, if HMRC believes that there has been an underpayment of tax due to the taxpayer's failure to comply with tax legislation.

(b) (i) Saving is encouraged by offering individuals tax incentives such as income tax and capital gains tax exemptions on individual savings accounts and income tax relief on pension contributions.

(ii) Charitable support is encouraged by giving individuals income tax relief on donations made through the gift aid scheme or by payroll deduction.

(iii) Entrepreneurs are encouraged to build their own businesses through various capital gains tax reliefs such as business asset disposal relief.

Investment in plant and machinery is encouraged through capital allowances.

42 Sugar plc

Course Book references

Chapter 19 deals with computing the corporation tax liability. Chapter 23 includes payment of tax by companies.

Top tips

The rules on associated companies are highly examinable and could be tested as an objective test question or in a constructed response question.

Easy marks

The calculation of the corporation tax liability in part (c) was straightforward.

Marking guide		Marks
(a) Definition		1
Honey plc		0.5
Molasses plc		0.5
Treacle plc		1
		3
(b) Year ended 31 March 2025		
Profit limit		0.5
Taxable total profits		0.5
Dividends		1
Profits, therefore large		0.5
Year ended 31 March 2026		
Taxable total profits = profits, therefore large		0.5
		3
(c) Year ended 31 March 2025		
Corporation tax		0.5
Date payable		0.5
Year ended 31 March 2026		
Corporation tax		0.5

Marking guide	Marks
Instalments	0.5
Dates payable	2
	4
Total	10

(a) Companies are associated if they are under the same control. This basically means a shareholding of more than 50%. Honey plc is not an associated company of Sugar plc because Sugar plc only directly owns 45% of the ordinary shares of Honey plc. Molasses plc is an associated company of Sugar plc because Sugar plc directly owns 75% of the ordinary shares of Molasses plc. We look for control (ie >50% shareholding) at each level and therefore Treacle plc is an associated company of Sugar plc.

(b) **Year ended 31 March 2025**

Sugar plc has two associated companies (Molasses plc and Treacle plc) at the end of the previous accounting period. The profit limit is therefore £1,500,000/3 = £500,000. Sugar plc's profits for the year to 31 March 2025 are:

	£
Taxable total profits	470,000
Dividends from non-group companies	50,000
Profits	520,000

Sugar plc is therefore a large company in the year to 31 March 2025.

Year ended 31 March 2026

The profit limit is the same and Sugar plc's taxable total profits of £600,000 are also its profits for these purposes. Sugar plc is therefore a large company in the year to 31 March 2026.

(c) **Year ended 31 March 2025**

	£
Corporation tax liability	
£470,000 × 25%	117,500

Since this is the first year that Sugar plc is a large company, its corporation tax liability will be due in one amount on 1 January 2026.

Year ended 31 March 2026

	£
Corporation tax liability	
£600,000 × 25%	150,000

This is payable in four equal instalments of £37,500. The instalments will be due on 14 October 2025, 14 January 2026, 14 April 2026 and 14 July 2026.

Part B: Income tax and NIC liabilities

Section A

OTQ bank – Income tax and NIC liabilities 1

43 The correct answer is: 90

> **ACCA Examining Team's Comments**
>
> This question examines the third automatic non-UK residency test. For an individual to meet this test, and therefore be treated as automatically not resident in the UK for the tax year 2024/25, they would have to work full-time overseas and spend less than 91 days in the UK. Therefore, because Hana worked full-time in Egypt throughout 2024/25, he will be treated as automatically not resident in the UK for the tax year as long as he spends no more than 90 days in the UK.
>
> The correct answer is therefore 90, however, answer option 15 was most commonly chosen. This would be the correct answer using the sufficient ties tests. However, the sufficient ties tests are only used to determine residence status if none of the automatic non-UK residence tests (and none of the automatic UK residence tests) is met.
>
> This suggests that candidates may not have been familiar enough with the residence tests and the procedure to determine residence.

44 The correct answers are:
- Premium bond prizes
- Dividends on shares held in an Individual Savings Account

Interest on an NS&I Investment account and interest on UK Government stocks ('gilts') are taxable as savings income.

45 The correct answer is: £2,500

	£
£3,000 @ 20%	600
£(5,000 – 3,000) = £2,000 @ 0% (starting rate band)	0
£1,000 @ 0% (savings income nil rate band)	0
£(12,500 – 2,000 – 1,000) = £9,500 @ 20%	1,900
Tax liability	2,500

The answer £2,900 does not apply the starting rate band. The answer £2,700 does not apply the savings income nil rate band. The answer £3,100 applies 20% to all income.

46   The correct answer is: £2,448

	£
Taxable income	13,500
Tax	
£13,500 × 20%	2,700
Less transferred personal allowance tax reducer £1,260 × 20%	(252)
Income tax liability	2,448

The answer £186 assumes that Delia can transfer her full personal allowance to Mike. The answer £1,440 deducts £1,260 as a tax reducer. The answer £2,700 is Mike's income tax liability with no transfer.

47   The correct answer is: £3,300

	£	£
Use: £3,600 × 20%		720
Gift:		
– Current market value	1,000	
or		
– Original value	3,600	
Less use:		
– 2023/24 £720 × 5/12	(300)	
– 2024/25	(720)	
	2,580	
The greater amount is taken		2,580
Total benefits 2024/25		3,300

Note. That the value of the asset when first provided to any employee is used rather than the value when first provided to John.

The answer £2,880 assumes the first year of provision was taxed in full. The answer £1,720 uses the lower value for the gift rather than the higher value. The answer £1,833 uses the value of £2,000 when the asset was provided to John.

48   The correct answer is: £60,203

	£
£(37,700 + 10,000) = £47,700 @ 20%	9,540
£(125,140 + 10,000) = £(135,140 – 47,700) = £87,440 @ 40%	34,976
£(170,000 – 135,140) = £34,860 @ 45%	15,687
Tax liability	60,203

The answer £60,703 does not adjust the higher rate limit. The answer £62,703 does not adjust either the basic rate limit or the higher rate limit. The answer £54,547 deducts the personal allowance.

49   The correct answer is: £333

	£
Net income	67,000
Less personal pension contributions (gross)	(2,000)
Adjusted net income	65,000
Less threshold	(60,000)
Excess	5,000
÷ £200	25
Child benefit income tax charge: 1% × £1,331 × 25	333

The answer £1,331 assumes there is full recovery of child benefit. The answer £532 is the child benefit times 40%. The answer £466 (benefit × 1% × 35) does not adjust for pension contributions.

50   The correct answer is: £22,500

The bonus received on 30 September 2024 is taxable in 2024/25 as the receipts basis applies to employment income.

The gratuity received on 1 December 2024 is taxable as employment income in 2024/25 as it is a reward of the employment even though it was not received from the employer.

51   The correct answers are:

- Travel from employer's office to visit a client
- Travel from home to visit a trade fair relevant to the employer's business 100 miles away from permanent place of work

Travel from home to a workplace to which an employee has been seconded for 36 months does not qualify as travel to a temporary workplace as the secondment exceeds 24 months. Travel from home to a permanent place of work is not a qualifying travel expense.

52   The correct answer is: £6,000

> **ACCA Examining Team's Comments**
>
> The provision of job-related accommodation does not give rise to a taxable benefit in kind for the employee however, where ancillary services are also provided (ie the household bills and furniture) an assessable benefit in kind does arise. Where the accommodation is job-related, the assessable amount for these benefits is limited to 10% of net remuneration excluding the household costs, giving £6,000 (10% of £60,000) in this example. However, the answer £9,000 was most commonly chosen. This would be the correct answer if the accommodation was not job-related. It is calculated as the cost to the employer of the household bills, plus the use of furniture, calculated at 20% of the cost of the asset, giving £9,000 (£7,000 + (20% × £10,000)). This suggests that candidates may not have been aware of the rule to restrict the assessable amount where the accommodation is job-related.

OTQ bank – Income tax and NIC liabilities 2

53 The correct answers are:

| £333 | Marion |
| £167 | Gerald |

	£
Marion	
Accrued interest deemed received 31.12.24 taxable savings income	
£20,000 × 5% × 4/12	333
Gerald	
Interest received 31.12.24	
£20,000 × 5% × 6/12	500
Less relief for accrued interest (amount taxable on Marion)	
£20,000 × 5% × 4/12	(333)
Taxable savings income	167

54 The correct answer is: £5,800

	£
CO_2 emission (rounded down)	100
Base figure	(55)
	45
Divided by 5	9
Starting percentage	16
Diesel addition	4
	29
Benefit £20,000 (list price) × 29%	£5,800

The answer £4,500 uses actual cost (not list price) and there is no diesel addition. The answer £5,220 uses actual cost. The answer £5,000 does not use the diesel addition.

55 £95,000

	£
2024/25 annual allowance	60,000
2023/24 annual allowance £(60,000 – 25,000)	35,000
	95,000

The annual allowance for 2021/22 and 2022/23 are not available as Troy was not a member of a pension scheme in those years.

The answer £60,000 is the current year annual allowance. The answer £175,000 brings forward allowances from all three previous tax years (£60,000 + £35,000 + £40,000 + £40,000). The answer £45,000 restricts the current year allowance to £10,000.

56 The correct answer is: £300

	£
Rental income £150 × 52	7,800
Less rent a room limit	(7,500)
	300

Luke should elect for the 'alternative basis' under rent a room relief, rather the normal basis which would give taxable property business income of £(150 – 20) = £130 × 52 = £6,760.

57 The correct answer is: £3,800

The replacement of an equivalent model of sofa is allowable as a deduction. It is restricted by the amount of proceeds realised by selling the first sofa.

£(4,000 – 200) = £3,800

The answer £5,500 allows the full cost of the enhancement of furniture. The answer £5,300 allows the cost of the enhancement of furniture less the proceeds of the first sofa. The answer £4,000 is the cost of the replacement sofa.

58 £2,470

	£
Rent received 3 × £900	2,700
Security deposit	0
Less:	
– Insurance premium paid	(150)
– Motoring expenses 178 × 45p	(80)
Taxable property business income 2024/25	2,470

The answer £1,932 uses the accruals basis for the rent and the insurance premium paid. The answer £2,970 includes the security deposit: this will only become a receipt when Amrul is legally entitled to retain some or all of it at the end of the tenancy.

The answer £2,505 uses the rate of 25p per mile for the motoring expenses.

59   £ 5,400

Depreciation and customer entertaining are not deductible and must be added back. The amount added back is therefore £(3,000 + 2,400) = £5,400.

Staff entertaining is fully deductible (the £150 limit applies to the taxable benefit for the employees).

60   £ 20,375

	£
Cash sales	41,000
Invoice sales £(4,000 – 1,500)	2,500
Less:	
– Cash expenses	(20,200)
– Motoring expenses 6,500 × 45p	(2,925)
Taxable trading income 2024/25	20,375

61   The correct answer is: £3,600

£(12,000 – 6,000) × 60% = £3,600

The answer £2,400 is the private use amount of £(12,000 – 6,000) × 40%.

The answer £648 uses the writing down allowance (WDA) and at the rate of 18% which does not apply to high emission cars.

The answer £216 uses the WDA at the rate of 6%.

> **ACCA Examining Team's Comments**
>
> This question required candidates to demonstrate their knowledge in respect of capital allowances on cars, where there was a disposal of a car during the year which was also used for private use by Olive.
>
> As the car was disposed of during the year, candidates need to recognise that a balancing allowance arose on its disposal, and that the amount of capital allowance Olive could claim was restricted to the business use element (ie 60%).
>
> Many candidates instead chose the fourth answer, continuing to write down the cost of the car, rather than calculating a balancing allowance. Candidates are reminded that cars which are used partly for private use by a sole trader are put into their own pool and on disposal a balancing charge or allowance may arise.

62   £417,667

	AIA	Main pool	Allowance
	£	£	£
p/e 5.4.25			
Plant	430,000		
AIA £1,000,000 × 5/12	(416,667)		416,667
Transfer to pool	13,333	13,333	
WDA @ 18% × 5/12		(1,000)	1,000

	AIA	Main pool	Allowance
	£	£	£
TWDV c/f		12,333	
Allowances			417,667

The answer £339,133 time apportions from the date of acquisition rather than the length of the period of account. The answer £419,067 does not time apportion the WDA. The answer £430,000 is the unrestricted annual investment allowance.

OTQ bank – Income tax and NIC liabilities 3

63 The correct answer is: 31 January 2027

> **ACCA Examining Team's Comments**
>
> This question examines knowledge of the deadline for an individual taxpayer to claim relief for a trading loss which they wish to offset in the tax year prior to the tax year in which the loss arose. The correct answer is the second option (31 January 2027), as a claim must be made within one year of 31 January following the end of the tax year in which the loss arose. Therefore, as the loss arose in the tax year 2024/25, a claim for relief must be made by 31 January 2027.
>
> The second option was the most common answer selected but a significant number of candidates also chose each of the other answer options, suggesting that many candidates were not well prepared for a question on this topic.
>
> The second most common answer was the first option (31 January 2026) which is the deadline for submitting a personal tax return online for the tax year 2024/25. Candidates may have selected this date as they are familiar with this deadline in relation to the tax year 2024/25 and assumed the deadline for claiming the loss would be the same.
>
> Administration deadlines, both for individuals and companies, are an important part of the syllabus and future candidates are reminded of the importance of learning, and being able to distinguish between, the different deadlines as part of their studies.

64 £ 44,150

	£
1.4.24 to 30.4.24 1/12 × £96,000 × 1/2	4,000
1.5.24 to 31.3.25 Salary 11/12 × £9,000	8,250
1.5.24 to 31.3.25 Profit share ((11/12 × £96,000) – 8,250) × 2/5	31,900
	44,150

65 £ 56

	£
Class 4 contributions £(13,500 – 12,570) × 6%	56

66   The correct answer is: £2,297

> **ACCA Examining Team's Comments**
>
> The correct answer is £2,297 [£(50,270 – 12,570) × 6% + £(52,000 – 50,270)] × 2%.
>
> The incorrect answers are:
>
> £3,155 which is calculated at the Class 1 NIC rates and includes property income
>
> £(50,270 – 12,570) × 8% + £(52,000 + 5,200 – 50,270) × 2%
>
> £3,051 which is calculated at the Class 1 NIC rates
>
> £(50,270 – 12,570) × 8% + £(52,000 – 50,270) × 2%
>
> £2,401 which is calculated at the Class 4 NIC rates but includes property income
>
> £(50,270 – 12,570) × 6% + £(52,000 + 5,200 – 50,270) × 2%

67   The correct answer is: £68,000

> **ACCA Examining Team's Comments**
>
> The correct answer is £68,000
>
> Class 1 national insurance contributions (NICs) are payable by both Mina and her employer on her earnings. Mina's earnings for this purpose is her salary of £68,000. The loan provided to Mina by her employer is a benefit and will be subject to Class 1A NICs, the contribution to the occupational pension scheme which Mina pays is not deductible when assessing earnings and the employer contribution is excluded from the definition of earnings.
>
> The incorrect answers are as follows:
>
> £69,500 incorrectly includes the taxable benefit of the loan;
>
> £72,000 incorrectly adds the employer's pension contribution and deducts Mina's own contribution; and
>
> £65,000 deducts Mina's own contribution to the pension fund.

68   £ 1,560

The emissions are between 1 g and 50 g per km so we need to use the electric range to determine the CO_2 percentage. The percentage for 39 miles is 12% and Katya had the car for six months. Therefore, the benefit is: £26,000 × 12% × 6/12 = £1,560.

69   The correct answer is: £124

> **ACCA Examining Team's Comments**
>
> The correct answer was £124 (900 × 13.8%). This is because class 1A NIC is only charged on the gym membership and it is calculated based on the cost to the employer (not what the employee would have paid). A number of candidates selected £373 as the correct answer. This was calculated by including the employer contributions into Bee's private pension in the calculation (ie (900 + 1,800) × 13.8%), which is incorrect as these contributions are exempt from class 1A NIC.

70   £ 500

The percentage for electric cars with zero CO_2 emissions is 2% (per tax tables).

	£
List price	30,000
Less capital contribution (maximum)	(5,000)

	£
	25,000
Car benefit £25,000 × 2%	£500

71 The correct answer is: £75,000

> **ACCA Examining Team's Comments**
>
> The correct answer is £75,000. This is because, the annual allowance of £60,000 is reduced by £1 for every £2 by which the individual's adjusted income exceeds the threshold of £260,000, subject to a minimum annual allowance of £10,000. So, Niamhe's annual allowance for the tax year 2024/25 is £60,000 – (£330,000 – £260,000)/2, giving £25,000. The annual allowance charge is the amount by which Niamhe's gross personal pension scheme contributions exceed her annual allowance (£100,000 – £25,000), giving £75,000. A number of candidates selected £25,000, which is the annual allowance, rather than the annual allowance charge.

72 The correct answers are:
- Zara's taxable income is £82,430.
- A child benefit charge of £2,213 will be added to Zara's income tax liability.

> **ACCA Examining Team's Comments**
>
> Zara's taxable income is £82,430, which is calculated as follows:
>
> | | £ |
> |---|---|
> | Employment income | 85,000 |
> | Property business income (£20,000 × 50%) | 10,000 |
> | | 95,000 |
> | Personal allowance | (12,570) |
> | Taxable income | 82,430 |
>
> The first statement is therefore correct. Note that income generated from assets which are owned jointly is split 50:50 between spouses regardless of the actual ownership percentage. Therefore, the property income of £20,000 is split evenly between Dane and Zara. A child benefit income tax charge arises when an individual is in receipt of child benefit and either they or their spouse/civil partner (or person with whom they live as if they are married or in a civil partnership) has adjusted net income above £60,000.
>
> Zara's adjusted net income is above £60,000, and so a child benefit income tax charge will arise. Since Zara's adjusted net income is above £80,000, the child benefit income tax charge is equal to the full amount of child benefit received by Dane, ie £2,213. Therefore, the fourth statement is correct.
>
> The second statement is incorrect. It is not possible for Zara to claim the transferable personal allowance from Dane, as she is a higher rate taxpayer. In order to claim the transferable personal allowance neither spouse/civil partner can be a higher or additional rate taxpayer. The third statement is also incorrect. It would not be beneficial to Zara to make a joint election to HMRC specifying their actual ownership share in the property. In doing so, Zara would be taxed on 75% of the property income, ie £15,000 (20,000 × 75%). This would increase Zara's tax liability for the tax year 2024/25 and it would also mean that more of the income would be taxed at the higher rate of 40%, than under the current 50:50 split.

OTQ bank – Income tax and NIC liabilities 4

73 The correct answers are:

For tax year 2024/25 to 2027/28, profit subject to class 4 national insurance will include any transitional profit.	TRUE	
A period of account ending on 5 April requires apportionment to calculate assessable profit.		FALSE
Transition profits are included as a separate entry in the income tax computation.	TRUE	
If accounts are not finalised on time, estimated profit figures are used for the later part of the profit apportionment.	TRUE	

74 £ 36,432

	£
Trading profit	106,000
Transitional profit	9,000
	115,000
Personal allowance (12,570 – (115,000 – 100,000)/2)	(5,070)
Taxable income	109,930
Income tax	
£37,700 @ 20%	7,540
£72,230 @ 40%	28,892
Tax liability	36,432

75 £ 69,300

Lamine will be taxed on his profits from 6 April 2024 to 5 April 2025.

6 April 2024 to 31 May 2024 = 2 months

1 June 2024 to 5 April 2025 = 10 months

Taxable profits = 2/12 × £63,800 + 10/12 × £70,400 = £69,300

Once the y/e 31 May 2025 figures have been finalised, the self-assessment tax return may need to be amended if the final taxable trading profit for y/e 31 May 2025 are not as estimated. This can be done within 12 months of the filing date, ie 31 January 2027.

76 £ 15,000

Date of commencement to trade up to 5 April 2025 = 1 February 2025 – 5 April 2025 = 2 months

2/11 × £82,500 = £15,000

77 £ 30,000

6 April 2024 – cessation = 6 April 2024 – 30 November 2024 = 8 months

8/12 × £45,000 = £30,000

Section B

OT case – Ann, Basil and Chloe (December 2008) (amended)

> **Course Book references**
>
> Pensions are covered in Chapter 5. The computation of taxable income and the income tax liability are dealt with in Chapter 2.
>
> **Top tips**
>
> Remember that higher rate tax relief for personal pension contributions made by higher rate taxpayers is given by increasing the basic rate limit.
>
> **Easy marks**
>
> There were some easy marks for working out a basic tax liability.

78 The correct answers are:

- Individuals can always make gross pension contributions of £3,600 in 2024/25 even if they do not have any relevant earnings in that tax year.
- Relevant earnings relate both to contributions to personal pension schemes and to occupational pension schemes.

Unused relevant earnings cannot be carried forward. Relevant earnings include trading income, employment income and income from furnished holiday lettings.

79 The correct answers are:

Employer contributions do not count towards the annual allowance.		FALSE
The annual allowance can be carried forward for three years to the extent that it is unused in the tax year.	TRUE	
The annual allowance is available even if the individual is not a member of a pension scheme in a tax year and so can be carried forward.		FALSE
If tax-relievable pension contributions exceed the annual allowance, there is a charge to income tax.	TRUE	

80 £ 15,200

The available annual allowance is £(60,000 + 20,000) = £80,000 and so there is no annual allowance charge for the tax year 2024/25. The basic rate band limit is £(37,700 + 49,000) = £86,700 so all of Ann's taxable income is within the basic rate band.

	£
Tax £76,000 × 20%	15,200

81   £ 6,750

The annual allowance must be tapered because Basil's adjusted income before any deduction for the pension contribution is more than £260,000. Basil is still an additional rate taxpayer because his higher rate limit is lifted by the gross pension contribution.

Annual allowance

	£
£60,000 − [½ × £(310,000 − 260,000)]	35,000

Excess pension contribution over annual allowance

	£
£(50,000 − 35,000) @ 45%	6,750

82   The correct answer is: £720

Maximum personal pension contribution is £3,600 since Chloe has no relevant earnings. The pension tax relief is therefore £3,600 × 20% = £720. This relief will have been given at source. The remaining £4,600 contribution is not given tax relief.

OT case – Rosie and Sam (December 2012) (amended)

> **Course Book references**
>
> Personal pensions are covered in Chapter 5. The income tax treatment of investments is covered in Chapter 2 and the capital gains tax implications of investments are dealt with in Chapter 13.
>
> **Top tips**
>
> Remember that there is useful information contained in the Tax Tables provided in the examination. For example, the annual allowance amounts were vital and could be found in the Tax Tables. The annual limit for ISAs is also in the Tax Tables.
>
> **Easy marks**
>
> There were easy marks for identifying the tax consequences of flexible access drawdown.

83   The correct answer is: £64,000

In 2024/25, Rosie's adjusted income is greater than £360,000 so her annual allowance is tapered to £10,000.

Rosie was not a member of a pension scheme in 2021/22, so no annual allowance is available to carry forward from that year.

In 2022/23, she had income of £130,000 so her annual allowance does not need to be tapered. She made a gross pension contribution of £26,000 during that year, and her employer made a contribution of £10,000 so she had £(40,000 − 26,000 − 10,000) £4,000 annual allowance available to carry forward.

In 2023/24, her income was also below the threshold so the annual allowance does not need to be tapered. She did not make any pension contributions, but her employer made a contribution of £10,000 leaving £50,000 available to carry forward.

Therefore, the available annual allowance for 2024/25 is:

	£
2024/25	10,000
2021/22	0
2022/23	4,000
2023/24	50,000
	64,000

The answer £104,000 does not restrict the 2024/25 annual allowance to the minimum amount (£50k + £4k + £50k). The answer £154,000 gives full allowances for the current year plus three years brought forward, after accounting for the contribution in 2022/23 and 2023/24 (£60k + £60k + £40k + £40k – £36k – £10k). The answer £84,000 includes an allowance of £60,000 (instead of £40,000) 2022/23.

84 If Rosie makes pension contributions in excess of her available annual allowances, there will be a charge to income tax at 45 % on the excess contributions.

The annual allowance charge is calculated by taxing the excess contribution as an extra amount of income received by Rosie and so is charged at her highest rate of income tax.

85 The correct answer is:

Lump sum	Rest of pension fund
Up to 25% of fund can be taken as tax-free lump sum	Taxable as pension income when received

86 £19,000

The ISA amount 2024/25 is £20,000. Sam has already invested £6,000 in the tax year, so can invest a further £(20,000 – 6,000) = £14,000.

He can also replace the £5,000 withdrawn in October 2024 so the total amount he can now invest is £(14,000 + 5,000) = £19,000.

87 The correct answers are:

Exempt from both income tax and capital gains tax	Premium bonds
Chargeable to income tax, exempt from capital gains tax	Government securities

 Videos can be viewed online by accessing your ebook version on VitalSource.

OT case – Chi (June 2014) (amended)

> **Course Book references**
>
> Chapter 2 covers the computation of taxable income and the income tax liability.
>
> National insurance contributions are the subject of Chapter 12.
>
> The cash basis of assessment is dealt with in Chapter 7.
>
> **Top tips**
>
> If the cash basis is used, there are no capital allowances on the office equipment but the expenditure is instead deducted in the same way as a revenue expense.
>
> **Easy marks**
>
> The computation of income tax should have been easy marks.
>
> There were some easy marks for identifying cash receipts and payments.

88 £ 8,632

	£
Trading income/net income	53,000
Less personal allowance	(12,570)
Taxable income	40,430
Tax	
£37,700 @ 20%	7,540
£2,730 (40,430 – 37,700) @ 40%	1,092
	8,632

89 £ 2,317

	£
£(50,270 – 12,570) = £37,700 @ 6%	2,262
£(53,000 – 50,270) = £2,730 @ 2%	55
Total Class 4 contributions	2,317

90 The correct answers are:

- The trader can deduct capital expenditure on plant and machinery (other than cars) as business expenses rather than using capital allowances.
- Under the cash basis, legal fees relating to a short lease on land are disallowable.

Accounts can be prepared to any date in the tax year as for the accruals basis of assessment.

Under the cash basis, there are no provisions because there has been no payment of cash.

Expenses for the renewal of a short lease for less than 50 years are allowable but disallowed under the cash basis if the expense relates to land.

91 The correct answer is: £5,300

	£
10,000 miles @ 45p	4,500
3,200 miles @ 25p	800
	5,300

Capital allowances are not relevant since purchases of equipment are deducted as an expense. The running and capital costs of owning a car are replaced by the deduction based on approved mileage allowances.

92 The correct answer is: Revenue £70,900, other expenses £7,300

Revenue £(72,500 − 1,600) = £70,900

Section C

93 Kagan

> **Course Book references**
>
> Income tax computations are the subject of Chapter 2. Pensions are covered in Chapter 4. Basic capital gains and inheritance tax are dealt with in Chapters 13 and 18.
>
> **Top tips**
>
> It is important to realise that the first two requirements only score 1 mark each and therefore the answers must be very straightforward. There is no need for lengthy and time-consuming calculations.
>
> **Easy marks**
>
> There were some easy marks in part (b)(ii) for dealing with the exempt income and personal allowance.
>
> **ACCA Examining Team's Comments**
>
> This question involved Kagan who had inherited quoted ordinary shares valued at £510,000. Kagan was unsure whether to retain the shares or sell some of them in order to make four alternative investments.
>
> Retain the inherited shares: Kagan would have received dividend income of £13,800 in addition to his employment income of £400,000 (for which the income tax liability was given) for the tax year 2024/25.
>
> Four alternative investments: These consisted of:
>
> (1) A personal pension contribution of £100,000, with Kagan having sufficient unused annual allowances to cover the pension contribution
>
>   He would immediately have withdrawn £25,000 of the pension fund tax-free.
>
> (2) Investing £50,000 in premium bonds
>
> (3) Investing £20,000 in a cash individual savings account (ISA)
>
> (4) Purchasing a freehold property for £295,000, with the property then let out unfurnished
>
> After making the four investments, Kagan would have been left with £65,000 of inherited shares, on which he would have received dividend income of £450 for the tax year 2024/25.
>
> Part (a) for 1 mark required candidates to calculate Kagan's revised income tax liability for the tax year 2024/25 if he retained the inherited shares.
>
> Although fairly well answered, many candidates used valuable time doing full before and after-tax computations. Kagan was clearly an additional rate taxpayer, so all that was required was to calculate the additional rate tax due on the dividend income and then add it to the provided figure of tax on the employment income.
>
> Part (b)(i) for 1 mark required an explanation as to why little or no capital gains tax would have been payable if Kagan had sold some of his inherited shares. This was because assets are inherited at the value at the time of the deceased's death. If these assets are sold soon after being inherited, there will generally be a minimal increase in value (this fact was stated in the question), so any gain is likely to be covered by the annual exempt amount.
>
> It was pleasing to see that this part was well answered by those candidates who appreciated the tax treatment.
>
> Part (b)(ii) for 6 marks required a calculation of Kagan's revised income tax liability for the tax year 2024/25 if he sold some of his inherited shares and made the four alternative investments.

This section was reasonably well answered, but several points should be noted:

- The question stated that a full tax computation was required, so exempt items (pension lump sum, premium bond prizes and the interest from the ISA) should simply have been listed within the main computation and indicated as such by the use of zero (0) – not by an explanation.
- The non-availability of the personal allowance should have been indicated in the same manner. There was no need to justify the non-availability given the level of Kagan's income.
- Although there might only be a ½ mark available for recognising an exemption, it is important to know the various exemptions so that time is not spent producing unnecessary, and more complicated workings – such as applying the savings income nil rate band where the interest from the ISA was included as savings income.

Part (c) for 2 marks required candidates to state, for each of the four alternative investments, whether the investment would reduce Kagan's potential inheritance tax liability compared to him retaining the inherited shares.

Unfortunately, this section was not well answered. Candidates need to remember, that unlike other taxes, there are few exemptions from inheritance tax. Therefore, the replacement of the quoted shares with either premium bonds, an ISA or freehold property would not have changed the value of Kagan's chargeable estate. However, the investment in the pension fund (which is not withdrawn) would have been outside of Kagan's estate, thereby reducing his potential IHT liability.

Marking guide

		Marks	
(a)	Revised income tax liability	1	
			1
(b) (i)	Base cost value inherited	1	
			1
(ii)	Employment income	0.5	
	Pension lump sum	0.5	
	Premium bond prizes	0.5	
	Interest from ISA	0.5	
	Property income	0.5	
	Dividend income	0.5	
	Personal allowance	0.5	
	Income tax liability	2.5	
			6
(c)	Pension fund outside estate	0.5	
	Other investments	1.5	
			2
Total			10

(a) Kagan's revised income tax liability will be £170,234 (165,000 + ((13,800 – 500) at 39.35%)).

(b) (i) The base cost of the shares will be their value at the time of the aunt's death (£510,000) and the minimal increase in value will be reduced by Kagan's annual exempt amount of £3,000.

(ii) **Kagan – Income tax liability 2024/25**

	£
Employment income	400,000
Pension lump sum	0
Premium bond prizes	0
Interest from ISA	0
Property income	9,600
Dividend income	450
	410,050
Personal allowance	0
Taxable income	410,050

Income tax

	£
£37,700 at 20%	7,540
£100,000 at 20%	20,000
£87,440 at 40%	34,976
£184,460 £(410,050 – 450 – 100,000 – 125,140) at 45%	83,007
£450 at 0%	0
£410,050	
Income tax liability	145,523

(c) Kagan's potential IHT liability:

(1) The amount invested in the pension fund (and not withdrawn) will be outside of Kagan's estate, reducing the potential IHT liability.

(2) The investments in premium bonds, the ISA and the freehold property will not affect Kagan's potential IHT liability because one asset is simply being replaced with another of equivalent value.

94 Michael and Sean (June 2012) (amended)

> **Course Book references**
>
> Chapter 10 deals with trading losses.
>
> **Top tips**
>
> Remember that if a taxpayer claims loss relief against general income, the benefit of the personal allowance may be lost.
>
> **Easy marks**
>
> There were some easy marks for identifying the possible loss relief claims.

Marking guide	Marks
Michael	
Early years relief against total income	1
Claims	1
Rate of tax saved – 2021/22	1
Rates of tax saved – 2022/23	1
Carry forward	0.5
Sean	
Available loss	1
Terminal loss relief	1
Claims	1
Rates of tax saved	1
Relief against total income	1.5
	10
Total	10

Michael

The loss of £26,230 for 2024/25 can be claimed against general income for the three preceding years, under early years loss relief, earliest year first, since the loss is incurred in one of the first four years of Michael's trade. The loss relief claim will therefore be £20,365 in 2021/22 and £(26,230 – 20,365) = £5,865 in 2022/23.

For 2021/22, this will waste Michael's personal allowance, with the balance of the claim of £(20,365 – 12,570) = £7,795 saving income tax at the basic rate of 20%.

For 2022/23, Michael has income of £(57,095 – 12,570 – 37,700) = £6,825 subject to income tax at the higher rate of 40%, so the claim of £5,865 will save tax at the higher rate. Alternatively, Michael could have carried the trading loss forward against future trading profits, but the trading profit of £9,665 for 2025/26 is covered by the personal allowance, and there is no information regarding future trading profits.

> **Tutorial note.** A claim for loss relief against general income for 2024/25 and/or 2023/24 is not possible since Michael does not have any income for either of these years.

Sean

The 2024/25 loss can be claimed as a terminal loss since it is for the final 12 months of trading. The claim is against trading income for the year of the loss (2024/25 – nil) and the three preceding years, latest first.

The terminal loss claim will therefore be £3,700 in 2023/24, £18,900 in 2022/23 and £(26,700 – 3,700 – 18,900) = £4,100 in 2021/22.

The property business profits are sufficient to utilise Sean's personal allowance for each year, so the loss relief claims will save income tax at the basic rate of 20%.

Alternatively, Sean could have initially claimed loss relief against his general income for 2024/25 and/or 2023/24, but this would have wasted his personal allowance in those years.

 Videos can be viewed online by accessing your ebook version on VitalSource.

95 Paul and Palu Ltd (March/June 2021) (amended)

Marking guide

	Marks
Business run as limited company	
(1) Trading profit	0.5
– Director's remuneration	0.5
– Corporation tax at 25%	0.5
(2) Income tax	
– Director's remuneration	0.5
– Dividend income	0.5
– Personal allowance	0.5
– Income tax at 20%	0.5
– Income tax at 0% (dividend)	0.5
– Income tax at 8.75%, 33.75%, 39.35%	1
(3) No Class 1 NIC as below threshold	0.5
Business run as a sole trader	0.5
(1) Taxable income	
– Income tax at 20%	0.5
– Income tax at 40%	0.5
– Income tax at 45%	0.5
(2) Class 4 NIC	1
– Conclusion	1.5
	10
Total	10

Business run as a limited company

(1) Palu Ltd's corporation tax liability for the year ended 5 April 2025 will be:

	£
Trading profit	275,000
Director's remuneration	(8,000)
Taxable total profits	267,000
Corporation tax (267,000 at 25%)	66,750

> **Tutorial note.** Equivalent marks will be awarded if the corporation tax liability is alternatively calculated as 275,000 – 8,000 – 200,250 = £66,750.

(2) Paul's income tax liability for 2024/25 will be:

	Non savings income	Dividend income	
	£	£	£
Director's remuneration	8,000		8,000
Dividend income		200,250	200,250
Net income	8,000	200,250	208,250
Personal allowance (income > £125,140)			0
Taxable income			208,250
£8,000 at 20%			1,600
£500 at 0%			0
£29,200 £(37,700 – 8,000 – 500) at 8.75%			2,555
£87,440 £(125,140 – 37,700) at 33.75%			29,511
£83,110 £(200,250 – 87,440 – 29,200 – 500) at 39.35%			32,704
£208,250			
Income tax liability			66,370

(3) There will be no class 1 NICs because the earnings of £8,000 are below the NIC lower thresholds.

Business run as a sole trader

(1) Paul's income tax liability for 2024/25 will be:

	£
Trading profit	275,000
Personal allowance	0
Taxable income	275,000
Income tax	
£37,700 at 20%	7,540
£87,440 at 40%	34,976
£149,860 at 45%	67,437
£275,000	
Income tax liability	109,953

(2) Class 4 NICs for 2024/25 will be:

	£
£37,700 £(50,270 – 12,570) at 6%	2,262
£224,730 £(275,000 – 50,270) at 2%	4,495
Class 4 NICs	6,757

Conclusion

If Paul runs his business as a limited company, then overall tax and NIC will be £16,410 more than if he ran his business as a sole trader:

	£
Limited company £(66,750 + 66,370)	133,120
Sole trader £(109,953 + 6,757)	(116,710)
Tax increase	16,410

96 Lucy

> **Course Book references**
>
> Chapter 2 deals with the income tax computation. Chapter 3 covers employment income and Chapter 7 covers trading income. National insurance contributions are dealt with in Chapter 12.
>
> **Top tips**
>
> Travel from home to work is not an allowable expense for tax purposes for an employee.
>
> **Easy marks**
>
> There were some easy marks for basic income tax and NIC computations for both the employment and self-employment work arrangements.

Marking guide

	Marks
Employee	
Income tax payable	1.5
Class 1 NIC	1.5
Income	1
Self-employed	
Income tax payable	2
Class 4 NIC	1
Income	2
Determination of working pattern with higher disposable income	1
	10
Total	10

Disposable income if Lucy is employee

Income tax

	£
Employment income/net income	36,000
Less personal allowance	(12,570)
Taxable income	23,430
Income tax @ 20%	4,686

192 Taxation (TX – UK) FA 2024

Class 1 NIC

	£
Salary	36,000
Less employee's threshold	(12,570)
	23,430
Class 1 NIC @ 8%	1,874

Disposable income

	£
Salary	36,000
Less:	
– Income tax	(4,686)
– Class 1 NIC	(1,874)
– Travel costs	(1,500)
	27,940

Disposable income if Lucy is self-employed

Income tax	£
Fees received	36,000
Less fixed rate mileage 4,600 @ 45p per mile	(2,070)
Trading income/net income	33,930
Less personal allowance	(12,570)
Taxable income	21,360
Income tax @ 20%	4,272

	£	£
Class 4 NIC		
Trading income	33,930	
Less lower limit	(12,570)	
	21,360	
Class 4 NIC @ 6%		1,282
Disposable income		
Fees received		36,000
Less		
– Income tax		(4,272)
– Class 4 NICs		(1,282)
– Travel costs 4,600 @ 40p		(1,840)
		28,606

Lucy will therefore have a higher disposable income by £(28,606 − 27,940) = £666 if she undertakes the self-employed work arrangement.

97 Poppy (March/June 2022)

> **Course Book references**
> Gilts are covered in Chapter 2. Benefits are covered in Chapter 4. Trading losses are covered in Chapter 10. Partnerships are covered in Chapter 11.
>
> **Top tips**
> Remember that the relevant figures for calculating accrued interest are the nominal value and the interest rate.
>
> **Easy marks**
> The calculation of the car benefit and 20% for the mobile phone provide easy marks.
>
> **ACCA Examining Team's Comments**
> A number of candidates struggled to correctly allocate the trading loss. The interaction of capital allowances and loss relief was a particular issue. The calculation of the accrued gilt income also caused problems.

(a) **Poppy – Taxable income 2024/25**

		£
Employment income		
Salary		65,000
Car benefit	(21,800 × (19% + 4%) × 8/12)	3,343
Mobile phone	(480 × 20%)	96
		68,439
Savings income	(40,000 at 3% × 3/12)	300
		68,739
Loss relief	(W1)	(9,350)
Personal allowance		(12,570)
Taxable income		46,819

Notes.

1 The exemption for mobile telephones does not apply to the second telephone.

2 Under the accrued income scheme, Poppy must include the accrued interest from the gilts as savings income for 2024/25, even though she has not received any actual interest.

Working

Trading loss

		£
Trading loss		19,500
Balancing allowance	((8,400 − 5,400) × 30%)	900
Revised trading loss		20,400

		£
Profit share		
6 April 2024 to 5 July 2024	20,400 × 3/12 × 1/3	1,700
6 July 2024 to 5 April 2025	20,400 × 9/12 × 1/2	7,650
		9,350

(b) Because Poppy's benefits are payrolled, the related income tax liability will have been collected under PAYE along with the tax on her salary.

Payrolled benefits do not have to be reported to HMRC on form P11D or otherwise.

(c) Interest will be charged for the period 31 January 2025 to 31 August 2025, so the charge will be £118 (2,600 × 7.75% × 7/12).

Two penalties of £130 (2,600 at 5%) will be imposed on the balancing payment, one when it is one month late and the other when it is six months late.

98 Kazuo

> **Course Book references**
>
> Employment income is covered in Chapter 3; the income tax computation in Chapter 2; and NICs are dealt with in Chapter 12. Corporation tax is covered in Chapter 19.
>
> **Top tips**
>
> For part (a), working in the margin is easier and quicker than using a full calculation approach. For part (b), remember to use your figure from part (a) instead of re-doing the calculation. Don't forget the corporation tax in part (c).
>
> **Easy marks**
>
> There were some easy marks for basic income tax and corporation tax computations.
>
> **ACCA Examining Team's Comments**
>
> Although there were a number of perfect answers, many candidates found this question quite challenging. One particular problem was that candidates did not appreciate that part (c) was essentially the same as part (a), but set a few years ahead with a lower tax rate. This future setting confused a significant minority of candidates, with a number calculating income and taxes over several years. However, the question clearly stated that the freelance work would only last for just one year.

(a) (i) Zaoku Ltd's corporation tax liability for the year ended 5 April 2025 will be £7,600 (40,000 at 19%).

(ii) Kazuo will receive dividend income of £32,400 (£40,000 – £7,600) and the income tax payable on this amount will be £12,553 ((£32,400 – £500) at 39.35%).

(b) (i) Corporation tax, income tax and NIC implications:

(1) Paying the director's remuneration and making the pension contribution will reduce Zaoku Ltd's taxable total profits (and corporation tax liability) to £0 (£40,000 – £8,000 – £32,000).

(2) Kazuo will pay income tax of just £3,600 (£8,000 at 45%) because the pension contribution will be an exempt benefit.

(3) There will be no class 1 NICs because the earnings of £8,000 are below the NIC lower threshold.

(ii) The overall tax saving compared to Alternative 1 will be £16,553 (£7,600 + £12,553 – £3,600).

(c) If Kazuo withdraws:

(1) Zaoku Ltd's corporation tax liability for the year ended 5 April 2025 will remain unchanged at £7,600.

(2) For 2028/29, Kazuo will be a higher rate taxpayer, so the income tax payable in respect of his dividend income will be reduced to £10,766 ((£32,400 – £500) at 33.75%).

(3) The overall tax saving compared to alternative 1 will be £1,787 (£12,553 – £10,766).

99 Joe (December 2010) (amended)

Course Book references

Chapters 3 and 4 deal with employment income and employment benefits.

Top tips

Don't forget to show that you know if a benefit is exempt by including it in your computation with a zero.

Easy marks

There were some easy marks for basic employment benefit computations such as the living accommodation.

Marking guide	Marks
Salary – Firstly plc	0.5
Occupational pension scheme contributions	1.5
Bonus	0.5
Salary – Secondly plc	0.5
Personal pension contributions	0.5
Beneficial loan – Average method	1.5
Beneficial loan – Strict method	1.5
Van benefit	1
Home entertainment system – Use	1.5
Home entertainment system – Acquisition	1.5
Living accommodation	2
Furniture	1.5
Working at home additional costs	1
	15
Total	**15**

Joe – employment income

	£
Salary – Firstly plc (6,360 × 9)	57,240
Pension contributions (57,240 × 6%) (N2)	(3,434)
	53,806
Bonus (N1)	0
Salary – Secondly plc (6,565 × 3)	19,695

Beneficial loan (W1)	1,331
Company van (£3,960 × 9/12)	2,970
Home entertainment system	
– Use (W2)	660
– Acquisition (W2)	3,860
Living accommodation (W3)	6,750
Furniture (W3)	816
Working at home additional costs (N3)	0
Employment income	89,888

Workings

1 **Loan benefit**

The benefit of the beneficial loan using the average method is £1,425 ((120,000 + 70,000)/2 = 95,000 at 2.25% × 8/12).

Using the strict method, the benefit is £1,331 ((120,000 at 2.25% × 3/12) + (70,000 at 2.25% × 5/12)).

Joe will therefore elect to have the taxable benefit calculated according to the strict method.

2 **Home entertainment system**

The benefit for the use of the home entertainment system is £660 (4,400 × 20% × 9/12).

The benefit for the acquisition of the home entertainment system is the market value of £3,860, as this is greater than £3,740 (4,400 – 660).

3 **Living accommodation and furniture**

The benefit for the living accommodation is the higher of the annual value of £2,600 (10,400 × 3/12) and the rent paid of £6,750 (2,250 × 3).

The benefit for the use of the furniture is £816 (16,320 × 20% × 3/12).

Notes.

1 The bonus of £12,000 will have been treated as being received during 2023/24 as Joe became entitled to it during that tax year.

2 The personal pension contributions will increase Joe's basic rate tax limit and are therefore irrelevant as regards the calculation of employment income. Firstly, plc's employer contributions are an exempt benefit.

3 Additional home working costs up to £26 per month does not give rise to a taxable benefit.

100 Esme (September/December 2023)

> **Course Book references**
> Chapters 3 and 4 deal with employment income and employment benefits.
>
> **Top tips**
> Don't forget to show that you know if a benefit is exempt by including it in your computation with a zero.
>
> **Easy marks**
> There were some easy marks for basic employment benefit computations such as the car and the mileage.

(a) **Esme – Income tax liability**

	A	B	C	D
1		Non-savings income	Dividend income	Total
2		£	£	£
3	Salary	45,000		
4	Pension contributions:			
5	Esme (45,000 × 4%)	(1,800)		
6	HHK plc (exempt)	0		
7	Bonus 1	0		
8	Bonus 2	22,000		
9	Car benefit (W1)	10,360		
10	Mileage (W2)	760		
11	Employment income	76,320		
12	Dividend income	——	4,500	——
13		76,320	4,500	80,820
14	Personal allowance	(12,570)	——	(12,570)
15	Taxable income	63,750	4,500	68,250
16		43,950 (37,700 + 5,000 × 100/80) at 20%		8,790
17		19,800 (63,750 – 43,950) at 40%		7,920
18			500 at 0%	0
19			4,000 at 33.75%	1,350
20	Income tax liability 2024/25			18,060

Workings

1 **Car benefit**

(1) The relevant percentage for the car benefit is 37% (16% + 24% ((175 – 55)/5) = 40%) but limited to 37%.

(2) The car was available during the period 6 April to 30 November 2024, so the benefit for 2024/25 is £10,360 (£42,000 × 37% × 8/12).

2 *Mileage*

	£	£
Mileage reimbursement		5,760
Approved mileage allowance		
10,000 miles at 45p	(4,500)	
2,000 miles at 25p	(500)	
		(5,000)
Mileage benefit		760

> **Tutorial note.** The bonus of £19,000 will have been treated as being received during the tax year 2023/24 even though it was paid on 10 April 2024 because Esme became entitled to it on 31 March 2024.
>
> The bonus of £22,000 will have been treated as being received during the tax year 2024/25 because it was paid to her on 22 March 2025.

(b)

1. The transferable amount is £1,260 of the personal allowance. This would reduce the personal allowance of the spouse/civil partner making the transfer to £11,310 (12,570 – 1,260).
2. The income tax liability of the receiving spouse/civil partner would be reduced by £252 (1,260 × 20%).
3. A claim is not possible in Esme and Andy's case because Esme is a higher rate taxpayer.

(c)

1. Andy currently receives dividend income of £8,500 each year from his own shareholdings. If Esme's quoted shares were transferred to Andy, his net income would increase to £13,000 (8,500 + 4,500). This would be partially relieved by Andy's personal allowance of £12,570 with the remainder covered by the dividend nil rate band of £500.
2. Esme's income tax liability would reduce by £4,000 (4,500 – 500) × 33.75% = £1,350.

101 Hannah and Gregor

> **Course Book references**
>
> Chapter 4 deals with employment benefits.
>
> **Top tips**
>
> Use headings for your workings.
>
> **Easy marks**
>
> There were easy marks for computing the mileage allowance and living accommodation.

(a) **Employment income for the tax year 2024/25**

	A	B
1		£
2	Salary (125,000 × 3/12)	31,250
3	Living accommodation (working 1)	4,985
4	Beneficial loan (working 2)	316
5	Mileage allowance (working 3)	300
6	Reimbursed expenses (exempt)	0
7		36,851

Workings

1 **Living accommodation**

	£
Annual value	16,000
Additional charge ((250,000 – 75,000) × 2.25%)	3,938
	19,938
Taxable benefit (19,938 × 3/12)	4,985

2 *Beneficial loan*

Average method

	£
Balance at 1 January 2025	60,000
Balance at 5 April 2025 (60,000 – (3 × 2,500))	52,500
	112,500
Average loan (112,500/2)	56,250
Taxable benefit (56,250 × 2.25% × 3/12)	316

3 *Mileage allowance*

	£
Mileage allowance received (6,000 miles at 50p)	3,000
Approved mileage allowance (6,000 miles at 45p)	(2,700)
Taxable benefit	300

(b) If the property provided to Hannah by Lomly Ltd qualified as job-related accommodation, there would be no taxable benefit.

(c) **Gregor – Trading loss carried forward**

	£
Trading loss	68,800
2023/24	
– Claim against total income £(14,700 + 4,600 + 1,300)	(20,600)
2024/25	
– Claim against total income	(900)
– Claim against chargeable gain (working)	(14,500)
Loss carried forward to 2025/26	32,800

Working

Claim against chargeable gain

The loss relief claim against the chargeable gain is restricted to £14,500 (chargeable gain of £17,400 less the capital loss brought forward of £2,900). Gregor can claim loss relief against his total income and chargeable gains for 2023/24 and 2024/25.

102 Alfred and Amaia (March/June 2021) (amended)

Marking guide	Marks
(a) Pre-trading expenditure	0.5
Client entertaining	0.5
Lease premium	
– Premium paid	0.5
– Less £5,400	0.5

– Deduction	1.5	
Capital allowances		
– Plant and machinery	0.5	
– AIA	0.5	
– Car WDA	1.5	
		6
(b) Salary	0.5	
Car	1.5	
Job related accommodation	1	
Personal allowance	0.5	
Income tax at 20%	0.5	
Income tax at 40%	0.5	
Interest relief	1	
PAYE	0.5	
Property income		
– Rent received	1	
– Insurance	1	
– Mortgage interest	1	
		9
Total		15

(a) **Alfred – tax adjusted trading loss for the seven-month period ended 31 March 2025**

	£
Trading profit	63,000
Pre-trading expenditure	(5,000)
Deduction for lease premium (W1)	(1,435)
Client entertaining	0
Capital allowances (W2)	(118,520)
Trading loss	(61,955)

Workings

1 **Deduction for lease premium**

	£
Premium paid	30,000
Less: 30,000 × 2% × (10 – 1)	(5,400)
Amount taxable on landlord	24,600
Deduction 24,600/10 × 7/12	1,435

2 Capital allowances

	£	Main pool £	Allowance £
Addition qualifying for AIA			
Plant and machinery	116,000		
AIA – 100%	(116,000)		116,000
Car		24,000	
WDA – 18% × 7/12		(2,520)	2,520
TWDV c/f		21,480	
Total allowances			118,520

Tutorial note. The cost of the marketing campaign is deductible because it was incurred in the seven years prior to the commencement of Alfred's trade and it would be deductible under general principles.

The car has CO_2 emissions between 1 and 50 grams per kilometre, and therefore qualifies for writing down allowances at the rate of 18%.

(b) **Amaia – income tax payable for the tax year 2024/25**

	£
Employment income	
Salary	80,000
Car (£25,000 × 15% × 3/12)	938
Job-related accommodation	0
Property income (working)	14,350
	95,288
Personal allowance	(12,570)
Taxable income	82,718
£37,700 at 20%	7,540
£45,018 (82,718 – 37,700) at 40%	18,007
	25,547
Interest relief (£2,600 at 20%)	(520)
Income tax liability	25,027
PAYE	(19,240)
Income tax payable	5,787

Working

Property income

	£
Rent received (£1,200 × 13)	15,600
Mortgage interest	0

	£
Insurance	(1,250)
Property income	14,350

103 John (June 2013) (amended)

> **Course Book references**
>
> Chapter 2 deals with the computation of taxable income and the income tax liability. Pensions are covered in Chapter 5. Employment income is dealt with in Chapters 3 and 4. Property income is the subject of Chapter 6.
>
> **Top tips**
>
> Make sure you distinguish between occupational pension contributions (which are given tax relief at all rates by being deducted in the computation of employment income) and personal pension contributions (which are given basic rate relief by the taxpayer making a net contribution and higher and additional rate relief by increasing the basic rate and higher rate limits).
>
> **Easy marks**
>
> The inclusion of salary, deduction of occupational pension contributions and calculation of the tax liability should have been straightforward in part (a).

Marking guide	**Marks**
(a) Remuneration	0.5
Occupational pension contributions	1
Beneficial loan
– Outstanding loan at end of tax year	1
– Average loan	1
– Interest paid	0.5
Property business profit	0.5
Letting agent fees	0.5
Personal allowance – not available	0.5
Personal pension contributions
– Unused allowances	1.5
– Available allowance 2024/25	1.5
Increase in basic and higher rate limits	1
Tax liability
– Basic rate	0.5
– Higher rate	0.5
– Additional rate	0.5
– Finance costs tax reducer	1
	12
(b) One for each relevant point (maximum of three)	3
Total	15

(a) **John – income tax computation 2024/25**

	Non-savings income £
Employment income	
Remuneration	338,318
Less occupational pension contributions	(18,000)
	320,318
Beneficial loan (W1)	1,530
Property business income (W2)	12,980
Net income	334,828
Less personal allowance	(0)
Taxable income	334,828

Tutorial note. No personal allowance is available as John's adjusted net income of £(334,828 – 10,000 (W3)) = £324,828 exceeds £125,140.

Tax

	£
£67,700 (W3) @ 20%	13,540
£87,440 (155,140(W3) – 67,700) @ 40%	34,976
£179,688 (334,828 – 155,140) @ 45%	80,860
	129,376
Less: finance costs tax reducer £7,500 × 20%	(1,500)
Income tax liability	127,876

Workings

1 **Beneficial loan**

John repaid £(12,000 + 12,000) = £24,000 of the loan during 2024/25, so the outstanding balance at 5 April 2025 is £(84,000 – 24,000) = £60,000.

The benefit calculated using the average method (specified in the question) is as follows:

	£
[(84,000 + 60,000)/2] × 2.25%	1,620
Less interest paid	(90)
Taxable benefit	1,530

2 **Property business income**

	£
Profit before interest	14,855
Less: Letting agent fees	(1,875)
Property business income	12,980

3 **Effect of personal pension contributions on tax limits**

John has adjusted income which is higher than £260,000 in the tax year 2024/25 so his annual allowance is reduced (tapered) for 2024/25 by £1 for every £2 the adjusted income exceeds £260,000. However, the annual allowance is not reduced to less than £10,000.

Unused allowances can be carried forward for three years.

The maximum gross personal pension contribution possible in 2024/25 is as follows:

	£
2024/25 (tapered)	10,000
Adjusted income = £(334,828 + 18,000 + 12,000) = £364,828 which is at least £360,000 so minimum annual allowance applies	
2023/24	60,000
No tapering required as adjusted income below tapering limit	
2022/23	40,000
No tapering required as adjusted income below tapering limit	
2021/22	40,000
No tapering required as adjusted income below tapering limit	
Occupational pension contributions already made £(18,000 + 12,000) × 4	(120,000)
Personal pension contribution allowable	30,000

John's basic and higher rate limits will be increased by this gross personal pension contribution to £(37,700 + 30,000) = £67,700 and £(125,140 + 30,000) = £155,140.

> **Tutorial note.** Adjusted income for an employee is net income plus employee pension contributions to occupational pension schemes under net pay arrangements plus employer contributions to occupational pension schemes and/or personal pension schemes.

(b) **Furnished holiday lettings**

Any three from:

(1) There is no restriction on finance costs.

(2) The cost of furniture purchased for use in the furnished holiday letting will be an allowable expense under the cash basis (or will qualify for capital allowances under the accruals basis) instead of replacement furniture relief.

(3) The profit from the furnished holiday letting will qualify as relevant earnings for pension tax relief purposes.

(4) Capital gains tax business asset disposal relief, relief for replacement of business assets and gift holdover relief for business assets will potentially be available on a disposal of the furnished holiday letting.

104 Wai (June 2015) (amended)

> **Course Book references**
>
> Employment income is covered in Chapters 3 and 4. The personal allowance is dealt with in Chapter 2.
>
> **Top tips**
>
> Make sure you are familiar with the tax rates and allowances which will be given to you in the exam. They include a lot of useful information such as mileage allowance, car benefit and the official rate of interest which will help you in answering this question.
>
> **Easy marks**
>
> There were some easy marks for calculation of basic employment benefits such as car benefit and living accommodation benefit.
>
> **ACCA Examining Team's Comments**
>
> Part (a) was generally very well answered. Surprisingly, the aspect that caused the biggest problem was the salary, because many candidates did not appreciate that it was necessary to calculate an annual figure. With calculations such as those for the mileage allowance, candidates are advised to study and replicate the layout followed in model answers rather than attempting their own style of short-cut. It is also a very poor approach to simply refer to a question note when answering, such as (5) instead of incidental expenses.
>
> Many candidates found part (b) difficult, and often based their answers on self-assessment tax return information or PAYE form P45. One clue should have been that the question said 'provided to Wai', so clearly a tax return could not be relevant.

Marking guide		Marks
(a)	Salary	0.5
	Bonus	1
	Mileage allowance	
	Reimbursement	0.5
	Ordinary commuting	0.5
	Travel to clients	0.5
	Temporary workplace	0.5
	Tax-free amount @ 45p	0.5
	Tax-free amount @ 25p	0.5
	Car benefit	
	Percentage	0.5
	Benefit	1
	Incidental expenses	0.5
	Mobile telephone	1
	Living accommodation	
	Annual value	0.5
	Additional benefit	
	– Cost	0.5

Marking guide	Marks
– Improvements	1
– Limit	1
– Benefit	0.5
Personal allowance	1
	12
(b) Form P60 contents	1.5
Date	0.5
Form P11D contents	0.5
Date	0.5
	3
Total	**15**

(a) **Wai – taxable income 2024/25**

	£
Employment income	
Salary (10,200 × 12)	122,400
Bonus	8,100
Mileage allowance (W1)	2,763
Car benefit (W2)	1,285
Incidental expenses (overseas, up to £10 per night – exempt)	0
Mobile telephone (400 × 20%)	80
Living accommodation	
– Annual value	4,828
– Additional benefit (W3)	2,052
	141,508
Less personal allowance	(0)
Taxable income	141,508

Tutorial note. The bonus of £4,600 will have been treated as being received during 2023/24 as Wai became entitled to it during that tax year. Similarly, the bonus of £2,900 will be treated as received during 2025/26.

The exemption for mobile telephones does not apply to the second telephone.

No personal allowance is available as Wai's adjusted net income of £141,508 exceeds £125,140.

Workings

1 **Mileage allowance**

	Miles	£
Reimbursement (13,860 at 55p)		7,623

	Miles	£
Business mileage		
Ordinary commuting	0	
Travel to clients' premises	8,580	
Temporary workplace	2,860	
	11,440	
Tax-free amount		
10,000 miles at 45p		(4,500)
1,440 miles at 25p		(360)
Taxable benefit		2,763

Tutorial note. Travel to the temporary workplace qualifies as business mileage because the 24-month limit was not exceeded.

2   The relevant percentage for the car benefit is 22% because the car has CO_2 emissions from 85 to 89 grams per kilometre. The diesel addition does not apply because the car meets the RDE2 standard.

The car was available during the period 1 September 2024 to 5 April 2025, so the benefit for 2024/25 is £1,285 (10,013 × 22% × 7/12).

3   The benefit is based on the cost of the property plus subsequent improvements incurred before the start of the tax year.

	£
Cost	142,000
Improvements (prior to 6 April 2024 only)	24,200
	166,200
Limit	(75,000)
	91,200

The additional benefit is therefore £2,052 (91,200 at 2.25%).

(b) **Form P60**

Form P60 will show Wai's taxable earnings, income tax deducted, final tax code, national insurance contributions (NIC), and Qaz plc's name and address.

This form should have been provided to Wai by 31 May 2025.

Form P11D

Form P11D will detail the expenses and benefits provided to Wai.

This form should have been provided to Wai by 6 July 2025.

 Videos can be viewed online by accessing your ebook version on VitalSource.

105 Samson and Delilah (September/December 2015) (amended)

> **Course Book references**
>
> The income tax computation is covered in Chapter 2. Chapters 3 and 4 deal with employment income and taxable and exempt benefits. Partnerships are the subject of Chapter 11.
>
> **Top tips**
>
> Trivial benefits (not exceeding £50) are exempt benefits.
>
> **Easy marks**
>
> There were some easy marks for dealing with the car benefit and computing income tax.
>
> **ACCA Examining Team's Comments**
>
> Part (a) of the question was a typical income tax liability calculation (for both the husband and wife), and it was generally very well answered.
>
> Part (b) of the question involved income tax planning, requiring a calculation of the husband's income tax saving for the tax year if the building society deposit account had been in his wife's sole name instead of in joint names for the entire year. Given that the husband's personal allowance restriction would be reduced, the answer was simply the amount of interest (after deducting the savings income nil rate band of £500) at 60%. However, half page answers were quite common.
>
> Once again, working at the margin (where appropriate) could have saved an enormous amount of time.

Marking guide Marks

(a) **Samson**	
Salary	0.5
Building society interest	0.5
Personal allowance	1
Income tax	2
Delilah	
Salary	0.5
Payroll giving	1
Car benefit	1
Chauffeur	0.5
Hamper	0.5
Business travel	0.5
Trading profit	1
Building society interest	0.5
Deductible interest	1
Personal allowance not available	0.5
Income tax	2
	13
(b) Transfer part of account from Samson to Delilah	2
	2
Total	15

210 Taxation (TX – UK) FA 2024

(a) **Samson – Income tax computation 2024/25**

	Non-savings income	Savings income	Total
	£	£	£
Employment income – Salary	112,000		
Building society interest £9,600/2		4,800	
Net income	112,000	4,800	116,800
Less personal allowance (W)	(4,170)		
Taxable income	107,830	4,800	112,630

Income tax

	£
£37,700 × 20%	7,540
£70,130 (107,830 – 37,700) × 40%	28,052
£500 × 0% (savings rate nil rate band)	0
£4,300 (4,800 – 500) × 40%	1,720
Income tax liability	37,312

Workings

1 Samson's adjusted net income exceeds £100,000, so his personal allowance of £12,570 is reduced to £4,170 (12,570 – 8,400 ((116,800 – 100,000)/2)).

Delilah – income tax computation 2024/25

	Non-savings income	Savings income	Total
	£	£	£
Employment income (W1)	213,248		
Trading profit £85,600 (93,600 – 8,000) × 40%	34,240		
Building society interest £9,600/2		4,800	
Total income	247,488	4,800	252,288
Less interest paid	(6,200)		
Net income/taxable income	241,288	4,800	246,088

2 **Employment income**

	£
Salary	184,000
Less charitable payroll deductions £250 × 12	(3,000)
	181,000
Car benefit (W2)	22,848
Chauffeur	9,400
Hamper	0

		£
	Reimbursement of travel to visit client	0
	Employment income	213,248

3 The relevant percentage for the car benefit is 34% (16% + (145 − 55)/5).

The car was available throughout 2024/25 so the benefit is £22,848 (67,200 × 34%).

Income

	£
£43,780 (W) × 20%	8,756
£87,440 (131,220 − 43,780) × 40%	34,976
£114,868 (246,088 − 131,220) × 45%	51,691
Income tax liability	95,423

4 Delilah's basic and higher rate tax limits are increased by:

$£4,864 \times \dfrac{100}{80} = £6,080$ to £43,780 (37,700 + 6,080) and £131,220 (125,140 + 6,080)

in respect of the charitable gift aid donations.

> **Tutorial note.** The car benefit does not cover the cost of a chauffeur, so this is an additional benefit.
>
> The hamper is a trivial benefit as it does not exceed £50.
>
> There is an automatic exemption for reimbursement of business expenses such as the train travel by Delilah (which would be a taxable benefit under general principles) provided that the expense would have been a deductible expense for the employee.
>
> The loan interest paid of £6,200 is deductible because the loan was used by Delilah for a qualifying purpose.
>
> No personal allowance is available as Delilah's adjusted net income of £240,008 (246,088 − 6,080) exceeds £125,140.
>
> No savings income nil rate band is available as Delilah is an additional rate taxpayer.

(b) If the building society deposit account had been in Delilah's sole name instead of in joint names for the entire year, this would have saved Samson income tax of £2,680 (£500 × 20% + £4,300 × 60%).

> **Tutorial note.** Samson's effective marginal rate on the savings income covered by the savings income nil rate band (£500) is 20%. This is 40% of half of the £500 (ie 20% of the whole of the £500) of the savings income which was used to restrict the personal allowance. Samson's effective marginal rate of income tax on the savings income not covered by the savings income nil rate band (ie £4,800 − 500 = £4,300) is 60%. This is 40% (the higher rate) plus 40% of half (ie 20% of the whole) of the remaining £4,300 of savings income which was used to restrict the personal allowance.

 Videos can be viewed online by accessing your ebook version on VitalSource.

106 Petula (March/June 2017)

Course Book references
Employment income is dealt with in Chapters 3 and 4. The income tax computation is covered in Chapter 2. Pensions are the subject of Chapter 5.

Top tips
Part (b) is quite challenging, and you need to adopt a logical approach by first working out the annual allowances that have been used and then working out the remaining allowances to be carried forward. Make sure you use the earliest available tax year brought forward allowance first. This maximises the amount that can be carried forward.

Easy marks
There were easy marks in part (a) for dealing with employment income benefits and expenses.

ACCA Examining Team's Comments
Part (a) was very well answered, and there were many perfect answers. However, the following points should be noted when answering this style of question:

(1) If a question requires just a calculation of taxable income, then that is where candidates should stop. Calculating the income tax liability wastes valuable time.

(2) As stated in the requirements, candidates should always clearly indicate (by the use of a zero) any items which are not taxable or deductible – such as the employer pension scheme contribution and the disallowable subscription.

(3) Candidates should think carefully about which workings can be included as one-line calculations within the main taxable income computation, and which need their own separate working. The only aspects which warranted separate workings here were the mileage allowance and property income. These workings should always have a heading or be obviously identifiable. Just referencing adjustments to the bullet list numbers used in the question is not good exam technique.

(4) The use of abbreviated numbers, such as 15.6k instead of 15,600 for the reimbursed mileage, should be avoided.

(5) With a computation containing both additions and deductions, candidates should be very careful to indicate which is which. A single column approach with deductions shown in brackets avoids any confusion.

(6) Where a result is obvious, such as no personal allowance being available (because the adjusted net income of £362,420 exceeded £125,140), all that is needed is a zero entry. There is no need for an explanation or a calculation of the reduction to nil.

(7) Candidates need to appreciate that each source of income is self-contained. It is not correct to show all the receipts from each source first (such as rent receivable), and then all the various expenses lumped together (such as property income deductions). With a separate working for property income, just the one figure for property income should then be included in the main taxable income computation.

Although most candidates scored some marks for part (b), few achieved full marks. The three marks available for this section should have been a good indication as to the complexity of the requirement.

Marking guide

		Marks
(a)	Salary	0.5
	Bonuses	1
	Mileage allowance	
	– Reimbursed	0.5

– First 10,000 miles	0.5
– Remaining miles	0.5
Pension contributions	0.5
Professional subscription	0.5
Golf club membership	0.5
Property income	
– Rent received	0.5
– Washing machine	1
– Dishwasher	1
– Other expenses	0.5
– Furnished room	1
Savings income	2
Interest paid	1
Personal allowance	0.5
	__12__
(b) 2024/25 annual allowance used in 2024/25	1
2021/22 annual allowance used in 2024/25	0.5
2022/23 annual allowance carried forward to 2025/26	0.5
2023/24 annual allowance carried forward to 2025/26	1
	__3__
Total	__15__

(a) **Petula – Taxable income 2024/25**

	£
Employment income	
Salary	300,000
Bonuses (18,600 + 22,400)	41,000
Mileage allowance (W1)	8,350
Pension contributions	__0__
	349,350
Less: Professional subscription	(630)
Less: Golf club membership	__0__
	348,720
Property income (W2)	11,340
Savings income (250,000 at 3% × 4/12)	2,500
Less: Interest paid	__(140)__
	362,420
Less: Personal allowance	__(0)__
Taxable income	__362,420__

214 Taxation (TX – UK) FA 2024

> **Tutorial note.** The bonus of £21,200 will have been treated as being received 2023/24 because Petula became entitled to it during that tax year.
>
> Under the accrued income scheme, Petula must include the accrued interest as savings income for 2024/25, even though she has not received any actual interest.
>
> No personal allowance is available because Petula's adjusted net income of £362,420 exceeds £125,140.

Workings

1 **Taxable benefit**

	£
Reimbursement (26,000 at 60p)	15,600
Tax free amount	
10,000 miles at 45p	(4,500)
11,000 miles at 25p	(2,750)
Taxable benefit	8,350

2 **Property income**

	£
Rent received	12,000
Replacement furniture relief	
– Washing machine	(420)
– Dishwasher	0
Other expenses paid	(1,640)
	9,940
Furnished room £(8,900 – 7,500)	1,400
Property income	11,340

> **Tutorial note.** No relief is given for that part of the cost of the washer-dryer which represents an improvement over the original washing machine. Relief is therefore restricted to the cost of a similar washing machine.
>
> No relief is available for the cost of the dishwasher because this is an initial cost rather than the cost of a replacement. Claiming rent-a-room relief in respect of the furnished room is more beneficial than the normal basis of assessment £(8,900 – 2,890 = 6,010).

(b) **Annual allowances carried forward to 2025/26**

First work out the annual allowance used in 2024/25, remembering to use the current tax year allowance first and then the previous three tax years, earlier years first:

	£
Used in 2024/25	
Annual allowance 2024/25 (N1)	10,000
Brought forward from 2021/22	
£(40,000 – 25,000)	15,000
Annual allowance used in 2024/25	25,000

Then work out the remaining annual allowances carried forward to 2025/26:

	£
Carried forward from 2022/23	
£(40,000 – 25,000)	15,000
Carried forward from 2023/24 (N2)	
£(60,000 – 25,000)	35,000
Annual allowance carried forward to 2025/26	50,000

Notes.

1. Petula's adjusted income for 2024/25 exceeds £360,000 so she is only entitled to the minimum annual allowance for this tax year.
2. Tapering of the annual allowance does not apply in 2021/22, 2022/23 and 2023/24 as Petula's adjusted income did not exceed £240,000 in those years.

107 Dill (September/December 2017) (amended)

Course Book references

Residence, exempt income and the restriction of the personal allowance are covered in Chapter 2. Employment income is the subject of Chapters 3 and 4.

Pensions are dealt with in Chapter 5. Trading losses are covered in Chapter 10.

Top tips

In part (a), keep your points brief and relevant to the facts given in the question.

Easy marks

In part (b) there were some easy marks for calculating taxable benefits and identifying exempt benefits.

ACCA Examining Team's Comments

Part (a) for 3 marks required candidates to explain why Dill was treated as not resident in the UK for the tax year 2023/24. Although reasonably well answered, very few candidates managed to pick up all the available marks for this section.

For example, most candidates simply stated that Dill had been in the UK for 60 days, rather than indicating that this fell in the 46- to 90-day band from the tax tables. A number of candidates wasted time by explaining the automatically resident and not resident tests, when it was obvious that these were not relevant. Then, when discussing UK ties, some candidates focused on those ties which were not met, rather than those which were. The three marks available should have been a clear indication that a long, detailed, explanation was not required.

Part (b) for 12 marks required candidates to calculate Dill's taxable income for the tax year 2024/25. This section was generally answered very well, with many candidates achieving high marks.

Common problems included:

- Not appreciating that the benefit of a workplace nursery is an exempt benefit.
- Treating subscriptions as benefits rather than as deductions.
- Omitting the personal allowance. Even when shown, it was obvious (given the level of Dill's income) that the personal allowance was not available, so all that was needed was a zero entry. There was no need for an explanation or a calculation of the reduction to nil.

- If a question requires just a calculation of taxable income, then that is where candidates should stop. Calculating the income tax liability just wastes valuable time.
- As stated in the requirements, candidates should always clearly indicate (by the use of a zero) any items which are not taxable or deductible – such as exempt benefits, non-deductible expenses and exempt income.
- Where a computation contains additions and deductions, candidates should be very careful to indicate which is which. A single column approach with deductions shown in brackets avoids any confusion.
- Candidates should think carefully about which workings can be included as one-line calculations within the main taxable income computation, and which need their own separate working. The only aspects which warranted a separate working here was the mileage allowance.
- The use of abbreviated numbers such as 45.5k instead of 45,500 for the bonuses should be avoided.

Marking guide

		Marks
(a)	Sufficient ties test relevant	0.5
	Number of sufficient ties needed	0.5
	Identification of UK ties	1.5
	Conclusion	0.5
		3
(b)	Salary	0.5
	Bonuses	1
	Gym	0.5
	Home entertainment system	1
	Workplace nursery	0.5
	Beneficial loan	1.5
	Health club membership	0.5
	Mileage allowance	1.5
	Professional subscription	0.5
	Golf club membership	0.5
	Occupational pension contribution	1
	Premium bond prize	0.5
	Interest from savings certificate	0.5
	Loss	1.5
	Personal allowance	0.5
		12
Total		**15**

(a) **Dill – residence status in the tax year 2023/24**

The sufficient ties test is relevant since Dill does not meet either of the automatic tests.

As Dill spends between 46 and 90 days in the UK in the tax year 2023/24 and was previously UK resident in at least one of the previous three tax years, she will be UK resident in that tax year if she has three or more UK ties.

Dill has two UK ties:

- Available UK accommodation in which she spent at least one night during the tax year; and
- More than 90 days spent in the UK in either or both of the previous two tax years.

On this basis, Dill is not UK resident in the tax 2023/24 as she has less than three UK ties.

> **Tutorial note.** Dill is not automatically non-UK resident in the tax year 2023/24 since she spends at least 16 days in the UK in that tax year and was resident in the UK for one or more of the three previous tax years, and does not work full-time overseas.
>
> Dill is not automatically UK resident in the tax year 2023/24 since she does not spend at least 183 days in the UK in that tax year, has an overseas home as well as a UK home, and does not work full-time in the UK.
>
> Dill might have a third UK tie which is that she was present in the UK at midnight for the same or more days in that tax year than in any other country. However, there is insufficient information to conclude on this point.

 Videos can be viewed online by accessing your ebook version on VitalSource.

(b) **Dill – Taxable income 2024/25**

	£
Employment income	
Salary	430,000
Bonuses £(16,200 + 29,100)	45,300
Company gym	0
Home entertainment system £5,900 × 20%	1,180
Workplace nursery	0
Beneficial loan £96,000 × 2.25% × 10/12	1,800
Health club membership	990
Less:	
– Mileage allowance (W)	(1,625)
– Professional subscription	(560)
– Golf club membership	(0)
– Occupational pension scheme contribution	(10,000)
	467,085
Premium bond prize	0
Interest from savings certificates	0
Total income	467,085
Less loss relief against total income	(58,000)
Net income	409,085
Less personal allowance	(0)
Taxable income	409,085

Working

	£
10,000 miles @ 45p	4,500
4,500 miles @ 25p	1,125
	5,625
Less mileage allowance paid 16,000 @ 25p	(4,000)
Allowable deduction	1,625

> **Tutorial note.** The bonuses are treated as received on the earlier of the time when payment is made and the time when Dill became entitled to the bonuses. These are 1 November 2024 for the first bonus and 1 March 2025 for the second bonus. Therefore, both bonuses are taxable in the tax year 2024/25.
>
> The use of the company gym is an exempt benefit as provision of sporting or recreational facilities available to employees generally and not to the general public.
>
> The golf club membership is not deductible as it is not incurred wholly, necessarily and exclusively for the purposes of Dill's employment.
>
> The maximum occupational pension scheme contribution that Dill can make without triggering an annual allowance charge is £10,000 since she has adjusted income of at least £360,000.
>
> The loss relief cap is the greater of £50,000 and 25% of Dill's adjusted total income of £467,085 which is £116,771. Therefore, Dill can relieve the whole of her trading loss of £58,000.

108 Danh (March/June 2018)

> **Course Book references**
>
> Residence, computing taxable income and the income tax liability are covered in Chapter 2. Property business income is dealt with in Chapter 6. Computing trading income is covered in Chapter 7, capital allowances in Chapter 8 and the basis of assessment in Chapter 9. Trading losses are covered in Chapter 10 and partnerships in Chapter 11.
>
> **Top tips**
>
> In part (a), you need to deal with Danh's residence position for both the tax years 2022/23 and 2023/24. Don't waste time dealing with ties that Danh does not satisfy, just state the ones which are relevant.
>
> **Easy marks**
>
> There are easy marks in part (b) for dealing with adjustment of profit. Watch out for the computation of the capital allowance on the car as you need to think about what rate of capital allowance will be given, private use and the length of the period of account.
>
> **ACCA Examining Team's Comments**
>
> Part (a) for 3 marks required candidates to explain whether Danh was treated as resident or not resident in the UK for each of the tax years 2022/23 and 2023/24.
>
> This section was reasonably well answered, although a number of candidates did not appreciate that there would be one additional UK tie for the tax year 2023/24. This is often the case where a question covers two tax years since for the second year a taxpayer will have the additional UK tie of being in the UK for more than 90 days during the previous tax year.

Where a question makes it clear that that the tests of automatic residence and automatic non-residence are not relevant, then there is nothing to be gained from explaining why this is the case. It should have been quite obvious from reading the question that only residence based on UK ties needed to be considered. The three marks available for this section was a good indication as to the length of answer required.

Part (b) for 12 marks required candidates to calculate Danh's income tax liability for the tax year 2024/25. This section was very well answered, and there were many perfect responses. However, the following points should be noted when answering this style of question:

- Candidates should think carefully about which workings can be included as one-line calculations within the main computation and which need their own separate working. For example, the partnership loss calculation of £12,600 × 7/12 × 20% = 1,470 was easily included within the main computation which would have saved candidates time. The only aspects which warranted separate workings here were the trading profit and property income.

- As mentioned above, the calculation for the partnership loss was fairly straightforward. There was no need to work out the loss allocations for the other partners and such workings simply used valuable time.

- Practise as many computations as possible. If this is done, basic mistakes such as applying the car benefit rules rather than claiming capital allowances should be avoided.

- As stated in the requirements, candidates should always clearly indicate (by the use of a zero) any items which do not require adjustment – the accountancy fees were deductible when calculating the trading profit, but this needed to be indicated.

- With computations containing both additions and deductions, candidates should be very careful to indicate which is which. A single column approach with deductions shown in brackets should avoid any confusion.

- Candidates need to appreciate that each source of income is self-contained. It is not technically correct to show all the receipts from each source first (such as rent receivable), and then the various deductions shown later in the main computation (such as property income deductions). With a separate working for property income, just the one figure for property income should then be included in the main taxable income computation.

Marking guide

		Marks
(a)	2022/23	2
	2023/24	1
		3
(b)	Trading profit	
	– Depreciation	0.5
	– Motor expenses	1
	– Accountancy	0.5
	– Legal fees	0.5
	– Use of office	1
	– Capital allowances	2
	Property business income	
	– Rent received	0.5
	– Other expenses	0.5
	Qualifying interest	1
	Partnership loss	2
	Personal allowance	0.5
	Income tax @ 20%	0.5

Marking guide	Marks
Income tax @ 40%	0.5
Tax reducer	1
	12
Total	15

(a) **Danh – residence status in the tax years 2022/23 and 2023/24**

2022/23

Danh was not resident in the UK. Danh would be UK resident if he had three or more UK ties because he was in the UK between 91 and 120 days and was not UK resident in any of the previous three tax years. Danh had two ties which were available UK accommodation in which he spent at least one night during the tax year and substantive UK work.

2023/24

Danh was resident in the UK. Again, Danh would be UK resident if he had three or more UK ties. Danh had an additional tie which was that he spent more than 90 days in the UK in the previous tax year.

(b) **Danh – income tax liability 2024/25**

	£
Trading income (W1)	73,176
Property business income £14,400 – £3,980	10,420
Total income	83,596
Less:	
– Qualifying interest	(875)
– Partnership loss £12,600 × 7/12 × 20%	(1,470)
Net income	81,251
Less: Personal allowance	(12,570)
Taxable income	68,681
Tax	
£37,700 @ 20%	7,540
£(68,681 – 37,700) = £30,981 @ 40%	12,392
Less: Property finance costs tax reducer £10,000 × 20%	(2,000)
Income tax liability	17,932

Working

Trading profit for the eight-month period ended 5 April 2025

	£
Net profit	70,200
Add:	
– Depreciation	2,300
– Motor expenses private use £3,300 × 4,000/12,000	1,100
– Accountancy	0
– Legal fees in connection with grant of short new lease	1,460
Less:	
– Use of office £4,200 × 1/6	(700)
– Capital allowances £(14,800 × 18% × 8/12 × 8,000/12,000)	(1,184)
Trading profit	73,176

109 Martin (September/December 2018)

Course Book references

The income tax computation is the subject of Chapter 2. Employment income is covered in Chapters 3 and 4. Property income is the subject of Chapter 6. Partnerships are dealt with in Chapter 9. Self-assessment for individuals is covered in Chapter 17.

Top tips

Make sure you indicate with a zero if a benefit or income received is exempt or a deduction is not allowable.

Easy marks

There were easy marks for recognising taxable and exempt benefits.

ACCA Examining Team's Comments

Part (a) was very well answered, and there were many perfect responses. However, the following points should be noted when answering this style of question:

- Candidates should think carefully about which workings can be included as one-line calculations within the main computation and which need their own separate working. For example, there were two car benefit calculations which were easily included within the main computation. The only aspect which warranted a separate working here was the partnership trading profit.

- When calculating Martin's share of the partnership's trading profit, it was only necessary to deal with his share. The allocations made to the other two partners were not relevant.

- Practise as many computations as possible. If this is done, basic mistakes such as claiming capital allowances rather than applying the car benefit rules can be avoided.

- As stated in the requirements, candidates should always clearly indicate (by the use of a zero) any items which do not require adjustment. The beneficial loan and the interest on the maturity of savings certificates were exempt, but this needed to be indicated.

- With computations containing both additions and deductions, candidates should be very careful to indicate which is which. A single column approach with deductions shown in brackets avoids any confusion.
- Candidates should appreciate that if expenses are paid privately by an employee, then they cannot possibly be taxable benefits – only a potential deduction against taxable income. In this case, Martin had paid a professional subscription (which was relevant to his employment with Global plc) and a membership fee to a health club (which he used to entertain Global plc's clients). It was clearly stated that Global plc did not reimburse Martin for either of these costs.
- Being aware of which benefits are exempt, such as the beneficial loan not exceeding £10,000, will avoid spending time on unnecessary calculations.
- Reading and understanding a question's requirements will avoid spending a lot of time calculating an income tax liability when it is not needed. The requirement was just to calculate Martin's taxable income.

Part (b)(i) was not answered particularly well. The deadline was 31 January 2027, but too many candidates gave a date of 12 months following the submission of Martin's self-assessment tax return. Answers for TX – UK need to be precise, so the explanation how HMRC will calculate interest should have said that this will be from the original due date (31 January 2026) to the date that the additional tax is paid. A general discussion of how HMRC charges interest was not sufficient.

Although part (b)(ii) was better answered than part (b)(i), too many candidates wrote everything they knew on compliance checks rather than focusing on the information given – it being clearly stated that this was not a random check.

Candidates should note that detailed answers are not required where just a few marks are involved as was the case for both aspects of part (b).

Marking guide

	Marks
(a) Employment income	
– Salary	0.5
– Bonuses	1
– Car benefit 1st car	1
– Car benefit 2nd car	1
– Beneficial loan	0.5
– Home entertainment system	1
– Charitable payroll deductions	0.5
– Professional subscription	0.5
– Health club membership	0.5
Trading profit	
– April to December	1
– January to March	1
Property income	1
Dividend income	0.5
Savings certificate income	0.5
Personal allowance	0.5
	11
(b) (i) Deadline for amending tax return	1
Interest	1
	2

> **Marking guide** | **Marks**
>
> (ii) Compliance check notice — 1
> Reasons for check — 1
> — 2
>
> **Total** — **15**

(a) **Martin – taxable income 2024/25**

	£
Employment income	
Salary	144,000
Bonuses (21,400 + 13,700)	35,100
Car benefit 18,450 × 16% × 9/12	2,214
Car benefit 24,905 × 19% × 3/12	1,183
Beneficial loan	0
Home entertainment system (7,400 × 20%)	1,480
Charitable payroll deductions	(1,000)
Professional subscription	(560)
Health club membership	0
	182,417
Trading profit (working)	20,930
Property income (9,200 – 7,500)	1,700
Dividend income	440
Interest from savings certificate	0
Net income	205,487
Less: Personal allowance	0
Taxable income	205,487

> **Tutorial note.** The bonus of £18,200 will have been treated as being received during 2023/24 because Martin became entitled to it during that tax year.
>
> There is no taxable benefit in respect of the beneficial loan because it did not exceed £10,000 at any time during 2024/25. No personal allowance is available because Martin's adjusted net income of £205,487 exceeds £125,140.

Working

Trading profit

	£
1 April to 31 December 2024 (54,600 × 9/12 × 40%)	16,380
1 January to 31 March 2025 (54,600 × 3/12 × 1/3)	4,550
	20,930

(b) (i) Martin's deadline for amending his self-assessment tax return for the tax year 2024/25 will be 31 January 2027 (12 months from the latest (electronic) filing date for the return of 31 January 2026).

Should additional tax become payable, then interest will be charged from 31 January 2026 to the day before the additional tax is paid.

(ii) If HMRC intend to carry out a compliance check into Martin's self-assessment tax return for 2024/25, then they will have to notify him by 26 December 2026 (12 months after they receive his tax return).

HMRC will carry out a compliance check because of a suspicion that income has been undeclared, or deductions have been incorrectly claimed.

110 Tonie (March/June 2019)

Course Book references

The income tax computation, including residence and the accrued income scheme, is covered in Chapter 2. Employment income is dealt with in Chapters 3 and 4. Property income is the subject of Chapter 6.

Top tips

In part (a) you only need to discuss the relevant UK ties which Tonie satisfied, not all of them. Be guided by the fact that there were only two marks for this part.

Easy marks

There were some easy ½ marks for showing that the premium bond prize and the interest from savings certificates were exempt income – but would you have got them by using a zero in your computation?

ACCA Examining Team's Comments

Part (a) was reasonably well answered, although candidates sometimes did not focus their answers on the information given. For example, there was no point mentioning the UK ties which were not met by Tonie. The section was for just two marks, so this should have been a good indication that only a few brief sentences were required and not a half page discussion on everything a candidate knew about the residence rules.

Part (b) was well answered. However, candidates should avoid repetition by, for example, stating that Tonie (1) attended weekly meetings at Droid plc's offices, and (2) received instructions – these were both indications of control. When asked for a list it is easiest to answer using a list format.

With the exception of the accrued gilt income, part (c) was generally very well answered.

- Candidates should note that most of the workings for this style of question can be included within the main computation. For example, the mileage allowance deduction was easily included within the main computation. The only aspect which warranted a separate working here was property income.
- With computations containing both additions and deductions, candidates should be very careful to indicate which is which. A single column approach with deductions included as such on the spreadsheet avoids any confusion.
- Candidates should note that taxable income is after the personal allowance has been deducted.
- Reading and understanding a question's requirements will avoid spending time calculating an income tax liability when it is not needed. The requirement was just to calculate Tonie's taxable income.

Marking guide		Marks
(a)	Three ties needed	0.5
	Two ties identified	1.5
		2
(b)	½ mark for each factor	2
		2
(c)	Employment income	
	– Salary	0.5
	– Mileage allowance	1
	– Leasing costs	1
	Property income	
	– Rent received	0.5
	– Mortgage interest – no relief	1
	– Washing machine	1
	– Dishwasher	1
	– Other expenses	0.5
	– Furnished room	1
	Accrued interest scheme income	2
	Premium bond prize	0.5
	Savings certificate interest	0.5
	Personal allowance	0.5
		11
Total		15

(a) Tonie was previously resident and was in the UK between 46 and 90 days. She therefore needed three UK ties or more to be treated as UK resident. Tonie only had two UK ties, which were being in the UK for more than 90 days during the previous tax year, and spending more time in the UK than in any other country during 2023/24.

(b) The contract was for a relatively long period of time.

Tonie did not take any financial risk. Tonie only worked for Droid plc.

Tonie was required to do the work personally.

Droid plc exercised control over Tonie via the weekly meetings and instructions.

(c) **Tonie – taxable income 2024/25**

	£
Employment income	
– Salary (6,200 × 12)	74,400
– Mileage allowance (2,300 at 15p (60p – 45p))	345
– Less leasing costs (180 × 12)	(2,160)
Property income (working)	7,570
Savings income (100,000 at 3% × 5/12)	1,250

	£
Premium bond prize	0
Interest from savings certificate	0
	81,405
Less personal allowance	(12,570)
Taxable income	68,835

> **Tutorial note.** Under the accrued income scheme, Tonie must include the accrued interest from the gilts as savings income for 2024/25, even though she has not received any actual interest.

Working

Property income

	£
Rent received	10,080
Less mortgage interest – relief as tax reducer	(0)
Less: Replacement furniture relief	
– Washing machine	(380)
– Dishwasher	(0)
Less other expenses	(3,210)
	6,490
Furnished room (8,580 – 7,500)	1,080
Property income	7,570

> **Tutorial note.** No relief is given for that part of the cost of the washer-dryer which represents an improvement over the original washing machine. Relief is therefore restricted to the cost of a similar washing machine.
>
> No relief is available for the cost of the dishwasher because this is an initial cost rather than the cost of a replacement.
>
> Claiming rent-a-room relief in respect of the furnished room is more beneficial than the normal basis of assessment £(8,580 – 870 = 7,710).

11 Alicia (September/December 2022)

> **Course Book references**
>
> Employment income is covered in Chapter 3; benefits in Chapter 4; the income tax computation in Chapter 2; and NICs are dealt with in Chapter 12.
>
> **Top tips**
>
> For parts (a) and (b), working in the margin is easier and quicker than using a full calculation approach.
>
> **Easy marks**
>
> There were some easy marks for parts (a) and (b) for working in the margin.

ACCA Examining Team's Comments

Parts (a) and (b) were generally well answered, with many candidates achieving maximum marks. Part (c) was not so well answered. Typically, candidates simply compared the tax and NIC costs of each alternative, with the more aware candidates also bringing in the additional car running costs. However, this was sufficient for many candidates to achieve a good overall mark provided they did well at parts (a) and (b).

(a) Alicia will be taxed on a car benefit of £3,360 (£22,400 × 15%).

Alicia's marginal rate of income tax is 40%, so her additional income tax liability in respect of the car benefit for 2024/25 will be £1,344 (£3,360 at 40%).

There are no national insurance contribution (NIC) implications in respect of the car benefit for Alicia.

> **Tutorial note.** The relevant percentage for the car benefit is 15% because the car has CO_2 emissions of 51 grams per kilometre.
>
> There is no fuel benefit because fuel is not provided for private journeys.

(b) Alicia's additional income tax liability for 2024/25 will be £4,000 (10,000 at 40%).

Her additional employee class 1 NIC will be £200 (10,000 at 2%).

HM Revenue and Customs (HMRC) rate of approved mileage allowance for the first 10,000 business miles is 45p per mile, so the mileage allowance will be tax free with no expense claim possible.

(c) If Alicia is provided with a company car, then she will have an additional tax liability of £1,344.

Under the additional salary alternative:

	A	B
1	Additional salary	10,000
2	Mileage allowance (8,000 at 45p)	3,600
3	Income tax	(4,000)
4	Employee NIC	(200)
5	Additional running costs	(6,200)
6		3,200

The additional salary alternative is therefore the most beneficial to Alicia because she is £4,544 (1,344 + 3,200) better off.

112 Dom (September/December 2022)

> **Course Book references**
>
> Employment income is covered in Chapter 3; benefits in Chapter 4; the income tax computation in Chapter 2; and NICs are dealt with in Chapter 12.
>
> **Top tips**
>
> For part (a), make sure you time apportion the salaries from Abacus Ltd and Brass Ltd. These salaries are subject to Class 1 employees NIC.
>
> **Easy marks**
>
> There were some easy marks throughout the question. The NIC calculation is straightforward if brackets are used correctly in the calculation.
>
> **ACCA Examining Team's Comments**
>
> This question overall was very well answered, especially part (a). All of the workings can be included in the main computation. With separate workings, it is all too easy to forget to include the result in the main computation. The most efficient approach is to use the SUM function of the spreadsheet, although, for this to work, deductible figures have to be included as negative numbers.
>
> For part (b), candidates should avoid putting workings for a computation such as this NIC one within the one cell. Apart from being difficult to mark, it is all too easy to make a mistake with the incorrect use of brackets.

(a) **Dom – Income tax computation 2024/25**

	A	B	C
1	Abacus Ltd		£
2	Salary	Formula in C2: =64,800*4/12	21,600
3	Exam reward – Briefcase		100
4	Approved mileage allowance claim	900 miles at 10p (45p – 35p)	(90)
5	Brass Ltd		
6	Salary	Formula in C6: =76,800*8/12	51,200
7	Car benefit	Formula in C7: =25,200*(28% + 4%)*7/12	4,704
8	Car fuel benefit	Formula in C8: =27,800*32%*7/12	5,189
9	Workplace nursery		0
10	Professional subscription		(300)
11	Employment income		82,403
12	Savings income		700
13	Dividend income		1,500
14			84,603

15	Personal allowance		
16	Taxable income		72,033
17			
18	Income tax		
19		Formula in C19: =37,700*20%	7,540
20		Formula in C20: =(240*100/80)*20%	60
21		Formula in C21: =(C11 − 37,700 − 300 − 12,570)*40%	12,733
22		Formula in C22: =500*0%	0
23		Formula in C23: =(700 − 500)*40%	80
24		Formula in C24: =500*0%	0
25		Formula in C25: =(1,500 − 500)*33.75%	338
26	Tax liability	Formula in C26: =SUM(C19:C25)	20,751

Tutorial note. The provision of a place in a workplace nursery does not give rise to a taxable benefit if it is available to all employees.

(b) **Total employee class 1 NICs**

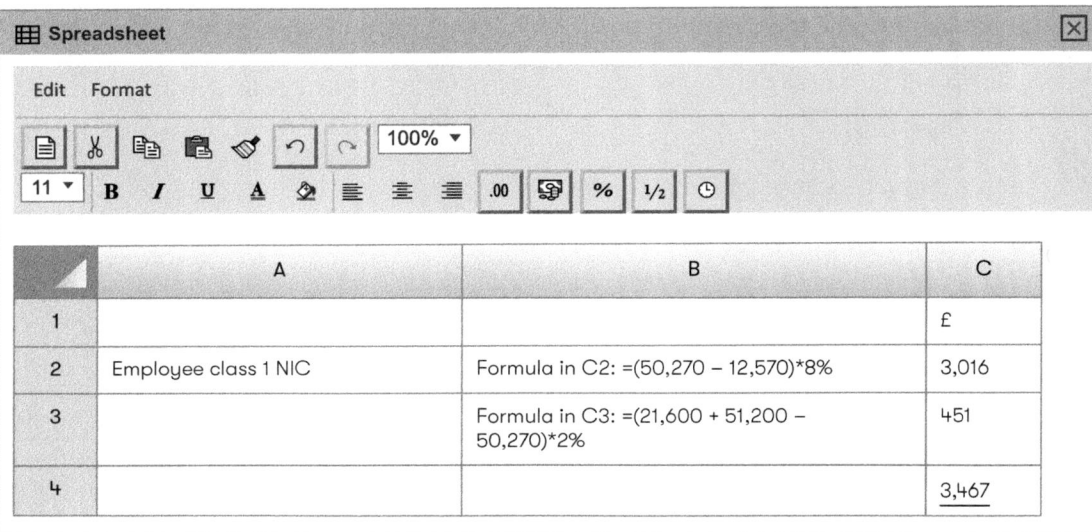

Tutorial note. Class 1 NIC is not due on benefits such as the briefcase provided as an exam reward.

(c)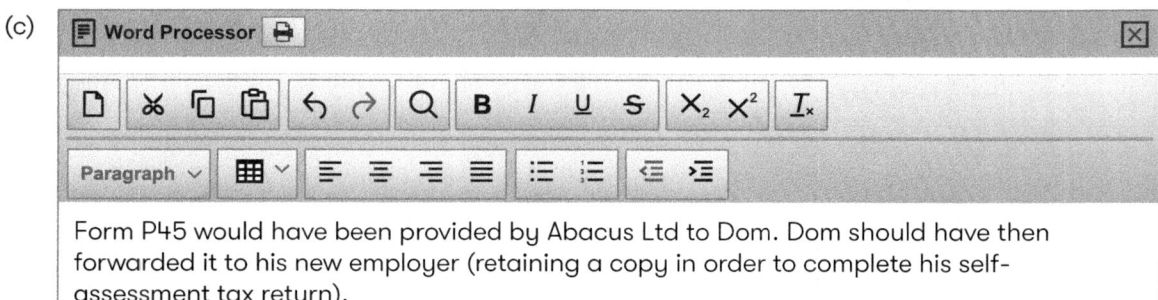

Part C: Chargeable gains for individuals

Section A

OTQ bank – Chargeable gains for individuals 1

113 The correct answer is: Gift of a motor boat valued at £10,000 (cost £5,000) to their aunt

The gift of the motor boat is exempt because this is a wasting chattel and is not plant and machinery eligible for capital allowances.

The gift of the unquoted shares is not a gift of tangible moveable property and so the chattels rules do not apply to it.

The gift of the antique jewellery is a gift of a non-wasting chattel but it would only be exempt if the proceeds (market value) were £6,000 or less. The gain cannot exceed 5/3 × (proceeds – £6,000).

The gift of the sculpture is a gift of a non-wasting chattel but results in a loss. The loss will be restricted by deeming the market value to be £6,000.

> **ACCA Examining Team's Comments**
>
> This question examines exempt gifts for capital gains tax purposes. The correct answer is gift of a motor boat valued at £10,000 (cost £5,000) to his aunt. This is an exempt gift because it is a wasting chattel (ie a tangible, movable asset with an expected life not exceeding 50 years). Wasting chattels (other than those eligible for capital allowances) are always treated as exempt disposals. The value and original cost are irrelevant.
>
> Answer option gift of unquoted shares in a United Kingdom company valued at £2,500 (cost £1,800) to his brother was the most commonly chosen, suggesting that candidates may not have known the special rules regarding chattels well enough.

114 The correct answer is: Gift holdover relief is available on the disposal of the interest in the partnership but not on the shares.

> **ACCA Examining Team's Comments**
>
> The correct answer is Gift holdover relief is only available on the disposal of the interest in the partnership; it is not available on the disposal of the shares because the shares are not held in a trading company.

115 The correct answer is: £2,635

	£
Chargeable gain	17,000
Less annual exempt amount	(3,000)
Taxable gains	14,000
Tax	
£(37,700 – 25,620) = 12,080 × 18% (residential property)	2,174
£(14,000 – 12,080) = 1,920 × 24% (residential property)	461
Total capital gains tax	2,635

The answer £3,360 uses 24% throughout. The answer £3,355 does not deduct the annual exempt amount. The answer £1,592 uses the rates of 10% and 20%.

116 £12,143

The amount of the cost attributable to the part sold is:

$$\frac{£36,000}{£36,000 + £90,000} \times £80,000 = £22,857$$

	£
Proceeds £(36,000 – 1,000)	35,000
Less cost (see above)	(22,857)
Gain	12,143

The answer £12,600 uses the net proceeds in the part disposal fraction. The answer £13,143 ignores the cost of disposal. The answer £11,000 uses 3/10 as the part disposal fraction.

117 The correct answer is: £11,400

	2022/23	2023/24	2024/25
	£	£	£
Gains	2,000	4,000	5,600
CY losses	(14,000)	(2,000)	(2,000)
	(12,000)	2,000	3,600
AEA	(0)	(2,000)	(3,000)
	0	0	600
B/f losses			(600)
Losses c/f	12,000	12,000	11,400

Current year losses must be set against current year gains. Brought forward losses are set off after the annual exempt amount.

118 £ 12,510

BRB remaining = £37,700 − £14,000 = £23,700

	Residential property £	Painting £
Chargeable gains	45,000	24,000
Annual exempt amount (best use, residential)	(3,000)	(0)
Taxable gain	42,000	24,000

	£
CGT payable	
£23,700 × 10%	2,370
£300 × 20%	60
£24,000	
£42,000 × 24% =	10,080
	12,510

119 The correct answer is: £1,667

	£
Proceeds	7,000
Less cost	(1,500)
Gain	5,500

The maximum gain is 5/3 × £(7,000 × 6,000) = £1,667.

The chargeable gain is the lower of £5,500 and £1,667, so it is £1,667.

The answer £1,000 is the excess over £6,000. The answer £0 assumes the chattel is an exempt asset.

120 The correct answers are:

The best use of the annual exempt amount is against the residential property gain first.	TRUE	
Any unused basic rate band should be used against the gain on disposal of the shares before the gain on the disposal of the residential property.	TRUE	
For disposal of the residential property, a payment on account must be made.	TRUE	
Any capital losses should be deducted from the gain on disposal of the shares in preference to the gain on residential property.		FALSE

121 The correct answers are:
- The annual exempt amount is deducted before any brought forward capital losses are utilised against current year gains.
- Excess current year capital losses are carried forward indefinitely until future chargeable gains arise.

> **ACCA Examining Team's Comments**
>
> Brought forward capital losses are deducted after the annual exempt amount (AEA) is deducted, thus ensuring that no AEA is wasted. Capital losses are generally not set against income but can be carried forward to be set off against future chargeable gains.

122 The correct answer is: £3,606

> **ACCA Examining Team's Comments**
>
> Because the asset being disposed of is a residential property, Naomi's chargeable gain will be taxed at 18%/24%, depending on how much of the basic rate band (BRB) is available. Naomi has taxable income (ie total income after personal allowance) of £29,500. The BRB is £37,700 but this is extended by the gross pension contribution of £2,500 (£2,000 × 100/80) to £40,200. Her taxable income therefore uses up £29,500 of this £40,200 leaving £10,700 BRB.
>
> The chargeable gain (ie before annual exempt amount (AEA)) is £20,700 against which the AEA of £3,000 can be deducted leaving a taxable gain of £17,700. Of this £17,700, £10,700 is within the remaining BRB and is taxable at 18% (tax of £1,926) and £7,000 is taxable at 24% (tax of £1,680) giving a total capital gains tax liability of £3,606.
>
> £4,326 forgets to deduct the AEA from the chargeable gain. (£10,700@18% + £10,000@24%)
>
> £3,756 forgets to extend the BRB by the gross pension contribution. (£8,200@18% + £9,500@24%)
>
> £4,476 does not deduct the AEA or extend the BRB. (£8,200@18% + £12,500@24%)

OTQ bank – Chargeable gains for individuals 2

123   £ 2,500

	£
Deemed proceeds	6,000
Less cost	(8,500)
Loss	(2,500)

124   14 years

	Exempt years	Chargeable years	Total years
Actual occupation	3		3
Deemed occupation – any time employed overseas	5		5
Actual occupation	2		2
Deemed occupation – up to 3 years any reason	3		3

	Exempt years	Chargeable years	Total years
Unoccupied		1	
Occupied (including last 9 months of ownership)	1	—	1
Totals	14	1	15

125 The correct answer is: 12 August 2034

When a depreciating asset is purchased to replace a non-depreciating asset the gain on the sale is deferred until the earliest of:

The sale of the depreciating asset – 14 October 2034

Ceasing to use the depreciating asset in a business – not applicable here

The ten-year anniversary of the purchase of the depreciating asset – 12 August 2034

126 £ 1,160

Gains subject to business asset disposal relief are taxed at 10%. Other gains will be reduced by the annual exempt amount and then taxed, in this case at 20%, because Louise has taxable income in excess of the basic rate limit of £37,700.

The capital gains tax (CGT) payable is therefore:

	£
£8,000 × 10%	800
£(4,800 – 3,000) = 1,800 × 20%	360
Total CGT	1,160

127 £ 13,650

	Number	Cost £
Purchase October 2004	1,000	1,500
Bonus issue November 2006		
1 for 2 bonus issue	500	0
	1,500	1,500
Rights issue July 2011		
3 for 1 rights issue @ £2.70	4,500	12,150
	6,000	13,650
Disposal February 2025	(6,000)	(13,650)

128 The correct answer is: £52,000

> **ACCA Examining Team's Comments**
>
> Lotte will claim rollover relief on the replacement of a business asset. The whole gain cannot be deferred as not all of the proceeds have been reinvested. As only part of the proceeds are reinvested, the gain equal to the amount which is not reinvested is chargeable immediately, in this case being £7,000 (71,000 – 64,000 = 7,000). This means that the gain which can be deferred is £12,000 (71,000 – 52,000) – 7,000 = 12,000) and therefore the base cost of the new asset is the amount reinvested less that gain which is rolled over/deferred £52,000 (64,000 – 12,000 = 52,000).
>
> The incorrect answers are:
>
> - £64,000 – (71,000 – 52,000) = £45,000 being the reinvested amount less the whole gain, ie no restriction on the amount of available rollover relief
> - £64,000 – (71,000 – 64,000) = £57,000 being the amount reinvested less the gain immediately chargeable to tax

129 The correct answer is: £16,200

	£
Proceeds	28,800
Less cost £21,000 × 9/15	(12,600)
Chargeable gain	16,200

A copyright is a wasting asset and so the cost is written down over its life on a straight-line basis.

130 £ 4,000

	£
Gain	15,100
Less current year loss	(10,000)
Net current year gain	5,100
Less annual exempt amount	(3,000)
	2,100
Less loss brought forward	(2,100)
Taxable gain	0
Loss carried forward £(6,100 – 2,100)	4,000

131 The correct answer is: £570

> **ACCA Examining Team's Comments**
>
> Brian has £7,270 of basic rate band available after taking account of his employment income (£43,000 less £12,570 = £30,430 of the basic rate band of £37,700 has been used up leaving £7,270). Brian's chargeable gain is £8,700 against which his annual exempt amount of £3,000 will be deducted leaving a taxable capital gain of £5,700. As all of this falls within the remaining basic rate band of £7,270, the £5,700 is taxed at 10% (the lower rate for capital gains tax) resulting in tax of £570.
>
> The incorrect answers are:
>
> £1,013 is the full chargeable gain of £8,700 (no annual exempt amount given) taxed at 10% for £7,270 and £1,430 at 20%; £1,740 is the full chargeable gain of £8,700 taxed at 20%; and £1,140 is the taxable gain (£8,700 less annual exemption £3,000) at 20% the higher rate of CGT.

132 The correct answers are:

1 August 2023	Earliest date
31 July 2027	Latest date

Section B

OT case – Aloi, Bon and Dinah (June 2011) (amended)

> **Course Book references**
>
> Business asset disposal relief is dealt with in Chapter 15. Shares are covered in Chapter 16. Transfers on death, computing chargeable gains and the calculation of capital gains tax will be found in Chapter 13.
>
> **Top tips**
>
> Par value means the face value of the shares. Aloi therefore had a cost of £50,000 for her first 50,000 £1 shares in Alphabet Ltd.
>
> **Easy marks**
>
> The dates should have been well known.

133 The correct answers are:

- Bon was not an officer or employee of Alphabet Ltd for the requisite time before disposal.
- Alphabet Ltd was not Dinah's personal company for the requisite time before disposal.

Bon only became a director on 1 February 2024, so this qualifying condition was not met for two years prior to the date of disposal. Her shareholding of 25% (25,000/100,000 × 100) means that Alphabet Ltd is her personal company and she also satisfies the minimum two years for this condition to be met prior to the date of disposal. Dinah was an employee for at least two years prior to the disposal but her shareholding of 3% (3,000/100,000 × 100) is less than the minimum required of 5% for Alphabet Ltd to be her personal company.

134 The correct answer is: £29,140

	£
Gain qualifying for business asset disposal relief	
Ordinary shares in Alphabet Ltd	
Proceeds of sale (60,000 × £6)	360,000
Less cost £(50,000 + 18,600)	(68,600)
Gain	291,400
CGT @ 10% on £291,400	29,140

135 The correct answers are:

5 October 2025	Notification
31 January 2026	Payment

136 The correct answer is: £34,320

	£
Deemed proceeds of sale (10,000 × £7.12 (W1))	71,200
Less cost (W2)	(36,880)
Gain	34,320

Workings

1 The shares in XYZ plc are valued at 7.10 + ½ × (7.14 − 7.10) = £7.12.

2 Following the takeover, Bon received 25,000 shares in XYZ plc. The cost of the original shareholding is passed on to the new shareholding so the cost attributable to the 10,000 shares sold is £36,880 (92,200 × 10,000/25,000).

137 The correct answer is: £0

There is no CGT liability on the sale of the XYZ plc shares as the gain of £5,000 (6,600 − (4,800 × 1,000/3,000)) is less than the annual exempt amount.

The transfer of the XYZ plc shares on Dinah's death is an exempt disposal.

OT case – Ginger, Innocent and Nigel (June 2013) (amended)

> **Course Book references**
>
> Chapter 13 covers the basics of computing chargeable gains. Chapter 15 deals with business reliefs.
>
> **Top tips**
>
> Think about why the disposals by Innocent and Nigel would give rise to different capital gains tax liabilities. Are there different rates of capital gains tax? When do those rates apply?
>
> **Easy marks**
>
> There were easy marks for working out the number of shares that could be sold without incurring a charge to CGT.

138 The correct answer is: £1.60

The disposal is at an undervalue, so only the gift element of the gain can be deferred under gift holdover relief. The consideration paid for each share will be immediately chargeable to capital gains tax to the extent that it exceeds the allowable cost. The chargeable amount is therefore £(4.00 − 2.40) = £1.60 per share.

139 The correct answer is: 8,506

Ginger's annual exempt amount for 2024/25 is £3,000 and she has a loss of £(10,100) brought forward from 2023/24. She can therefore sell (13,100/1.54) = 8,506 shares to her daughter without this resulting in any capital gains tax liability for 2024/25.

140 The correct answers are:
- There is a lifetime limit of £1,000,000 for business asset disposal relief.
- Business asset disposal relief is only available on shareholdings if they are held in a trading company.

The individual can be an officer (eg a director) or an employee of the company in which the shares are held. The conditions for business asset disposal relief must be satisfied for two years before the disposal.

141   £ 6,300

Innocent makes disposal

	£
Disposal proceeds	65,000
Less cost	(2,000)
Gain	63,000
CGT on £63,000 @ 10%	6,300

142   £ 6,840

Nigel makes disposal

	£
Disposal proceeds	65,000
Less cost (£46,200 × 2,000/3,000)	(30,800)
Gain	34,200
CGT on £34,200 @ 20%	6,840

OT case – Jerome (March/June 2016) (amended)

> **Course Book references**
>
> Computing chargeable gains is dealt with in Chapter 13. Chattels are covered in Chapter 14. Business reliefs are the subject of Chapter 15.
>
> **Top tips**
>
> If you are dealing with the disposal of a chattel, do not assume that the 5/3 rule always applies. Test it against the actual gain.
>
> **Easy marks**
>
> There were some easy marks for identifying the base cost of the house for Jerome's wife and for the administrative aspects of the election to hold over the gain on the Reward Ltd shares.

143   The correct answer is: £112,800

The disposal of the house does not give rise to a gain or a loss because it is a transfer between spouses. The base cost of the house for Jerome's wife is therefore Jerome's base cost which was the value of the house at the uncle's death.

144   £ 50,600

	£
Deemed proceeds	98,400
Less cost	(39,000)
Gain before gift holdover relief	59,400

Gift holdover relief is restricted to £50,600 (£59,400 × 460,000/540,000), being the proportion of chargeable business assets to chargeable assets.

145 The correct answers are:

5 April 2029	Latest date for election
Jerome and his son	Person(s) making election

146 £10,100

	£
Proceeds	12,200
Less cost	(2,100)
Chargeable gain	10,100

The maximum gain is 5/3 × £(12,200 × 6,000) = £10,333. The chargeable gain is the lower of £10,333 and £10,100, so it is £10,100.

If your choice was £3,900, make sure you do not confuse the rules on gains and the rules on losses – the deemed proceeds are only £6,000 for computing the restricted loss.

147 The correct answer is: £51,940

	£
Proceeds	78,400
Less cost (W)	(26,460)
Chargeable gain	51,940

Working

The amount of the cost attributable to the part sold is:

$$\frac{£78,400}{£78,400 + £33,600} \times £37,800 = £26,460$$

OT case – Hali and Goma (March/June 2019)

Course Book references

Capital gains tax (CGT) computation is covered in Chapter 13 and business reliefs in Chapter 15.

Top tips

Remember that current year losses are set against gains before the annual exempt amount (AEA), but brought forward losses are set against gains remaining after the AEA.

Easy marks

There were easy marks for knowledge of exempt assets for CGT.

148 The correct answer is:

Option	Hali £	Goma £
4	35,300	2,200

Hali

	£
Gains	7,000
Less: AEA	(3,000)
	4,000
Less: Losses b/f	(4,000)
	0
Losses c/f £(39,300 – 4,000)	35,300

Goma

	£
Gains	6,900
Less: Current year losses	(9,100)
Losses c/f	(2,200)

For Hali, the answer £32,300 ignores the annual exempt amount (£39,300 – £7,000). For Goma, the answer £13,000 uses the annual exempt amount first so that there are no gains left to relieve.

149 The correct answer is:

Option	Cost figure £	Value per share £
1	5,000	4.95

The transfer of the shares between Goma and Hali was on a no gain/ no loss basis so Hali's cost is Goma's cost of £1 per share (par value). His cost of 5,000 shares is therefore 5,000 × £1 = £5,000.

The answer £14,500 is the value of 5,000 shares at the time of the transfer between Goma and Hali.

The value per share is £4.95.

The answer £5.30 could be the market value per share. This is used where there is a sale which is not at arm's length but not just because Hali wanted a quick sale.

150 The correct answer is: Lima Ltd must be a trading company.

The first option is incorrect because the condition is that that they are either officers (could include company secretary, not just directors) or employees of the company.

The third option is incorrect because the condition is at least 5%.

The fourth option is incorrect because the qualifying period is two years.

151 The correct answer is: £45,600

	£
Proceeds (compensation received)	62,000
Less cost	(44,000)
Gain	18,000

All proceeds reinvested so whole gain can be rolled over into the cost of the replacement asset.

The base cost of the replacement antique table is £(63,600 – 18,000) = £45,600.

The answer £62,000 is the compensation received. The answer £63,200 is the cost of the replacement antique table (ie no roll-over). The answer £44,000 is the cost of the original table.

152 The correct answer is: Three

Qualifying corporate bonds sold for £38,300

A car (suitable for private use) sold for £11,600

Quoted shares held within an individual savings account (ISA) sold for £24,700

The antique vase sold for £6,200 is a chargeable asset but the restriction applies of the gain to 5/3 × proceeds.

The copyright (with an unexpired life of eight years when purchased) sold for £5,400 is a chargeable asset but the cost will be written down on a straight-line basis so that only the remaining eight years of cost will be available.

OT Case – Lily (March/June 2021)

153 The correct answer is: £17,600

> **ACCA Examining Team's Comments**
>
> The copyright is a wasting asset; a useful life of 50 years or less, and the original value will depreciate over time.
>
> £17,600 is the cost of £22,000 proportionate to the remaining life of the copyright
>
> £22,000 × 12/15 = £17,600
>
> The alternative, incorrect options are:
>
> £22,000 is the original cost.
>
> £4,400 is the value by which the asset has depreciated: 3/15 × 22,000 = £4,400.
>
> £19,067 is calculated using a remaining life of 13 years: 13/15 × 22,000 = £19,067.

154 The correct answer is: £73,200

> **ACCA Examining Team's Comments**
>
> The cost of the land originally purchased was for six acres but only four acres are sold. Unlike the copyright, the land is not a wasting asset, therefore the original cost must be apportioned proportionate to the current market value.
>
> The current market value is £200,000, being £140,000 (for the four acres sold) plus £60,000 (for the two acres not sold). Lily is also allowed to deduct any capital costs relating to the sale of this land; being the £14,400 for clearing and levelling those four acres.
>
> The correct answer is the second option £73,200, being the proportion of the original cost £84,000 × (140,000/200,000) = £58,800 plus the costs of clearing and levelling of £14,400 = £73,200.
>
> The alternative, incorrect answer options are:
>
> The first option apportions the clearing and levelling costs across the six acres (84,000 + 14,400) × 140,000/200,000 = £68,880.
>
> The third option apportions the cost by the number of acres and adds the capital cost (84,000 × 4/6) + 14,400 = £70,400.
>
> The fourth option takes the correct proportion of the original cost but does not add the capital costs (84,000 × 140,000/200,000) = £58,800.

155 The correct answer is: 145 months

> **ACCA Examining Team's Comments**
>
> The months of actual occupation are shown clearly as 32 + 20 = 52. The deemed occupation must be preceded and succeeded by periods of occupation, so the first period of 36 months is covered as absence for any reason (up to three years) and the second period of working elsewhere in the UK is covered for 48 months. The final period of travelling is not covered as deemed occupation since there was no actual occupation afterwards. However, nine months of the final period of ownership are covered as deemed occupation, even if not actually occupied.
>
> The correct answer is the first option 145 being, 32 + 20 + 36 + 48 + 9 = 145.
>
> The alternative, incorrect answer options are:
>
> The second option 157 gives the full period of working in the UK (32 + 20 + 36 + 60 + 9) = 157.
>
> The third option 168 gives the full period of ownership.
>
> The fourth option 136 forgets the last nine months (32 + 20 + 36 + 48) = 136.

156 The correct answer is: £11,880

> **ACCA Examining Team's Comments**
>
> The cash received on the takeover is treated as a part disposal and the original cost is apportioned according to current market value of £19,800 cash plus £48,400 (22,000 shares at £2.20) = £68,200. Applying this to the original cost of £27,780 gives £7,920 (£27,280 × £19,800/£68,200).
>
> The correct answer is £11,880, being proceeds of £19,800 cash, less apportioned cost of £7,920 = £11,880.
>
> The alternative, incorrect options are:
>
> £6,878 where the shares are valued at par and not current market value (19,800 − (27,280 × 19,800/(19,800 + 22,000)) = £6,878).
>
> £19,800 is the cash received.
>
> £8,640 apportions the cost by the market value of the shares only (19,800 − (27,280 × 19,800/(22,000 × 2.2) = £8,640).

157 The correct answer is: £27,244

> **ACCA Examining Team's Comments**
>
> Lily's sister has no taxable income for the year 2024/25 therefore her basic rate band is available. The chargeable gains (rather than taxable gains) are given and so the annual exempt amount (AEA) is also available of £3,000.
>
> It is more beneficial to set off the AEA against the residential gain; since residential property is subject to tax at 18% and 24%, whereas the other gain is taxed at 10% only.
>
> However, this gain qualifying for business asset disposal relief will use up the full basic rate band. So, this gain will be £44,200 which will be taxed at 10% = £4,420. The residential gain will be £98,100 less AEA of £3,000 = £95,100 which will be taxed at 24% = £22,824.
>
> The correct answer is £27,244, being £4,420 as above plus £22,824 as above = £27,244.
>
> The alternative incorrect options are:
>
> £27,964 forgets about AEA and correctly taxes the gain qualifying for business asset disposal relief (98,100 × 24% = £23,544 plus £4,420) = £27,964.
>
> £24,982 applies 18% to the £37,700 of the gain on residential property forgetting that the other gain will use this basic rate band first (£98,100 − £3,000 = £95,100 taxed as £37,700 × 18% = £6,786 and remaining £57,400 × 24% = £13,776 plus the gain of £44,200 at 10% = £4,420) = a total of £24,982.
>
> £27,664 applies the AEA against the gain qualifying for business asset disposal relief rather than against the residential gain. (£98,100 × 24% + ((£44,200 − £3,000) × 10%)) = £27,664.

Section C

158 Jorge (December 2011) (amended)

> **Course Book references**
> Chapter 13 deals with the basic computation of chargeable gains, including the annual exempt amount. Chapter 14 covers wasting assets, chattels, and the private residence exemption.
>
> **Top tips**
> Remember that deemed periods of occupation for private residence relief must usually be preceded by a period of actual occupation and followed by a period of actual occupation.
>
> **Easy marks**
> The painting and the car were easy half marks. Don't forget to deduct the annual exempt amount for another easy half mark.

Marking guide	Marks
House	
Proceeds	0.5
Cost	0.5
Enhancement expenditure	0.5
Period of exemption	3
Private residence exemption	1
Copyright	
Proceeds	0.5
Cost	1.5
Painting	0.5
Car	0.5
Annual exempt amount	0.5
Capital loss bf	1
	10
Total	10

Jorge – taxable gains computation 2024/25

	£
House (W1)	31,000
Copyright (W4)	24,300
Painting – exempt as proceeds and cost £6,000 or less	0
Car – exempt asset so loss not allowable	0
Chargeable gains	55,300
Less annual exempt amount	(3,000)
Less capital loss bf	(25,000)
Taxable gains	27,300

Workings

1 **House**

	£
Proceeds	308,000
Less cost	(93,000)
Less enhancement expenditure (defending title to property)	(5,000)
Gain	210,000
Less private residence exemption (W2)	(179,000)
Gain after exemptions	31,000

2 **Private residence exemption**

	Exempt months	Chargeable months	Total months
Actual occupation	34		34
Deemed occupation – up to 3 years any reason	18		18
Deemed occupation – any time employed overseas	24		24
Actual occupation	11		11
Deemed occupation – up to 4 years working elsewhere in UK	30		30
Deemed occupation – up to 3 years any reason balance (36 – 18) = 18, (22 – 18) = 4 chargeable	18	4	22
Deemed occupation – up to 4 years working elsewhere in UK balance (48 – 30) = 18, (26 – 18) = 8 chargeable	18	8	26
Actual occupation	17		17
Working overseas – not followed by actual occupation		12	12
Unoccupied – travelling		7	7
Last 9 months – always treated as period of occupation	9		9
Totals	179	31	210

Private residence exemption £210,000 × 179/210   £179,000

> **Tutorial note.** In calculating the private residence exemption, any periods of absence while working overseas, a maximum of four years' absence while working elsewhere in the UK, and a maximum of three years' absence for any reason are treated as deemed occupation, usually provided that they are preceded and followed by a period of actual occupation. The second period working overseas is therefore not a period of deemed occupation as it was not followed by a period of actual occupation.
>
> No letting relief is available since Jorge let out the whole property while he was away, rather than sharing occupation.

3 **Alternative approach**

An alternative approach to calculate the chargeable months as follows:

	Months
Total period of ownership	210
Less actual occupation (34 + 11 + 17)	(62)

	Months
Deemed occupation:	
– any reason up to 3 years	(36)
– employed overseas without limit	(24)
– working in UK up to 4 years	(48)
Last 9 months – always treated as period of occupation	(9)
Chargeable months	31

4 **Copyright**

	£
Proceeds	80,300
Less cost £70,000 × 8/10 (N)	(56,000)
Gain	24,300

Tutorial note. The copyright is a wasting asset. The cost of £70,000 must therefore be depreciated based on an unexpired life of ten years at the date of acquisition and an unexpired life of eight years at the date of disposal.

159 Winston (June 2012) (amended)

Course Book references

Chapter 13 covers transfers on death, computing chargeable gains, transfers between spouses, part disposals and CGT liability.

Chapter 15 includes business asset disposal relief.

Top tips

Losses on assets not qualifying for business asset disposal relief and the annual exempt amount should be deducted to produce the lowest CGT liability. This means that they should be deducted from gains taxed at 20% in priority to gains taxed at 10%.

Easy marks

The calculation of capital gains tax in part (a)(i) was straightforward.

Marking guide

			Marks
(a)	(i)	Annual exempt amount	1
		Unused basic rate band	0.5
		Capital gains tax	1.5
			3
	(ii)	Freehold shop	0.5
		Painting	0.5
		Capital loss	1
		Annual exempt amount	0.5
		Capital gains tax	1.5
			4

Marking guide	Marks
(b) Net proceeds	1
Cost – probate value taken over on transfer from spouse	1
Apportionment of cost	1
	3
Total	**10**

(a) (i) **Winston – CGT liability 2024/25**

	£
Chargeable gain on painting	38,260
Less annual exempt amount	(3,000)
Taxable gain	35,260
CGT liability:	
– £(37,700 – 25,100) = 12,600 @ 10%	1,260
– £(35,260 – 12,600) = 22,660 @ 20%	4,532
	5,792

(ii) **Winston – revised CGT liability 2024/25**

	£
Gain qualifying for business asset disposal relief	
Gain on freehold shop £(140,000 – 80,000)	60,000
Gain not qualifying for business asset disposal relief	
Painting	38,260
Less allowable loss on warehouse £(102,000 – 88,000)	(14,000)
Net gain	24,260
Less annual exempt amount	(3,000)
Taxable gain	21,260
CGT liability:	
– £60,000 @ 10%	6,000
– £21,260 @ 20%	4,252
	10,252

Tutorial note. The capital loss on the sale of the freehold warehouse and the annual exempt amount are set against the chargeable gain from the sale of the painting as this saves CGT at the higher rate of 20%. Although the warehouse is being sold with the business, it was never actually used in the business, and so this aspect of the sale does not qualify for business asset disposal relief.

> If it had been used in the business, the loss of £14,000 would have been deducted from the gain on the shop to give a net gain on sale of the business of £46,000. CGT would then be charged on £46,000 at 10%.
>
> The unused basic rate tax band of £12,600 is effectively used by the gain qualifying for business asset disposal relief of £60,000 even though this has no effect on the 10% tax rate.

(b) **Renaldo – chargeable gain 3 December 2024**

	£
Gross proceeds	92,000
Less auctioneers' commission (cost of disposal) £92,000 × 5%	(4,600)
Net proceeds	87,400
Less cost £28,600 × $\frac{92,000}{92,000 + 38,000}$	(20,240)
Chargeable gain	67,160

> **Tutorial note.** The cost of the land is £28,600 which is the value when Renaldo's father-in-law died. Renaldo would have taken over this cost when his wife transferred the land to him. The gross proceeds of sale are used in the part-disposal fraction.

160 Mick (June 2014) (amended)

> **Course Book references**
>
> The computation of chargeable gains for individuals is covered in Chapter 13. Shares are the subject of Chapter 16. Business reliefs are dealt with in Chapter 15.
>
> **Top tips**
>
> In part (b) you need to think about how you would use replacement of business asset relief and business asset disposal relief to identify the missing information.
>
> **Easy marks**
>
> The share pool in part (a) should have scored easy marks.

Marking guide	Marks
(a) Warehouse	
Disposal proceeds	0.5
Cost	0.5
Extension	0.5
Floor	0.5
Shares in Rolling Ltd	
Disposal proceeds	0.5
Purchase	0.5
Bonus issue	0.5
Disposal cost	0.5
	4

Marking guide

	Marks
(b) Warehouse	
Replacement of business assets relief	1
Acquisition date of new warehouse	1
Cost of new warehouse	1
Shares in Rolling Ltd	
Business asset disposal relief	1
Rolling Ltd share capital	1
Previous claims	1
	6
Total	**10**

(a) **Mick – chargeable gains 2024/25**

Freehold warehouse

	£	£
Disposal proceeds		522,000
Less:		
– Cost	258,000	
– Enhancement expenditure: extension	99,000	
– Enhancement expenditure: floor	0	
		(357,000)
Chargeable gain		165,000

> **Tutorial note.** The cost of replacing the warehouse's floor is revenue expenditure as the floor is a subsidiary part of the property.

Shares in Rolling Ltd

	£
Disposal proceeds	3,675,000
Less cost (W)	(537,600)
Chargeable gain	3,137,400

Working

Share pool

	Number	Cost
		£
Purchase June 2007	500,000	960,000
Bonus issue December 2012		
– 500,000 × 3/2	750,00	0

	Number	Cost
		£
Disposal September 2024	1,250,000	960,000
– 960,000 × 700,000/1,250,000	(700,000)	(537,600)
Balance carried forward	550,000	422,400

(b) **Freehold warehouse**

Replacement of business assets relief (rollover relief) may be available in respect of the chargeable gain arising on the disposal of the freehold warehouse.

The acquisition date of the replacement warehouse is required since relief will only be available if this is after 19 May 2023 (one year before the date of disposal).

The cost of the replacement warehouse is required since relief will be restricted if the sale proceeds of £522,000 have not been fully reinvested.

Shares in Rolling Ltd

Business asset disposal relief may be available in respect of the chargeable gain arising on the disposal of the shares in Rolling Ltd.

Details of Rolling Ltd's share capital are required, since relief will only be available if Mick had the minimum required holding of 5%.

Details of any previous business asset disposal relief claims made by Mick are required, since there is a lifetime limit of £1 million of gains.

161 Ruby (September/December 2015) (amended)

Course Book references

The computation of chargeable gains and capital gains tax is covered in Chapter 13.

Business reliefs are the subject of Chapter 15.

Shares are dealt with in Chapter 16.

Top tips

The annual exempt amount should be set against gains which do not qualify for investors' relief in priority to those which do qualify for the relief.

Easy marks

There were easy marks in part (a) for a basic computation of capital gains tax.

ACCA Examining Team's Comments

Part (a) of the question was well answered.

In part (b), the main problem was that candidates did not appreciate that both disposals would impact on the capital gains tax payable in respect of the disposal of the investment property.

The disposal of the shares in the unquoted trading company (qualifying for investors' relief) would utilise the remaining basic rate tax band, meaning that the 24% rate was now applicable. The capital loss arising on the disposal of the shares in the quoted trading company would be offset against the chargeable gain on the investment property.

Another common problem was the 50p nominal value of the shares in the quoted trading company. This did not impact on the calculation of the capital loss, although many candidates incorrectly divided their cost figure by two.

Marking guide

		Marks
(a)	Annual exempt amount	0.5
	CGT at 18%	1
	CGT at 24%	0.5
		2
(b)	**Pola Ltd**	
	Disposal proceeds	0.5
	Cost	0.5
	Investment property	0.5
	Annual exempt amount (best use)	1
	CGT at 10%	1
	CGT at 24%	1
	Aplo plc	
	Disposal proceeds	0.5
	Cost	1.5
	Investment property	0.5
	Annual exempt amount	0.5
	CGT at 18%	0.5
		8
Total		**10**

(a) **Ruby's CGT liability**

	£
Chargeable gain on investment property	37,700
Less annual exempt amount	(3,000)
	34,700
Capital gains tax	
£14,185 (37,700 – 23,515) @ 18% (residential property)	2,553
£20,515 (34,700 – 14,185) @ 24% (residential property)	4,924
	7,477

(b) **Choice of disposal**

Shareholding in Pola Ltd

	Investors' relief £	No reliefs £
Pola Ltd shares £(61,000 – 23,700)	37,300	
Investment property (part (a))		37,700
Less annual exempt amount (best use)		(3,000)
	37,300	34,700

	Investors' relief £	No reliefs £
Capital gains tax		
£37,300 @ 10%	3,730	
£34,700 @ 24%		8,328
Total CGT £(3,730 + 8,328)		12,058

Tutorial note. The shares in Pola Ltd qualify for investors' relief because they are shares in an unlisted trading company of which Ruby is neither an officer nor an employee, were subscribed for by Ruby on or after 17 March 2016 and held by her for at least three years before the disposal.

Shareholding in Aplo plc

	£
Aplo plc shares £59,000 – (40,000 × £2.15(W))	(27,000)
Investment property (part (a))	37,700
Less annual exempt amount	(3,000)
Taxable gain	7,700
Capital gains tax	
£7,700 @ 18%	1,386

Working

The Aplo plc shares are valued at £2.12 + ½ × (£2.18 – £2.12) = £2.15.

 Videos can be viewed online by accessing your ebook version on VitalSource.

Part D: Inheritance tax

Section A

OTQ bank – Inheritance tax 1

162 £ 150,000

	£
Before the gift: 70% shareholding	350,000
After the gift: 50% shareholding	(200,000)
Transfer of value	150,000

163 £461,250

	£
Sunita's unused nil rate band £325,000 × 65%	211,250
Joel's nil rate band	325,000
	536,250
Less used against Joel's PET now chargeable	(75,000)
Available nil rate band to set against Joel's death estate	461,250

Sunita's nil rate band is increased pro-rata to that available at the time of Joel's death.

The answer £325,000 does not involve a spouse transfer and does not take account of the PET. The answer £452,800 transfers 65% of £312,000. The answer £536,250 does not deduct the PET.

164 The correct answer is: £29,750

	£
Gift	190,000
Less AE × 2 (current year + b/f)	(6,000)
	184,000
Less nil rate band available £(325,000 – 260,000)	(65,000)
	119,000
IHT @ $^{20}/_{80}$	29,750

The answer £28,250 deducts annual exemptions from the earlier transfer. The answer £31,250 does not deduct annual exemptions from the current transfer. The answer £23,800 does not gross up, ie uses a rate of 20%.

165 The correct answer is: £0

The gift to the granddaughter is covered by the marriage exemption of £2,500 by a remoter ancestor.

The sale of the vase is not a transfer of value because there is no gratuitous intent as Donald and Alan believed that the vase was worth what Alan paid for it.

166 The correct answers are:

| £0 | June 2021 |
| £22,080 | November 2024 |

ACCA Examining Team's Comments

£0 is the IHT payable at the time of the gift in June 2021 since the gift is a potentially exempt transfer. £22,080 of IHT was payable by Petra at the time of Roman's death in November 2024. The gift of £400,000 will have been reduced by the £3,000 annual exemption for both the tax years 2021/22 and 2020/21 giving a value of £394,000. At the time of death in November 2024, being within seven years from the date of the gift, this amount will be reduced by the available nil rate band of £325,000 thus the value chargeable to tax becomes £394,000 – £325,000 = £69,000. The rate of tax on this is 40% but this is reduced by taper relief of 20% because the gift was made more than three but less than four years before death (these rates are given in the Tax Tables in the exam). Thus, the tax is £22,080 ((69,000 at 40%) less 20%).

The incorrect answers are:

£13,800 being the £69,000 at the lifetime tax rate of 20%

£15,000 with no lifetime allowances and taxed at the lifetime rate ((400,000 – 325,000) at 20%

£24,000 calculated without the lifetime allowances at death rates of 40%, less 20% taper relief ((400,000 – 325,000) at 40% less 20%)

£27,600 calculated with lifetime allowances but no taper relief given (400,000 – 6,000 – 325,000) at 40%).

OTQ bank – Inheritance tax 2

167 The correct answer is: £350

The gifts to the grandson are exempt as normal expenditure out of income because they are part of the normal expenditure of the donor, made out of income and left the donor with sufficient income to maintain her usual standard of living.

The small gifts exemption only applies to gifts up to £250 per donee per tax year. If gifts total more than £250, the whole amount is chargeable. Since the gifts to the grandnephew totalled £(100 + 250) = £350 in the year, this exemption does not apply.

168 £66,000

	£
Before the gift: 100% shareholding 1,000 × £150	150,000
After the gift: 70% shareholding 700 × £120	(84,000)
Transfer of value	66,000

169   £ 15,200

> **ACCA Examining Team's Comments**
>
> Firstly, a review of the lifetime gifts at time of death shows that the chargeable lifetime transfer (CLT) in October 2017 is more than seven years before death so that falls out of consideration.
>
> The CLT in June 2021 is within seven years of death so that will have to be reassessed on death. The NRB on death is £325,000, less the CLT in June 2021 of £118,000, gives a remaining NRB of £207,000.
>
> Death liability on the estate is therefore the chargeable death estate of £245,000 less the remaining NRB after reviewing the lifetime transfers of £207,000, giving a taxable estate of £38,000 at the death rate of 40% = £15,200.

170   £ 351,000

	£
Cash to nephews £200 × 5	1,000
ISA investments	350,000
Chargeable estate	351,000

The small gifts exemption only applies to lifetime transfers. The ISA exemption only applies for income tax and capital gains tax. The residue to the wife is covered by the spouse exemption.

171   The correct answer is: Sandeep is liable to make the payment by 31 May 2025

> **ACCA Examining Team's Comments**
>
> This question tested candidates' knowledge of the payment of IHT on a chargeable lifetime transfer (CLT) to a trust. The donor, Sandeep, is primarily liable for the tax due on a CLT and the due date is the later of the following:
>
> - Six months after the end of the month of transfer
> - 30 April after the end of the tax year of transfer
>
> The later of these dates is therefore 31 May 2025 and so the correct answer was the third option. Many candidates were able to select the correct date but were less successful in determining who was primarily liable for payment.
>
> Tax administration and the payment of tax are important aspects of the syllabus and candidates are reminded to devote sufficient attention to these topics when preparing for the TX – UK exam.

172 £234,000

	£
Estate	890,000
Less:	
– IHT	(276,000)
– Legacy to wife	(260,000)
– Legacy to brother	(120,000)
Residue to grandchildren	234,000

173 The correct answers are:

Changing the terms of her will so that the residue of her estate goes to her grandchildren rather than her children		WILL NOT ACHIEVE
Making lifetime gifts to trusts up to the value of the nil rate band every seven years	WILL ACHIEVE	
Changing the terms of her will so that the residue of her estate goes to her husband rather than her children	WILL ACHIEVE	
Making lifetime gifts to her grandchildren early in life	WILL ACHIEVE	

There will be the same amount of inheritance tax on the residue of the estate if it is left to Heng's children or grandchildren. However, if the estate is left to her husband the spouse exemption will apply. Heng could reduce the potential inheritance tax liability on her estate when she dies by making lifetime gifts to trusts up to the value of the nil rate band every seven years as these will reduce her assets and will not be cumulated if she survives seven years. She could also make lifetime gifts to her grandchildren early in life as these would be potentially exempt transfers and she is more likely to survive seven years the earlier in life she makes the gifts.

174 The correct answers are:

30 April 2021	In Yuna's lifetime
30 November 2024	As a result of Yuna's death

ACCA Examining Team's Comments

The correct answer for the lifetime gift is 30 April 2021 (being the later of 30 April following the end of the tax year of the transfer and six months after the end of the month of transfer) and as a result of Yuna's gift 30 November 2024 (being six months from the end of the month of death).

175 The correct answer is: £220,000

Nadia is entitled to her husband's residence nil rate band (as it was unused at the date of his death). It is assumed to be £175,000. The maximum residence nil rate band is therefore £(175,000 + 175,000) = £350,000.

The residence nil rate band is the lower of the maximum residence nil rate band of £350,000 and the net value of the main residence of £(360,000 – 140,000) = £220,000, ie £220,000.

176 The inheritance tax liability on Rachel's estate will [decrease] by [£70,000] if she leaves her main residence to her son rather than her brother.

The inheritance tax liability on Rachel's estate will decrease by £70,000 if she leaves her main residence to her son rather than her brother.

This is because the residence nil rate band will apply since Rachel will be leaving her main residence to a direct descendent. The available residence nil rate band is the lower of £175,000 and £300,000 ie £175,000. This gives a decrease in the inheritance tax liability of £175,000 × 40% = £70,000.

Section B

OT case – Dianne (September/December 2023)

177 £ 31,840

> **ACCA Examining Team's Comments**
>
> The correct answer is £31,840. Each gift made by Dianne's father within seven years of his death on 14 September 2023 is reviewed again and so both the gift on 4 May 2018 and 10 June 2018 need to be taken into account. The gift on 4 May 2018 will use £84,000 of the available nil rate band (NRB) leaving only £241,000 to reduce the gift on 10 June 2018. Thus, the amount chargeable is £199,000 (being 440,000 – 241,000) chargeable at 40% giving a liability of £79,600. This is further reduced by taper relief of 60%, because the gift in June 2018 was made more than 5 but less than 6 years before death. Thus, the answer is £79,600 less 60% = £31,840.

178 The correct answer is: £357,600

> **ACCA Examining Team's Comments**
>
> The correct answer is £357,600. Dianne's father's NRB has been used up by the potentially exempt transfers (PETs) within seven years of his death and his spouse (her mother) had used all of her NRB. The residence nil rate band (RNRB) is available as the main residence is left to Dianne (direct descendant) and so is the RNRB from her mother (since this had not been used). However, the total RNRB is restricted to the net value of the property which is £240,000. Thus, the answer is £(1,134,000 – 240,000 (RNRBs restricted)) × 40% = £357,600.
>
> The incorrect options are as follows:
>
> £313,600 which deducts the full RNRB for both mother and father £(1,134,000 – 350,000) × 40%
>
> £453,600 which does not deduct any RNRB £1,134,000 × 40%
>
> £383,600 which only deducts one amount of RNRB £(1,134,000 – 175,000) × 40%

179 The correct answers are:

- Capital gains tax payable in respect of the tax year 2022/23
- Credit card debts

> **ACCA Examining Team's Comments**
>
> The promise to pay the friend's legal fees is not legally enforceable, and the electricity bill was paid before the date of death.

180 The correct answer is:

Lifetime gift	Chargeable estate
31 March 2024	31 March 2024

The correct answer is 31 March 2024 for both the lifetime gift and the chargeable estate, both falling due six months after the end of the month in which the father died.

181 The correct answer is: £66,250

> **ACCA Examining Team's Comments**
>
> The correct answer is £66,250. On the date of the gift, Dianne has used up £70,000 of her NRB in respect of the chargeable lifetime transfer (CLT) to the trust on 10 June 2023; the PET does not use any NRB since this will only happen if Dianne dies within seven years of making the PET to her sister. This gives a chargeable amount of £265,000 (520,000 – (325,000 – 70,000)) and because Dianne is paying the tax on this gift to the trust the tax must be grossed up (265,000 × 20/80 = 66,250).
>
> The incorrect options are as follows:
>
> £73,750 where the PET to her sister reduces the NRB further (520,000 – (325,000 – 70,000 – 30,000)) × 20/80 = 73,750
>
> £53,000 where the tax on the CLT is only at 20%; not taking account of the fact that Dianne is paying the tax (520,000 – (325,000 – 70,000)) × 20% = 53,000
>
> £48,750 where the full NRB is given with no reduction for the CLT (520,000 – 325,000) × 20/80 = 48,750

OT case – Rishi and Nagina (March/June 2022) (amended)

182   £ 362,500

> **ACCA Examining Team's Comments**
>
> When calculating lifetime tax, the nil rate band at the date of gift should be used. Rishi has agreed to pay the IHT, so the rate is 25% (being 20% of the gift plus the tax, ie 20% × 100/80). Thus, the chargeable lifetime transfer of £355,000 less NRB of £325,000 at 25% gives tax of £7,500. This is the gross chargeable transfer being the value of the gift (after exemptions) plus the tax paid.
>
> £355,000 + £7,500 = £362,500

183   The correct answer is: £120,000

> **ACCA Examining Team's Comments**
>
> Before the gift, Rishi had 8,000 shares in Altion Ltd, a holding of 80%. Each of Rishi's shares before the gift therefore had a value of £30 per share.
>
> After the gift Rishi owned 6,000 shares in Altion Ltd, mean the holding had fallen to 60%. Each of his shares after the gift therefore had a value of £20 per share for IHT.
>
> | | £ |
> |---|---:|
> | Value of estate before gift (£30 × 8,000) | 240,000 |
> | Value of estate after gift (£20 × 6,000) | (120,000) |
> | Diminution in value | 120,000 |
>
> The incorrect options are as follows:
>
> £20,000 = 2,000 shares gifted at a value of £10 per share (for a 20% holding)
>
> £60,000 = 2,000 at a value of £30 (all valued at the 80% holding)
>
> £180,000 = 8,000 at £30 less 6,000 at a 20% holding value of £10

184 The correct answer is: £8,500

> **ACCA Examining Team's Comments**
>
> As this was a gift made to her grandchild, the marriage exemption available was £2,500. The gift will also qualify for the annual exemptions for the tax year 2020/21 and 2019/20. £2,500 + (2 × £3,000) = £8,500.
>
> The incorrect options are:
>
> £7,000 is the answer if a marriage allowance of only £1,000 is given.
>
> £6,000 is calculated by not allocating a marriage allowance.
>
> £5,500 is given if only the current year's annual exemption is claimed with £2,500 marriage allowance.

185 The correct answer is: £8,000

> **ACCA Examining Team's Comments**
>
> There were no previous chargeable transfers in the seven years before this gift, so the full nil rate band is available. As Nagina lived more than three years but less than four years from making the gift, taper relief is available to reduce the tax. The available reduction here is 20%.
>
> (PET of £350,000 less NRB of £325,000) at 40% = £10,000
>
> Less (20% × £10,000) = £8,000
>
> The incorrect options are as follows:
>
> £10,000 is the answer before deduction of taper relief.
>
> £140,000 is given by treating the nil rate band as not being available and not giving taper relief (£350,000 @40% = £140,000).
>
> £112,000 is given by treating the nil rate band as being unavailable but giving a deduction for taper relief (£350,000 @ 40% × 80% = £112,000).

186 The correct answers are:

Grandson	By whom paid
31 December 2024	Due date

> **ACCA Examining Team's Comments**
>
> The correct answer is death tax on lifetime gifts made by the deceased individual is paid by the recipient of the gift. Thus, it is payable by the **Grandson**. It is due six months from the end of the month of death; the end of the month of death was 30 June 2024 and therefore six months after this is 31 **December 2024**.
>
> Death tax is payable by the executors of the estate only on the estate left by the deceased individual.

OT case – Zoe and Luke (June 2015) (amended)

> **Course Book reference**
>
> Inheritance tax is the subject of Chapter 18.
>
> **Top tips**
>
> Be careful to read the question thoroughly. You were told that Zoe always used her annual exemption in April each year.
>
> **Easy marks**
>
> There were some easy marks for working out the additional IHT due.

187 The correct answers are:

- The payments could be exempt without any cash limit under the normal expenditure out of income exemption.
- The payments must have left Luke with sufficient income to maintain his usual standard of living to qualify for the normal expenditure out of income exemption.

Payments can qualify for the normal expenditure out of income exemption even if they are not paid directly to the individual who benefits from them. The payments did not have been reported each tax year to HM Revenue & Customs in Luke's income tax return to qualify for the normal expenditure out of income exemption (they will be reported in the inheritance tax account submitted on Luke's death).

188 The correct answer is: £710,000

	£
Net chargeable transfer (AEs already used)	633,000
IHT	
£325,000 × 0%	0
£308,000 × 20/80	77,000
£633,000	77,000
Gross chargeable transfer £(633,000 + 77,000)	710,000

The answer £702,500 deducts two annual exemptions. The answer £694,600 treats the transfer as a gross chargeable transfer so uses the rate of 20%. The answer £756,200 uses the death rate of 40%.

189   £24,000

	£
Gross chargeable transfer	200,000
IHT on death (nil rate band already used)	
£200,000 × 40%	80,000
Less taper relief (3 to 4 years) £80,000 × 20%	(16,000)
	64,000
Less lifetime tax £200,000 × 20%	(40,000)
Additional IHT payable	24,000

The answer £40,000 does not deduct taper relief. The answer £80,000 is the death tax without deducting taper relief or lifetime tax. The answer £64,000 does not deduct lifetime tax.

190   £259,000

	£
Gift	270,000
Less:	
– Marriage exemption	(5,000)
– Annual exemption current year	(3,000)
– Annual exemption b/f	(3,000)
Potentially exempt transfer	259,000

191   The correct answer is: £75,000

	£
Unused nil rate band at wife's death £(312,000 – 240,000)	72,000
Amount to transfer £325,000 × 72,000/312,000	75,000

The answer £72,000 does not adjust for the change in the nil rate band between the death of Luke's wife and Luke. The answer £312,000 is the nil rate band at the date of Luke's wife's death. The answer £325,000 is the nil rate band at Luke's death.

OT case – Marcus (September/December 2015) (amended)

> **Course Book references**
>
> Inheritance tax is dealt with in Chapter 18.
>
> **Top tips**
>
> Don't mix up the rules for transfers between spouses for capital gains tax (no gain/no loss transfer) and inheritance tax (exempt transfer).
>
> **Easy marks**
>
> There were some easy marks for a basic inheritance tax computation provided that you remembered that the nil rate band at the date of the transfer should be used.

192 £ 600

	£		£
IHT	325,000	× 0% =	Nil
	3,000	× 20% =	600
	328,000		600

193 The correct answer is: £98,250

	£		£
IHT	0	(325,000 − 328,000) × 0% =	Nil
	491,250	× 20% =	98,250
	491,250		98,250

Although Marcus pays the inheritance tax due, since the gross chargeable transfer is given, to work out the tax he pays, this is 20% of the excess over the available nil rate band.

The answer £122,812 grosses up (ie uses 20/80). The answer £33,250 uses the full nil rate band. The answer £41,562 uses the full nil rate band and grosses up.

194 £78,600

	£		£
IHT	0	× 0% =	Nil
	491,250	× 40% =	196,500
	491,250		196,500
Taper relief (4 to 5 years) £196,500 @ 40%			78,600

The answer £117,900 is the tax payable after taper relief. The answer £26,600 does not take account of the brought forward transfer. The answer £39,900 is does not take account of the brought forward transfer and is the tax payable after taper relief.

195 The correct answer is: £570,000

	£
Before: 100,000 × £12	1,200,000
After: 70,000 × £9	(630,000)
Potentially exempt transfer of value	570,000

The answer £360,000 is 30,000 shares at £12 each. The answer £270,000 is 30,000 shares at £9 each. The answer £150,000 is 30,000 shares at £5 each.

196 The correct answers are:
- If Barbara remarries, any unused nil rate band on her death can be transferred to her spouse if they survive her.
- The transfer of Marcus's estate to Barbara on his death is an exempt transfer.

Married couples (and registered civil partnerships) are not chargeable persons for inheritance tax (IHT) purposes, because each spouse (or civil partner) is taxed separately.

The gift of the land on 29 June 2022 by Marcus to Barbara is an exempt transfer.

OT case – Lebna and Lulu (March/June 2019)

> **Course Book references**
>
> Inheritance tax (IHT) is the subject of Chapter 18.
>
> **Top tips**
>
> Remember that IHT is charged on the diminution of the donor's estate, not on the value of the property transferred.
>
> **Easy marks**
>
> The taper relief percentage will be found in the Tax Rates and Allowances in the exam, and you should have known the payment date for IHT as a result of death.

197 The correct answer is: £205,000

	£
Nil rate band at Lulu's death	325,000
Less: PET now chargeable (within 7 years of death)	(80,000)
Legacy to brother	(40,000)
Lulu's nil rate band for transfer to Lebna	205,000

Since the nil rate band at the date of both Lulu's and Lebna's death is the same (£325,000) there is no need to adjust the amount available to transfer.

The chargeable lifetime transfer (CLT) is more than seven years before Lulu's death and is therefore not cumulated on death. It would be cumulated to work out any inheritance tax on the PET (although in this case the cumulative amount would be within the nil rate band at Lulu's death and so no tax would be payable on the PET).

The answer £155,000 cumulates the CLT. The answer £35,000 deducts the PET twice, the legacy twice and the CLT once. The answer £285,000 only deducts the legacy.

198 The correct answer is: £188,000

	£	£
Lebna's available RNRB is lower of:		
– Value of house	340,000	
– Less mortgage	(152,000)	
		188,000
Maximum RNRB at date of death = £175,000	175,000	
Lulu's RNRB	175,000	
Maximum RNRB		350,000
Available RNRB		188,000

The whole of Lulu's RNRB is available for transfer because she died before 6 April 2017 (so even if she had had a main residence at her death, it could not have been used since this was the date of introduction of the RNRB). It is not necessary that Lulu had a main residence at her death, the condition is that Lebnar has a main residence at his death which he leaves to a direct descendent (his son).

The answer £175,000 is just Lebna's RNRB. The answer £350,000 is the maximum RNRB. The answer £340,000 is the gross value of Lebna's main residence.

199 The correct answer is: £536,000

	£
Before transfer: 100,000 @ £7.10	710,000
Less After transfer: 40,000 @ £4.20	(168,000)
Transfer of value (diminution in value)	542,000
Less Current year and previous year annual exemptions £3,000 × 2	(6,000)
Potentially exempt transfer	536,000

The answer £542,000 does not deduct the annual exemptions (make sure you read the question carefully if you chose this answer!). The answer £372,000 is the value of the gifted holding (60,000 @ £6.30) less annual exemptions. The answer £378,000 is just the value of the gifted holding.

200 The correct answer is: Option 1

The period between the date of the PET (22 February 2020) and the date of Lebna's death (1 March 2025) is between five and six years so the taper relief reduction is 60% (in the Tax Rates and Allowance available in the exam).

The answer 40% is the amount of the transfer on which tax will be charged at the death rate.

The due date for payable of death tax on a PET is the end of six months following the month of death which is 30 September 2025.

The answer 1 September 2025 is exactly six months from the date of Lebna's death.

201 The correct answer is: £225

Only the gift of £225 is exempt under the small gifts exemption. The limit of £250 applies per donee per tax year so the gifts of £(85 + 190) = £275 and £490 both exceed the limit. The answer £500 exempts the gifts of £85, £225 and £190. The answer £990 exempts all the gifts. The answer £275 exempts the gifts of £85 and £190.

Section C

202 Pere and Phil (June 2013) (amended)

> **Course Book references**
> Inheritance tax is dealt with in Chapter 18. Chargeable gains and the computation of capital gains tax are in Chapter 13. The points on distinguishing between revenue and capital expenditure are covered in Chapter 7.
>
> **Top tips**
> You don't need to know names of tax cases in the Taxation (TX – UK) exam, but you are expected to know, and be able to apply, the principles decided, as in part (b) here.
>
> **Easy marks**
> There were some easy marks in part (a) for using the exemptions.

Marking guide

	Marks
(a) Lifetime gift	
Marriage exemption	1
Annual exemption – current year	0.5
Annual exemption – brought forward	0.5
Potentially exempt transfer	0.5
IHT @ 0%	0.5
IHT @ 40%	0.5
Taper relief	1
Death estate	
Spouse exemption	1
IHT @ 40%	0.5
	6
(b) Disposal proceeds	0.5
Cost	1
Enhancement	1
Annual exempt amount	0.5
Capital gains tax @ 18%	0.5
Capital gains tax @ 24%	0.5
	4
Total	**10**

(a) **Pere – Inheritance tax (IHT) arising on death**

Lifetime transfer 23 August 2018

	£
Gift	420,000
Less	
– Marriage exemption	(5,000)

	£
– Annual exemption current year	(3,000)
– Annual exemption b/f	(3,000)
Potentially exempt transfer	409,000
IHT	
£325,000 @ 0%	0
£84,000 @ 40%	33,600
£409,000	
Less taper relief (6 to 7 years @ 80%)	(26,880)
IHT payable	6,720

> **Tutorial note.** The potentially exempt transfer becomes chargeable as a result of Pere dying within seven years of making it.

Death estate

	£
Value of estate	880,000
Less spouse exemption £880,000/2	(440,000)
Chargeable estate	440,000
IHT on £440,000 @ 40%	176,000

(b) **Phil – capital gains tax computation 2024/25**

	£
Net disposal proceeds	487,400
Less:	
– Cost	(420,000)
– Enhancement expenditure	(5,200)
Gain	62,200
Less annual exempt amount	(3,000)
Taxable gain	59,200
CGT on £23,550 (37,700 – 14,150) @ 18%	4,239
CGT on £35,650 (59,200 – 23,550) @ 24%	8,556
	12,795

> **Tutorial note.** The cost of replacing the property's chimney is revenue expenditure because the chimney is a part of the house and so this is a repair to the house. The cost of the new boundary wall is capital expenditure because the wall is a separate structure which is not part of the house.
>
> Because the house is residential property, the gain is taxed at 18% and 24% rather than 10% and 20%.

203 Afiya (December 2013) (amended)

> **Course Book references**
>
> Inheritance tax is covered in Chapter 18.
>
> **Top tips**
>
> A potentially exempt transfer is treated as if it were an exempt transfer during the lifetime of the donor, so it does not affect the computation of lifetime tax on subsequent chargeable lifetime transfers.
>
> **Easy marks**
>
> The calculation of the residue in part (b) was an easy mark.

Marking guide	Marks
(a) Lifetime transfers	
Cassava Ltd shares	
– Value of shares before transfer	1
– Value of shares after transfer	1
– Annual exemption current year	0.5
– Annual exemption brought forward	0.5
Cash	
– Nil rate band	0.5
– Balance @ 20/80	0.5
Additional liabilities arising on death	
Cassava Ltd shares	
– Potentially exempt transfer now chargeable	1
Cash	
– Gross chargeable transfer	0.5
– Nil rate band	0.5
– Balance @ 40%	0.5
– Lifetime tax already paid	0.5
Death tax	
Value of estate	0.5
Spouse exemption	0.5
Residence nil rate band	0.5
Charge @ 40%	0.5
	9
(b) Residue of estate	1
Total	10

(a) **Afiya – Inheritance tax on death**

Lifetime transfers

14 September 2023

	£
Value of shares held before transfer 8,000 × £8	64,000
Less value of shares held after transfer 1,500 × £3	(4,500)
Transfer of value	59,500
Less:	
– Annual exemption current year	(3,000)
– Annual exemption b/f	(3,000)
Potentially exempt transfer	53,500

27 January 2024

	£
Net chargeable transfer	400,000
IHT	
325,000 × 0%	0
75,000 × 20/80 (donor pays tax)	18,750
400,000	18,750
Gross chargeable transfer £(400,000 + 18,750)	418,750

Additional tax on lifetime transfer on death of donor

14 September 2023

Potentially exempt transfer of £53,500 becomes chargeable as donor dies within seven years.

Within nil rate band at death, no tax to pay.

27 January 2024

Nil rate band available £(325,000 – 53,500) = £271,500.

	£
Gross chargeable transfer	418,750
IHT	
271,500 × 0%	0
147,250 × 40%	58,900
418,750	58,900
No taper relief (death within three years of transfer)	
Less lifetime tax paid	(18,750)
Additional tax payable on death	40,150

Death estate	£
Assets at death	623,000
Less funeral expenses	(3,000)
Value of estate for IHT purposes	620,000
Less exempt legacy to spouse	(150,000)
Chargeable estate	470,000
Less residence NRB (lower of £90,000 and £175,000)	(90,000)
Taxable estate	380,000
IHT liability £380,000 × 40%	152,000

The nil rate band was used by lifetime transfers.

(b) Her children inherit the residue of £(620,000 − 150,000 − 40,000 − 152,000) = **£278,000**

204 Kendra (June 2014) (amended)

> **Course Book references**
> Inheritance tax is covered in Chapter 18.
>
> **Top tips**
> Lifetime gifts may involve both inheritance tax and capital gains tax.
>
> Sometimes it will be preferable for a gift to be made on death since there is no capital gains tax charge on death and the assets will pass to the beneficiary at death (probate) value.
>
> **Easy marks**
> The calculation of the death estate should have been easy marks.

Marking guide		Marks
(a)	Property	0.5
	Building society deposits	0.5
	ISAs	0.5
	NS&I certificates	0.5
	Proceeds of life assurance policy	1
	Income tax	0.5
	Loan	0.5
	Inheritance tax	1
		5
(b)	No IHT benefit	1.5
	No CGT benefit	1.5
		3
(c)	Skip a generation	1
	Avoids double charge to IHT	1
		2
Total		**10**

(a) **Kendra – inheritance tax on death**

	£
Property	970,000
Building society deposits	387,000
Individual savings accounts	39,000
NS&I certificates	17,000
Proceeds of life policy	225,000
Gross estate	1,638,000
Less:	
– Income tax	(12,800)
– Loan	(1,200)
Net estate	1,624,000
Inheritance tax	
£325,000 @ 0%	0
£1,299,000 @ 40%	519,600
Inheritance tax liability	519,600

(b) As the property is not expected to increase in value in the near future, there is no inheritance tax benefit in making a lifetime gift. Kendra would need to live for three more years for taper relief to be available.

Also, a lifetime gift would result in a capital gains tax liability of £41,760 (£174,000 at 24%) for 2024/25, whereas a transfer on death would be an exempt disposal.

(c) It can be beneficial to skip a generation so that gifts are made to grandchildren rather than children, particularly if the children already have significant assets.

This avoids a further charge to inheritance tax when the children die. Gifts will then only be taxed once before being inherited by the grandchildren, rather than twice.

205 James (March/June 2016)

> **Course Book references**
> Chapter 18 deals with inheritance tax.
>
> **Top tips**
> When working out the inheritance death tax on the lifetime transfer, remember to look back seven years from the date of the lifetime transfer (not the date of death) to see whether there are any previous transfers to cumulate.
>
> **Easy marks**
> The nil rate band is used up on the first gift so the calculation of the inheritance tax on the CLT and death estate are easy.

Marking guide	Marks
(a) Potentially exempt transfer (after annual exemptions)	1
Nil rate band available	1.5

Inheritance tax		0.5
Daughter to pay		0.5
Chargeable lifetime transfer		0.5
Inheritance tax		0.5
Trustees to pay		0.5
Death estate – IHT liability		0.5
James's personal representatives to pay		0.5
		6
(b) Avoidance of double taxation		2
		2
(c) Taper relief		0.5
Lifetime transfer values fixed		0.5
IHT saving		1
		2
Total		**10**

(a) **James – Inheritance tax arising on death**

Lifetime transfers within seven years of death

14 May 2023

	£
Gift	420,000
Less:	
– Annual exemption – current year	(3,000)
– Annual exemption – b/f	(3,000)
Potentially exempt transfer	414,000
Inheritance tax liability	
– £296,000 (W) @ 0%	0
– £118,000 @ 40%	47,200
	47,200

James's daughter will be responsible for paying the inheritance tax of £47,200.

2 August 2023

	£
Chargeable lifetime transfer	260,000
Inheritance tax liability £260,000 @ 40%	104,000

The trustees will be responsible for paying the inheritance tax of £104,000.

Death estate

	£
Chargeable estate	870,000
Inheritance tax liability £870,000 @ 40%	348,000

The personal representatives of James's estate will be responsible for paying the inheritance tax of £348,000.

Working

Available nil rate band

	£	£
Nil rate band at date of death		325,000
Gift 9 October 2017	35,000	
Less:		
– Annual exemption – current year	(3,000)	
– Annual exemption – b/f	(3,000)	(29,000)
Nil rate band available		296,000

(b) Skipping a generation avoids a further charge to inheritance tax when the children die. Gifts will then only be taxed once before being inherited by the grandchildren, rather than twice.

(c) Even if the donor does not survive for seven years, taper relief will reduce the amount of IHT payable after three years.

The value of potentially exempt transfers and chargeable lifetime transfers are fixed at the time they are made.

James therefore saved inheritance tax of £20,000 (£(310,000 – 260,000) @ 40%) by making the lifetime gift of property.

206 Dembe (March/June 2019)

Course Book references

The income tax computation is covered in Chapter 2 and pensions in Chapter 5. Chargeable gains computation is dealt with in Chapter 13. Inheritance tax is the subject of Chapter 18.

Top tips

In part (c) think about the nil rate bands available for each spouse. What happens if the first spouse dies without using up their nil rate bands?

Easy marks

There were some easy marks for basic computation of capital gains tax in part (b) but you should make sure that you clearly show which individual is making the disposal in each case.

ACCA Examining Team's Comments

Although there were some good answers to part (a), many candidates used up valuable time by producing full tax computations. The question stated that these were not required, indicating that workings were to be done at the margin.

Many candidates did not appreciate that the personal pension contribution would have no impact on NICs. This fact should have just been stated, without any need to perform calculations. Many candidates did not realise that the personal pension contribution would bring Dembe's adjusted net income down from £125,140, to less than £100,000. Therefore, the personal allowance would have been fully reinstated. This shows the importance of carefully considering the impact of all the information provided.

Part (b) was generally well answered provided the basic tax planning involved was understood. Transferring the property to Kato prior to its disposal meant a lower rate of capital gains tax (CGT) on part of the gain, plus Kato's annual exempt amount was available (Dembe's was not).

Somewhat surprisingly, quite a few candidates used the incorrect rates of CGT, despite the fact that these rates are provided in the tax rates and allowances. The £2,000 in additional legal fees were often not taken into account in the comparison.

Part (c) was not particularly well answered, with many candidates not appreciating how straightforward the answer actually was.

The couple's estate, with a value of £950,000, would have been fully covered by the available nil rate bands totalling £1,000,000 (two nil rate bands of £325,000, and two residence nil rate bands of £175,000). The IHT liability was therefore nil.

Even if IHT were payable (for example, if the value of the estate increased faster than the available nil rate bands), then there would be no advantage to leaving assets to children on the first death. This is because unused nil rate bands can be transferred to the surviving spouse. This very basic IHT planning was often overlooked.

Marking guide

		Marks	
(a)	Extension of basic rate band	2	
	Reinstatement of personal allowance	1.5	
	National insurance contributions	0.5	
			4
(b)	Disposal by Dembe	0.5	
	Disposal by Kato		
	– Taxable at basic rate	1	
	– Taxable at higher rate	1	
	Overall saving	0.5	
			3
(c)	Spouse exemption	0.5	
	Residence nil rate bands	0.5	
	Nil rate bands	0.5	
	Chargeable at death rate	0.5	
	Transfer of unused nil rate band	1	
			3
Total			**10**

(a) Reduction in Dembe's income tax liability and NICs:

	£
Extension of basic rate tax band: 60,000 (48,000 × 100/80) at 20% (40% – 20%)	12,000
Reinstatement of personal allowance: 12,570 at 40%	5,028
Reduction in income tax liability	17,028
National insurance contributions (NICs)	0
Total tax reduction	17,028

> **Tutorial note.** Before making the personal pension contribution, Dembe's adjusted net income was £125,140, so no personal allowance is available.
>
> The personal pension contribution will reduce Dembe's adjusted net income to less than £100,000 (125,140 – 60,000 = 65,140), so the personal allowance will be fully reinstated.
>
> Pension contributions have no impact on NICs.

(b) Overall saving:

	£	£
Disposal made by Dembe		
– 67,000 at 24%		16,080
Disposal made by Kato		
– 16,350 (37,700 – 21,350) at 18%	2,943	
– 45,650 (65,000 – 3,000 – 16,350) at 24%	10,956	(13,899)
Capital gains tax (CGT) saving		2,181
Additional legal fees		(2,000)
Overall saving		181

(c) On first death, there will be no inheritance tax (IHT) liability because of the spouse exemption.

There will also be no IHT liability on second death because the couple's residence nil rate bands and nil rate bands will exceed the value of the combined chargeable estate:

	£
Combined chargeable estate	950,000
Residence nil rate bands (175,000 × 2)	(350,000)
Nil rate bands (325,000 × 2)	(650,000)
Chargeable at 40%	0

Even if IHT were payable (eg if the value of the estate increases faster than the available nil rate bands), there is no advantage to leaving assets to children on the first death. This is because unused nil rate bands can be transferred to the surviving spouse.

Part E: Corporation tax liabilities

Section A

OTQ bank – Corporation tax liabilities 1

207 The correct answers are:

Legal expenses relating to the acquisition of a new 40-year lease on its factory		NOT ALLOWABLE
Cost of arranging a new bank loan to purchase machinery for trade	ALLOWABLE	
Write off of an irrecoverable loan to a former employee		NOT ALLOWABLE
Donation to local charity with mention of Jet Ltd's support in programme for fundraising concert (not a qualifying charitable donation)	ALLOWABLE	

Legal expenses in respect of leases are only allowable if they relate to the **renewal** of a short lease. The cost of arranging a bank loan for trade purposes is allowable. A debt written off in respect of a former employee is accounted for under the non-trade loan relationship rules as it does not relate to the trade of the company. A small donation to a local charity with publicity would normally be allowable as being for the purposes of the trade.

208 The correct answer is: 12 months to 30 November 2024, 4 months to 31 March 2025

If the company has a long period of account, it is divided into one period of 12 months and one of the remainder.

209 £ 40,500

£1,800,000 × 3% × 9/12 = £40,500

The qualifying cost for SBAs excludes acquisition fees. The SBA must be time-apportioned in the year of acquisition from the date the building is brought into use.

210 £3,198

	Main pool	Special rate pool	Allowances
	£	£	£
Additions	30,400	15,400	
WDA			
6% × 6/12		(462)	462
18% × 6/12	(2,736)		2,736
TWDV c/f /allowances	27,664	14,938	3,198

Do not forget to pro-rate writing down allowances in a short accounting period. No adjustment is made for private use by a director for a company.

The answer £4,122 uses 18% for both WDAs. The answer £6,396 is the full year's WDAs. The answer £3,106 adjusts for private use – this is a common mistake. Remember that there is never any private use by a company!

211 The correct answer is: £0

	£
Proceeds	70,000
Less cost 15,000 × £3.50	(52,500)
Unindexed gain	17,500
Less indexation allowance	
0.578 × £52,500 = £30,345 restricted to	(17,500)
Indexed gain	0

The answer £12,845 allows the indexation allowance to create a loss. The answer £105,000 loss uses the cost of all 50,000 of the shares. The answer £17,500 is the unindexed gain.

> **ACCA Examining Team's Comments**
>
> This was a straightforward chargeable gain computation on the disposal of shares. The correct answer is £0. However, the vast majority of candidates chose £12,845, suggesting they simply forgot that indexation cannot create a loss.

212 £ 33,300

Crane plc can make a carry forward loss relief claim against total profits but can leave sufficient profits to cover the qualifying charitable donation, thus maximising the unrelieved loss carried forward to the next accounting period. The most beneficial claim is therefore £(30,000 + 6,000 − 2,700) = £33,300. The remaining £(40,000 − 33,300) = £6,700 will be carried forward to the accounting period ending 31 December 2026.

213 £ 83,750

	£
Loss	160,000
Less loss relief y/e 31.12.25	(5,000)
Less loss relief p/e 31.12.24 (40,000 + 15,500)	(55,500)
Less loss relief y/e 31.3.24 3/12 × (45,000 + 18,000)	(15,750)
Loss c/f	83,750

214 The correct answer is: £38,000

> **ACCA Examining Team's Comments**
>
> This calculative question tested candidates' knowledge of group relief. The question asked candidates to calculate the maximum amount of group relief which Boon Ltd could claim from Bab Ltd. The correct answer was £38,000. Boon Ltd can claim group relief against its taxable total profits, in this case £40,000 (£36,000 + £4,000). Bab Ltd does not need to use its trading loss against its own profits first, so it can surrender the full amount of £38,000 to Boon Ltd.
>
> Most candidates answered £31,000, indicating that they may have thought that Bab Ltd had to use the loss against its chargeable gains first. Many candidates answered £36,000, perhaps because they thought that group relief can only be set against trading income.
>
> Group relief is an important aspect of the syllabus in respect of corporation tax, and candidates should ensure they are familiar with the rules and can apply them to a given scenario.

215 The correct answers are:

Daffodil plc	YES	
Geranium Inc		NO
Flora Ltd	YES	
Hellebore Ltd		NO

Group relief can be made to UK companies only, so not to Geranium Inc, and where there is a ≥75% direct and indirect holding by the controlling company. Daffodil plc only has a (80% × 90%) = 72% interest in Hellebore Ltd.

216 The correct answers are:

Pine plc	YES	
Willow Ltd	YES	
Juniper Ltd	YES	
Lime Inc		NO

Losses can only be transferred to UK companies where there is a ≥75% direct interest at each level and >50% indirect holding by the top company. Pine plc has a (75% × 75%) = 56.25% interest in Maple Ltd.

OTQ bank – Corporation tax liabilities 2

217 £ 32,000

> **ACCA Examining Team's Comments**
> Loan interest receivable will always be non-trade interest unless the company is in the trade of money lending. The amount which will be included in the accounts of Flower Ltd for the year to 31 March 2025 will be the received and accrued amount totalling £40,000. From this figure, the non-trade loan interest payable will be deducted. The loan to purchase the delivery vehicles is for trade purposes therefore the amount of £10,000 will be deducted from the trading profits. However, the loan to buy shares in another company is an investment and is not for trading purposes and so this amount will be deducted from the £40,000. The answer is £40,000 – £8,000 = £32,000.

218 £ 83,000

The most beneficial manner is to carry forward the loss and make a partial claim to bring profits to the lower limit of £50,000 and prevent QCD becoming unrelieved.

£(130,000 + 10,000 – 7,000 – 50,000) = £83,000

	31.3.26
	£
Trading income	130,000
Interest income	10,000
Total profits	140,000
Carry forward loss claim	(83,000)
	57,000
Qualifying charitable donations	(7,000)
TTP	50,000

219 £ 12,500

Do not forget to include the parent company in the number of associated companies.

£50,000/4 = £12,500

220 £ 26,550

Upper limit = £250,000/2 × 10/12 = £104,167
Lower limit = £50,000/2 × 10/12 = £20,833

	£
Trading profits	60,000
Property business income	30,000
Chargeable gains	16,200
	106,200
Corporation tax at 25%	26,550

221 £ 46,957

	£
Taxable total profits	190,000
Dividends	20,000
Augmented profits	210,000
Corporation tax liability	
£190,000 × 25%	47,500
Less marginal relief	
– (250,000 – 210,000) × 3/200 × 190,000/210,000	(543)
	46,957

222 The correct answers are:
- Xtra Ltd can claim group relief of £135,000 from Zeus Ltd.
- Yak Ltd cannot claim group relief from Zeus Ltd.

> **ACCA Examining Team's Comments**
>
> Zeus Ltd can surrender the lower of £180,000 (240,000 × 9/12) and £135,000 (180,000 × 9/12) to Xtra Ltd. Yak Ltd is not in a 75% group with Xtra Ltd and Zeus Ltd, and so cannot claim group relief for the accounting period (120,000 × 9/12 = £90,000).

223 The correct answer is: £150,000 on 14 July 2024

> **ACCA Examining Team's Comments**
>
> The correct answer is £150,000 on 14 July 2024. This is because the period ended 31 August 2024 is a short period of less than 12 months, meaning that only three instalment payments will be made. The first instalment is due six months and 14 days (ie in month 7) following the start of the period commencing on 1 January 2024 (ie by 14 July 2024) and is calculated as £400,000 × 3/8, giving £150,000. A number of candidates selected £100,000 on 14 July 2024, which is the correct due date however the instalment amount (calculated as £400,000 × 3/12, giving £100,000) is incorrect because £100,000 would be the amount payable if the period had been 12 months (rather than eight months).

224 The correct answer is: When plant and machinery on which the 130% super deduction was claimed is sold, the sale proceeds are deducted from the main pool.

When plant and machinery (on which the 130% super deduction has been claimed) is subsequently sold after 31 March 2024, the sale proceeds are **not** deducted from the main pool. Instead, the proceeds are brought in as a balancing charge.

225 £ 210,000

Balancing charge

		£
Machinery (130% super deduction was claimed on full cost)	(Proceeds = BC)	(100,000)
Special rate expenditure (50% FYA was claimed)	(Proceeds × 50% = BC)	(80,000)
Special rate pool	TWDV b/f less proceeds × 50% (50,000 − (160,000 × 50%))	(30,000)
Overall balancing charge		(210,000)

226 £ 257,800

Remember, when plant and machinery on which the 130% super deduction was claimed is subsequently sold, the sale proceeds are not deducted from the main pool. They are brought in as a balancing charge.

When plant and machinery on which the 50% FYA was claimed is subsequently sold, 50% of the sale proceeds are deducted from the special rate pool and the other 50% brought in as a balancing charge.

	AIA/FYA	Main pool	Special rate pool	Allowances
	£	£	£	£
TWDV b/f		200,000	100,000	
Additions qualifying for AIA	350,000			
AIA	(350,000)			350,000
Disposals (130% item proceeds = BC)				(60,000)
Disposals (50% FYA item, 50% proceeds = deduction, 50% proceeds = BC)			(70,000)	(70,000)
		200,000	30,000	
WDA @ 18%/6%		(36,000)	(1,800)	37,800
TWDV c/f		164,000	28,300	
Allowances				257,800

Section B

OT case – Luna Ltd (June 2015) (amended)

> **Course Book references**
> Chargeable gains for companies are covered in Chapter 20.
>
> **Top tips**
> Learn the proforma for dealing with a pool of shares owned by a company. In this scenario you only needed to include the indexed cost column.
>
> **Easy marks**
> There were easy marks for identifying the correct statement about indexation allowance.

227 The correct answers are:

Indexation allowance can reduce a gain to nil but not create a loss.	**TRUE**	
Indexation allowance can increase an unindexed loss.		**FALSE**

Indexation allowance cannot increase or create a loss, although it can reduce a gain to nil.

228 £ 6,186

	£
Proceeds	53,400
Less cost	(36,800)
	16,600
Less indexation allowance to December 2017 0.283 × £36,800	(10,414)
Gain	6,186

229 The correct answer is: £14,928

	No. of shares	Indexed cost
		£
Acquisition	16,000	32,000
Indexed rise to December 2017		
0.244 × £32,000		7,808
		39,808
Disposal	(10,000)	(24,880)
	6,000	14,928

The answer £12,000 is the unindexed pool of cost immediately after the sale. The answer £39,808 is the indexed cost of the pool immediately before the disposal. The answer £24,880 is the amount of indexed cost used on the disposal.

230 The correct answer is: £13,125

	No. of shares	Cost £
Acquisition	5,000	7,500
Bonus 1 for 1	5,000	0
	10,000	7,500
Rights 1 for 4 @ £2.25	2,500	5,625
	12,500	13,125

231 £ 19,500

$$£33,000 \times \frac{(£6.50 \times 10,000)}{(£6.50 \times 10,000) + (£4.50 \times 10,000)} \quad £19,500$$

OT case – Tay Ltd

Course Book references
Chargeable gains for companies is the subject of Chapter 20.

Top tips
The application of the rules on the destruction of assets in is similar to rollover relief for replacement of business assets.

Easy marks
The chattels rules should have been well known.

232 The correct answer is: £155,000

	£
Proceeds	180,000
Less indexed cost	(155,000)
Gain	25,000
Gain immediately chargeable £(180,000 – 162,000)	(18,000)
Deduction from base cost of new warehouse	7,000

The base cost of the new warehouse is £(162,000 – 7,000) = £155,000. The answer £162,000 does not give any relief. The answer £144,000 deducts the gain immediately chargeable. The answer £140,000 uses the unindexed cost to work out the gain.

233 The correct answer is: £8,000 gain

	Market value £	Indexed cost £	Gain £
20,000 £1 ordinary shares @ £4 each	80,000	64,000	
£40,000 (20,000 × £2) cash	40,000	32,000	8,000
	120,000	96,000	

The answer £24,000 gain is the total gain if the acquisition of the shares was treated as a disposal. The answer £16,000 gain is the gain on the shares if the acquisition of the shares was treated as a disposal. The answer £(24,000) loss is the loss on cash if the nominal value of the shares of £1 is used for the apportionment.

234 The correct answer is: £5,000

Although the general rule is that wasting chattels are exempt, there is an exception for assets used for the purpose of a trade in respect of which capital allowances have been or could have been claimed. The usual chattel rules therefore apply as follows:

	£
Proceeds	9,000
Less indexed cost	(3,500)
Gain	5,500

The maximum gain is 5/3 × £(9,000 × 6,000) = £5,000.

The chargeable gain is the lower of £5,500 and £5,000, so it is £5,000.

235 The correct answer is: £15,732

	£
Proceeds	45,000
Less:	
– Cost	(20,000)
– Enhancement (drainage)	(2,000)
Unindexed gain	23,000
Less:	
– Indexation on cost £20,000 × 0.342	(6,840)
– Indexation on enhancement £2,000 × 0.214	(428)
Chargeable gain	15,732

The answer £16,160 does not index the enhancement. The answer £15,476 uses the indexation factor on cost for both cost and enhancement. The answer £15,134 indexes the unindexed gain using the indexation factor on cost.

236 The correct answer is: 2 and 4

The capital loss can be set against chargeable gains made in the year ended 31 March 2026 and the capital loss can be carried forward and set against the first available chargeable gains.

Capital losses cannot be carried back and cannot be set against profits other than chargeable gains.

OT case – Hyde plc group

> **Course Book references**
> Groups are the subject of Chapter 22.
>
> **Top tips**
> Make sure you know the difference between the rules for relationships between companies for group relief and those applying to chargeable gains groups.
>
> **Easy marks**
> The identification of the base cost of the factory should have been easy marks if you remembered that transfers between chargeable gains group companies are on a no gain, no loss basis.

237 The correct answers are:

Hampstead plc	YES	
Regent plc	YES	
Richmond plc		NO
Primrose plc	YES	

A company is in a group relief group where there is a ≥75% direct and indirect holding by the controlling company (Hyde plc). Hyde plc has a (95% × 80%) = 76% interest in Primrose Ltd but only has a (85% × 85%) = 72.25% interest in Richmond Ltd.

238 The correct answer is: £70,000

	£
Trading loss	68,000
Excess qualifying charitable donations £(5,000 – 3,000)	2,000
Maximum current period group relief	70,000

239 £50,500

	£
Chargeable gain	48,000
Interest income	12,000
Trading loss	(8,000)
Qualifying charitable donations	(1,500)
Available taxable total profits	50,500

Hyde plc is assumed to use its own current year losses in working out the taxable total profits against which it may claim current group relief, even if it does not in fact claim relief for current losses against total profits. Group relief is set against taxable total profits after all other reliefs for the current period such as qualifying charitable donations.

240 The correct answers are:
- A claim for current period group relief will be ineffective unless Greenwich plc gives a notice of consent.
- The claim for current period group relief would be made on Hyde plc's corporation tax return.

Any payment by Hyde plc for current period group relief, up to the amount of the loss surrendered, is ignored for all corporation tax purposes. A claim for current period group relief between Greenwich plc and Hyde plc will be available against 9/12ths of the taxable total profits of Hyde plc for the year to 31 March 2026, since surrendered losses must be set against taxable total profits of a corresponding accounting period (1 April 2025 to 31 December 2025).

241 The correct answer is: £120,000

	£
Cost	100,000
Indexation allowance to date of transfer £100,000 × 0.200	20,000
Base cost for Primrose plc	120,000

The transfer of assets within a chargeable gains group is on a no gain/no loss basis including indexation to the date of the transfer.

Section C

242 Problematic Ltd (June 2010) (amended)

> **Course Book references**
> Chargeable gains for companies are covered in Chapter 20.
>
> **Top tips**
> Make sure you use the three column proforma for the FA 1985 pool.
>
> **Easy marks**
> The base cost required in part (b) is easy provided you remember that the leasehold factory is a depreciating asset, and so do not reduce the base cost by rollover relief.

Marking guide

	Marks
(a) Easy plc	
FA 1985 pool	
Purchase	0.5
Rights issue	1
Indexation	2
Disposal	1
Chargeable gain	1.5
Freehold factory	
Disposal proceeds	0.5
Indexed cost	0.5
Rollover relief	2
	9
(b) Leasehold factory	1
	1
Total	**10**

(a) **Easy plc shares**

FA85 pool

	No. of shares	Cost £	Indexed cost £
Purchase 26.6.05	15,000	12,600	12,600
Index to September 2008			
0.136 × £12,600			1,714
Rights issue 1 for 3 @ £2.20	5,000	11,000	11,000
c/f	20,000	23,600	25,314

	No. of shares	Cost £	Indexed cost £
Index to December 2017			
0.273 × £25,314			6,911
			32,225
Sale	(16,000)	(18,880)	(25,780)
c/f	4,000	4,720	6,445

Gain

	£
Proceeds	54,400
Less cost	(18,880)
	35,520
Less indexation £(25,780 – 18,880)	(6,900)
Chargeable gain	28,620

Freehold factory

	£
Proceeds	171,000
Less indexed cost	(127,000)
	44,000
Less gain deferred on purchase of leasehold factory £(44,000 – 16,200)	(27,800)
Chargeable gain (amount not reinvested £(171,000 – 154,800))	16,200

(b) The leasehold factory is a depreciating asset, so there is no adjustment to the base cost of £154,800.

> **Tutorial note.** When a replacement asset is a depreciating asset then the gain is not rolled over by reducing the cost of the replacement asset. Instead, the gain is deferred until it crystallises on the earliest of:
> - The disposal of the replacement asset
> - The date the replacement asset is no longer used in the business
> - Ten years after the acquisition of the replacement asset which in this case is 10 December 2034

 Videos can be viewed online by accessing your ebook version on VitalSource.

243 Volatile Ltd (December 2009) (amended)

Course Book references

Corporation tax losses are covered in Chapter 21.

> **Top tips**
> Don't forget to set up a loss memorandum for each loss so that you can see how the loss is utilised.
>
> **Easy marks**
> You should have been able to state at least two of the principles of claiming loss relief in part (a).

Marking guide

		Marks	
(a)	Rate of tax	1	
	Timing of relief	1	
	Loss of QCDs	1	
			3
(b)	Trading income	0.5	
	Property business income	0.5	
	Chargeable gains	0.5	
	Loss relief – y/e 31 December 2023	2	
	Loss relief – y/e 30 September 2027	2.5	
	Qualifying charitable donations	0.5	
	Unrelieved losses	0.5	
			7
Total			**10**

(a) **Choice of loss relief**

The three factors that will influence a company's choice of loss relief claims are:

(1) The rate at which relief will be obtained: 26.5% if marginal relief applies (best use), 25% at the main rate (second best use), 19% at the small profits rate (third best use)

(2) Timing of relief: both in terms of tax rate and cash flow (saving tax sooner is beneficial for cash flow)

(3) The extent to which relief for qualifying charitable donations might be lost, so it may be beneficial to restrict carry forward loss relief claims to keep an amount of total profits in charge after loss relief to match donations

(b) **Volatile Ltd**

	p/e 31.12.23	y/e 31.12.24	y/e 31.12.25	p/e 30.9.26
	£	£	£	£
Trading income	44,000	0	86,500	78,700
Property business income	9,400	6,600	6,500	0
Chargeable gains (11,700 – 2,000)	5,100	0	0	9,700
Total profits	58,500	6,600	93,000	88,400
Less current period loss relief	(0)	(6,600)	(0)	(0)
Less carry back loss relief	(58,500)		(23,250)	(88,400)
Less carry forward loss relief	(0)	(0)	(8,700)	(0)
Less qualifying charitable donations	(0)	(0)	(1,200)	(0)
Taxable total profits	0	0	59,850	0

Loss memorandum

	£
Loss in y/e 31.12.24	73,800
Less used y/e 31.12.24	(6,600)
Less used p/e 31.12.23	(58,500)
Less used y/e 31.12.25	(8,700)
Loss remaining unrelieved	0
Loss in y/e 30.9.27	186,800
Less used p/e 30.9.26	(88,400)
3 months to 31.12.25 £93,000 × 3/12	(23,250)
Loss remaining unrelieved at 30.9.27	75,150

The loss of y/e 30.9.27 can be carried back against total profits of the previous 12 months ie against the nine-month period ending 30.9.26 and three months of the y/e 31.12.25.

244 Maison Ltd (September/December 2019)

> **Course Book references**
>
> Corporation tax computations are covered in Chapter 19, and gains for companies are covered in Chapter 20.
>
> **Top tips**
>
> Given that a draft layout was provided in the question, this should have been replicated in the answer.
>
> **Easy marks**
>
> There is a full mark for using figures given in the question in the TTP pro forma and two more half marks for picking up the gains figures provided.
>
> **ACCA Examining Team's Comments**
>
> The corporation tax question involved Maison Ltd, for which a partly completed draft corporation tax computation had been prepared for the year ended 31 March 2025. The figures provided were correct, but there were four uncompleted sections, all related to property. These were:
>
> - A deduction for the payment of a lease premium
> - Capital allowances in respect of the construction of an extension adjacent to the company's existing freehold office building
> - Property business income from the letting of a warehouse which was purchased in a dilapidated state
> - Chargeable gains on the disposal of two investment properties
>
> The sole requirement for 15 marks was to prepare a completed version of Maison Ltd's corporation tax computation for the year ended 31 March 2025 after dealing with the uncompleted sections. The question was generally very well answered.
>
> As regards layout, candidates should again include as many workings as possible within the main computation. Given that a draft layout was provided, then this layout should have been followed by candidates in their answers, thereby allowing candidates to achieve as many of the available marks as possible.

Lease premium: A number of candidates did not appreciate that this was a deduction rather than an addition.

Property business income: Many candidates were not aware that the cost of initial repairs was disallowable capital expenditure because the property could not have been let out in its original state and this was reflected in the purchase price paid.

Chargeable gains: Figures for the two chargeable gains were given, so candidates should not have recalculated them. The reason for giving more information (proceeds and expenditure) was so that the indexation allowance could be calculated. Candidates should always deal with each gain separately, and not combine the figures.

Marking guide	Marks
(W1) Deduction for lease premium	
Premium paid	0.5
Deduction	1
Per annum and time apportioned	1
(W2) Capital allowances	
Main pool	0.5
Allowable costs	1
AIA	1
SBA on building costs	1
(W3) Property income	
Rent receivable	1
Security deposit	0.5
Insurance	1
Initial repairs	1
Advertising	0.5
(W4) Chargeable gains	
First property	
– Gain	0.5
– Indexation allowance	1
– Enhancement expenditure	0.5
Second property	
– Gain	0.5
– Indexation allowance	1
Corporation tax	0.5
Figures provided in question	1
	15
Total	15

Maison Ltd – Corporation tax computation for the year ended 31 March 2025

	£
Operating profit	892,900*
Non-deductible expenditure	22,340*
Deduction for lease premium (W1)	(715)
Capital allowances (W2)	(70,500)

	£
Trading profit	844,025
Property business income (W3)	28,685
Loan interest receivable	1,460*
Chargeable gains (W4)	77,985
Taxable total profits	952,155
Corporation tax (952,155 at 25%)	238,039

*Figures provided in question

Workings

1 Deduction for lease premium

	£
Premium paid	44,000
Less: 44,000 × 2% × (12 − 1)	(9,680)
Amount assessed on the landlord as income	34,320
Deduction (34,320/12 years × 3/12)	715

2 Capital allowances

	£	£
Main pool		22,867
Capital allowances		
Building costs	0	
Ventilation system	6,700	
Heating system	3,900	
Furniture and furnishings	33,500	
Refrigerator and microwave cooker	2,600	
AIA @ 100%		46,700
Structures and buildings allowance (£93,300 × 3% × 4/12)		933
Total allowances		70,500

3 Property business income

	£
Rent receivable (18,300 + (18,300 × 2/3))	30,500
Security deposit	0
Insurance	(1,035)
Initial repairs	0
Advertising	(780)
Property business income	28,685

Tutorial note. A security deposit, less the cost of making good any damage, is returned to the tenant on the cessation of a letting. It is therefore initially not treated as income.

The cost of insurance for the period 1 July to 1 November 2024 is deductible as pre-trading expenditure.

The cost of the initial repairs to the warehouse are disallowable capital expenditure as the warehouse could not be let out in its original state and this was reflected in the purchase price paid.

4 **Chargeable gains**

	£
First property	
Gain	109,800
Indexation allowance	
– Cost (101,000 × 0.315)	(31,815)
– Enhancement expenditure	0
Chargeable gain	77,985
Second property	
Gain	26,000
Indexation allowance	
– Cost (117,000 × 0.315) – Restricted	(26,000)
Chargeable gain	0

Tutorial note. There is no indexation allowance for the first property's enhancement expenditure of £26,200 because this was incurred after December 2017.

For the second property, the indexation allowance cannot create a capital loss.

 Videos can be viewed online by accessing your ebook version on VitalSource.

245 Black Ltd (Dec 2011) and Gastron Ltd (June 2009) (amended)

Course Book references

Groups are covered in Chapter 22.

Top tips

It is very important that you read the questions carefully and comply with any detailed instructions. For example, in part (a) you were given a note about what you were not expected to do.

Easy marks

You should have been able to outline the group structure in part (b)(i).

Marking guide	Marks
(a) Maximum potential claim by Black Ltd in relation to White Ltd	1
Maximum surrender by White Ltd	
– Current period trading loss – maximum claim	0.5

	– Qualifying charitable donations	1	
	Maximum group relief claim Black Ltd and White Ltd	0.5	
	Maximum potential claim by Black Ltd in relation to Grey Ltd	0.5	
	Maximum surrender by Grey Ltd		
	– Carried forward trading loss – maximum claim	1	
	Maximum group relief claim Black Ltd and Grey Ltd	0.5	
			5
(b) (i)	75% shareholding	1	
	50% effective interest	1	
			2
(ii)	Set-off of capital loss	1	
	Rate of tax for relief	2	
			3
Total			10

(a) **Black Ltd – Group relief claims for year ended 31 March 2025**

Maximum potential claim by Black Ltd from White Ltd

Group relief is against taxable total profits after all other reliefs for the current period (eg qualifying charitable donations).

The maximum potential current period group relief claim by Black Ltd in relation to White Ltd is therefore £(338,900 + 21,100 – 4,400) = £355,600.

Maximum potential surrender by White Ltd to Black Ltd

White Ltd may surrender its current period trading losses of £351,300.

White Ltd may also surrender excess qualifying charitable donations (ie to the extent that they exceed total profits before taking account of any losses). Since the qualifying charitable donations of £5,600 do not exceed the total profits of £26,700, there is no excess.

The maximum potential surrender by White Ltd is therefore £351,300.

Maximum group relief claim by Black Ltd from White Ltd

The maximum current period group relief claim is the lower of the claim that can be made by Black Ltd and the surrender that can be made by White Ltd, ie £351,300.

Maximum potential claim by Black Ltd from Grey Ltd

Current period group relief is taken before carry forward group relief. The maximum potential claim by Black Ltd in relation to Grey Ltd is therefore £(355,600 – 351,300) = £4,300.

Maximum potential surrender by Grey Ltd

Grey Ltd may surrender its carried forward trading losses after deducting the amount it can set against its own current period total profits ie £(57,500 – 50,000 – 4,500) = £3,000.

Maximum group relief claim by Black Ltd from Grey Ltd

The maximum carry forward group relief claim is the lower of the claim that can be made by Black Ltd and the surrender that can be made by Grey Ltd, ie £3,000.

(b) (i) Companies form a chargeable gains group if at each level in the group structure there is a 75% shareholding.

However, the parent company must also have an effective interest of over 50% in each group company.

(ii) The election will enable the capital loss of £16,000 to be set against the capital gain of £24,800 and so save tax in the current year. Otherwise, the loss would have to be carried forward by Culinary Ltd and set against future gains.

Gastron Ltd is a marginal rate company since its augmented profits fall between the lower limit of £50,000/2 = £25,000 and the upper limit of £250,000/2 = £125,000 (as adjusted for Culinary Ltd as an associate). It is therefore also beneficial for the balance of the chargeable gain of £(24,800 – 16,000) = £8,800 to arise in Culinary Ltd as it will only be taxed at the rate of 19%, instead of at the marginal rate in Gastron Ltd.

246 Crumble Ltd (September/December 2022)

Course Book references

Computing taxable total profits, including capital allowances, and the corporation tax liability are dealt with in Chapter 19. Losses are covered in Chapter 21.

Top tips

Make sure you start with the operating loss figure in part (a) and read the requirements carefully. Part (a) states that notes 5 and 6 are not relevant for that part of the question. Use negative figures for the loss and for interest and then you can use the SUM function in the spreadsheet for the total tax adjusted trading loss.

Easy marks

There were 3.5 easy marks for indicating non-adjustable items with a zero in part (a). Part (b) was fairly straight forward.

(a) **Crumble Ltd – Tax-adjusted trading loss for the nine-month period ended 31 March 2025**

	A	B
1		£
2	Operating loss	(187,800)
3	Accountancy fees	0
4	Compliance check	0
5	Legal fees in connection with varying the terms of loan notes	0
6	Legal fees in connection with the issue of share capital	9,300
7	Legal fees in connection with the registration of trademarks	0
8	Construction of new car park	7,300
9	Repairing the wall of an office building	0
10	Qualifying charitable donations	3,400
11	Removal expenses	0
12	Fine for infringing health and safety regulations	1,200

	A	B
13	Remaining expenses – allowable	0
14	Interest payable (8,750 + (5,000 × 3/6))	(11,250)
15	Trading loss	(177,850)

(b) Crumble Ltd – Taxable total profits for the nine-month period ended 31 March 2025

	A	B
1		£
2	Property business income	
3	Rent receivable (6,600 × 4/6)	4,400
4	Security deposit	0
5	Insurance (840 × 9/12)	(630)
6		3,770
7	Chargeable gain (25,200 – 13,600)	11,600
8		15,370
9	Qualifying charitable donations	(3,400)
10	Taxable total profits	11,970

Tutorial note. A security deposit, less the cost of making good any damage, is returned to the tenant on the cessation of a letting. It is therefore initially not treated as income.

(c) (i) **Claim**

A claim must be made by 31 March 2027 (within two years of the end of the period ended 31 March 2025, the loss-making period).

(ii) **Choice of loss relief**

The three factors that will influence Crumble Ltd's choice of loss relief claims are:

- The rate at which relief will be obtained:
    - 26.5% if marginal relief applies (best use)
    - 25% at the main rate (second best use)
    - 19% at the small profits rate (third best use)
- How quickly relief will be obtained

    Loss relief against total profits is quicker than carry forward loss relief.
- The extent to which relief for qualifying charitable donations might be lost

Crumble Ltd should make a carry forward claim for the year ended 31 March 2026 where tax can be saved at the highest rate (ie when marginal relief applies).

247 Hopi Ltd (March/June 2018)

Course Book references

The income tax computation is covered in Chapter 2. National insurance contributions are the subject of Chapter 12. Corporation tax liability is dealt with in Chapter 19.

Top tips

When computing Kaya's income tax liability, simply calculate the additional tax on the dividend income rather than rework the whole income tax computation.

Easy marks

There were easy marks for stating that, if Kaya receives additional dividend income, there will be no change to the national insurance contributions for Kaya and Hopi Ltd and no change to Hopi Ltd's corporation tax liability.

ACCA Examining Team's Comments

The requirement for 10 marks was to calculate the revised tax and national insurance contributions (NICs) for Kaya and Hopi Ltd for the year ended 5 April 2025 if, on 31 March 2025, Kaya paid herself a bonus of £25,000 (1) as additional director's remuneration or (2) as an additional dividend. Candidates who understood tax rules had no difficulty.

As warned in previous reports, where tax figures are given for the original scenario, candidates should never attempt to recalculate these figures for themselves. All this does is lose valuable time with candidates producing three sets of workings rather than the expected two.

Candidates should always read the requirements very carefully. These types of questions often require a summary or a conclusion, but neither was necessary for this question – again those candidates who provided one lost a bit more time. Where computations are required for two different scenarios, candidates should clearly indicate which scenario is being answered. It is much better to deal with one scenario first, then the second, rather than have a mix of computations dealing with one tax at a time, such as all the income tax and class 1 NIC computations for Kaya, then the corporation tax and class 1 NIC calculations for Hopi Ltd.

Although full marks are awarded for correct answers however the information is presented, dealing with one scenario at a time can help candidates to ensure they have covered all aspects in their answers. Some of the calculations in this question required full computations (such as Kaya's income tax liability under the additional director's remuneration alternative), whereas others (such as Kaya's income tax liability under the additional dividend alternative) could be calculated by working at the margin. Appreciating where full computations can be avoided saves time as well as reducing the complexity of the workings. Also, under the additional dividend alternative, many candidates did not appreciate that the class 1 NICs and Hopi Ltd's corporation tax liability would not change from the original figures provided.

In summary, although many candidates correctly calculated most, if not all, of the revised tax and NICs, they often took a much longer route in reaching their answer than was necessary. Working through past examination questions will help candidates familiarise themselves with the best approach to be taken when answering these types of questions. Also, it is important that candidates appreciate the interactions which can arise in these questions, and an article has been published covering many of the scenarios which could be examined.

Marking guide   **Marks**

Revised liabilities if Kaya receives additional director's remuneration

Kaya income tax liability
– Director's remuneration   0.5

– Personal allowance		0.5
Income tax (½ mark for each amount)		2
Kaya Class 1 national insurance contributions		1.5
Hopi Ltd Class 1 national insurance contributions		1
Hopi Ltd corporation tax		1
Revised liabilities if Kaya receives additional dividend income		
Kaya income tax liability		1.5
Kaya and Hopi Ltd Class 1 national insurance contributions		1
Hopi Ltd corporation tax		0.5
		10
Total		10

Revised liabilities if Kaya receives additional director's remuneration

Kaya – Income tax liability 2024/25

	Non-savings income	Dividend income
	£	£
Director's remuneration £(30,000 + 25,000)	55,000	
Dividend income		44,000
Net income	55,000	44,000
Less: Personal allowance	(12,570)	
Taxable income	42,430	44,000
Tax		
£37,700 @ 20%		7,540
£(42,430 – 37,700) = £4,730 @ 40%		1,892
£500 @ 0% (dividend nil rate band)		0
£(44,000 – 500) = £43,500 @ 33.75%		14,681
Revised income tax liability		24,113

Kaya and Hopi Ltd – National insurance contributions 2024/25

	£
£(50,270 – 12,570) = 37,700 @ 8%	3,016
£(55,000 – 50,270) = 4,730 @ 2%	95
Revised employee Class 1 NICs	3,111
Revised employer Class 1 NICs £(55,000 – 9100) = £45,900 @ 13.8%	6,334

Hopi Ltd – Corporation tax liability for year ended 5 April 2025

	£
Trading profit before additional director's remuneration	70,000
Less:	
– Additional director's remuneration	(25,000)
– Additional employer's Class 1 NIC £(6,334 – 2,884)	(3,450)

	£
Taxable total profits	41,550
Tax	
£41,550 @ 19%	7,895

Revised liabilities if Kaya receives additional dividend income

Kaya – Income tax liability 2024/25

	£
Original income tax	13,225
Add: tax on additional dividend income £25,000 @ 33.75%	8,438
	21,663

Kaya and Hopi Ltd – National insurance contributions 2024/25

There are no NICs payable on dividends so the Class 1 NICs for Kaya and Hopi Ltd will remain unchanged.

Hopi Ltd – Corporation tax liability for year ended 5 April 2025

Hopi Ltd's corporation tax liability will remain unchanged.

248 Kat (September/December 2018)

> **Course Book references**
>
> The income tax computation is the subject of Chapter 2. Property income is dealt with in Chapter 6. Corporation tax computation is covered in Chapter 19. The computation of chargeable gains for individuals is covered in Chapter 13 and for companies in Chapter 20.
>
> **Top tips**
>
> When you are given a figure for a tax liability in the question don't waste time proving that the figure is correct – just use it!
>
> **Easy marks**
>
> There were some easy marks for basic income tax and corporation tax computations, but you needed to keep them separate and then compare them at the end of your answer.
>
> **ACCA Examining Team's Comments**
>
> In part (a), those candidates who made sure that they understood the scenario and worked carefully through each calculation had no difficulty answering this section.
>
> As warned in previous reports, where a tax figure is given for one of the scenarios (in this case, the corporation tax figure), candidates should never attempt to recalculate the figure for themselves. All this does is use up valuable time. As regards the conclusion, this should have just been a calculation of the tax difference between the two scenarios.
>
> There was no need for a detailed explanation.
>
> Where computations are required for two different scenarios, candidates should clearly indicate which scenario is being answered. This is particularly important where some of the same information is used in both scenarios. In this case employment income and the personal allowance were common across both scenarios. Some candidates attempted to answer this question with just the one computation; impossible given that property income formed part of the first computation, with dividend income included in the second.
>
> It should have been quite clear from the information provided that full computations were necessary for both scenarios. Those candidates who calculated the tax liability for a personal purchase and then attempted to adjust the figures for a corporate purchase invariably ended

up with a very confused answer. Candidates should be particularly aware of recent tax changes, and this is why an annual Finance Act update article is published.

Working through past examination questions will help candidates familiarise themselves with the best approach to be taken when answering questions which examine more than one tax. Also, it is important that candidates appreciate the interactions that can arise in such questions, and an article has been published covering many of the scenarios which could be examined. Although there were many good answers to part (b), some candidates discussed the finance costs restriction when this has nothing to do with taxable gains. All that was required was a brief mention (not a detailed answer) of the annual exempt amount.

Marking guide

	Marks
(a) Property purchased personally	
Employment income	0.5
Property income	
– Rent received	1
– Other expenses	0.5
Personal allowance	0.5
Income tax at basic rate	0.5
Income tax at higher rate	0.5
Finance costs tax reducer	1
Property purchased via limited company	
Employment income	0.5
Dividend income	0.5
Personal allowance	0.5
Income tax on non-savings income at basic rate	0.5
Income tax on non-savings income at higher rate	0.5
Dividend nil rate band	0.5
Income tax on dividend income at higher rate	0.5
Conclusion	1
	9
(b) Annual exempt amount	1
	1
Total	**10**

(a) **Property purchased personally**

	Non-savings income
	£
Employment income	60,000
Property income (W)	23,600
Net income	83,600
Less: Personal allowance	(12,570)
Taxable income	71,030
Income tax	
£37,700 at 20%	7,540

	Non-savings income
	£
£33,330 at 40%	13,332
£71,030	
	20,872
Interest relief (12,000 at 20%)	(2,400)
Income tax liability	18,472
Working – Property income	
Rent receivable (2,600 × 12)	31,200
Other expenses	(7,600)
Property income	23,600

Property purchased via a limited company

	Non-savings income	Dividend income
	£	£
Employment income	60,000	
Dividends		4,500
Net income	60,000	4,500
Less: Personal allowance	(12,570)	
Taxable income	47,430	4,500
Income tax		
Non-savings income		
– £37,700 at 20%	7,540	
– £9,730 at 40%	3,892	
– £47,430		
Dividend income		
– £500 at 0%	0	
– £4,000 at 33.75%	1,350	
– £4,500		
Income tax liability	12,782	

Conclusion

If Kat purchases the property via a limited company, then the overall tax saving will be £3,486 compared to purchasing the property personally:

	£
Property purchased personally	18,472
Property purchased via a limited company (2,204 + 12,782)	(14,986)
Tax saving	3,486

> **Tutorial note.** The comparison ignores the fact that not all of the profits are withdrawn under the company purchase option. However, profits might typically be retained within a company to repay the mortgage borrowing or to fund a future property purchase.

(b) Annual exempt amount of £3,000 not available if gain occurs within limited company.

249 Venus Ltd (March/June 2023)

Course Book references
Corporation tax computations are covered in Chapter 19 and gains for companies in 20.

Top tips
There are 5.5 marks available for capital allowances so care is needed here.

Easy marks
There were some easy marks throughout the question.

ACCA Examining Team's Comments
This question was generally very well answered, with many candidates scoring high marks.

For disallowable expenditure, most candidates adjusted for four or five of the items, although the amortisation and/or qualifying charitable donations were missed. Many had no difficulty calculating the correct deduction for the grant of a 12-year lease. One common mistake was to work out the non-chargeable portion of the lease and use that for the basis of the lease deduction rather than the chargeable portion.

Venus Ltd – Corporation tax computation for the year ended 31 March 2025

	A	B
1		£
2	Operating profit	200,692
3	Depreciation	32,046
4	Amortisation	4,000
5	Entertaining UK customers	3,600
6	Gifts of hampers	2,730
7	Qualifying charitable donation	1,410
8	Leasehold premium (working 1)	(3,120)
9	Capital allowances (working 2)	(80,324)
10	Trading profit	161,034
11	Bank interest (18,050 + 350)	18,400
12	Dividends from Mars Ltd	0
13	Chargeable gain	62,880
14		242,314
15	Qualifying charitable donation	(1,410)
16		240,904
17	Group relief	(7,635)
18	Taxable total profits	233,269
19	Corporation tax (233,269 at 25%)	58,317

> **Tutorial note.** The dividends received from Mars Ltd are exempt income. The upper limit for corporation tax = £250,000/2 = £125,000. Thus, Venus Ltd will pay the main rate.

Workings

1 **Leasehold premium**

	£
Premium received	96,000
Less: 96,000 × 2% × (12 – 1)	(21,120)
	74,880
Deduction 74,880/12 × 6/12	3,120

2 **Capital allowances**

	AIA	Main pool	Special rate pool	Allowances
	£	£	£	£
WDV brought forward		8,400	12,740	
Additions qualifying for AIA:				
Equipment	52,112			
AIA – 100%	(52,112)			52,112
New delivery van	20,800			
AIA	(20,800)			20,800
Car (1)			22,930	
Proceeds			(16,750)	
Car (2)		26,470		
		34,870	18,920	
WDA – 18%		(6,277)		6,277
WDA – 6%			(1,135)	1,135
WDV carried forward		28,593	17,785	
Total allowances				80,324

> **Tutorial note.** Car (1) has CO_2 emissions over 50 grams per kilometre, and therefore qualifies for writing down allowances at the rate of 6%.
>
> Car (2) has CO_2 emissions up to 50 grams per kilometre, and therefore qualifies for writing down allowances at the rate of 18%.

250 Mooncake Ltd (March/June 2021 amended)

> **Course Book references**
>
> Corporation tax computations are covered in Chapter 19 and gains for companies are covered in Chapter 20. Losses are covered in Chapter 21.
>
> **Top tips**
>
> For part (a), be careful to stick to the allotted time. The fact that this requirement is just for 2 marks, together with the use of 'state' indicates that only a short set of answers is required.
>
> For part (b) construct your answer in the same order as the information given in the question. This helps to ensure all items are covered.
>
> In part (c), remember that indexation allowance cannot create a capital loss.
>
> **Easy marks**
>
> There were some easy marks throughout the question but part (a) was very straightforward.

Marking guide	**Marks**

			Marks	
(a)	Rate		1	
	Timing		0.5	
	Qualifying charitable donations		0.5	
				2
(b)	Depreciation		0.5	
	Lease of office equipment		0.5	
	Lease of car		1	
	Entertaining staff		0.5	
	Entertaining overseas customers		0.5	
	QCDs		0.5	
	Capital allowances		0.5	
	– WDV b/f		0.5	
	– Proceeds – van		1	
	– Proceeds – car		1	
	– Proceeds – car		0.5	
	– WDA		0.5	
				7
(c)	(i)	Trading profit	0.5	
		Property business income	0.5	
		Chargeable gain	1	
		Trading loss	0.5	
		QCDs	0.5	
		Corporation tax	0.5	
				4
	(ii)	Trading loss	0.5	
		Property business loss	0.5	

308   Taxation (TX – UK) FA 2024

Marking guide	Marks
Capital loss	0.5
QCDs	0.5
	2
Total	**15**

(a) Factors which will influence a company's choice of loss relief claim:

(1) The rate at which relief will be obtained: 26.5% if marginal relief applies (best use), 25% at the main rate (second best use), 19% at the small profits rate (third best use)

(2) The timing and cash flow in relation to the relief obtained, with an earlier claim generally being preferable

(3) The extent to which relief for qualifying charitable donations will be lost

(b) **Mooncake Ltd – Trading loss for the year ended 31 March 2025**

	£
Operating loss	(93,820)
Depreciation	7,230
Lease of office equipment	0
Lease of car (3,400 × 15%)	510
Entertaining staff	0
Entertaining overseas customers	8,720
Qualifying charitable donations	1,600
Capital allowances (working)	(3,240)
Trading loss	(79,000)

Working

Capital allowances

	Main pool	Allowances
	£	£
WDV b/f	43,200	
Proceeds		
– Delivery van (130% item, proceeds = BC)		(2,124)
– Car [1]	(8,100)	
– Car [2]	(5,300)	
	29,800	
WDA – 18%	(5,364)	5,364
WDV c/f	24,436	
Total allowances		3,240

Answers 309

(c) (i) **Corporation tax liabilities for the years ended 31 March 2024 and 2025**

	y/e 31.3.24 £	y/e 31.3.25 £
Trading profit	138,200	0
Property business income	23,700	0
Chargeable gain	0	0
	161,900	0
Trading loss	(79,000)	0
Qualifying charitable donations	(1,400)	0
Taxable total profits	81,500	0
Corporation tax at 25%	20,375	0
Less marginal relief (250,000 − 81,500) × 3/200	(2,528)	
Corporation tax payable	17,847	

> **Tutorial note.** There is no chargeable gain for the year ended 31 March 2025 because the indexation allowance of £6,700 exceeds the gain of £3,700.

(ii) **Carry forward to the year ending 31 March 2026**

	£
Trading loss	0
Property business loss	4,400
Capital loss	4,900
Qualifying charitable donations	0

> **Tutorial note.** Indexation allowance cannot be used to create a capital loss.

251 Maximum Ltd (September/December 2023)

> **Course Book references**
>
> Corporation tax computations are covered in Chapter 19 and gains for companies are covered in Chapter 20.
>
> **Easy marks**
>
> There were some easy marks throughout the question.
>
> **ACCA Examining Team's Comments**
>
> This question was generally well answered.

(a) **Maximum Ltd – Taxable total profits for the year ended 31 March 2025**

	A	B
1		£
2	Trading profit	127,200
3	Deduction for lease premium ((22,320/8) × 8/12)	(1,860)
4	Lease of first car	0
5	Lease of second car (3,900 × 15%)	585
6	Employee bonus paid November 2025	(20,000)
7	Employee bonus paid February 2026	0
8	Revised trading profit	105,925
9	Property business income (W1)	7,950
10	Chargeable gains (W2)	38,400
11		152,275
12	Qualifying charitable donations	(2,800)
13	Political donations	0
14	Taxable total profits	149,475

Tutorial note. Only the employee bonuses of £20,000 paid within nine months of the end of Maximum Ltd's period of account are deductible. The bonuses of £16,000 will be deducted in calculating the trading profit for the year ended 31 March 2026.

Workings

1 **Property business income**

	£
Rent receivable ((8,400 × 3/6) + 5,600)	9,800
Insurance (1,320 – 190)	(1,130)
Security deposit	0
Advertising	(720)
Property business income	7,950

Tutorial note. A security deposit, less the cost of making good any damage, is returned to the tenant on the cessation of a letting. It is not treated as income when received by the landlord and, therefore, is not an allowable expense when returned to the tenant.

2   *Chargeable gains*

	£	£
Warehouse		43,300
Factory	29,100	
Rollover relief	(29,100)	0
Capital loss		(4,900)
Chargeable gains		38,400

Tutorial note. The sale proceeds of the factory are fully reinvested, so the chargeable gain of £29,100 can be rolled over. No rollover relief claim is possible in respect of the chargeable gain made on the disposal of the warehouse because this property was not used for business purposes.

(b) **Maximum Ltd – Unused losses carried forward**

	A	B
1		£
2	Unused losses brought forward	
3	Trading loss	288,200
4	Property business loss	3,800
5		292,000
6	Maximum Ltd – Loss relief	(149,475)
7	Xim Ltd – Group relief	(21,400)
8	Mum Ltd – Group relief	0
9	Unused losses carried forward	121,125

Tutorial note. The carried forward loss of £121,125 consists entirely of trading loss because the property business loss of £3,800 is used first.

252 Lucky Ltd (September/December 2015) (amended)

Course Book references

The computation of taxable total profits and the computation of the corporation tax liability are covered in Chapter 19. The adjustment to trading profits is dealt with in Chapter 7 and capital allowances in Chapter 8. National insurance contributions are covered in Chapter 12.

Top tips.

Administrative aspects of corporation tax are very likely to be examined so don't omit them from your revision.

Easy marks

There were some easy marks for the adjustment to trading profit and computation of corporation tax in part (b).

ACCA Examining Team's Comments

In part (a), most candidates appreciated that an accounting period starts when a company commences to trade, but many could not provide any other circumstances. For example, an accounting period will also start when a company otherwise becomes liable to corporation tax.

In part (b), the aspect of this question which appeared to cause candidates the most difficulties was the lease premium deduction and the difficulties were largely due to a failure to read the question carefully. Candidates were given the amount of the premium assessed on the landlord as income. However, a lot of candidates misread this figure as being the total premium paid. Part (c) of the question was reasonably well answered.

[**BPP note.** Part (d) has been added to this question and there are no relevant examining team's comments.]

Marking guide		Marks
(a)	After end of previous period	1
	Other situations	1
		2
(b)	**Trading profit**	
	Advertising	0.5
	Depreciation	0.5
	Amortisation	0.5
	Lease premium deduction	1.5
	Capital allowances	
	Integral feature addition	0.5
	AIA in preference to integral feature	0.5
	Computer addition	0.5
	Office equipment addition	0.5
	AIA	1
	WDA	0.5
	Car addition	0.5
	FYA	0.5
	Interest income	0.5
	Corporation tax	1
		9

Marking guide	Marks
(c) Date for retention	1
Penalty	<u>1</u>
	2
(d) Capital allowances	1
National insurance contributions	<u>1</u>
	2
Total	<u><u>15</u></u>

(a) An accounting period will normally start immediately after the end of the preceding accounting period.

An accounting period will also start when a company commences to trade, or otherwise becomes liable to corporation tax.

(b) **Lucky Ltd – Corporation tax computation for the four-month period ended 31 March 2025**

	£
Operating profit	699,266
Advertising	0
Depreciation	14,700
Amortisation	9,000
Deduction for lease premium £46,800/12 × 4/12	(1,300)
Capital allowances (W1)	<u>(346,957)</u>
Trading profit	374,709
Interest income	<u>700</u>
Taxable total profits	<u>375,409</u>
Corporation tax £375,409 @ 25%	93,852

> **Tutorial note.** The advertising expenditure incurred during September 2024 is pre-trading and is treated as incurred on 1 December 2024. It is therefore deductible, and no adjustment is required.

Workings

1 **Capital allowances**

	AIA/FYA	Main pool	Allowances
	£	£	£
Integral features	291,200		
AIA (W2)	(291,200)		291,200
Computer		6,300	
Office equipment		<u>48,689</u>	
		54,989	

314 Taxation (TX – UK) FA 2024

	AIA/FYA	Main pool	Allowances
	£	£	£
AIA (W2) 333,333 – 291,200	(42,133)		42,133
	12,856		
FYA full expensing 100%	(12,856)		12,856
Car		12,800	
WDA 18% × 4/12		(768)	768
TWDV carried forward		12,032	
Total allowances			346,957

2 **Annual investment allowances**

The annual investment allowance is reduced to £333,333 (£1,000,000 × 4/12) because Lucky Ltd's accounting period is four months long.

> **Tutorial note.** Lucky Ltd would want to avoid a balancing charge on disposal and would therefore claim the annual investment allowance in priority to first year allowances. Capital allowances should therefore be claimed in the following order:
>
> (1) 100% AIA against second-hand assets (those qualifying for 6% WDA first, then those qualifying for 18% WDA) – N/A for Lucky Ltd in this case
>
> (2) 100% AIA against new assets falling into the special rate pool – the integral features in this case
>
> (3) 100% AIA against new assets falling into the main pool – the computer and office equipment in this case
>
> (4) 100% and 50% FYAs
>
> It is beneficial to claim the annual investment allowance against the integral features expenditure, as it would otherwise only qualify for first year allowance of 50% with the balance going into the special rate pool.
>
> The computer purchased on 19 August 2024 is pre-trading and is treated as incurred on 1 December 2024.
>
> The car has CO_2 emissions up to 50 grams per kilometre and therefore qualifies for the 18% WDA in the main pool.

 Videos can be viewed online by accessing your ebook version on VitalSource.

(c) Lucky Ltd must retain the records used in preparing its self-assessment corporation tax return until six years after the end of the accounting period, which is 31 March 2031.

A failure to retain records could result in a penalty of up to £3,000 per accounting period. However, the maximum penalty will only be charged in serious cases.

(d) The cost of the car will be included in Lucky Ltd's capital allowance computation and written down at the appropriate rate each year depending on the car's CO_2 emissions.

Lucky Ltd will also have to pay Class 1A national insurance contributions on the company car. Class 1A is deductible from taxable trading profits.

253 Jump Ltd (March/June 2016)

Course Book references

The computation of taxable total profits and the corporation tax liability are covered in Chapter 19.

Groups of companies are covered in Chapter 22.

Top tips

In part (a), remember to include a zero when an item needs no adjustment; otherwise, you will not be credited for this knowledge.

Easy marks

Most of the adjustments to profit appear regularly in corporation tax questions.

Marking guide			Marks
(a)	**Trading loss**		
	Depreciation		0.5
	Employee training courses		0.5
	Employee pension contributions0		0.5
	Staff party		0.5
	Car lease		1
	Accountancy		0.5
	Legal fees – share capital		0.5
	Legal fees – renewal of short lease		0.5
	Entertaining UK customers		0.5
	Entertaining overseas customers		0.5
	Political donations		0.5
	Balancing charge adjustment		0.5
	Capital allowances		
	Tax written down values b/f		0.5
	Car 1		1
	Car 2		0.5
	Balancing charge		0.5
	Writing down allowance		1
			10
(b)	(i) Choice of relief		1
			1
	(ii) Maximum relief claim – 7 m/e 31.12.24		0.5
	Maximum relief claim – y/e 31.5.24		1.5
			2
	(iii) Maximum surrender		1.5
	Skip Ltd		0.5
			2
Total			**15**

316 Taxation (TX – UK) FA 2024

(a) **Jump Ltd – Trading loss for the three-month period ended 31 March 2025**

	£
Loss before taxation	(144,700)
Depreciation	8,100
Employee training courses	0
Employee pension contributions	0
Staff party	0
Lease of car £1,200 × 15%	180
Accountancy	0
Legal fees	
– Issue of share capital	3,800
– Renewal of short lease	0
Entertaining UK customers	1,700
Entertaining overseas customers	790
Political donations	800
Balancing charge (W)	3,330
Trading loss	(126,000)

Working

Capital allowances

	Main pool	Special rate pool	Allowances
	£	£	£
TWDV brought forward	12,100	5,700	
Proceeds – Car [1]		(9,300)	
Proceeds – Car [2]	(6,100)		
Balancing charge		3,600	(3,600)
	6,000		
WDA – 18% × 3/12	(270)		270
TWDV carried forward	5,730		
Net balancing charge			(3,330)

> **Tutorial note.** The proceeds for car [1] are restricted to the original cost figure of £9,300.

(b) (i) The main factor which will influence Jump Ltd's choice of loss relief or group relief claims is the rate at which relief will be obtained: 26.5% if marginal relief applies (best use), 25% at the main rate (second best use), 19% at the small profits rate (third best use).

> **Tutorial note.** The extent to which relief for qualifying charitable donations will be lost is not relevant here given that Jump Ltd has not made any charitable donations.

(ii) The maximum loss relief claim for the seven-month period to 31 December 2024 is £42,400, being the total profits for this period. The loss relief claim for the year ended 31 May 2024 is restricted to £33,250 ((78,600 + 1,200) × 5/12).

(iii) The maximum amount of trading loss which can be surrendered to Hop Ltd is £23,625, being the lower of £23,625 (63,000 × 3/8) and £126,000.

Skip Ltd is not a 75% subsidiary of Jump Ltd, so no group relief claim is possible.

254 Online Ltd (March/June 2017)

Course Book references

Computing taxable total profits is covered in Chapter 19.

Chargeable gains for companies is the subject of Chapter 20.

The use of losses is dealt with in Chapter 21.

Payment of tax by companies is covered in Chapter 22.

Top tips

Don't forget to answer both parts of the question. In part (b) you only needed to make a couple of points in order to gain the marks.

Easy marks

There should have been easy marks for well-known adjustments such as depreciation and amortisation. The capital allowances computation was quite straightforward.

ACCA Examining Team's Comments

Part (a) was well answered. Surprisingly, the one aspect which consistently caused difficulty was the qualifying charitable donation. Many candidates added this back prior to deducting it, with others grossing up the deduction.

Also, it is important that candidates know basic tax rules.

Even though all of the items included in the capital allowances special rate pool had been sold, there was no balancing allowance because Online Ltd's trade did not cease. This was another computation where candidates needed to think carefully about where to show workings. In this case, the deduction for the lease premium, capital allowances and the chargeable gain warranted separate workings. It was not a good idea for candidates to attempt a short-cut approach to any of these workings. As regards the chargeable gain, quite a few candidates included the gain from the disposal made three years previously. This shows just how much care needs to be taken over dates.

In part (b), many candidates appreciated that acquiring an associated company would mean that the profit threshold for establishing whether Online Ltd is a large company would be reduced to £750,000. It would therefore be likely that the company's corporation tax would in future be payable by quarterly instalments. Having established this point, there was no need to then go on and explain quarterly instalments in detail. If such detail was needed, then this would have been made clear in the requirement. Few candidates correctly stated that the dividends received from Offline Ltd, being group dividends, would not form part of Online Ltd's profits when establishing its large company status.

Marking guide	Marks
(a) Depreciation	0.5
Amortisation	0.5
Property loss brought forward	1
Qualifying charitable donations	0.5
Lease premium	
Amount assessed on landlord	1
Deduction	1
Capital allowances	
Tax written down values b/f	0.5
Disposal – car	1
Disposal – pool	0.5
WDA @ 18%	0.5
WDA @ 6%	1
Chargeable gain	
Disposal proceeds	0.5
Share pool – original cost	0.5
Share pool – indexation to October 2013	0.5
Share pool – disposal October 2013	1
Share pool – indexation to December 2017	0.5
Share pool – disposal March 2025	0.5
Capital loss brought forward	0.5
	13
(b) Profit threshold reduced	1.5
Group dividends	0.5
	2
Total	**15**

(a) **Online Ltd – Corporation tax computation for the year ended 31 March 2025**

	£
Operating profit	896,700
Depreciation	21,660
Amortisation	9,000
Deduction for lease premium (W1)	(7,380)
Capital allowances (W2)	(9,824)
Trading profit	910,156
Chargeable gain (W3)	59,967
	970,123

	£
Property business loss brought forward	(12,500)
Qualifying charitable donations	(6,800)
Taxable total profits	950,823

Workings

1 **Deduction for lease premium**

	£
Premium paid	90,000
Less: 90,000 × 2% × (10 – 1)	(16,200)
Amount assessed on the landlord	73,800
Deduction (73,800/10)	7,380

2 **Capital allowances**

	Main pool £	Special rate pool £	Allowances £
WDV brought forward	56,700	13,433	
Addition – Car	13,700		
Disposals – Car	(17,200)		
Disposals – Pool		(9,300)	
	53,200	4,133	
WDA – 18%	(9,576)		9,576
WDA – 6%		(248)	248
WDV carried forward	43,624	3,885	
Total allowances			9,824

> **Tutorial note.** The car purchased has CO_2 emissions between 1 and 50 grams per kilometre, and therefore qualifies for writing down allowances at the rate of 18%.
>
> The proceeds for the car which was sold are restricted to the original cost figure of £17,200.
>
> Although all of the items included in the special rate pool have been sold, there is no balancing allowance because the business has not ceased.

3 **Chargeable gain**

	£
Disposal proceeds	90,600
Less: Indexed cost (W4)	(27,529)
	63,071
Less: Capital loss brought forward	(3,104)
Chargeable gain	59,967

4 *Share pool*

	Number	Indexed cost
	£	£
Purchase June 2010	40,000	49,300
Indexation to October 2013 (49,300 × 0.124)		6,113
		55,413
Disposal October 2013 (55,413 × 22,000/40,000)	(22,000)	(30,477)
	18,000	24,936
Indexation to December 2017 (24,936 × 0.104)		2,593
		27,529
Disposal March 2025	(18,000)	(27,529)

(b) The profit threshold for establishing whether Online Ltd is a large company will be reduced to £750,000 (1,500,000/2), so it is likely that the company's corporation tax will have to be paid by quarterly instalments.

The dividends received from Offline Ltd, being group dividends, will not form part of Online Ltd's profits.

255 Last-Orders Ltd (September/December 2017)

Course Book references

The computation of taxable total profits is covered in Chapter 19. Chargeable gains for companies are covered in Chapter 20. Corporate losses are the subject of Chapter 21 and group relief is dealt with in Chapter 22.

Top tips

When a company ceases to trade, no writing down allowances are given in the final accounting period but there will be a balancing adjustment.

Easy marks

In part (a) there were plenty of easy marks for adjustment to profit items but be careful to identify the effect of each of the adjustments on the trading loss. An item added back, such as depreciation, will reduce the loss, but an item deducted, such as capital allowances, will increase the loss.

ACCA Examining Team's Comments

Although section (a) was very well answered by many candidates, it caused problems for others. The section did not require any detailed workings, with any adjustments easily contained within the single computation.

When commencing with a loss figure, candidates should be particularly careful to indicate which adjustments are deductions and which are additions. A single column approach with deductions shown in brackets avoids any confusion. Many candidates did not show those items not requiring any adjustment, despite being instructed specifically to do so – easy marks thereby being lost. Also, candidates should appreciate that there is no need to adjust for items of income which occur in the statement of profit or loss **after** the figure used to commence the loss adjustment. Last-Orders Ltd had ceased trading, so this meant that there was a balancing allowance. Many candidates missed this point, instead calculating capital allowances for the period.

Section (b) was generally well answered, with a number of perfect answers. However, candidates do not impress if they make basic mistakes such as deducting the annual exempt amount when calculating a corporate chargeable gain. Also, candidates should always be careful to follow the requirements – an easy half-mark was sometimes missed by not showing a figure for the amount of unused trading loss despite this being specifically requested.

In section (c), given that the company had ceased trading, candidates should really have realised that the loss could not be carried forward. Vague answers such as 'claim terminal loss relief' are not sufficient. Instead, candidates should have stated that relief was against total profits, for the previous three years and on a latest year first (LIFO) basis.

Marking guide

		Marks
(a)	Depreciation	0.5
	Counselling services	0.5
	Employee pension contributions	0.5
	Employer Class 1 NICs	0.5
	Employer Class 1A NICs	0.5
	Unpaid bonuses	0.5
	Lease of car	0.5
	Entertaining UK suppliers	0.5
	Entertaining overseas customers	0.5
	Qualifying charitable donations	0.5
	Balancing allowance	1
		6
(b)	**Property business income**	
	Rent receivable	1
	Insurance	1
	Repairs	0.5
	Chargeable gain	1
	Trading loss	0.5
	Qualifying charitable donation	0.5
	Unused trading loss	0.5
		5
(c)	Terminal loss relief	1.5
	Group relief to Gastro Ltd	2
	No group relief to Gourmet Ltd	0.5
		4
Total		**15**

(a) **Last-Orders Ltd – Trading loss for the ten-month period ended 31 January 2025**

	£
Operating loss	(276,480)
Add:	
– Depreciation	9,460
– Counselling services	0
– Employee pension contributions	0

	£
– Employer Class 1 NICs	0
– Employer Class 1A NICs	0
– Unpaid bonuses	10,400
– Lease of car	0
– Entertaining UK suppliers	1,920
– Entertaining overseas customers	440
– Employer Class 1A NICs	0
– Employer Class 1A NICs	0
– Qualifying charitable donations	800
Less: Balancing allowance £(24,200 – 13,600)	(10,600)
Trading loss	(264,060)

> **Tutorial note.** No deduction is permitted where earnings are not paid within nine months of the end of the period of account.
>
> No adjustment is required where the CO_2 emissions of a leased car do not exceed 50 grams per kilometre.
>
> All business entertaining is disallowable. The distinction between UK and overseas is only relevant for value added tax (VAT) purposes.

(b) **Last-Orders Ltd – Taxable total profits for the ten-month period ended 31 January 2025**

	£
Property business income (W)	22,800
Chargeable gain £(126,800 – 79,400 – 12,900)	34,500
Total profits	57,300
Less	
– Trading loss	(57,300)
– Qualifying charitable donations	(0)
Taxable total profits	0
Unused trading loss £(264,060 – 57,300)	206,760

Working

	£
Rent receivable £19,200 × 2 × 10/12	32,000
Less	
– Insurance £1,800 × 10/12	(1,500)
– Repairs	(7,700)
Property business income	22,800

> **Tutorial note.** The accruals basis is always used by companies in computing property business income.

(c) The trading loss can be relieved against Last-Orders Ltd's total profits for the previous three years, later years first, because it is a terminal loss.

The trading loss can be surrendered to Gastro Ltd because there is a 75% group relationship. The amount surrendered will be restricted to 10/12ths of Gastro Ltd's taxable total profits for the year ended 31 March 2025.

There is not a 75% group relationship with Gourmet Ltd, so no group relief claim is possible.

256 Solo Ltd (March/June 2018)

Course Book references

The computation of taxable total profits is covered in Chapter 19. Chargeable gains for companies are covered in Chapter 20. Corporate losses are the subject of Chapter 21.

Top tips

Think about why you are given capital losses for the two previous accounting periods. How can capital losses be relieved?

Easy marks

You should have gained two easy marks for dealing with the deduction for the lease premium in part (a) as this topic is regularly examined and a further two easy marks in part (b) for the calculation of property business income.

ACCA Examining Team's Comments

Part (a) for 3 marks required candidates to calculate Solo Ltd's revised tax-adjusted trading loss for the year ended 31 March 2025. This section was quite well answered. However, when dealing with a trading loss, candidates need to be very careful that adjustments are correctly added or deducted. Treating the loss as a negative means that there is no need to change the approach from that used for a trading profit. A number of candidates did not appreciate that there was a balancing charge because the disposal proceeds for the plant and machinery main pool exceeded the written down value brought forward.

Part (b) for 8 marks asked candidates to prepare a corporation tax computation for the year ended 31 March 2025 showing taxable total profits. This was on the basis that Solo Ltd claimed relief for its trading loss against its total profits. The requirement meant that candidates had to calculate property business income, calculate a chargeable gain on a share disposal, deduct brought forward capital losses from the gain, and then deduct the trading loss so that taxable total profits were nil. This section was again well answered. One aspect which consistently caused difficulty was candidates not preparing a separate gain calculation for the share purchase made during the preceding nine days.

A number of candidates incorrectly restricted the insurance deduction in the property business income calculation to 8/12ths because the building was unoccupied from 1 April to 31 July 2024.

Information was provided in date order, and candidates often tried to use the details provided for the year ended 31 December 2023 and the period ended 31 March 2024 in this section of the question. The only details which were relevant were the capital losses, and these were often omitted in any case.

Part (c) for 4 marks required candidates to calculate Solo Ltd's taxable total profits for the year ended 31 December 2023 and the three-month period ended 31 March 2024. This was on the basis that the company claimed relief for the remainder of its trading loss as early as possible. This section was very well answered, and it was pleasing to see most candidates correctly restricting the trading loss set off for the year ended 31 December 2023 to 9/12ths of the total profits.

Candidates should note that where two accounting periods are involved, then a two-column approach avoids the need to type out descriptions twice.

Marking guide	Marks	
(a) **Deduction for lease premium**		
Premium received	0.5	
Amount treated as capital	1	
Trading income deduction	0.5	
Balancing charge	1	
		3
(b) **Property business income**		
Rent receivable	1	
Security deposit	0.5	
Insurance	1	
Chargeable gain		
Disposal proceeds on shares purchased in previous 9 days	0.5	
Cost of shares purchased in previous 9 days	0.5	
Disposal proceeds on shares from share pool	0.5	
Share pool		
– Original purchase	0.5	
– Indexation to December 2017	1	
– Disposal	1	
Capital losses relieved	1	
Trading loss relieved	0.5	
		8
(c) Trading profits	0.5	
Property business income	0.5	
Chargeable gains	0.5	
Trading loss relieved	1.5	
Qualifying charitable donations	1	
		4
Total		15

(a) **Solo Ltd – Trading loss for the year ended 31 March 2025**

	£
Trading loss	(151,300)
Less: Deduction for lease premium (W)	(2,150)
Add: Balancing charge	4,300
Trading loss	(149,150)

Working

	£
Premium received	20,000
Less: £20,000 × 2% × (8 – 1)	(2,800)

	£
Amount assessable on landlord	17,200
Trading income deduction £17,200/8	2,150

(b) **Solo Ltd – Corporation tax computation for the year ended 31 March 2025**

	£
Property business income (W1)	9,480
Net chargeable gains £(16,198(W2) – 3,300 – 2,100)	10,798
Total profits	20,278
Less: Trading loss	(20,278)
Taxable total profits	0

Workings

1 **Property business income**

	£
Rent receivable £(7,800 + (7,800 × 2/6))	10,400
Security deposit	0
Less: Insurance	(920)
Property business income	9,480

> **Tutorial note.** The accruals basis is always used by companies in computing property business income. A security deposit is not treated as income when received. It will be treated as income if the landlord uses it, for example to cover unpaid rent at the end of the tenancy. Any amount repaid to the tenant is not treated as an expense.

2 **Chargeable gains**

	£	£
Purchase 8 December 2024		
Disposal proceeds £31,200 × 1,000/6,500	4,800	
Less: Cost	(4,600)	
		200
Share pool		
Disposal proceeds £31,200 × 5,500/6,500	26,400	
Less: Cost (W3)	(10,402)	
		15,998
Chargeable gains		16,198

326 Taxation (TX – UK) FA 2024

3   *Share pool*

	Number	Cost £
Purchase June 2006	20,000	27,000
Indexation to December 2017 £27,000 × 0.401		10,827
		37,827
Disposal December 2024 £37,827 × 5,500/20,000	(5,500)	(10,402)
c/f	14,500	27,425

Tutorial note. The disposal is first matched with the shares purchased in the nine days before the disposal and then against the share pool.

Indexation is frozen at December 2017.

(c) **Solo Ltd – Taxable total profits for the periods ended 31 December 2023 and 31 March 2024**

	y/e 31 December 2023 £	p/e 31 March 2024 £
Trading profit	35,900	12,300
Property business income	12,100	4,200
Chargeable gain	0	0
Total profits	48,000	16,500
Less		
– Trading loss relief	(W) (36,000)	(16,500)
– Qualifying charitable donations	(1,200)	Wasted
Taxable total profits	10,800	0

Working

	£
Year ended 31 December 2023 £48,000 × 9/12	36,000

257 Ash Ltd, Beech Ltd and Cedar Ltd (September/December 2018)

Course Book references

Computing taxable total profits (including residence of companies and accounting periods) and the corporation tax liability are covered in Chapter 19. Chargeable gains for companies is the subject of Chapter 20. Losses for a single company are dealt with in Chapter 21 and group relief in Chapter 22.

Top tips

Take care you answer all three parts of the question.

Easy marks

These were available for basic adjustments to profits in part (b).

ACCA Examining Team's Comments

Part (a)(i) was quite well answered. However, if asked to identify a company's accounting periods throughout a given period, then candidates should make sure that all relevant periods are stated. It does not create a good impression if there are gaps between the accounting periods stated by a candidate, or if a stated period ends before it has started.

In part (a)(ii), again candidates should be careful not to confuse the rules for companies with those applicable to individuals.

If a limited company is incorporated in the UK, then nothing else is relevant. So, as regards the majority of Ash Ltd's director/shareholders moving overseas, candidates should just have stated that this did not have any impact on the company's residence status.

Part (b) was very well answered. When making adjustments to a trading profit, candidates need to be very careful that adjustments are correctly added and not deducted.

Part (c) was again well answered. When calculating chargeable gains for a corporate share disposal, then carefully check the dates that have been given. There was a rights issue which had taken place in the month of purchase, so there was no need to index prior to adding the new shares into the share pool.

Marking guide

			Marks	
(a)	(i)	First accounting period	1	
		Second accounting period	0.5	
		Third accounting period	0.5	
				2
	(ii)	Incorporated in UK	1	
		Move overseas by director/shareholders	1	
				2
(b)		Depreciation	0.5	
		Gifts to customers	0.5	
		Gifts to staff	0.5	
		Qualifying charitable donations added back	0.5	
		Impairment loss	0.5	
		Lease of cars	1	
		Fine	0.5	
		Legal fees	0.5	
		Interest payable	0.5	
		Qualifying charitable donations deducted from total profits	0.5	
		Corporation tax liability	0.5	
				6
(c)		Disposal proceeds	0.5	
		Indexed cost		
		Purchase	0.5	
		Rights issue	1	
		Indexation allowance	1	
		Capital loss	1	

Marking guide	Marks
Loss relief	0.5
Group relief	0.5
	5
Total	**15**

(a) **Ash Ltd**

(i) **Accounting periods**

1 February 2023 to 31 January 2024

1 February 2024 to 31 March 2024

Year ended 31 March 2025

> **Tutorial note.** The bank account opened by Ash Ltd on 1 December 2022 is not a source of income, and therefore does not trigger the start of an accounting period.
>
> An accounting period cannot be longer than 12 months, so the period of account ended 31 March 2024 must be split into two accounting periods.
>
> The move overseas of a majority of Ash Ltd's director/shareholders on 1 October 2024 has no impact on the company's accounting periods.

(ii) **Residence status**

(1) Ash Ltd was incorporated in the UK, so the company is therefore resident in the UK throughout the period 1 December 2022 to 31 March 2025.

(2) The move overseas of a majority of Ash Ltd's director/shareholders on 1 October 2024 does not have any impact on the company's residence status.

(b) **Beech Ltd**

Corporation tax computation for the year ended 31 March 2025

	£
Profit before taxation	305,500
Depreciation	14,700
Gifts to customers	3,500
Gifts to staff	0
Qualifying charitable donations	1,100
Impairment loss	0
Lease of cars (12,600 × 15%)	1,890
Data protection fine	6,400
Legal fees – renewal of short lease	0
Interest payable	0
Trading profit/total profits	333,090
Less qualifying charitable donations	(1,100)
Taxable total profits	331,990

	£
Corporation tax	
331,990 at 25%	82,998

> **Tutorial note.** Gifts to customers are only an allowable deduction if they cost less than £50 per recipient per year, are not of food, drink, tobacco or vouchers for exchangeable goods and carry a conspicuous advertisement for the company making the gift. Gifts to staff are allowable.

(c) **Cedar Ltd**

Taxable total profits for the year ended 31 March 2025

	£
Disposal proceeds (25,000 × 6.00)	150,000
Indexed cost (W)	(38,004)
Chargeable gain	111,996
Capital loss	(8,800)
Loss relief	(19,700)
Group relief	(20,800)
Taxable total profits	62,696

Working

Indexed cost

Share pool

	Number	Indexed cost
	£	£
Purchase July 2010	20,000	24,800
Rights issue July 2010		
20,000 × 1/4 × £1.15	5,000	5,750
	25,000	30,550
Indexation to December 2017 (frozen)		
30,550 × 0.244		7,454
		38,004
Disposal December 2024	(25,000)	(38,004)

> **Tutorial note.** A joint election can be made so that Cedar Ltd is treated as having incurred Timber Ltd's capital loss.
>
> Indexation allowance is frozen at December 2017.

258 Aoede Ltd, Bianca Ltd and Charon Ltd (March/June 2019)

> **Course Book references**
>
> Computing taxable total profits is covered in Chapter 19, losses for a single company in Chapter 21 and group relief in Chapter 22. Chargeable gains for companies is the subject of Chapter 20.
>
> **Top tips**
>
> It is important that you attempt all three parts of this question in order to gain reasonable marks.
>
> **Easy marks**
>
> There were easy marks for straightforward adjustments to profits in part (b).
>
> **ACCA Examining Team's Comments**
>
> Although Moon Ltd was often overlooked, part (a)(i) was generally well answered.
>
> For the year ended 31 March 2024, many candidates did not appreciate that loss relief was claimed against Aoede Ltd's chargeable gain in priority to offsetting the qualifying charitable donations.
>
> Part (a)(ii) was often not answered. The answer was simply that it was not beneficial for Aoede Ltd to make the loss relief claim against total income for the year ended 31 March 2024 because the income would have otherwise been covered by qualifying charitable donations.
>
> Part (b) was very well answered. Candidates should note that, when dealing with straightforward capital allowance computations such as those involved in this context, it is quicker to include them in the main computation rather than producing a full capital allowances working.
>
> Part (c) was also well answered. However, a few candidates combined the two computations.
>
> Where a question involves more than one disposal, then the gain or loss for each disposal must be calculated separately.

Marking guide	**Marks**
(a) (i) **Aoede Ltd y/e 31.3.24**
Total profits	0.5
Current period loss relief	1
Qualifying charitable donation unrelieved	0.5
Aoede Ltd y/e 31.3.25
Total profits	0.5
Carry forward loss relief	1
Qualifying charitable donation	0.5
Moon Ltd y/e 31.3.25
Trading profit	0.5
Group relief	0.5
	5
(ii) Loss relief claim not beneficial	1
	1
(b) Advertising expenditure	0.5
Lease of cars	1.5
Laptops	1

> **Marking guide**

	Marks
Car [1]	1
Car [2]	1
	5
(c) First property	
Disposal proceeds	0.5
Cost	0.5
Enhancement expenditure	0.5
Indexation allowance	1
Second property	
Disposal proceeds	0.5
Cost	0.5
Indexation allowance	0.5
	4
Total	15

(a) (i) **Aoede Ltd – Taxable total profits**

	y/e 31.3.24	y/e 31.3.25
	£	£
Trading profit	0	67,800
Property business income	0	23,400
Chargeable gain	5,800	16,200
Total profits	5,800	107,400
Less:		
– Current period trading loss relief	(5,800)	(0)
– Carry forward trading loss relief	(0)	(100,800)
– Qualifying charitable donation	(0)	(6,600)
Taxable total profits	0	0

(ii) **Moon Ltd – Taxable total profits**

	y/e 31.3.25
	£
Trading profit	19,700
Less:	
– Trading loss carry forward group relief	(4,700)
– Property business loss carry forward group relief	(15,000)
Taxable total profits	0

332 Taxation (TX – UK) FA 2024

> **Tutorial note.**
>
> **Loss memorandum**
>
> | | Trading loss | Property business loss |
> |---|---:|---:|
> | | £ | £ |
> | y/e 31.3.24 | 111,300 | 26,400 |
> | Used in y/e 31.3.24 against own profits | (5,800) | (0) |
> | Used in y/e 31.3.25 against own profits | (100,800) | (0) |
> | Used in y/e 31.3.25 as group relief | (4,700) | (15,000) |
> | Losses c/f | 0 | 11,400 |
>
> There are independent claims for Aoede Ltd's trading loss and property business loss. We have used the trading loss in priority to the property business loss but it would be possible to use the property business loss first – the result for these two accounting periods would be the same. Aoede Ltd's current period loss relief claim must be taken against total profits as far as possible. It is not possible to restrict it to preserve relief on the qualifying charitable donation of £6,000.
>
> Aoede Ltd will automatically carry forward its unused losses to y/e 31 March 2025 but can make a partial relief claim to keep sufficient total profits in charge to cover the qualifying charitable donation of £6,600. Aoede Ltd must use its carried forward losses itself before surrendering losses under carry forward group relief.
>
> It is not beneficial for Aoede Ltd to make the loss relief claim against total income for the year ended 31 March 2024 because the income would have otherwise been covered by the qualifying charitable donations of £6,000.

(b) **Bianca Ltd – Tax adjusted trading profit for the year ended 31 March 2025**

	£
Trading profit	256,300
Less: Advertising expenditure	(5,800)
Add: Lease of cars (5,100 × 15%)	765
Less: Capital allowances	
– Laptops (1,000 × 4 × 100%)	(4,000)
– Car [1] (12,400 × 18%)	(2,232)
– Car [2] (13,900 × 6%)	(834)
Revised trading profit	244,199

> **Tutorial note.** The advertising expenditure incurred during January 2023 is pre-trading and is therefore treated as incurred on 1 April 2024.
>
> The original cost of the laptops is irrelevant. Car [2] has CO_2 emissions over 50 grams per kilometre and therefore qualifies for writing down allowances at the rate of 6%.

(c) **Charon Ltd – Chargeable gains and capital losses for the year ended 31 March 2025**

First property

	£
Disposal proceeds	368,000
Less: Cost	(147,000)

	£
Less: Enhancement expenditure	(39,000)
	182,000
Indexation allowance	
– 147,000 × 0.856	(125,832)
Chargeable gain	56,168

Second property

	£
Disposal proceeds	167,000
Less: Cost	(172,000)
Indexation allowance	0
Less: Capital loss	(5,000)

> **Tutorial note.** There is no indexation allowance for the first property's enhancement expenditure of £39,000 because this was incurred after December 2017.

259 Mixture Ltd (March/June 2022)

Course Book references

Computing taxable total profits (including property income) and corporation tax are covered in Chapter 19. Large companies and instalments are covered in Chapter 23. Capital allowances are covered in Chapter 8.

Top tips

Remember that dividends received from other companies are not included in taxable total profits but they are included in augmented profits. For part (b), list all the assets and include a value for expenditure that does qualify and a zero for expenditure that does not qualify. Note that the cash basis for property income is not relevant for limited companies.

Easy marks

There were easy marks for calculating the corporation tax liability, dividing it by four and stating that it was due on the 14th of each month.

ACCA Examining Team's Comments

The corporation tax question was generally reasonably well answered, especially parts (a)(i), (b) and (d) which accounted for 10 of the marks. For part (c), few candidates seemed to appreciate that there is no benefit in making a short life asset election where the 100% annual investment allowance can be claimed.

Negative figures should be included by entering them as such on the spreadsheet. It is very difficult for markers to pick up negative figures if all figures are shown positive, with the total calculated within the cell on the lines of A1 + A2 – A3 + A4. It is also very easy to make mistakes using this approach. If negative figures are entered, the total is simply SUM(A1:A4).

(a) (i) Mixture Ltd is classed as a large company for the year ended 31 March 2025 because its profits of £515,000 (470,000 + 45,000) exceed the threshold of £500,000 (1,500,000/3).

Notes.
1 The threshold is divided by three because Mixture Ltd has two associated group companies.
2 No exception applies because Mixture Ltd would have also been a large company for the year ended 31 March 2024.

(ii) Mixture Ltd's corporation tax liability for the year ended 31 March 2025 is £117,500 (470,000 at 25%). The company will have paid this in four quarterly instalments of £29,375 (117,500/4). The instalments will have been due on the 14th of October 2024, January 2025, April 2025 and July 2025.

(b) **Expenditure qualifying as plant and machinery**

	£
Staircase	0
Sprinkler equipment and fire alarm system	16,400
Doors and windows	0
Ventilation system	27,100
Machinery	76,600
Building alterations	9,200
Moveable partition walls	33,800
Decorative wall	0

Note. The costs of building alterations necessary for the installation of plant and machinery are treated as plant and machinery for the purposes of the capital allowances legislation.

(c) Short-life asset election:
(1) A short-life asset election will be beneficial when an asset is disposed of for less than its tax written down value within eight years of the accounting period in which it was purchased.
(2) However, there is no benefit to a short-life asset election where the 100% annual investment allowance can be claimed in respect of the asset.
(3) The balancing allowance given when the asset is disposed of accelerates the allowances rather than these being given on a reducing balance basis.

Any of these three points up to a maximum of 2.

(d) **Mixture Ltd – Property business income for the year ended 31 March 2025**

	£
Premium received	18,000
Less: 18,000 × 2% × (5 – 1)	(1,440)
	16,560
Rent receivable (7,800 + 5,200 + (8,400 × 1/3))	15,800
	32,360
Advertising	(900)
Insurance ((1,700 × 9/12) + (1,900 × 3/12))	(1,750)
Property business income	29,710

Part F: Value added tax

Section A

OTQ bank – Value added tax 1

260 The correct answers are:

18 August	Deposit
2 September	Balancing payment

The basic tax point is the date the goods were supplied (26 August). Where payment is received before the basic tax point, then this date becomes the actual tax point. The tax point for the 10% deposit is therefore the date that it is received (18 August). The actual tax point for the balancing payment is the date the invoice was issued (2 September) as this was within 14 days of the basic tax point.

261 The correct answer is: 1 January 2025

> **ACCA Examining Team's Comments**
>
> Frances' taxable turnover exceeds £90,000 on 30 November 2024 (15,000 + 25,000 + 30,000 + 2/3 × 33,000) = £92,000. She has 30 days to notify HM Revenue and Customs and is registered from 1 January 2025.
>
> The alternative, incorrect answer options are as follows:
>
> - 30 December 2024 being 30 days after historic test exceeded
> - 31 January 2025 being one month after quarter end when historic test exceeded
> - 1 February 2025 which would be correct if the historic test was met on 31 December 2024

262 The correct answer is: £64

	£
Output VAT: £368 × 1/6	61
Less input VAT: £625 × 20%	(125)
VAT due	(64)

Input VAT on the car is not recoverable because there is private use. The answer £51 treats the scale charge as VAT-exclusive but recovers the correct amount on the petrol. The answer £74 treats the scale charge as VAT-exclusive and fails to recover the VAT on the actual petrol purchase. The answer £43 treats petrol as inclusive, instead of exclusive, of VAT.

263 The correct answers are:
- A business which buys standard rated supplies and sells zero rated goods to members of the public
- A business which buys standard rated supplies and sells standard rated goods to other VAT-registered businesses

> **ACCA Examining Team's Comments**
>
> Voluntary registration is beneficial for traders who can recover their input VAT and either make zero rated supplies (so will not have to charge higher prices inclusive of VAT), or make supplies to other VAT registered businesses (who can recover the additional cost of the output VAT charged).
>
> A business which buys zero rated supplies and sells standard rated goods to members of the public, will not benefit by voluntary registration since it will not recover VAT on its purchases (as these have no VAT being zero rated) and will have to charge members of the public an extra 20% to recover the VAT on sales.
>
> A business which buys zero rated supplies and sells zero rated goods to members of the public will not benefit from voluntary registration as there is no VAT to be charged on sales or recovered on expenses.

264 The correct answer is: VAT quarter ended 30 June 2025

The value added tax (VAT) on an impaired debt may only be reclaimed once the debt has been outstanding for six months from the due date. The due date in this instance is 10 October 2024, therefore the VAT can be reclaimed in the quarter ended 30 June 2025.

OTQ bank – Value added tax 2

265 £ 333

Input tax on the car is not recoverable because there is private use. However, since there is some use of the car for business purposes, then any VAT charged on repairs and maintenance costs can be treated as input tax without apportionment for private use. The input VAT recoverable is therefore £2,000 × 1/6 = £333.

266 £2,320

	£
New car for salesperson	0
New van £10,320 × 1/6	1,720
Entertaining UK customers	0
Entertaining overseas customers £3,600 × 1/6	600
Total input tax recoverable	2,320

The answer £5,360 allows full input tax recovery. The answer £4,192 allows business use recovery of input tax on the car. The answer £3,020 allows recovery of input tax on the entertaining of UK customers.

267 £ 270

The following rules apply to pre-registration input tax:

Goods – if acquired within four years prior to registration and still held on registration date (so the VAT on the inventory of spare parts is recoverable)

Services – if supplied within six months prior to registration (so the VAT on the accountancy fees is recoverable but not that on the legal fees)

268 The correct answer is: 1 August 2024

Scott is required to notify HMRC within 30 days of exceeding the £90,000 registration threshold, ie 30 July 2024 (30 days after the year to 30 June 2024). He will then be registered from 1 August 2024.

269 £ 960

> **ACCA Examining Team's Comments**
>
> The flat rate percentage is applied to the tax inclusive turnover. In this case, that is the standard rated sales of £10,000 plus 20% VAT (£12,000), at 8% giving VAT of £960.

270 The correct answer is: 0%

Charlie will charge VAT at zero rate because exports of goods to anywhere in the world are zero rated.

271 The correct answers are:

- Date of payment or receipt determines the VAT period in which the transaction is dealt with
- Gives automatic impairment loss relief (bad debt relief)

272 The correct answer is: £16,500

> **ACCA Examining Team's Comments**
>
> The correct answer was the first option (£16,500). Total sales including VAT are £150,000 (100,000 × 120/100 plus 30,000) and the flat rate percentage of 11% applied to this is £16,500.
>
> The incorrect answers are:
>
> £14,300 – flat rate percentage applied to the net figure of standard and zero rated sales 11% × (100,000 + 30,000)
>
> £14,520 – standard rated purchases deducted from standard rated sales before being grossed up and the flat rate percentage applied (((100,000 – 15,000) × 120/100) + 30,000) × 11%
>
> £13,200 – where the flat rate percentage is applied only to the gross standard rated sales (100,000 × 120/100) × 11%

273   The correct answer is: £8,500

	£
Standard rated sales (£50,000 × 120%)	60,000
Zero rated sales	20,000
Exempt sales	5,000
Total VAT inclusive sales	85,000
Value added tax £85,000 × 10%	8,500

ACCA Examining Team's Comments

This question on value added tax (VAT) required candidates to calculate the amount of VAT payable by an individual taxpayer who calculates their liability based on the flat rate scheme. The taxpayer made standard rated, zero rated and exempt sales so it was crucial for candidates to know that the flat rate percentage is applied to total VAT-inclusive turnover under the flat rate scheme in order to answer this question correctly.

The correct answer was the first option (£8,500).

The most common answer was the third option (£7,500) which is the answer arrived at if VAT at the standard rate is not included on the standard rated sales ((£50,000 + £20,000 + £5,000) × 10%). This demonstrates that many candidates did not appreciate the need to calculate VAT using VAT inclusive figures, or had not realised that the figures provided excluded VAT.

Candidates are reminded of the importance of the VAT special schemes for the TX – UK exam and also of the importance of reading questions carefully before calculating and selecting an answer.

274   The correct answers are:

Tax exclusive annual taxable turnover up to £150,000	Join scheme
Tax inclusive annual turnover up to £230,000	Leave scheme

Section B

OT case – Anne (June 2009) (amended)

> **Course Book references**
>
> Value added tax liability is covered in Chapter 24. Special schemes are dealt with in Chapter 25.
>
> **Top tips**
>
> Make sure that you read all the information given in the question – you are given this information by the examining team for a reason so you must make use of it when answering the question.
>
> **Easy marks**
>
> The output tax on cash sales should have been easy to deal with.

275 £ 5,600

Cash sales £28,000 (adult clothes standard rated) × 20% = £5,600

276 The correct answer is: £2,292

	£
Credit sales with discount £12,000 × 95% × 90% × 20%	2,052
Credit sales without discount £12,000 × 10% × 20%	240
	2,292

The calculation of output VAT on the credit sales only takes into account the discount for prompt payment for the 90% of customers that took it.

The answer £2,052 is just the output VAT on the discounted sales. The answer £2,280 is the output tax if all sales are treated as discounted. The answer £2,400 is the answer if no sales are treated as discounted.

277 £ 2,400

	£
Purchases and expenses £11,200 × 20%	2,240
Impairment loss £800 × 20%	160
	2,400

Relief for an impairment loss is not given until six months from the time that payment is due. Therefore, relief can only be claimed in respect of the invoice due for payment on 10 April 2024. Obviously, the customer did not take up the discount for prompt payment.

278 The correct answers are:

- Anne will be permitted to join the scheme if her expected taxable turnover for the next 12 months does not exceed £1,350,000.
- If the value of Anne's taxable supplies exceeds £1,600,000 in the 12 months to the end of a VAT period, she must leave the scheme immediately.

Anne will be permitted to join the scheme if she is up to date with both her VAT payments and her VAT returns. Payment in nine monthly instalments is a feature of the annual accounting scheme.

279 The correct answers are:

Reduced amount of output VAT payable		NOT ADVANTAGE
Automatic impairment loss relief (bad debt relief)	ADVANTAGE	
Only one VAT return each year		NOT ADVANTAGE
Output VAT on 10% of credit sales will be accounted for up to 1 month later than at present	ADVANTAGE	

The output VAT payable will remain the same and accounting for VAT will also remain the same.

OT case – Auy and Bim (June 2010) (amended)

> **Course Book references**
>
> The tax point and VAT liability are covered in Chapter 24. Special schemes are dealt with in Chapter 25.
>
> **Top tips**
>
> Learn the rules about the tax point – they are often examined! For the basic tax point, you need to distinguish between supplies of goods (date goods are removed or made available to the customer) and services (date on which services are completed).
>
> **Easy marks**
>
> There were easy marks for the computation of the VAT paid or payable by the partnership.

280 The correct answers are:
- If the VAT invoice is issued within 14 days after the basic tax point and payment has not been received before the basic tax point, the invoice date becomes the tax point.
- The tax point determines the VAT period in which output tax must be accounted for and credit for input tax will be allowed.

The basic tax point for services is the date that services are completed. If the VAT invoice is issued and payment is received before the basic tax point, the actual tax point is the earlier of those two dates.

281 The correct answer is: £25,280

The partnership's output VAT for the year ended 5 April 2025 is £25,600 and its total input VAT for the year is £(180 + 140) = £320.

Therefore, VAT of £25,280 (25,600 – 320) will have been paid to HM Revenue & Customs for the year ended 5 April 2025.

282 The correct answers are:
- Businesses using the scheme must still issue VAT invoices to their VAT registered customers.
- Businesses using the scheme cannot reclaim any input tax suffered.

Under the scheme, businesses calculate VAT by applying a fixed percentage to all their income (ie, including reduced rate, zero rated and exempt income). A 1% reduction off the flat rate percentage can be made by businesses in the first year that they use the flat rate scheme only if it is also the first year of registration.

283 The correct answer is:

Join	Continue to use
Expected taxable turnover (excluding VAT) for the next 12 months does not exceed £150,000.	Until its total turnover (including VAT) for the previous year exceeds £230,000

284 The correct answer is: £23,291

If the partnership had used the flat rate scheme throughout the year ended 5 April 2025, then it would have paid VAT of £(140,762 + 25,600) = £166,362 @ 14% = £23,291.

OT case – Mabel (March/June 2023)

Course Book references

The VAT liability and sale of a business as a going concern are covered in Chapter 24. Special schemes are dealt with in Chapter 25.

Top tips

Remember, input tax is not recoverable on cars, UK customer entertaining and non-business purchases.

Easy marks

There were easy marks for the two narrative questions.

285 The correct answer is: £18,424

ACCA Examining Team's Comments

(98,000 × 40% × 20%) + (98,000 × 60% × 90% × 20%) = £18,424 with 60% of customers receiving the 10% discount and VAT calculated on the exclusive of VAT sales figures.

The incorrect options are:

- £17,640: (98,000 × 90% × 20%) applying the discount to all sales
- £15,353: (98,000 × 40% × 20/120) + (98,000 × 60% × 90% × 20/120) treating the sales figures as if they are inclusive of VAT
- £19,600: (98,000 × 20%) not applying any discount

286 The correct answer is: £5,805

ACCA Examining Team's Comments

((35,700 – 690 – (900 × 20%)) × 20/120) = £5,805 allowing the VAT on entertaining overseas customers but not allowing the VAT for entertaining UK customers or the private element of the telephone calls.

The incorrect options are:

- £5,920: (35,700 – (900 × 20%)) × 20/120 which allows all entertaining costs
- £5,835: (35,700 – 690) × 20/120 which does not disallow the private element of telephone calls
- £5,605: (35,700 – 690 – 1,200 – (900 × 20%)) × 20/120 which disallows the entertaining of overseas customers

287 The correct answer is: Notification: 30 April 2025. Deregistration: 31 March 2025

> **ACCA Examining Team's Comments**
>
> HMRC should be notified within 30 days of ceasing to make taxable supplies, and the VAT registration is cancelled from the date of cessation.

288 The correct answer is: £1,480

> **ACCA Examining Team's Comments**
>
> £7,400 × 20% = £1,480, being the VAT on the office equipment
>
> The computer equipment has already been sold and so is no longer held by Mabel and no VAT will have been claimed on the car, because it is used for both business and private use.
>
> The incorrect options are:
>
> - £3,400: (7,400 + 9,600) × 20% for the car and the office equipment
> - £2,300: (7,400 + 4,100) × 20% including the computer equipment at cost
> - £2,230: (7,400 + 4,100 – 350) × 20% including the loss on sale of the computer equipment

289 The correct answer is: No output VAT will be payable in respect of the sale of the business

> **ACCA Examining Team's Comments**
>
> No output VAT will be payable in respect of the sale of the business.

OT case – Starfish Ltd (December 2011) (amended)

> **Course Book references**
>
> Calculation of value added tax (VAT) and transfer of a business as a going concern are covered in Chapter 24. Default interest is dealt with in Chapter 25.
>
> **Top tips**
>
> In the last question, you need to identify the supplies which will not be subject to VAT as a result of the transfer of going concern rules.
>
> **Easy marks**
>
> There were some easy marks available in the computation of VAT in the second question.

290 The correct answer is: £390

	£
Credit sales revenue discount taken up £2,000 × (100 – 4)% × 60% × 20%	230
Credit sales revenue discount not taken up £2,000 × 40% × 20%	160
	390

291   The correct answer is: £16,420

	£
Cash sales revenue £38,520 × 20/120	6,420
Sale of inventory on cessation £28,800 × 20/120	4,800
Sale of non-current assets £31,200 × 20/120	5,200
	16,420

There is no VAT charged on the sale of the car, as none was recovered on purchase (owing to private usage).

292   The correct answer is: £11,324

	£
Expenses £([69,960 − 4,320] = £65,640) × 20/120	10,940
Impairment loss	384
	11,324

Input VAT on business entertainment for UK customers is not recoverable.

Relief for the impairment loss is available because the claim is made more than six months from the time that payment was due, and the debt has been written off in the company's books.

293   The correct answers are:

It will incur a penalty point for the late payment.		FALSE
A fixed late penalty charge of 4% will apply.	TRUE	
It will incur a daily late penalty charge of 4% for 10 days.	TRUE	
Late payment interest will be charged at 7.75% for 40 days.	TRUE	

The first statement is false. Penalty points are incurred for late filing (not late payment).

The other three statements are true. The payment is over 30 days late and this leads to a 4% penalty, a daily penalty after the initial 30-day period (ie 10 days) and late payment interest (at the late payment interest rate).

294   The correct answer is: No output VAT would have been due on the sale of the inventory or the sale of the non-current assets.

A sale of a business as a going concern is outside the scope of VAT, and therefore output VAT would not have been due on either the sale of the inventory or the sale of the non-current assets.

OT case – Greenzone Ltd (June 2013)

> **Course Book references**
> All the VAT aspects in this question are dealt with in Chapter 24.
>
> **Top tips**
> Watch out for the difference between entertaining UK customers and overseas customers.
>
> **Easy marks**
> There were easy marks for working out the output VAT.

295 The correct answer is: £42,540

	£
Sales	38,210
Group sales	4,330
Output VAT	42,540

The tax point for the deposit is the date of payment, so no adjustment is required to the output VAT figure of £38,210.

The answer £38,210 does not include group sales. The answer £42,140 does not include the deposit. The answer £37,810 does not include either group sales or the deposit.

296 The correct answer is: £27 recoverable

	£
Output VAT	
Fuel scale charge £334 × 20/120	56
Input VAT	
Fuel purchased £500 × 20/120	(83)
VAT recoverable	(27)

The answer £23 payable adjusts the input tax for private mileage, so the input VAT is £500 × 20/120 = £33. The answer £33 recoverable treats the amounts as VAT exclusive. The answer £56 payable is just the fuel scale charge.

297 £ 12,560

	£
Total input VAT	12,770
Entertaining UK customers	(210)
Entertaining overseas customers	0
Repainting office building	0
New reception area	0
	12,560

Input VAT on business entertaining is not recoverable unless it relates to the cost of entertaining overseas customers.

There is no distinction between capital and revenue expenditure for VAT so input tax is recoverable on both the repainting of the office building (revenue) and the building of the new reception area (capital).

298 The correct answers are:

ARE LTD	YES	
BE LTD		NO
DOER INC		NO

Are Ltd can register with Greenzone Ltd as a group for VAT purposes as it is UK resident and controlled by Greenzone Ltd.

Be Ltd is not controlled by Greenzone Ltd and Doer Inc is not UK resident and does not have a fixed establishment in the UK.

299 The correct answers are:
- Each VAT group must appoint a representative member which accounts for the group's output tax and input tax.
- Any supply of goods or services by a member of the group to another member of the group is disregarded for VAT purposes.

All members of the group are jointly and severally liable for any VAT due from the representative member. It is not necessary for each company, which is eligible for group registration, to join a particular VAT group.

OT case – Long Ltd group (B) (June 2014) (amended)

Course Book references
Value added tax (VAT) calculation and group registration will be found in Chapter 24.

Top tips
It is vital to understand the difference between making exempt supplies and zero-rated supplies – think about whether input VAT can be recovered in either case.

Easy marks
There were some easy marks for dealing with input VAT.

300 £ 53,780

	£
Sales £(52,640 – 1,760)	50,880
Group sales £(1,940 + 960)	2,900
	53,780

The tax point for the deposit is the date of payment, so this will have been included in output VAT for the quarter ended 31 December 2024.

301 The correct answer is: £15,638

	£
Expenses	14,720
Hire of photocopier	
– £18 × [(4 years × 12 = 48 months) + 3 months]	918
	15,638

Refunds of VAT are subject to a four-year time limit so, in addition to the input VAT for the hire of the photocopier incurred during the quarter ended 31 March 2025, Long Ltd can claim for the input VAT incurred during the period 1 January 2021 to 31 December 2024.

The answer £14,720 does not include the hire of the photocopies. The answer £14,774 includes only three months of the hire of the photocopier. The answer £14,882 includes an additional six months of hire of the photocopier giving nine months in total – this is a confusion between the rules for recovery of goods and of services.

302 £ 0

Wind Ltd's sales are exempt from VAT, so the company cannot be registered for VAT and thus cannot recover input tax.

303 £3,500

	£
Expenses	3,120
Advertising	380
	3,500

Input VAT on services incurred prior to registration is subject to a six-month time limit, so the input VAT of £640 in respect of the advertising expenditure incurred during April 2024 cannot be recovered.

The answer £3,120 does not include the advertising at all. The answer £4,140 includes all the advertising. The answer £3,760 includes only the £640 of advertising expenditure.

304 The correct answers are:
- Supplies of goods or services to Road Ltd from outside the group will be treated as a supply to Long Ltd.
- The supplies by Long Ltd to Wind Ltd and Road Ltd would be disregarded for VAT purposes.

Two or more companies are eligible to be treated as members of a group if one of them controls each of the others, or one person (which could be an individual or a holding company) controls all of them, or two or more persons carrying on a business in partnership control all of them.

The controlling entity therefore does not need to be a company. It is not necessary for each company, which meets the requirements, to join a particular VAT group.

OT case – Zim (June 2015) (amended)

> **Course Book references**
> Value added tax is dealt with in Chapters 24 and 25.
>
> **Top tips**
> You must make sure you know the thresholds for entering and leaving the flat rate scheme as they are not given in the rates and allowances available in the examination.
>
> **Easy marks**
> There are easy marks for working out the net VAT payable.

305 £ 12,000

	£	£
Sales		
– Standard rated £115,200 × 20/120		19,200
– Zero rated		0
Purchases		
– Standard rated £43,200 × 20/120	7,200	
– Zero rated	0	
		(7,200)
Net VAT payable		12,000

306 The correct answer is: £240

Impairment losses £(780 + 660) = 1,440 × 20/120 = £240

Relief for impairment losses is given once six months have expired from the time when payment was due, so relief can be claimed in respect of both impairment losses.

The answer £0 assumes no relief for impairment losses is available. The answer £130 gives relief only on the loss of £780. The answer £110 gives relief only on the loss of £660.

307 The correct answer is:

Mobile phone	Customers
£260	£40

Mobile phone £2,600 × 60% (100% – 40%) × 20/120 = £260

An apportionment is made where a service such as the use of a telephone is partly for business purposes and partly for private purposes.

Customer entertainment £240 × 20/120 = £40

Input VAT on business entertainment is not recoverable unless it relates to the cost of entertaining overseas customers.

308 The correct answers are:

Taxable turnover excluding VAT not more than £150,000 in next 12 months	Join
Total turnover including VAT more than £230,000 in previous 12 months	Leave

309 £15,120

Using the flat rate scheme to calculate his VAT liability, Zim would have paid VAT of £126,000 × 12% = £15,120 for the year ended 31 March 2025.

The answer £13,860 assumes that the 1% reduction is available – be careful of this rule as it only applies in the first year of VAT registration. The answer £13,824 only charges standard rated sales. The answer £9,216 charges the flat rate on sales less expenses.

OT case – Smart Ltd (September/December 2015) (amended)

Course Book references

VAT registration, accounting for VAT and the tax point will be found in Chapter 24. Penalties and special schemes are dealt with in Chapter 25.

Top tips

There is a common penalty regime for errors which can apply to VAT errors as well as, for example, income tax or corporation tax errors.

Easy marks

There were some easy marks for identifying the date of registration and the date of notification.

310 The correct answers are:

1 November 2024	Register
30 November 2024	Notification

Smart Ltd was liable to register for VAT from 1 November 2024 because this is the date when it signed the contract valued at £91,000. The company would therefore have known that its taxable supplies for the following 30-day period would have exceeded £90,000. Registration is required from the start of the 30-day period.

Smart Ltd would have had to notify HM Revenue & Customs by 30 November 2024, being the end of the 30-day period.

311 The correct answers are:

Smart Ltd can file its VAT returns by entering figures manually on HMRC's website.		FALSE
Smart Ltd can choose whether to pay the VAT which is due electronically or by cheque.		FALSE
The deadline for paying any VAT which is due is one month after the end of each quarter.		FALSE
The deadline for filing the VAT return is one month and seven days after the end of each quarter.	TRUE	

Smart Ltd must use the Making Tax Digital software to directly submit its VAT returns to HMRC.

Smart Ltd must pay the VAT which is due electronically. The deadline for paying any VAT which is due is one month and seven days after the end of each quarter.

312 The correct answers are:
- The basic tax point is the date on which services are completed.
- If a customer pays for services before the basic tax point, the payment date will be the tax point.

313 The correct answer is: 1 and 4

The scheme will provide automatic relief for an impairment loss should a customer default on the payment of a debt. Output VAT will be accounted for 60 days later than at present, because the scheme will result in the tax point becoming the date when payment is received from customers.

314 The correct answer is:

Maximum penalty

30% of the VAT underpaid

Minimum penalty for prompted disclosure

15% of the VAT underpaid

OT case – Thidar (March/June 2019)

Course Book references
Value added tax (VAT) is covered in Chapters 24 and 25.

Top tips
In the first question, make sure you only have 12-months of sales when testing against the registration limit.

Easy marks
The rules on invoices should have been easy marks if you had studied the required knowledge of VAT.

315 The correct answer is: Month 14

	£	£
Months 1 to 12 Standard rated and zero-rated		84,400
Month 13 Standard rated and zero-rated	3,700	

	£	£
Less: Month 1 Standard rated and zero-rated	(3,400)	
		300
		84,700
Month 14 Standard rated and zero-rated	7,900	
Less: Month 2 Standard rated and zero-rated	(1,900)	
		6,000
		90,700

VAT registration threshold of £90,000 exceeded at the end of Month 14.

The answer Month 15 ignores the month where no supplies are made as one of the 12 months. The answer Month 13 uses the first 13-months of trading (ie does not take out Month 1). The answer Not yet exceeded only uses the standard rated supplies.

316 The correct answer is: £0

Pre-registration input tax suffered on the supply of services within six months prior to registration can be reclaimed. The supply on 10 June 2023 is earlier than six months before registration on 1 January 2024. The input tax on the supply on 8 December 2023, whilst it is within six months before registration, cannot be reclaimed as Thidar does not have evidence for the supply.

The answer £360 allows reclaim for the 10 June 2023 supply only. The answer £60 allows reclaim for the 8 December 2023 supply only. The answer £420 allows reclaim for both supplies.

317 The correct answer is: Option 2

VAT invoices must be issued within 30 days. VAT records (including invoices) must be retained for six years.

318 The correct answer is: Because separate disclosure of the VAT underpayment was not required

Default interest on unpaid VAT as a result of an error is only charged where the limit is exceeded for the error to be corrected on the next VAT return (here £10,000) such that it must be separately disclosed to HM Revenue & Customs.

The 12-month period is not relevant for penalties for errors (it applies to penalties for failure to notify chargeability). There can be a penalty for a careless (ie not deliberate) error. Default interest runs from the date the VAT should have been paid if the error had not been made.

319 The correct answer is: Option 3

The input tax of £800 × 20% = £160 on entertaining UK customers is non-deductible (but would be deductible for entertaining overseas customers). The answer £0 permits deduction of input tax on entertaining UK customers.

50% of the input tax is deductible on leased cars where there is some private use so the remaining 50% × £700 × 20% = £70 is non-deductible. The answer £105 is 75% × £700 × 20% = £105 (ie based on the amount of private use).

Section C

320 Jogger Ltd (B) (December 2008) (amended)

Course Book references

Value added tax penalties and special schemes are covered in Chapter 25.

Top tips

In part (b), make sure that you make four points to get the available marks.

Easy marks

The conditions for Jogger Ltd to join the annual accounting scheme in part (b) should have been easy marks.

Marking guide

		Marks	
(a)	Quarter ended 30 September 2023	3	
	Quarter ended 31 March 2024	3	
	Quarter ended 31 March 2025	4	
		—	6
(b)	One VAT return	1	
	Payments on account	2	
	Limit	1	
	VAT payments up to date	1	
		—	4
Total			10

(a) The late **submission** of the VAT return for the quarter ended 30 September 2023 will have resulted in HM Revenue & Customs (HMRC) issuing a penalty point. The late **payment** (between 16 and 30 days late) will have resulted in a 2% penalty of £854 (£42,700 × 2%) and late payment interest of £272 (£42,700 × 7.75% × 30/365).

The late **submission** of the VAT return for the quarter ended 31 March 2024 will have resulted in HM Revenue & Customs (HMRC) issuing a further penalty point (making two cumulatively). The late **payment** (between 16 and 30 days late) will have resulted in a 2% penalty of £778 (£38,900 × 2%) and late payment interest of £248 (£38,900 × 7.75% × 30/365).

The late **submission** of the VAT return for the quarter ended 31 March 2025 will have resulted in HM Revenue & Customs (HMRC) issuing a further penalty point (making three cumulatively). The late **payment** (paid later than 30 days of the due date) will have resulted in a 4% penalty of £3,564 (£89,100 × 4%), a daily penalty for 30 days (60 days less the initial 30 days) of £293 (£89,100 × 4% × 30/365) and late payment interest of £1,135 (£89,100 × 7.75% × 60/365).

(b) The reduced administration from only having to submit one VAT return each year should mean that penalties are avoided in respect of the late submission of VAT returns.

In addition, making payments on account based on the previous year's VAT liability will improve both budgeting and possibly cash flow if Jogger Ltd's business is expanding.

Jogger Ltd can apply to use the annual accounting scheme if its expected taxable turnover for the next 12 months does not exceed £1,350,000 exclusive of VAT. However, the company must be up to date with its VAT payments before it is allowed to use the scheme.

321 Flick (June 2012) (amended)

> **Course Book references**
>
> The flat rate scheme is dealt with in Chapter 25. Registration is covered in Chapter 24 as is the tax point.
>
> **Top tips**
>
> In a multiple part question such as this, it is really important to attempt all the parts.
>
> **Easy marks**
>
> Part (c) might have looked a little unusual but was really a basic question on the tax point.

Marking guide

	Marks
(a) Flat rate scheme	1
Normal basis	1
Conclusion	1
	3
(b) No recovery of VAT by customers	1
Possible need to absorb VAT	1
Conclusion	1
	3
(c) VAT period	1
Basic tax point	1
Deposit	1
Balance	1
	4
Total	**10**

(a) Using the flat rate scheme to calculate its VAT liability, the partnership will have paid VAT of £(59,700 × 12%) = £7,164 for the quarter ended 31 March 2025.

If the partnership had used the normal basis, it would have paid VAT of £(59,700 – 27,300 = 32,400 × 20/120) = £5,400.

It was therefore not beneficial to use the flat rate scheme as the additional cost of £(7,164 – 5,400) = £1,764 for the quarter would appear to outweigh the advantage of simplified VAT administration.

(b) The partnership's sales are all to members of the general public, who cannot recover the input VAT.

It may not therefore be possible to pass the output VAT on to customers in the prices charged. To the extent this is not possible the partnership would have had to absorb all or some of this amount itself as a cost.

It was therefore not beneficial for the partnership to have voluntarily registered for VAT from 1 January 2025. For the quarter ended 31 March 2025, voluntary registration reduced the partnership's profits by a maximum of £7,164 (£5,400 if the normal basis had been used).

(c) Output VAT must be accounted for according to the VAT period in which the supply is treated as being made. This is determined by the tax point.

The basic tax point is the date when the service is completed, which will be the date that a film is screened.

Where payment is received before the basic tax point, then this date becomes the actual tax point. The tax point for each 25% deposit is therefore the date that it is received.

Invoices are issued on the same day as the basic tax point, so this is the tax point for the balance of 75%.

322 Richard (December 2013) (amended)

> **Course Book references**
>
> Registration for VAT is covered in Chapter 24 as is VAT administration. VAT invoices are dealt with in Chapter 25. Ethical considerations are covered in Chapter 1.
>
> **Top tips**
>
> Ethical considerations are an important part of the Taxation (TX – UK) syllabus and you might be asked about them in relation to any tax.
>
> **Easy marks**
>
> The calculation of the date for registration for VAT in part (a) was straightforward.

Marking guide

		Marks	
(a)	Compulsory registration limit	0.5	
	Date registration required	1.5	
	Date registration effective	1	
	Consequences of non-registration	1	
			4
(b)	Honesty and integrity	0.5	
	Cease to act and inform HMRC	1	
	Money laundering notification	0.5	
			2
(c)	Simplified invoice	1	
	Request for invoice	0.5	
	Details on invoice: 0.5 mark per item to maximum	2.5	
			4
Total			**10**

(a) Richard would have been liable to compulsory VAT registration when his taxable supplies during any 12-month period (or from the commencement of trade, if less) exceeded £90,000.

This happened on 31 October 2024 when taxable supplies were £([10,500 × 4] + [17,000 × 3]) = £93,000.

Registration is required from the end of the month following the month in which the limit is exceeded, so Richard should have been registered from 1 December 2024.

If Richard continued to trade after 1 December 2024 without registering for VAT, he would still have to pay the VAT due from the time he should have been registered.

(b) The matter is one of professional judgement and a trainee chartered certified accountant would be expected to act honestly and with integrity. If Richard refuses to register for VAT, you should cease to act for him. You must notify HM Revenue & Customs (HMRC) that you no longer act for Richard although you should not provide any reason for this.

You would also be obliged to make a report under the money laundering regulations.

(c) A simplified (or less detailed) VAT invoice can be issued by a trader where the VAT inclusive total of the invoice is less than £250.

Such an invoice should be issued when a customer requests a VAT invoice.

A simplified VAT invoice must show the following information:

- The supplier's name and address
- The supplier's registration number
- The date of the supply
- A description of the goods or services supplied
- The rate of VAT chargeable
- The total amount chargeable including VAT

323 Clueless Ltd (December 2012) (amended)

Course Book references
Special schemes for VAT and overseas aspects of VAT are in Chapter 25.

Top tips
The question stated that the company incurred considerable overtime costs due to its employees working late in order to meet tax return filing deadlines which should have alerted you to one of the advantages of the annual accounting scheme.

Easy marks
There were some easy marks in part (a) for the conditions for the cash accounting and annual accounting schemes.

Marking guide

			Marks	
(a)	Eligible for both schemes on turnover		1.5	
	Up to date with payments for both schemes		1	
	Up to date with returns for cash accounting scheme		0.5	
	Output tax under cash accounting scheme		1	
	Input tax under cash accounting scheme		1	
	Annual accounting scheme – one return		1	
				6
(b)	(i)	Payment on importation	1	
		Input tax recovery	1	
	(ii)	Output tax on date of acquisition	1	
		Input tax reclaimed on same return	1	
				4
Total				10

(a) Clueless Ltd can use both schemes because its expected taxable turnover for the next 12 months does not exceed £1,350,000 exclusive of VAT.

In addition, for both schemes the company is up to date with its VAT payments, and for the cash accounting scheme it is up to date with its VAT returns.

With the cash accounting scheme, output VAT will be accounted for two months later than at present as the date of the cash receipt determines the return in which the transaction is dealt with rather than the invoice date.

The recovery of input VAT on expenses will not be affected as these are dealt with on a cash basis. With the annual accounting scheme, the reduced administration in only having to file one VAT return each year should save on overtime costs.

(b) (i) **Import without postponed accounting**

Clueless Ltd will have to pay VAT of £22,000 @ 20% = £4,400 to HM Revenue & Customs at the time of importation.

This will then be reclaimed as input VAT on the VAT return for the period during which the machinery is imported.

(ii) **Import with postponed accounting**

Import VAT is declared as output VAT on the VAT return covering the date that the machinery is imported. It is reclaimed as input VAT on the same VAT return, so there is no VAT cost.

> Videos can be viewed online by accessing your ebook version on VitalSource.

324 Garfield (March/June 2016)

Course Book references

Computation of value added tax (VAT), including deduction of input tax and relief for impairment losses, is dealt with in Chapter 24. Overseas trade and special schemes for VAT are covered in Chapter 25.

Top tips

Remember the input VAT on entertaining UK customers is not recoverable but that suffered on entertaining overseas customers is recoverable.

Easy marks

Most of the content of this question has appeared a number of times in previous questions and so there were easy marks in part (a) for computing VAT payable.

Marking guide — Marks

(a) **Output VAT**
	Marks
Discounted sale	1
Equipment	1
Input VAT	
Equipment	0.5
Impairment losses	1
Entertaining	1
Motor expenses	1.5
VAT payable (including figures provided in question)	1
	7

Marking guide	Marks
(b) Possible schemes	1
Identify cash accounting scheme as beneficial	0.5
Benefits of cash accounting scheme (½ mark each)	1.5
	3
Total	**10**

(a) Garfield – Value added tax (VAT) return for the quarter ended 31 March 2025

	£
Output VAT	
Sales	*22,500
Discounted sale £4,300 × 90% × 20%	774
Equipment £12,400 × 20%	2,480
Fuel scale charge	*414
Input VAT	
Purchases	*(11,200)
Car	*0
Equipment	(2,480)
Impairment losses £1,400 × 20%	(280)
Entertaining	
– UK customers	*0
– Overseas customers £960 × 20/120	(160)
Motor expenses £1,668 (1,008 + 660) × 20/120	(278)
VAT payable	11,770

*Figures provided in question

> **Tutorial note.** Relief for an impairment loss is only available if the claim is made more than six months from the time when payment was due.
>
> Therefore, relief can only be claimed in respect of the invoice due for payment on 29 August 2024.
>
> Input VAT on business entertainment is recoverable if it relates to the cost of entertaining overseas customers.

(b) Given Garfield's current annual turnover of £450,000, he can use the cash accounting scheme and the annual accounting scheme, but not the flat rate scheme.

The cash accounting scheme would appear to be the most beneficial scheme for Garfield to use.

The scheme will provide automatic VAT relief for the impairment losses which Garfield is incurring.

Where credit is given to customers, output VAT could be accounted for later than at present.

The recovery of input VAT on most purchases and expenses will not be affected as Garfield pays for these on a cash basis.

> **Tutorial note.** The annual turnover limit for both the annual accounting scheme and the cash accounting scheme is £1,350,000, but for the flat rate scheme it is £150,000.
>
> Although the annual accounting scheme would mean only having to submit one VAT return each year (reducing the risk of late return penalties), payments on account are based on the VAT payable for the previous year. From a cash flow viewpoint, this is not beneficial where turnover is decreasing.

325 Zhi (March/June 2017)

Course Book references

Self-assessment and payment of tax by individuals is covered in Chapter 17. Capital gains tax business reliefs are the subject of Chapter 15. The VAT tax point is dealt with in Chapter 24. Computation of income tax is covered in Chapter 2 and national insurance contributions in Chapter 12. The PAYE system is dealt with in Chapter 4.

Top tips

If you are asked to calculate a reduction in tax, don't waste time setting out a full tax computation. Just work out the reduction using the marginal rate of tax.

This is a similar process to working out additional tax covered in Chapter 2 of the Course Book.

Easy marks

There were some easy marks in part (c) for applying the rules on the tax point.

ACCA Examining Team's Comments

This 10-mark question had a focus on higher skills.

Part (a) was not very well answered and was not attempted by some candidates. Essentially, all that candidates had to do was select the two relevant tax years (out of the three provided), deduct one set of figures from the other, and divide by two.

Part (b) was the only part of the question which was consistently well answered. One particular issue, however, was that some candidates worked out the current capital gains tax liability (prior to the rollover relief claim) despite this being provided.

Carefully noting which information has been provided in the question will avoid time being wasted in this manner.

Whether or not candidates did well in part (c) depended on them realising that 1 February 2025 was more than 14 days after 12 December 2024. This being the case, postponing the sales invoice would not affect the basic tax point.

Candidates should appreciate that a suggested tax planning strategy might not necessarily be effective, and they need to have the courage to base their answer on this conclusion if led there following the application of basic principles.

However, some candidates either did not read the question carefully or chose to answer a question they would have preferred to have been asked and based their answer on the amount of VAT which could be postponed.

There were some good answers to part (d). However, only a few candidates appreciated that by far the quickest and easiest way to calculate the tax reductions was to work at the margin – rather than producing full before and after-tax computations.

Of course, it was also important to realise that the first employee was a basic rate taxpayer, subject to employee national insurance contributions at 8%, whereas the second employee was a higher rate taxpayer and only subject to employee national insurance contributions at 2%.

Marking guide

		Marks
(a)	No reduction in balancing payment	0.5
	Reduction in payment on account	1.5
		2
(b)	Current CGT liability	0.5
	Proceeds not reinvested	1
	Annual exempt amount	1
	CGT computation	0.5
		3
(c)	Basic tax point	0.5
	Invoice does not displace	1
	Cannot reduce VAT payable	0.5
		2
(d)	**First employee**	
	PAYE	0.5
	NIC – employee	0.5
	NIC – employer	0.5
	Second employee	
	PAYE	0.5
	NIC – employee	0.5
	NIC – employer	0.5
	Payment date	0.5
		3
Total		**10**

(a) The balancing payment for 2023/24 due on 31 January 2025 cannot be reduced. A claim can be made to reduce the payment by £5,040:

	£
Current POA (27,600 + 4,204) × 50%	15,902
Revised POA (18,000 + 3,724) × 50%	(10,862)
Reduction	5,040

(b) CGT liability due:

	£	£
Current CGT liability		14,600
Revised CGT liability		
Proceeds not reinvested (210,000 – 164,000)	46,000	
Annual exempt amount	(3,000)	
	43,000	
CGT: 43,000 at 20%		(8,600)
Reduction		6,000

> **Tutorial note.** Equivalent marks will be awarded if the reduction is alternatively calculated as 30,000 (76,000 – (210,000 – 164,000)) at 20% = £6,000.

(c) The basic tax point for goods is the date when they are made available to the customer, which in the case of Zhi's sale is 12 December 2024. An invoice date of 1 February 2025 will not affect this because the invoice will not have been issued within 14 days of the basic tax point.

Zhi therefore cannot reduce the amount of VAT payable on 7 February 2025.

(d) PAYE and NICs:

	£
First employee	
PAYE (1,500 at 20%)	300
NIC	
– Employee (1,500 at 8%)	120
– Employer (1,500 at 13.8%)	207
Second employee	
PAYE (5,000 at 40%)	2,000
NIC	
– Employee (5,000 at 2%)	100
– Employer (5,000 at 13.8%)	690
Reduction	3,417

The postponed PAYE and NICs of £3,417 will be payable one month later on 22 February 2025.

Mock Exams

ACCA

Taxation (TX – UK) FA 2024

Mock Exam 1

September 2016 (amended to FA 2024)

Questions	
Time allowed	3 hours
ALL questions are compulsory and MUST be attempted	

DO NOT OPEN THIS EXAM UNTIL YOU ARE READY TO START UNDER EXAMINATION CONDITIONS

Section A

ALL 15 questions are compulsory and MUST be attempted.

1. On 1 July 2023, Sameer made a cash gift of £2,500 to his sister.

   On 1 May 2024, he made a cash gift of £2,000 to a friend.

   On 1 June 2024, he made a cash gift of £50,000 to a trust.

   Sameer has not made any other lifetime gifts.

   In respect of Sameer's cash gift of £50,000 to the trust, what is the lifetime transfer of value for inheritance tax purposes after taking account of all available exemptions?

   ○ £48,500

   ○ £44,000

   ○ £46,000

   ○ £46,500   (2 marks)

---

2. On 31 March 2025, Angus sold a house, which he had bought on 31 March 2011.

   Angus occupied the house as his main residence until 31 March 2016, when he left for employment abroad.

   Angus returned to the UK on 1 April 2018 and lived in the house until 31 March 2019, when he bought a flat in a neighbouring town and made that his private residence.

   What is Angus's total number of qualifying months of occupation for private residence relief on the sale of the house?

   ○ 72 months

   ○ 141 months

   ○ 105 months

   ○ 96 months   (2 marks)

---

3. Abena has made the following gross contributions to her personal pension scheme over the past three tax years:

Tax year	£
2021/22	42,000
2022/23	27,000
2023/24	28,000

   Abena is entitled to an annual allowance of £40,000 in tax years 2021/22 and 2022/23.

   What is the maximum gross contribution which Abena can make to her personal pension scheme for the tax year 2024/25 without giving rise to an annual allowance charge?

   ○ £92,000

   ○ £60,000

   ○ £105,000

   ○ £107,000   (2 marks)

4   Triangle Ltd is registered for value added tax (VAT) and uses the annual accounting scheme.

For the year ended 31 December 2024, the net VAT payable by Triangle Ltd was £73,500.

For the year ended 31 December 2023, the net VAT payable by Triangle Ltd was £47,700.

Indicate, by clicking on the relevant boxes in the table below, the number and amount of the monthly payments on account of VAT which Triangle Ltd must make in respect of the year ended 31 December 2024 prior to submitting its VAT return for that year.

Options	Selection	Category
Nine	**Nine**	Number of monthly payments
Ten		
£4,770	**£4,770**	Monthly payment amount
£7,350		

(2 marks)

---

5   Lili Ltd commenced trading on 1 January 2024. The company incurred the following expenditure prior to 1 January 2025:

		£
30 November 2016	Initial market research	15,000
6 June 2019	Research into competitors	12,000
31 July 2023	Entertaining potential customers and suppliers	8,000
15 December 2023	Donation to local school fair in exchange for advertising	2,000

What is the amount of Lili Ltd's deductible pre-trading expenditure in respect of the year ended 31 December 2024?

£ ⬜

(2 marks)

---

6   Paloma has been trading for a number of years. Her tax adjusted trading profit for the year ended 31 March 2025 was £53,150.

What is the amount of class 4 national insurance contributions (NIC) payable by Paloma for the tax year 2024/25?

○ £3,074
○ £2,435
○ £2,262
○ £2,320

(2 marks)

7 Identify, by clicking on the relevant boxes in the table, whether the following are true or false.

Corporation tax is a direct tax on the turnover of companies.	TRUE	FALSE
National insurance is a direct tax suffered by employees, employers and the self-employed on earnings.	TRUE	FALSE
Inheritance tax is a direct tax on transfers of income by individuals.	TRUE	FALSE
Value added tax is a direct tax on the supply of goods and services by businesses.	TRUE	FALSE

(2 marks)

8 Which of the following statements concerning self-assessment tax returns for individuals is TRUE?

○ Individuals with tax payable of less than £1,000 for a tax year are not required to file a tax return.

○ Individuals are only required to file a tax return for a tax year if they receive a notice to deliver from HM Revenue & Customs (HMRC).

○ All individuals who submit a tax return on time are able to have their tax payable calculated by HMRC.

○ The tax return for an individual covers income tax, class 1 and class 4 national insurance contributions and capital gains tax liabilities.

(2 marks)

9 In certain circumstances, an individual is automatically not resident in the UK. Indicate, by clicking on the relevant boxes in the table below, whether the following two individuals satisfy or do not satisfy the tests to be treated as automatically not resident in the UK for the tax year 2024/25.

Eric, who has never previously been resident in the UK. In the tax year 2024/25, he was in the UK for 40 days. Fran, who was resident in the UK for the two tax years prior to the tax year 2024/25. In the tax year 2024/25, she was in the UK for 18 days.

Eric	SATISFIES	DOES NOT SATISFY
Fran	SATISFIES	DOES NOT SATISFY

(2 marks)

10 Max is employed by Star Ltd. On 6 April 2023, Star Ltd provided him a camera for personal use. The camera had a market value of £2,000 on 6 April 2023. On 6 April 2024, Star Ltd gave the camera to Max for free. The camera had a market value of £1,400 on 6 April 2024.

What is Max's taxable benefit in respect of the camera for the tax year 2024/25?

[Pull down list ▼]

Pull down list
- £1,000
- £1,400
- £1,600
- £2,000

(2 marks)

---

11 Cora made a cash gift of £300,000 to her niece on 30 April 2019. She then made a cash gift of £500,000 to her nephew on 31 May 2020. Both of these amounts are stated after deducting available exemptions.

Cora subsequently died on 31 October 2024.

What amount of inheritance tax was payable as a result of Cora's death in respect of the cash gift of £500,000 to her nephew?

O £190,000
O £110,000
O £114,000
O £105,000

(2 marks)

---

12 Rajesh is a sole trader. He correctly calculated his self-assessment payments on account for the tax year 2024/25 and paid these on the due dates.

Rajesh paid the correct balancing payment of £1,200 for the tax year 2024/25 on 30 June 2026.

Indicate, by clicking on the relevant boxes in the table below, what penalties and interest Rajesh may be charged as a result of his late balancing payment for the tax year 2024/25.

Options		Category
£0		Penalty
£60		Interest
£39		
£93		

(2 marks)

13 Oblong Ltd has had the following results:

	y/e 31 March 2024	y/e 31 March 2025
	£	£
Trading profit/(loss)	79,400	(102,800)
Property business income	6,800	10,100
Qualifying charitable donations	(1,600)	(1,300)

If Oblong Ltd makes a claim to relieve its trading loss of £102,800 for the year ended 31 March 2025 against total profits for the year ended 31 March 2024, how much of this loss will remain unrelieved?

○ £6,500
○ £16,600
○ £9,400
○ £23,400

(2 marks)

14 Putting an asset into joint names with a spouse (or a partner in a registered civil partnership) prior to the asset's disposal can be sensible capital gains tax (CGT) planning.

Which of the following CANNOT be achieved as a direct result of using this type of tax planning?

Pull down list

- Deferring the CGT due date
- Making the best use of annual exempt amounts
- Making the best use of capital losses
- Reducing the amount of CGT payable

(2 marks)

15 Eva's income tax liability and class 4 national insurance contributions (NIC) for the tax year 2024/25 are £4,840. Her income tax liability and class 4 NICs for the tax year 2023/24 were £6,360.

What is the lowest amount to which Eva could make a claim to reduce each of her payments on account for the tax year 2024/25 without being charged interest?

£ ☐

(2 marks)

Section B

ALL 15 questions are compulsory and MUST be attempted.

Adana

Adana died on 17 March 2025, and inheritance tax (IHT) of £566,000 is payable in respect of her chargeable estate. Under the terms of her will, Adana left her entire estate to her children.

At the date of her death, Adana did not own a main residence. She had these debts and liabilities:

(1) An outstanding interest-only mortgage of £220,000

(2) Income tax of £43,700 payable in respect of the tax year 2024/25

(3) Legal fees of £4,600 incurred by Adana's sister which Adana had verbally promised to pay

Adana's husband had died on 28 May 2006, and only 20% of his inheritance tax nil rate band was used on his death. The nil rate band for the tax year 2006/07 was £285,000.

On 22 April 2012, Adana had made a chargeable lifetime transfer of shares valued at £500,000 to a trust. Adana paid the lifetime IHT of £52,250 arising from this gift. If Adana had not made this gift, her chargeable estate at the time of her death would have been £650,000 higher than it otherwise was. This was because of the subsequent increase in the value of the gifted shares.

16   What is the maximum nil rate band which will have been available when calculating the IHT of £566,000 payable in respect of Adana's chargeable estate?

Pull down list
- £325,000
- £390,000
- £553,000
- £585,000

(2 marks)

---

17   What is the total amount of deductions which would have been permitted in calculating Adana's chargeable estate for IHT purposes?

£ ⬚

(2 marks)

18 Indicate, by clicking on the relevant boxes in the table below, who will be responsible for paying the IHT of £566,000 in respect of Adana's chargeable estate, and what is the due date for the payment of this liability.

Beneficiaries of Adana's estate (her children)		Responsible persons
Personal representatives of Adana's estate		Due date for payment
17 September 2025		
30 September 2025		

(2 marks)

19 How much of the IHT payable in respect of Adana's estate would have been saved if, under the terms of her will, Adana had made specific gifts of £400,000 to a trust and £200,000 to her grandchildren, instead of leaving her entire estate to her children?

○ £240,000
○ £160,000
○ £0
○ £80,000

(2 marks)

20 How much IHT did Adana save by making the chargeable lifetime transfer of £500,000 to a trust on 22 April 2012, rather than retaining the gifted investments until her death?

○ £260,000
○ £207,750
○ £147,750
○ £200,000

(2 marks)

(Total = 10 marks)

Kat Ltd and Kitten

Kitten is the controlling shareholder in Kat Ltd, an unquoted trading company.

Kat Ltd

Kat Ltd sold a freehold factory on 31 May 2025 for £364,000, which resulted in a chargeable gain of £120,700. The factory was purchased on 1 October 2005 for £138,600, and further capital improvements were immediately made at a cost of £23,400 during the month of purchase. Further improvements to the factory were made during the month of disposal. The relevant indexation factor is 0.439.

Kat Ltd is unsure how to reinvest the proceeds from the sale of the factory. The company is considering either purchasing a freehold warehouse for £272,000 or acquiring a leasehold office building on a 40-year lease for a premium of £370,000. If either reinvestment is made, it will take place on 30 September 2025.

All of the above buildings have been, or will be, used for the purposes of Kat Ltd's trade.

Kitten

Kitten sold 20,000 £1 ordinary shares in Kat Ltd on 5 October 2024, which resulted in a chargeable gain of £142,200. This disposal qualified for business asset disposal relief.

Kitten had originally subscribed for 90,000 shares in Kat Ltd on 7 July 2010 at their par value. On 22 September 2013, Kat Ltd made a 2 for 3 rights issue. Kitten took up her allocation under the rights issue in full, paying £6.40 for each new share issued.

Kitten also sold an antique vase on 16 January 2025, which resulted in a chargeable gain of £19,600.

For the tax year 2024/25, Kitten had taxable income of £12,000.

21 **What amount of indexation allowance will have been deducted in calculating the chargeable gain of £120,700 on the disposal of Kat Ltd's factory?**

£ ☐ (2 marks)

22 **If Kat Ltd decides to purchase the freehold warehouse and makes a claim to roll over the chargeable gain on the factory under the rollover relief rules, what will be the base cost of the warehouse for chargeable gains purposes?**

○ £243,300
○ £272,000
○ £180,000
○ £151,300 (2 marks)

23 **If Kat Ltd decides to acquire the leasehold office building and makes a claim to hold over the chargeable gain on the factory under the rollover relief rules, what is the latest date by which the held-over gain will crystallise?**

[▼]

Pull down list

- 10 years from 30 September 2025
- 10 years from 31 May 2025
- 40 years from 30 September 2025
- The date when the office building is sold

(2 marks)

24 **What cost figure will have been used in calculating the chargeable gain on Kitten's disposal of 20,000 ordinary shares in Kat Ltd?**

○ £12,000
○ £63,200
○ £84,800
○ £20,000 (2 marks)

25 What is Kitten's capital gains tax (CGT) liability for the tax year 2024/25?

- ○ £15,880
- ○ £17,840
- ○ £18,140
- ○ £17,540

(2 marks)

(Total = 10 marks)

Alisa

Alisa commenced trading on 1 January 2024. Her sales since commencement have been:

January to April 2024	£7,500 per month
May to August 2024	£10,000 per month
September to December 2024	£20,500 per month

The above figures are stated exclusive of value added tax (VAT). Alisa only supplies services, and these are all standard rated for VAT purposes. Alisa notified her liability to compulsorily register for VAT by the appropriate deadline.

For each of the eight months prior to the date on which she registered for VAT, Alisa paid £240 per month (inclusive of VAT) for website design services and £180 per month (exclusive of VAT) for advertising. Both of these supplies are standard rated for VAT purposes and relate to Alisa's business activity after the date from when she registered for VAT.

After registering for VAT, Alisa purchased a car on 1 January 2025. The car is used 60% for business mileage. During the quarter ended 31 March 2025, Alisa spent £456 on repairs to the car and £624 on fuel for both her business and private mileage. The relevant quarterly scale charge is £290. All of these figures are inclusive of VAT. All of Alisa's customers are registered for VAT, so she appreciates that she has to issue VAT invoices when services are supplied.

26 **From what date would Alisa have been required to be compulsorily registered for VAT and therefore have had to charge output VAT on her supplies of services?**

[▼]

Pull down list

- 1 November 2024
- 1 October 2024
- 30 October 2024
- 30 September 2024

(2 marks)

27 **What amount of pre-registration input VAT would Alisa have been able to recover in respect of inputs incurred prior to the date on which she registered for VAT?**

- ○ £468
- ○ £608
- ○ £536
- ○ £456

(2 marks)

28 What is the maximum amount of input VAT which Alisa can reclaim in respect of her motor expenses for the quarter ended 31 March 2025?

   ○ £108
   ○ £138
   ○ £180
   ○ £125   (2 marks)

29 Complete the following sentence by matching the correct due date and payment method into the relevant target area.

   Alisa has to pay any VAT liability for the quarter ended 31 March 2025 by

   [(1) ▼] using [(2) ▼] method.

   Pull down list 1
   - 30 April 2025
   - 7 May 2025

   Pull down list 2
   - An electronic payment
   - Any payment

   (2 marks)

30 Which of the following items of information is NOT required to be included by Alisa on a valid VAT invoice.

   ○ The customer's VAT registration number
   ○ The customer's address
   ○ An invoice number
   ○ A description of the services provided   (2 marks)

   (Total = 10 marks)

Section C

ALL three questions are compulsory and MUST be attempted.

31 Joe

Joe is the managing director and 100% shareholder of OK-Joe Ltd. He has always withdrawn the entire profits of the company as director's remuneration but given a recent increase in profitability he wants to know whether this basis of extracting the profits is beneficial.

For the year ended 5 April 2025, OK-Joe Ltd's taxable total profits, before taking account of director's remuneration, are £65,000. After allowing for employer's class 1 national insurance contributions (NIC) of £6,779 Joe's gross director's remuneration is £58,221.

The figure for employer's NIC of £6,779 does not deduct the £5,000 employment allowance as this is not available since Joe is the only employee of OK-Joe Ltd.

Required

Calculate the overall saving of tax and NIC for the year ended 5 April 2025 if Joe had instead paid himself gross director's remuneration of £8,000 and dividends of £45,645.

Notes.

1. You are expected to calculate the income tax payable by Joe, the class 1 NIC payable by both Joe and OK-Joe Ltd, and the corporation tax liability of OK-Joe Ltd for the year ended 5 April 2025.
2. You should assume that the rate of corporation tax remains unchanged. **(10 marks)**

32 Ashura

Ashura has been employed by Rift plc since 1 January 2022. She has also been self-employed since 1 July 2024, preparing her first accounts for the nine-month period ended 5 April 2025. The following information is available for the tax year 2024/25:

Employment

(1) During the tax year 2024/25, Ashura was paid a gross annual salary of £56,600.

(2) On 1 January 2025, Ashura personally paid two subscriptions. The first was a professional subscription of £320 paid to a professional body. The second was a subscription of £680 to a health club which Ashura regularly uses to meet Rift plc's clients. Ashura was not reimbursed for the costs of either of these subscriptions by Rift plc.

(3) During the tax year 2024/25, Ashura used her private car for business purposes. She drove 3,400 miles in the performance of her duties for Rift plc, for which the company paid her an allowance of 55 pence per mile.

(4) During the tax year 2024/25, Ashura contributed £2,800 into Rift plc's occupational pension scheme and £3,400 (gross) into a personal pension scheme.

Self-employment

(1) Ashura's tax adjusted trading loss based on her draft accounts for the nine-month period ended 5 April 2025 under the accruals basis is £3,300. This figure is before making any adjustments required for:

   (i) Advertising expenditure of £800 incurred during January 2024

   This expenditure has not been deducted in calculating the loss of £3,300.

   (ii) The cost of Ashura's office (see note (2) below)

   (iii) Capital allowances

(2) Ashura runs her business using one of the five rooms in her private house as an office. The total running costs of the house for the nine-month period ended 5 April 2025 were £4,350. No deduction has been made for the cost of the office in calculating the loss of £3,300.

(3) On 10 June 2024, Ashura purchased a laptop computer for £2,600.

On 1 July 2024, Ashura purchased a car for £25,600. The car has a CO_2 emission rate of 117 grams per kilometre. During the nine-month period ended 5 April 2025, Ashura drove a total of 8,000 miles, of which 2,500 were for self-employed business journeys.

Other information

Ashura's total income for the previous four tax years is as follows:

Tax year	Total income
	£
2020/21	11,100
2021/22	10,800
2022/23	48,800
2023/24	54,300

Required

(a) Calculate Ashura's revised tax adjusted trading loss for the nine-month period ended 5 April 2025. **(6 marks)**

(b) State the factors that will influence an individual's choice of loss relief claims and explain why it would not be beneficial for Ashura to claim loss relief under the provisions giving relief to a loss incurred in the early years of trade.

Note. You should assume that the tax rates and allowances for the tax year 2024/25 also applied in all previous tax years. **(4 marks)**

(c) Assuming that Ashura claims loss relief against her total income for the tax year 2024/25, calculate her taxable income for this tax year. **(5 marks)**

(Total = 15 marks)

33 Mable

Mable is a serial entrepreneur, regularly starting and disposing of businesses. On 31 July 2024, Tenth Ltd, a company owned by Mable, ceased trading. On 1 October 2024, Eleventh Ltd, another company owned by Mable, commenced trading. The following information is available:

Tenth Ltd

(1) For the final four-month period of trading ended 31 July 2024, Tenth Ltd had a tax adjusted trading profit of £52,400. This figure is **before** taking account of capital allowances.

(2) On 1 April 2024, the tax written down value of the company's main pool was £12,400. On 3 June 2024, Tenth Ltd purchased a laptop computer for £1,800.

On 31 July 2024, the company sold all of the items included in the main pool at the start of the period for £28,200 and the laptop computer for £1,300. None of the items included in the main pool was sold for more than its original cost and no enhanced capital allowances had been claimed.

(3) On 31 July 2024, Tenth Ltd sold the company's freehold office building for £180,300. The building was purchased on 3 May 2014 for £151,334, and its indexed cost to December 2017 was £164,500.

(4) During the four-month period ended 31 July 2024, Tenth Ltd let out one floor of its freehold office building which was always surplus to requirements. The floor was rented at £1,200 per month, but the tenant left owing the rent for July 2024 which Tenth Ltd was unable to recover. The total running costs of the office building for the four-month period ended 31 July 2024 were £6,300, of which one-third related to the let floor. The other two-thirds of the

running costs have been deducted in calculating Tenth Ltd's tax-adjusted trading profit of £52,400.

(5) During the four-month period ended 31 July 2024, Tenth Ltd made qualifying charitable donations of £800.

Eleventh Ltd

(1) Eleventh Ltd's operating profit for the six-month period ended 31 March 2025 is £122,900. Depreciation of £2,580 and amortisation of leasehold property of £2,000 (see note (2) below) have been deducted in arriving at this figure.

(2) On 1 October 2024, Eleventh Ltd acquired a leasehold office building, paying a premium of £60,000 for the grant of a 15-year lease. The office building was used for business purposes by Eleventh Ltd throughout the six-month period ended 31 March 2025.

(3) On 1 October 2024, Eleventh Ltd purchased two new cars. The first car cost £12,600 and has a CO_2 emission rate of 40 grams per kilometre. This car is used as a pool car by the company's employees. The second car cost £13,200 and has a zero CO_2 emission rate per kilometre. This car is used by Mable, and 45% of the mileage is for private journeys.

(4) On 1 October 2024, Mable made a loan of £100,000 to Eleventh Ltd at an annual interest rate of 5%. This is a commercial rate of interest, and no loan repayments were made during the period ended 31 March 2025. The loan was used to finance the company's trading activities.

Required

(a) Calculate Tenth Ltd's taxable total profits for the four-month period ended 31 July 2024.

(7 marks)

(b) Calculate Eleventh Ltd's tax adjusted trading profit for the six-month period ended 31 March 2025.

(8 marks)

(Total = 15 marks)

Answers

DO NOT TURN THIS PAGE UNTIL YOU HAVE COMPLETED THE MOCK EXAM

A plan of attack

If this were the real Taxation (TX – UK) exam and you had been told to turn over and begin, what would be going through your mind?

Perhaps you're having a panic. You've spent most of your study time on income tax and corporation tax computations (because that's what your tutor/BPP Course Book told you to do), plus a selection of other topics, and you're really not sure that you know enough. So calm down. Spend the first few moments or so **looking at the exam** and develop a **plan of attack**.

Looking through the exam.

Section A contains **15 Objective Test (OT) questions** each worth **2 marks**. These will cover all sections of the syllabus. Some you may find easy and some more difficult. In Question 8, where you are asked to identify the true statement about self-assessment tax returns for individuals, read the possible answers at least twice before you decide which one to select. Don't spend a lot of time on anything you really don't know. For multiple choice questions you are not penalised for wrong answers, so you should answer all of them. If all else fails – guess!

Section B contains **three OT Case** scenarios. These each have **five questions** each worth **2 marks**. Make sure you read the scenario carefully before you start to answer the OTQs.

- **Questions 16 to 20** test your knowledge of inheritance tax (IHT). Question 18 is a quick question as you only need to select two answers, one is the persons responsible for payment of tax and the other is the date for payment.

- **Questions 21 to 25** concern chargeable gains for a company and for an individual. Make sure to double check your calculations to avoid losing marks for simple mistakes. This is particularly applicable to Question 25.

- **Questions 26 to 30** are about value added tax (VAT). Read the questions carefully to make sure you answer the question set. For example, in Question 26 you need to identify the date from which Alisa would have been required to be compulsorily registered, not the date on which the registration limit was exceeded.

In **Section C** you have **three constructed response (long) questions**:

- **Question 31** for **10 marks** is about whether there is an overall tax saving by taking a mixture of dividends and remuneration from a company rather than just remuneration. You need to work out the individual's income tax, the national insurance contributions for an employee and corporation tax.

- **Question 32** for **15 marks** is an income tax computation and also deals with choice of accounting date.

- **Question 33** for **15 marks** is a corporation tax question dealing with a company ceasing to trade and one commencing to trade.

Allocating your time

BPP's advice is always allocate your time **according to the marks for the question** in total and for the parts of the question. But **use common sense**. If you're confronted by an OTQ on a topic of which you know nothing, pick an answer and move on. Use the time to pick up marks elsewhere.

After the exam... **Forget about it!**

And don't worry if you found the exam difficult. More than likely other candidates will too. If this were the real thing you would need to **forget** the exam the minute you left the exam hall and **think about the next one**. Or, if it's the last one, **celebrate**!

Section A

1 The correct answer is: £48,500

	£
Gift 1 June 2024	50,000
Less:	
– AE 2024/25 £(3,000 – 2,000 PET 1 May 2024)	(1,000)
– AE 2023/24 b/f £(3,000 – 2,500 PET 1 July 2023)	(500)
Chargeable lifetime transfer	48,500

Note the current tax year annual exemption is used first (against the PET on 1 May 2024 and then the CLT on 1 June 2024) and then the balance brought forward from the previous tax year.

2 The correct answer is: 105 months

Qualifying period		Months
31.3.11–31.3.16	Actual occupation	60
1.4.16–31.3.18	Employed abroad (any length with reoccupation)	24
1.4.18–31.3.19	Actual occupation	12
1.7.24–31.3.25	Last nine months ownership	9
Qualifying months		105

Check: non-qualifying months 1.4.19–30.6.24 = 63 months, total period of ownership 31.3.11–31.3.25 = 168 months = (105 + 63) months

3 The correct answer is: £105,000

	£
2024/25	60,000
2021/22 £(40,000 – 42,000) = £(2,000) excess	0
2022/23 £(40,000 – 27,000)	13,000
2023/24 £(60,000 – 28,000)	32,000
Available annual allowance	105,000

Use the current tax year allowance first and then start working forwards from the earliest available tax year (maximum three tax years before current year).

4 The correct answers are:

Nine	Number of monthly payments
£4,770	Monthly payment amount

$$\frac{90\% \times £47,700 \text{ (previous year VAT payable)}}{9} = £4,770$$

5   £ 14,000

	£
30.11.16: More than seven years before commencement	0
6.6.19: Research deductible	12,000
31.7.23: Entertaining not deductible under general rules	0
15.12.23: Donation for trade purposes deductible	2,000
Deductible pre-trading expenditure	14,000

6   The correct answer is: £2,320

	£
£(53,150 – 50,270) = 2,880 @ 2%	58
£(50,270 – 12,570) = 37,700 @ 6%	2,262
Class 4 NIC payable	2,320

The answer £3,074 uses the class 1 rates of 8% and 2% rather than class 4 rates. The answer £2,435 uses a rate of 6% throughout. The answer £2,262 is just the amount chargeable at 6%.

7   The correct answers are:

Corporation tax is a direct tax on the turnover of companies.		FALSE
National insurance is a direct tax suffered by employees, employers and the self-employed on earnings.	TRUE	
Inheritance tax is a direct tax on transfers of income by individuals.		FALSE
Value added tax is a direct tax on the supply of goods and services by businesses.		FALSE

Corporation tax is a direct tax on profits (not turnover).

National insurance is a direct tax (collected directly from taxpayer either through PAYE or by self-assessment) suffered by employees (Class 1 employee's), employers (Class 1 employer's) and the self-employed (Class 4).

Inheritance tax is a direct tax on transfers of capital (not income) by individuals.

Value added tax is an indirect tax (collected by businesses not customers) on the supply of goods and services by businesses.

8   The correct answer is: All individuals who submit a tax return on time are able to have their tax payable calculated by HMRC.

ACCA Examining Team's Comments

This question tested candidates' knowledge of various aspects of the income tax self-assessment system. The majority of candidates appreciated that there can be a requirement to file a tax return despite not receiving a notice to do so from HMRC. However, a significant number of candidates chose the last option, despite class 1 national insurance contributions (NIC) not being part of the self-assessment system.

Many candidates chose the first option, not remembering that the de minimis limit of £1,000 instead relates to payments on account. All individuals who submit a tax return on time (either a paper return or electronically) are able to have the tax payable calculated by HMRC therefore the third option was the correct answer.

This should have been a fairly straightforward question and it demonstrates the need to carefully read and consider each alternative – not just quickly jump to the first one that seems to fit.

9 The correct answers are:

| Eric | SATISFIES | |
| Fran | | DOES NOT SATISFY |

Eric satisfies the tests. He was not previously UK resident and was present in the UK for between 16 and 45 days (see table in Tax Rates and Allowances).

Fran does not satisfy the tests. She was resident during the previous three years, so to be automatically not resident she must be in the UK for less than 16 days.

10 £1,600

	£	£
2023/24 Use benefit £2,000 × 20%	400	
2024/25 Gift		
Greater of:		
(1) Market value at gift	1,400	
(2) Original cost	2,000	
Less: Use benefit	(400)	
	1,600	
		1,600

11 The correct answer is: £114,000

	£	£
31.5.20 PET now chargeable		500,000
Nil rate band at death	325,000	
Less: 30.4.19 PET now chargeable	(300,000)	
		(25,000)
Transfer chargeable to IHT @ 40%		475,000
£475,000 @ 40%		190,000
Less: Taper relief (4 to 5 years) @ 40%		(76,000)
IHT payable as a result of Cora's death		114,000

12 The correct answers are:

£60	Penalty

£39	Interest

The due date for payment of the balancing payment was 31 January 2026.

Interest is due for the period February 2026 to June 2026 (working in whole months) so is £1,200 × 7.75% × 5/12 = £39. The answer £93 is the interest for a 12-month period.

The penalty date was 30 days after the due date and so payment was less than five months after the penalty date. The penalty due is £1,200 × 5% = £60.

13 The correct answer is: £6,500

	y/e 31.3.24	y/e 31.3.25
	£	£
Trading income	79,400	0
Property business income	6,800	10,100
Total profits	86,200	10,100
Less: Loss against total profits	(86,200)	(10,100)
Taxable trading profits	0	0

Loss memorandum

	£
Trading loss incurred in y/e 31.3.25	102,800
Less:	
– Used in y/e 31.3.25	(10,100)
– Used in y/e 31.3.24	(86,200)
Loss unrelieved	6,500

The qualifying charitable donations are unrelieved.

14 Deferring the CGT due date

The CGT due date will be 31 January following the end of the tax year of the disposal for both spouses/civil partners.

Note the three ways in which tax planning for spouses can be used: making the best use of annual exempt amounts; reducing the amount of CGT payable (eg if one spouse has unused basic rate band); and making best use of capital losses.

15 £ 2,420

2024/25: Relevant amount = £4,840 / 2 = £2,420

Section B

Adana

> **Course Book references**
>
> Inheritance tax (IHT) is the subject of Chapter 18.
>
> **Top Tips**
>
> In Question 20, you need to think about the lifetime IHT paid as well as the death tax on the estate.
>
> **Easy Marks**
>
> There were easy marks in Questions 16 and 17 for basic IHT knowledge.
>
> **ACCA Examining Team's Comments**
>
> The first two questions (involving the available nil rate band and the amount of deductions permitted in calculating the taxpayer's chargeable estate) were well answered.
>
> One of the questions asked who was responsible for paying the IHT liability in respect of the taxpayer's chargeable estate, and also the due date. The due date was not a problem, but many candidates opted for the beneficiaries of the taxpayer's estate as responsible rather than the personal representatives of the estate.
>
> A further question asked for how much of the IHT payable in respect of taxpayer's estate would have been saved if specific gifts had been made to a trust and to the taxpayer's grandchildren (instead of the entire estate being left to the taxpayer's children). Although most candidates chose the correct answer (that there was no tax saving), a significant number opted for either of the gifts resulting in an IHT saving at 40%.
>
> There was also a question that asked for how much IHT was saved as a result of the taxpayer making a chargeable lifetime transfer (CLT) rather than retaining the gifted assets until death. Again, the correct answer (based on the value at death less the amount of lifetime IHT paid) was most popular, but a significant number of candidates instead based their answer on the initial value of the CLT.
>
> These three, less well answered questions, demonstrate the need for a good grasp of how a tax such as IHT is applied, rather than just rote learning the basic mechanics of tax calculation. These questions show how tax planning can feature within a case question.

16 £585,000

	£
Adana: own nil rate band (lifetime transfer more than 7 years before death)	325,000
Adana's husband: 80% × £325,000 (use 2024/25 nil rate band)	260,000
Maximum nil rate band available	585,000

17   £ 263,700

	£
Mortgage (debt incurred for consideration)	220,000
Income tax (statutory debt)	43,700
Total deductions	263,700

The legal fees are not deductible as the agreement to pay them is not legally enforceable because no consideration is received.

18   The correct answers are:

Personal representatives of Adana's estate	Responsible persons
30 September 2025	Due date for payment

The beneficiaries of Adana's estate will bear the IHT, as it will reduce the amount due to them from the estate, but it is her personal representatives (the executors of her will) who are responsible for making the payment. The IHT on a death estate is due by the end of six months from the end of the month of death.

19   The correct answer is: £0

There would be no IHT saving by making either of these gifts as both are chargeable in the same way as gifting the entire estate to Adana's children. The only exempt transfer in relation to the death estate for Taxation (TX – UK) purposes is a gift to a spouse/civil partner.

20   The correct answer is: £207,750

	£
Extra IHT on death estate: £650,000 × 40%	260,000
Less: lifetime IHT paid	(52,250)
IHT saving	207,750

Kat Ltd and Kitten

> **Course Book references**
>
> Chargeable gains for companies are dealt with in Chapter 20. Computation of CGT is covered in Chapter 13 and business reliefs in Chapter 15.
>
> **Top tips**
>
> Double check your computations! Just because your answer is one of those given, it does not necessarily mean that it is correct.
>
> **Easy marks**
>
> The indexation allowance in Question 21 was made easier by both the cost and the enhancement expenditure being incurred in the same month.
>
> **ACCA Examining Team's Comments**
>
> Questions involving the indexation allowance, the crystallisation date for a heldover gain and the base cost of shares following a rights issue were well answered.

One of the questions asked for the base cost of an asset against which a rollover relief claim had been made. Although the correct answer was the most popular (with candidates appreciating that the amount of proceeds not reinvested could not be rolled over), a significant number of candidates ignored the amount of proceeds not reinvested and rolled over the full amount of gain.

Another question asked for the taxpayer's CGT liability. Again, the correct answer (the disposal qualifying for business asset disposal relief utilised the available basic rate tax band, with the other gain therefore taxed at 20%) was marginally the most popular. However, many candidates ignored the impact of business asset disposal relief on the basic rate band or did not deduct the annual exempt amount.

These two less well answered questions demonstrate the need to be very careful with all aspects of a calculation. One simple mistake means the loss of the two marks available.

21 £ 71,118

	£
0.439 × £162,000 (138,600 + 23,400)	71,118

22 The correct answer is: £243,300

	£
Gain	120,700
Immediately chargeable = amount not reinvested £(364,000 – 272,000)	(92,000)
Deduction from base cost of new warehouse	28,700

The base cost of the new warehouse is £(272,000 – 28,700) = £243,300.

23 10 years from 30 September 2025

The gain will become chargeable on the latest of: the date of disposal of the replacement asset; the date it ceases to be used in the trade; and ten years from its acquisition.

24 The correct answer is: £63,200

Date	Transaction	No. of shares	Cost £
7.7.10	Acquisition at par £1 cost for each £1 share bought	90,000	90,000
22.9.13	Rights issue 2 new shares for every 3 original shares held @ £6.40	60,000	384,000
		150,000	474,000
5.10.24	Sale	(20,000)	(63,200)
c/f		130,000	410,800

25 The correct answer is: £17,540

	BADR gain £	Non-BADR gain £
Gains	142,200	19,600
Less: annual exempt amount (best use)		(3,000)
Taxable gains	142,200	16,600

	BADR gain	Non-BADR gain
	£	£
Tax @ 10%/20%	14,220	3,320
Total CGT payable	£17,540	

The basic rate band is treated as being used first by the gain qualifying for business asset disposal relief. This means that the band is entirely used up and so the tax on the gain not qualifying for business asset disposal relief is taxable at 20%.

The answer £15,880 uses the basic rate of 10% on the gain not qualifying for business asset disposal relief. The answer £18,140 does not deduct the annual exempt amount. The answer £17,840 sets the annual exempt amount against the gain qualifying for business asset disposal relief.

Alisa

Course Book references

Value added tax is covered in Chapters 24 and 25.

Top tips

For Question 28 note that the fuel scale charge is the basis for **output** tax charged in relation to private use fuel. You were asked to identify the **input** tax which could be reclaimed.

Easy marks

There were easy marks in Question 26 for identifying the date from which the trader would have been required to be compulsorily registered for VAT. However, it was important to read the question carefully to see exactly what was being asked – it was **not** the date on which the registration threshold was reached.

ACCA Examining Team's Comment

Generally, this case question was not as well answered as the previous two. However, candidates made reasonable attempts at questions on the recovery of pre-registration input VAT, how and by when the VAT liability would be paid, and the information included on a valid VAT invoice.

A further question asked for the date of compulsory VAT registration. Although the correct answer was the most popular, many candidates opted for the end of the month in which the registration limit was exceeded.

One of the questions asked for the maximum amount of input VAT which could be reclaimed in respect of motor expenses. The correct answer (ignoring private use) was by a long way the most popular, but a significant number of candidates either adjusted for private use or used the fuel scale charge instead of the actual fuel figure.

26 1 November 2024

	£
January to April: 4 × £7,500	30,000
May to August: 4 × £10,000	40,000
September	20,500
	90,500

The registration threshold of £90,000 is met by 30 September 2024. Alisa should therefore have notified HMRC by 30 October 2024, with registration effective from 1 November 2024.

27 The correct answer is: £456

	£
Website design service: £240 × 6 × 1/6	240
Advertising: £180 × 6 × 20%	216
Input tax reclaimable	456

Pre-registration input tax is recoverable on services which are supplied within six months prior to registration. Note the different calculations for VAT-inclusive and VAT-exclusive amounts.

28 The correct answer is: £180

	£
Repairs	456
Fuel	624
	1,080
Input tax reclaimable £1,080 × 1/6	180

Full input tax can be reclaimed on the repairs to the car – the private use of the car is not relevant.

All the input tax will be reclaimed on fuel and the adjustment to private use will be made by charging output tax based on the fuel scale charge.

29 Alisa has to pay any VAT liability for the quarter ended 31 March 2025 by 7 May 2025 using an electronic payment method.

Alisa has to pay any VAT liability for the quarter ended 31 March 2025 by 7 May 2025 using an electronic payment method.

30 The correct answer is: The customer's VAT registration number

Section C

31 Joe

> **Course Book references**
>
> Employment income is covered in Chapter 3, and income tax computation in Chapter 2. NICs are dealt with in Chapter 12. Corporation tax is covered in Chapter 19.
>
> **Top Tips**
>
> A good start would be to look at the list of taxes in note 1 and consider whether they apply to each of the two scenarios.
>
> **Easy marks**
>
> There were some easy marks for basic income tax and corporation tax computations. However, you needed to be methodical in the way in which you set out your computations.
>
> **ACCA Examining Team's Comments**
>
> Although there were good attempts at this question, aspects consistently caused problems.
>
> - It was often not clear as to which section of the scenario was being answered, particularly as regards the corporation tax calculations.
> - The majority of candidates did not appreciate that where all of a company's profits are paid out as director's remuneration (and the related employer's class 1 NIC) then there is no corporation tax liability.
> - Similarly, it was not appreciated that with director's remuneration of just £8,000 (which is below the NIC lower thresholds) then there were no NICs.
> - Many candidates incorrectly calculated NICs on the dividends.

Marking guide	Marks
Profits withdrawn as director's remuneration	
Income tax	1.5
Class 1 employee's NIC	1.5
Corporation tax	0.5
Profits withdrawn as a mix of director's remuneration and dividends	
Income tax	3
Class 1 NIC	1
Corporation tax	1.5
Overall tax saving	1
	10
Total	10

Joe – Income tax liability 2024/25 if just remuneration

	Non-savings income
	£
Director's remuneration/net income	58,221
Less personal allowance	(12,570)
Taxable income	45,651

	Non-savings income
Tax	£
£37,700 @ 20%	7,540
£(45,651 − 37,700) = 7,951 @ 40%	3,180
Income tax payable	10,720

Joe – National insurance contributions 2024/25 if just remuneration

	£
£(58,221 − 50,270) = 7,951 @ 2%	159
£(50,270 − 12,570) = 37,700 @ 8%	3,016
Class 1 employee's NIC payable	3,175

There will be no corporation tax payable since the profits are entirely withdrawn as director's remuneration (including Class 1 employer's NIC).

Joe – Income tax liability 2024/25 if mix of remuneration and dividends

	Non-savings income	Dividend income	Total income
	£	£	£
Director's remuneration	8,000		
Dividends		45,645	
Net income	8,000	45,645	53,645
Less personal allowance	(8,000)	(4,570)	
Taxable income	0	41,075	41,075
Tax			
£500 @ 0% (dividend nil rate band)			0
£(37,700 − 500) = 37,200 @ 8.75%			3,255
£(41,075 − 37,700) = 3,375 @ 33.75%			1,139
Income tax payable			4,394

There will be no Class 1 NIC for either OK-Joe Ltd or Joe as the earnings are below the NIC employee's and employer's thresholds.

Corporation tax liability of OK-Joe Ltd for the year ended 5 April 2025 if mix of remuneration and dividends

	£
Trading profit	65,000
Less: Director's remuneration	(8,000)
Taxable trading profit	57,000
£57,000 @ 25%	14,250
Less marginal relief (250,000 − 57,000) × 3/200	(2,895)
Corporation tax	11,355

Summary of tax and NIC liabilities

	Remuneration only	Mix of remuneration and dividends
	£	£
Income tax	10,720	4,394
Class 1 NIC employee's	3,175	0
Class 1 NIC employer's (given in question)	6,779	0
Corporation tax	0	11,355
Total tax and NIC	20,674	15,749

Therefore, the overall tax and NIC saving if Joe extracts profits using a mix of director's remuneration and dividends is £(**20,674** – 15,749) = £4,925.

32 Ashura

Course Book References

Assessable trading income is dealt with in Chapter 9, capital allowances in Chapter 8 and losses in Chapter 10. Employment income is dealt with in Chapters 3 and 4. Taxable income is covered in Chapter 2.

Top Tips

In part (c), note the difference between the tax treatment of occupational pension contributions (paid gross and deducted in the income computation giving tax relief at all rates) and personal pension contributions (basic rate relief given by being paid net and further tax relief being given by increasing the basic rate limit so not relevant to this question which only required a calculation of taxable income).

Easy marks

There were some easy marks in part (a) for straightforward adjustments to profit. Part (c) had some easy marks for dealing with the mileage allowance and subscriptions.

ACCA Examining Team's Comments

Part (a) required a calculation of the taxpayer's revised tax adjusted trading loss for the first period of account. This meant adjusting for pre-trading expenditure, use of one of the five rooms in the taxpayer's private house as an office, and capital allowances. There were many good answers to this section, although a common mistake was to not appreciate that each of the three adjustments increased (not decreased) the trading loss.

For part (b), candidates had to explain why it was not beneficial for the taxpayer to claim loss relief under the provisions giving relief to a loss incurred in the early years of trade. It should have been fairly obvious that such a claim would have wasted the personal allowance and not resulted in any tax saving. This section was not as well answered, with many candidates not appreciating that the loss could only be carried back for three years. Some candidates actually explained why a claim would be beneficial.

Part (c) required a calculation of the taxpayer's taxable income (on the basis that loss relief was claimed against total income). This meant taking account of two subscriptions (only one of which was deductible), a mileage allowance deduction for the use of a private car for business purposes, and pension contributions (both to an occupational scheme and a personal pension scheme). This section was generally well answered, although many candidates wasted time by calculating the tax liability. The occupational pension scheme contribution was often grossed up (such contributions are not paid net of tax). Many candidates made things more difficult than they needed to be by attempting this section before section (a).

Marking guide		Marks
(a)	Trading loss	2.5
	Capital allowances	3.5
		6
(b)	Choice of loss relief claim	2
	Early years loss relief	2
		4
(c)	Salary	0.5
	Mileage	1
	Pension	1
	Subscriptions	1
	Loss	1
	Personal allowance	0.5
		5
Total		**15**

(a) **Ashura – Trading loss for the nine-month period ended 5 April 2025**

	£
Trading loss	(3,300)
Less:	
– Pre-trading expenditure	(800)
– Use of office £4,350 × 1/5	(870)
– Capital allowance (W)	(2,960)
Adjusted trading loss	(7,930)

Working

Capital allowances

9 months to 5 April 2025	AIA	Main pool	Car		Allowances
	£	£	£		£
Additions					
Laptop	2,600				
AIA	(2,600)				2,600
Transfer to pool	0	0			
Car			25,600		
WDA @ 6% × 9/12			(1,152)	× 2,500/8,000	360
WDA c/f		0	24,448		
Allowances					2,960

Tutorial note. The advertising expenditure incurred in January 2024 is pre-trading expenditure which is treated as incurred on the first day of trading. An adjustment is therefore required. Ashura's car has CO_2 emissions over 50 g/km and therefore only qualifies for writing down allowance at the rate of 6%.

The laptop computer purchased on 10 June 2024 is pre-trading capital expenditure and is therefore treated as incurred on the first day of trading.

(b)

Factors that affect choice of loss relief

- The rate of income tax or capital gains tax at which relief will be obtained, with preference being given to income charged at the additional rate of 45%, then the higher rate of 40%.
- The timing of the relief obtained, with a claim against general income/capital gains of the current year or preceding year resulting in earlier relief than a carry forward claim against future trading profits.
- The extent to which the income tax personal allowance and the capital gains annual exempt amount will be wasted.

Early years trading loss relief

Under early years trading loss relief, the loss of £7,930 in 2024/25 would be relieved against her total income of £10,800 in 2021/22 since this is the earliest of the three years 2021/22, 2022/23 and 2023/24. However, since Ashura's total income for 2021/22 is covered by her personal allowance of £12,570 (assumed), there would be no tax saving by making an early years loss relief claim.

(c) Ashura – Taxable income 2024/25

	£
Salary	56,600
Mileage allowance 3,400 × 10p (55p – 45p)	340
Pension contributions	
– Occupational	(2,800)
– Personal	(0)
Subscriptions	
– Professional	(320)
– Health club	(0)
Total income	53,820
Less: Loss relief against total income	(7,930)
Net income	45,890
Less: Personal allowance	(12,570)
Taxable income	33,320

Tutorial note. The personal pension scheme contribution does not affect the calculation of taxable income but will instead increase Ashura's basic rate limit by the gross contribution of £3,400.

The health club subscription is not an allowable deduction because membership is not a necessary expense for Ashura to carry out the duties of her employment.

The loss relief cap does not apply because Ashura's trading loss is less than the greater of £50,000 and 25% of her total income.

33 Mable

Course Book references

The computation of taxable total profits is covered in Chapter 19. The adjustment to trading profits is dealt with in Chapter 7 and capital allowances in Chapter 8. Property business income is covered in Chapter 5.

Top tips

Be careful when working with short accounting periods. For example, in part (b) you needed to adjust the writing down allowance so that only six months of allowances were given.

Easy marks

There were some easy marks in part (b) for adjustments to profits which should have been well-known.

ACCA Examining Team's Comments

Part (a) was generally very well answered, requiring a calculation of the first company's taxable total profits for the final period of trading. This involved calculating the balancing charge on cessation (all of the items included in the company's main pool being sold), the chargeable gain on the sale of the company's freehold office building and the property business income in respect of one floor of the office building which had been let out. The company has also made qualifying charitable donations.

The only consistent problem here was the capital allowances, with many candidates not appreciating that neither the annual investment allowance (a laptop computer had been purchased during the period) nor writing down allowances are given in the period of cessation. A few candidates ignored the cessation altogether and therefore did not calculate a balancing charge.

Part (b) was also well answered on the whole, requiring a calculation of the second company's tax adjusted trading profit for the initial period of trading. This involved adjusting for depreciation and amortisation, calculating the deduction in respect of a lease premium, calculating capital allowances for two cars (one car was used as a pool car by the company's employees, with the other having private use by a director) and deducting loan interest in respect of a loan made to the company by a director/owner.

Some candidates attempted to calculate benefits in respect of the cars and loan which, although correct as regards the cars, had no relevance to the requirement. Perhaps not surprisingly, the deduction for the lease premium caused quite a few problems.

Marking guide	Marks
(a) Taxable total profits	2.5
Balancing charge	3
Property business income	1.5
	7

Marking guide	Marks
(b) Profit and add-backs	1.5
Interest payable	1
Lease premium	2.5
Capital allowances	3
	8
Total	15

(a) **Tenth Ltd – Taxable total profits for the four-month period ended 31 July 2024**

	£
Trading profits	52,400
Balancing charge (W1)	15,300
Adjusted trading profits	67,700
Property business income (W2)	1,500
Chargeable gain £(180,300 – 164,500)	15,800
Total profits	85,000
Less qualifying charitable donations	(800)
Taxable total profits	84,200

Workings

1 **Capital allowances**

	Main pool	Allowances
	£	£
TWDV brought forward	12,400	
Addition		
Laptop computer	1,800	
Disposal		
Main pool items £(28,200 + 1,300)	(29,500)	
Balancing charge	15,300	(15,300)

2 **Property business income**

	£
Rent receivable £1,200 × 4	4,800
Less:	
– Impairment loss	(1,200)
– Running costs £6,300 × 1/3	(2,100)
Property business income	1,500

Answers 399

(b) **Eleventh Ltd – Tax adjusted trading profit for the six-month period ended 31 March 2025**

	£
Operating profit	122,900
Add:	
– Depreciation	2,580
– Amortisation	2,000
Less:	
– Deduction for lease premium (W1)	(1,440)
– Interest payable £100,000 × 5% × 6/12	(2,500)
– Capital allowances (W2)	(14,334)
Tax adjusted trading profit	109,206

Workings

1 **Deduction for lease premium**

	£
Premium paid	60,000
Less: £60,000 × 2% × (15 –1)	(16,800)
Amount taxable on landlord as property business income	43,200
Deduction £43,200/15 × 6/12	1,440

2 **Capital allowances**

	FYA	Main pool	Allowances
	£	£	£
Addition not qualifying for FYA			
Car [1]		12,600	
WDA @ 18% × 6/12		(1,134)	1,134
Addition qualifying for FYA			
Car [2]	13,200		
FYA @ 100%	(13,200)		13,200
Transfer to pool	0	0	
TWDV carried forward		11,466	
Allowances			14,334

Tutorial note. Car [1] has CO_2 emissions of below 50 g/km. It therefore goes into the main pool and has writing down allowances at 18% scaled down for the short accounting period.

Car [2] is new and has zero CO_2 emissions so therefore qualifies for the 100% first year allowance. This is not scaled down for the short accounting period. The private use of the car is not relevant for the company.

ACCA

Taxation (TX – UK) FA 2024

Mock Exam 2

ACCA Specimen exam (updated to FA 2024)

Questions	
Time allowed	3 hours
ALL questions are compulsory and MUST be attempted	

DO NOT OPEN THIS EXAM UNTIL YOU ARE READY TO START UNDER EXAMINATION CONDITIONS

Section A

ALL 15 questions are compulsory and MUST be attempted.

1. William is self-employed, and his tax adjusted trading profit for the year ended 5 April 2025 was £84,050. During the tax year 2024/25, William contributed £5,400 (gross) into a personal pension scheme.

   What amount of Class 4 national insurance contributions (NIC) will William pay for the tax year 2024/25?

   - ○ £3,692
   - ○ £4,289
   - ○ £2,938
   - ○ £2,262

   (2 marks)

2. You are a trainee chartered certified accountant, and your firm has a client who has refused to disclose a chargeable gain to HM Revenue & Customs (HMRC).

   From an ethical viewpoint, which TWO of the following actions could be expected of your firm?

   - ☐ Reporting under the money laundering regulations
   - ☐ Advising the client to make disclosure
   - ☐ Informing HMRC of the non-disclosure
   - ☐ Warning the client that your firm will be reporting the non-disclosure

   (2 marks)

3. Martin is self-employed and for the year ended 5 April 2025 his trading profit was £109,400. During the tax year 2024/25, Martin made a gift aid donation of £800 (gross) to a national charity.

   What amount of personal allowance will Martin be entitled to for the tax year 2024/25?

   £ [   ]

   (2 marks)

4. For the year ended 31 March 2025, Halo Ltd made a trading loss of £180,000.

   Halo Ltd has owned 100% of the ordinary share capital of Shallow Ltd since it began trading on 1 July 2024. For the year ended 30 June 2025, Shallow Ltd will make a trading profit of £224,000.

   Neither company has any other taxable profits or allowable losses.

   What is the maximum amount of group relief which Shallow Ltd can claim from Halo Ltd in respect of the trading loss of £180,000 for the year ended 31 March 2025?

   - ○ £180,000
   - ○ £168,000
   - ○ £45,000
   - ○ £135,000

   (2 marks)

5 For the year ended 31 March 2024, Sizeable Ltd had taxable total profits of £820,000, and for the year ended 31 March 2025 had taxable total profits of £970,000. The profits accrue evenly throughout the year.

Sizeable Ltd has had one associated company for many years.

How will Sizeable Ltd pay its corporation tax liability for the year ended 31 March 2025?

- ○ Nine instalments of £20,500 and a balancing payment of £58,000
- ○ Four instalments of £60,625
- ○ Four instalments of £51,250 and a balancing payment of £37,500
- ○ One payment of £242,500

(2 marks)

6 For the year ended 31 December 2024, Lateness Ltd had a corporation tax liability of £60,000, which it did not pay until 31 March 2026. Lateness Ltd is not a large company.

How much interest will Lateness Ltd be charged by HM Revenue & Customs (HMRC) in respect of the late payment of its corporation tax liability for the year ended 31 December 2024?

[▼]

Pull down list
- £1,163
- £2,325
- £5,813
- £775

(2 marks)

7 On 26 November 2024, Alice sold an antique table for £8,700. The antique table had been purchased on 16 May 2014 for £3,800.

What is Alice's chargeable gain in respect of the disposal of the antique table?

- ○ £4,500
- ○ £1,620
- ○ £4,900
- ○ £0

(2 marks)

8 On 14 November 2024, Jane made a cash gift to a trust of £800,000 (after deducting all available exemptions). Jane paid the inheritance tax arising from this gift. Jane has not made any other lifetime gifts.

What amount of lifetime inheritance tax would have been payable in respect of Jane's gift to the trust?

£ [   ]

(2 marks)

9   During the tax year 2024/25, Mildred made four cash gifts to her grandchildren.

For each of the gifts listed below, click in the box to indicate whether the gift will be exempt or not exempt from inheritance tax under the small gifts exemption.

£400 to Alfred	EXEMPT	NOT EXEMPT
£140 to Minnie	EXEMPT	NOT EXEMPT
A further £280 to Minnie	EXEMPT	NOT EXEMPT
£175 to Winifred	EXEMPT	NOT EXEMPT

(2 marks)

---

10 For the quarter ended 31 March 2025, Zim had standard rated sales of £49,750 and standard rated expenses of £22,750. Both figures are exclusive of value added tax (VAT).

Zim uses the flat rate scheme to calculate the amount of VAT payable, with the relevant scheme percentage for her trade being 12%. The percentage reduction for the first year of VAT registration is not available.

How much VAT will Zim have to pay to HM Revenue & Customs (HMRC) for the quarter ended 31 March 2025?

○ £5,970
○ £3,888
○ £5,400
○ £7,164

(2 marks)

---

11 **Which TWO of the following assets will ALWAYS be exempt from capital gains tax?**

☐ A car suitable for private use
☐ A chattel
☐ A UK government security (gilt)
☐ A house

(2 marks)

---

12 Winston invested £8,000 into a cash individual savings account (ISA) during the tax year 2024/25. Still within tax year 2024/25, Winston wants to invest into a stocks and shares ISA.

What is the maximum possible amount which Winston can invest into a stocks and shares ISA for the tax year 2024/25?

○ £20,000
○ £12,000
○ £0
○ £10,000

(2 marks)

13 Ming is self-employed.

For each of the types of records listed below, click in the box to indicate the date until which Ming must retain the records used in preparing her self-assessment tax return for the tax year 2024/25.

Business records	31 JANUARY 2027	31 JANUARY 2031
Non-business records	31 JANUARY 2027	31 JANUARY 2031

(2 marks)

14 Moon Ltd has had the following results:

Period	Profit/(loss)
	£
Year ended 31 December 2024	(105,000)
Four-month period ended 31 December 2023	43,000
Year ended 31 August 2023	96,000

The company does not have any other income.

How much of Moon Ltd's trading loss for the year ended 31 December 2024 can be relieved against its total profits of £96,000 for the year ended 31 August 2023?

- ○ £64,000
- ○ £96,000
- ○ £70,000
- ○ £62,000

(2 marks)

15 Nigel has not previously been resident in the UK, being in the UK for less than 20 days each tax year. For the tax year 2024/25, he has three ties with the UK.

What is the maximum number of days which Nigel could spend in the UK during the tax year 2024/25 without being treated as resident in the UK for that year?

- ○ 90 days
- ○ 182 days
- ○ 45 days
- ○ 120 days

(2 marks)

Section B

ALL 15 questions are compulsory and MUST be attempted.

Delroy and Marlon

Delroy and Grant

On 10 January 2025, Delroy made a gift of 25,000 £1 ordinary shares in Dub Ltd, an unquoted trading company, to his son, Grant. The market value of the shares on that date was £240,000. Delroy had subscribed for the 25,000 shares in Dub Ltd at par on 1 July 2008. Delroy and Grant have elected to hold over the gain as a gift of a business asset. Grant sold the 25,000 shares in Dub Ltd on 18 March 2025 for £240,000. Dub Ltd has a share capital of 100,000 £1 ordinary shares. Delroy was the sales director of the company from its incorporation on 1 July 2008 until 10 January 2025. Grant has never been an employee or a director of Dub Ltd.

For the tax year 2024/25 Delroy and Grant are both higher rate taxpayers. They have each made other disposals of assets during the tax year 2024/25, and therefore they have both already utilised their annual exempt amounts for this year.

Marlon and Alvita

On 28 March 2025, Marlon sold a residential property for £497,000, which he had owned individually. The property had been purchased on 22 October 2007 for £152,600. Throughout the period of ownership, the property was occupied by Marlon and his wife, Alvita, as their main residence. One-third of the property was always used exclusively for business purposes by the couple. Business asset disposal relief is not available in respect of this disposal.

For the tax year 2024/25, Marlon is a higher rate taxpayer, but Alvita did not have any taxable income. This will remain the case for the tax year 2025/26. Neither of them has made any other disposals of assets during the year.

16   What is Grant's capital gains tax (CGT) liability for the tax year 2024/25 in respect of the disposal of the shares in Dub Ltd?

   ○ £43,000
   ○ £21,500
   ○ £0
   ○ £42,400 (2 marks)

17   Which TWO of the following statements would have been true in relation to the CGT implications if Delroy had instead sold the 25,000 shares in Dub Ltd himself for £240,000 on 10 January 2025, and then gifted the cash proceeds to Grant?

   ☐ Business asset disposal relief would have been available.
   ☐ The CGT liability would have been paid later.
   ☐ The cash gift would not have been a chargeable disposal.
   ☐ The cash gift would have qualified for gift holdover relief. (2 marks)

18   What is Marlon's chargeable gain for the tax year 2024/25?

   ○ £229,600
   ○ £0
   ○ £114,800
   ○ £344,400 (2 marks)

19 What is the amount of CGT which could have been saved if Marlon had transferred 50% ownership of the residential property to Alvita prior to its disposal?

○ £720
○ £2,982
○ £2,262
○ £9,768

(2 marks)

20 What is the payment date for the capital gains tax payable on the disposal of the residential property on 28 March 2025?

[▼]

Pull down list
- 27 May 2025
- 31 January 2026
- 31 January 2027
- 31 May 2025

(2 marks)

(Total = 10 marks)

Opal

You should assume that today's date is 15 March 2025.

Opal is aged 71 and has a chargeable estate for inheritance tax (IHT) purposes valued at £950,000. She owns a property which is valued at £374,000 and has an outstanding repayment mortgage of £160,000. She also holds life insurance on her own life, currently valued at £350,000, but which will pay proceeds of £442,000 in the event of her death.

Opal owes £22,400 in respect of a personal loan from a bank, and she has also verbally promised to pay legal fees of £4,600 incurred by her nephew. Opal expects the cost of her funeral to be £5,200, and this cost will be covered by the £6,000 she has invested in an individual savings account (ISA). Under the terms of her will, Opal has left all of her estate to her children. Opal's husband is still alive.

On 14 August 2015, Opal had made a gift of £100,000 to her daughter, and on 7 November 2024, she made a gift of £220,000 to her son. Both these figures are after deducting all available exemptions.

The nil rate band for the tax year 2015/16 is £325,000. You should assume that both the value of Opal's estate and the nil rate band will remain unchanged for future years.

21 What is the net value for the property and insurance policy, which will have been included in the calculation of Opal's chargeable estate of £950,000?

○ £816,000
○ £564,000
○ £656,000
○ £724,000

(2 marks)

22 Which TWO of the following amounts will have been deducted in calculating Opal's chargeable estate of £950,000?

☐ Personal loan from a bank of £22,400
☐ Promise to pay legal fees of £4,600
☐ Funeral cost of £5,200
☐ ISA investment of £6,000

(2 marks)

23 What amount of IHT will be payable in respect of Opal's chargeable estate valued at £950,000 were she to die on 20 March 2025?

○ £250,000
○ £338,000
○ £378,000
○ £335,600

(2 marks)

24 By how much would the IHT payable on Opal's death be reduced if she were to live for another seven years until 20 March 2032, compared to if she were to die on 20 March 2025?

[▼]

Pull down list

- £0
- £128,000
- £40,000
- £88,000

(2 marks)

25 Which TWO of the following conditions must be met if Opal wants to make gifts out of her income, so that these gifts are exempt from IHT?

☐ The gifts cannot exceed 10% of income.
☐ The gifts must be habitual.
☐ Opal must have enough remaining income to maintain her normal standard of living.
☐ Opal must make the gifts monthly or quarterly.

(2 marks)

(Total = 10 marks)

Glacier Ltd

The following information is available in respect of Glacier Ltd's value added tax (VAT) for the quarter ended 31 March 2025:

(1) Invoices were issued for sales of £44,600 to VAT registered customers. Of this figure, £35,200 was in respect of exempt sales and the balance in respect of standard rated sales. The standard rated sales figure is exclusive of VAT.

(2) In addition to the above, on 1 March 2025 Glacier Ltd issued a VAT invoice for £8,000 plus VAT of £1,600 to a VAT registered customer in respect of a contract which will be completed on 15 April 2025.

The customer paid for the contract in two instalments of £4,800 on 31 March 2025 and 30 April 2025.

(3) The managing director of Glacier Ltd is provided with free fuel for private mileage driven in her company car. During the quarter ended 31 March 2025, the total cost of fuel for business and private mileage was £720, of which £270 was for private mileage.

The relevant quarterly scale charge is £490. All of these figures are inclusive of VAT.

For the quarters ended 30 September 2023 and 30 June 2024, Glacier Ltd was one month late in submitting its VAT returns and in paying the related VAT liabilities.

All of the company's other VAT returns have been submitted on time.

26 **What is the amount of output VAT payable by Glacier Ltd in respect of its sales for the quarter ended 31 March 2025?**

[▼]

Pull down list
- £1,880
- £10,520
- £2,680
- £3,480

(2 marks)

27 **Calculate the amounts required to complete the following sentence:**

Glacier Ltd will include:

Output VAT of £ [ ]

Input VAT of £ [ ]

On its VAT return for the quarter ended 31 March 2025 in respect of the managing director's company car. **(2 marks)**

28 **What penalties will Glacier Ltd be charged if the company is 30 days late in paying its VAT liability for the quarter ended 31 March 2025?**
- ○ 2% of the VAT liability and late payment interest
- ○ 2% of the VAT liability, daily penalty 4% of the VAT liability and late payment interest
- ○ No penalty
- ○ 4% of the VAT liability, daily penalty 4% of the VAT liability and late payment interest

(2 marks)

29 **Which TWO of the following statements about late filing penalties are true?**
- ☐ A business incurs a penalty of £200 for every quarterly return that it submits late.
- ☐ Once the threshold is reached, four quarterly returns must be submitted on time to reset penalty points to zero.
- ☐ A business incurs a penalty point once four quarterly returns have been submitted late.
- ☐ Penalty points expire after two years unless the threshold of four points has been reached.

(2 marks)

30 Glacier Ltd will be required to issue a VAT invoice in certain circumstances.

Complete the following sentence by matching one of the 'types of supply' and one of the 'types of customer' into each target area.

Glacier Ltd will be required to issue a VAT invoice when [(1) ▼] is made to [(2) ▼].

Pull down list 1
- A standard rated supply
- Any type of supply

Pull down list 2
- A VAT registered customer
- Any customer

(2 marks)

(Total = 10 marks)

Section C

ALL three questions are compulsory and MUST be attempted.

31 Sarah

You should assume that today's date is 1 March 2024.

Sarah is currently self-employed. If she continues to trade on a self-employed basis, her total income tax liability and national insurance contributions (NIC) for the tax year 2024/25 will be £9,732.

However, Sarah is considering incorporating her business on 6 April 2024. The forecast taxable total profits of the new limited company for the year ended 5 April 2025 will be £50,000 (before taking account of any director's remuneration). Sarah will pay herself gross director's remuneration of £30,000 and dividends of £10,000. The balance of the profits will remain undrawn within the new company.

Required

(a) Determine whether or not there will be an overall saving of tax and national insurance contributions (NIC) for the year ended 5 April 2025 if Sarah incorporates her business on 6 April 2024.

Notes.

1. You are expected to calculate the income tax payable by Sarah, the Class 1 NIC payable by Sarah and the new limited company, and the corporation tax liability of the new limited company for the year ended 5 April 2025.

2. The new limited company will not be entitled to the NIC annual employment allowance.

3. You should assume that the rates of corporation tax remain unchanged. **(8 marks)**

(b) Advise Sarah as to why her proposed basis of extracting profits from the new limited company is not optimum for tax purposes and suggest how the mix of director's remuneration and dividends could therefore be improved.

Note. You are not expected to calculate any revised tax or NIC figures. **(2 marks)**

(Total = 10 marks)

32 Simon

On 6 April 2024, Simon commenced employment with Echo Ltd. He was already in partnership with Art, preparing accounts to 5 April and he continued this partnership. The following information is available for the tax year 2024/25:

Employment

(1) During the tax year 2024/25, Simon was paid a gross annual salary of £24,010.

(2) Throughout the tax year 2024/25, Echo Ltd provided Simon with living accommodation. The company had purchased the property in 2012 for £89,000, and it was valued at £143,000 on 6 April 2024. The annual value of the property is £4,600. The property was furnished by Echo Ltd during March 2024 at a cost of £9,400. The living accommodation is not job related.

(3) On 1 December 2024, Echo Ltd provided Simon with an interest-free loan of £84,000, which he used to purchase a holiday cottage.

Partnership

(1) The partnership's tax adjusted trading profit for the year ended 5 April 2025 is £29,700. This figure is before taking account of capital allowances.

(2) The only item of plant and machinery owned by the partnership is a car which cost £8,333 on 1 February 2025. The car has a CO_2 emission rate of 125 grams per kilometre. It is used by Art, and 40% of the mileage is for private journeys.

(3) Profits are shared 40% to Simon and 60% to Art. This is after paying an annual salary of £2,000 to Art.

Property income

(1) Simon owns a freehold house which is let out furnished. The property was let throughout the tax year 2024/25 at a monthly rent of £660, all of which was received during the tax year.

(2) During the tax year 2024/25, Simon paid council tax and water rates totalling £1,320 in respect of the property. He also replaced the property's washing machine during March 2025. The old washing machine was sold for £70, being replaced by a washer-dryer costing £970. The cost of a similar washing machine would have been £730.

Required

(a) Calculate Simon's taxable income for the tax year 2024/25. **(13 marks)**

(b) State the period during which HM Revenue and Customs (HMRC) will have to notify Simon if they intend to carry out a compliance check in respect of his self-assessment tax return for the tax year 2024/25 and a possible reason why such a check would be made. **(2 marks)**

(Total = 15 marks)

33 Naive Ltd

You are a trainee accountant and your manager has asked you to correct a corporation tax computation which has been prepared by the managing director of Naive Ltd. The corporation tax computation is for the year ended 31 March 2025 and contains a significant number of errors:

Naive Ltd – Corporation tax computation for the year ended 31 March 2025

	£
Trading profit (W1)	372,900
Loan interest received (W2)	32,100
	405,000
Corporation tax (405,000 at 19%)	76,950

Workings

(1) Trading profit

	£
Operating profit before interest and taxation	274,530
Depreciation	15,740
Donations to political parties	400
Qualifying charitable donations	900
Accountancy	2,300
Legal fees in connection with the issue of loan notes (the loan was used to finance the company's trading activities)	5,700
Entertaining suppliers	3,600

	£
Entertaining employees	1,700
Gifts to customers (pens costing £40 each and displaying Naive Ltd's name)	920
Gifts to customers (food hampers costing £45 each and displaying Naive Ltd's name)	1,650
Capital allowances (working 3)	65,460
Trading profit	372,900

(2) *Loan interest received*

	£
Loan interest receivable	32,800
Accrued at 1 April 2024	10,600
Accrued at 31 March 2025	(11,300)
Loan interest received	32,100

The loan was made for non-trading purposes.

(3) *Capital allowances*

	Main pool	Car	Special rate pool	Allowances
	£	£	£	£
WDV brought forward	12,400		13,600	
Additions				
Machinery	42,300			
Car [1]	13,800			
Car [2]		14,000		
	68,500			
AIA	(68,500)			68,500
Disposal proceeds			(9,300)	
			4,300	
Balancing allowance			(4,300)	(4,300)
WDA – 18%		(2,520)	× 50%	1,260
WDV carried forward	0	11,480		
Total allowances				65,460

- Car [1] has a CO_2 emission rate of 40 grams per kilometre.
- Car [2] has a CO_2 emission rate of 125 grams per kilometre. This car is used by the sales manager and 50% of the mileage is for private journeys.
- All of the items included in the special rate pool at 1 April 2024 were sold for £9,300 during the year ended 31 March 2025. The original cost of these items was £16,200 and no enhanced capital allowances were claimed on acquisition.

Required

(a) Prepare a corrected version of Naive Ltd's corporation tax computation for the year ended 31 March 2025.

   Note. Your calculations should commence with the operating profit before interest and taxation figure of £274,530, and you should indicate by the use of zero (0) any items in the computation of the trading profit for which no adjustment is required. **(12 marks)**

(b) The managing director of Naive Ltd understands that the company will have to file its self-assessment corporation tax returns online, and that the supporting accounts and tax computations will have to be filed using the inline eXtensible Business Reporting Language (iXBRL). The managing director is concerned with how the company will be able to produce the documents in this format.

   Required

   Explain the options available to Naive Ltd regarding the production of accounts and tax computations in the iXBRL format. **(3 marks)**

   (Total = 15 marks)

Answers

DO NOT TURN THIS PAGE UNTIL YOU HAVE COMPLETED THE MOCK EXAM

A plan of attack

If this were the real Taxation (TX – UK) exam and you had been told to turn over and begin, what would be going through your mind?

Perhaps you're having a panic. You've spent most of your study time on income tax and corporation tax computations (because that's what your tutor/BPP Course Book told you to do), plus a selection of other topics, and you're really not sure that you know enough. So calm down. Spend the first few moments or so **looking at the exam** and develop a **plan of attack**.

Looking through the exam.

Section A contains **15 Objective Test (OT) questions** each worth **2 marks**. These will cover all sections of the syllabus. Some you may find easy and some more difficult. For example, Question 13 on keeping records for tax should be easy marks and you just need to pick the right answers from the table. Don't spend a lot of time on anything you really don't know. For multiple choice questions you are not penalised for wrong answers, so you should answer all of them. If all else fails – guess!

Section B contains **three OT Case** scenarios. These each have **five questions** each worth **2 marks**. Make sure you read the scenario carefully before you start to answer the OTQs.

- **Questions 16 to 20** are about chargeable gains for individuals. In Question 19, note that you are asked for the amount of CGT which could have been **saved** if Marlon had transferred 50% ownership of the residential property to Alvita prior to its disposal so you need to think about how CGT is computed for Alvita bearing in mind that she has no taxable income or other disposals in the year.
- **Questions 21 to 25** concern inheritance tax (IHT). In Question 24, you need to consider how the seven year accumulation period works.
- **Questions 26 to 30** test topics in value added tax (VAT). For Question 26, you need to think about the tax point for the contract in part (2).

In Section C you have three constructed response (long) questions:

- **Question 31** for **10 marks** is about the potential tax saving by incorporating a sole trader business. You need to work out the individual's income tax, the national insurance contributions for an employee and corporation tax.
- **Question 32** for **15 marks** is an income tax computation.
- **Question 33** for **15 marks** is a corporation tax question and includes capital allowances. Part (b) is about how a company files its corporation tax return and supporting accounts.

Allocating your time

BPP's advice is always allocate your time **according to the marks for the question** in total and for the parts of the question. But **use common sense**. If you're confronted by an OTQ on a topic of which you know nothing, pick an answer and move on. Use the time to pick up marks elsewhere.

After the exam... **Forget about it!**

And don't worry if you found the exam difficult. More than likely other candidates will too. If this were the real thing you would need to **forget** the exam the minute you left the exam hall and **think about the next one**. Or, if it's the last one, **celebrate!**

Section A

1   The correct answer is: £2,938

	£
£(50,270 – 12,570) = £37,700 × 6%	2,262
£(84,050 – 50,270) = £33,780 × 2%	676
Class 4 NICs	2,938

The answer £3,692 the Class 1 rate of 8%. The answer £4,289 uses 6% throughout. The answer £2,262 is just the 6% band liability.

2   The correct answers are:
   - Reporting under the money laundering regulations
   - Advising the client to make disclosure

Your firm should advise the client to make disclosure. Your firm should make a report under the money laundering regulations.

You should not inform HMRC of the non-disclosure. Your firm also should not warn the client that it will be reporting the non-disclosure as this might constitute the criminal offence of 'tipping-off.'

3   £ 8,270

	£
Personal allowance	12,570
Less restriction £(109,400 – 800 – 100,000) = £8,600/2	(4,300)
Restricted personal allowance	8,270

4   The correct answer is: £135,000

	£
Lower of:	
Taxable total profits of Shallow Ltd for the corresponding accounting period (1.7.24 – 31.3.25) £224,000 × 9/12	168,000
Losses of Halo Ltd for the corresponding accounting period £180,000 × 9/12	135,000

5   The correct answer is: Four instalments of £60,625

	£
Profits threshold £1,500,000/2 (one associated company)	750,000

Sizeable Ltd was therefore a large company in both years.

Upper limit = £250,000/2 (one associated company) = £125,000

Sizeable Ltd will therefore be charged corporation tax at the main rate.

Each instalment for the year to 31 March 2025 is £(970,000 @ 25%) = 242,500/4	60,625

The answer nine instalments of £20,500 (£820,000@25% × 10%) and a balancing payment of £58,000 (£242,500 – 9 × £20,500) is based on the previous accounting period's profits with each of the instalments being 10% of the liability. This is the VAT annual accounting schedule of payments. The answer instalments of £51,250 (£820,000@25% ÷ 4) and a balancing payment of £37,500 (£242,500 – 4 × £51,250) is based on the previous year's profits, similar to self-assessment for individuals. The answer £242,500 is the full amount of corporation tax which would be payable if Sizeable Ltd was not a large company.

6   £2,325

Interest runs from due date (1 October 2025) to the date of payment (31 March 2026) which is six months.

£60,000 × 7.75% × 6/12   £2,325

The answer £5,813 is for a 15-month period from 31 January 2025 to 31 March 2026. The answer £775 is for a two-month period from 31 January 2026 to 31 March 2026. The answer £1,163 is for a three-month period from the filing date of 1 January 2026 to 31 March 2026.

7   The correct answer is: £4,500

	£
Proceeds	8,700
Less cost	(3,800)
Gain	4,900

The maximum gain is 5/3 × £(8,700 – 6,000) = £4,500.

The chargeable gain is the lower of £4,900 and £4,500, so it is £4,500.

The answer £0 assumes that this is an exempt chattel.

8   £ 118,750

	£
Net chargeable transfer	800,000
Less nil rate band	(325,000)
	475,000
IHT £475,000 × 20/80 (donor paid tax)	118,750

9   The correct answers are:

£400 to Alfred		NOT EXEMPT
£140 to Minnie		NOT EXEMPT
A further £280 to Minnie		NOT EXEMPT
£175 to Winifred	EXEMPT	

Outright gifts to individuals totalling £250 or less per donee in any one tax year are exempt under the small gifts exemption. The £400 gift to Alfred is therefore not exempt under the small gifts exemption. If gifts total more than £250, the whole amount is chargeable. Neither of the gifts to Minnie which total £(140 + 280) = £420 are exempt under the small gifts exemption. The gift of £175 to Winifred is exempt under the small gifts exemption.

10 The correct answer is: £7,164

£(49,750 × 120/100) = 59,700 × 12% = £7,164

Under the flat rate scheme, a business calculates VAT by applying a fixed percentage to its tax inclusive turnover. However, the business cannot reclaim any input tax suffered.

11 The correct answers are:
- A car suitable for private use
- A UK government security (gilt)

A wasting chattel is exempt, as is a chattel sold for gross proceeds of £6,000 or less. Other chattels are chargeable assets. A house may be exempt if private residence relief applies but is otherwise a chargeable asset.

12 The correct answer is: £12,000

£(20,000 − 8,000) = £12,000

The answer £20,000 is the full ISA allowance. The answer £0 assumes that only one ISA can be opened in a tax year and so Winston cannot invest into a stocks and shares ISA having invested in a cash ISA. The answer £10,000 assumes that the ISA limit is divided equally.

13 The correct answers are:

Business records		31 JANUARY 2031
Non-business records		31 JANUARY 2031

Records must be retained until five years after the 31 January following the tax year where the taxpayer is in business. This applies to all of the records, not only the business records.

14   The correct answer is: £62,000

	£
Loss incurred in y/e 31.12.24	105,000
p/e 31.12.23	(43,000)
	62,000
y/e 31.8.23	
Lower of £96,000 × 8/12 = £64,000 and unused loss	(62,000)
C/f	0

Loss relief by deduction from total profits may be given by deduction from current period profits and from the previous 12 months. Therefore, relief can be given in the four-month period ended 31 December 2023 and for eight months of the year ended 31 August 2023.

The answer £64,000 is the time apportioned amount of profits. The answer £96,000 assumes that the earlier accounting period profits can be relieved first. The answer £70,000 is £105,000 × 8/12.

15   The correct answer is: 90 days

Nigel was not previously resident in the UK. He will be UK resident for 2024/25 with three UK ties if he spends at least 91 days in the UK during that tax year. Therefore, the maximum number of days that Nigel could spend in the UK during the tax year 2024/25 without being treated as UK resident for that year is 90 days.

Section B

Delroy and Marlon

> **Course Book references**
>
> Computing chargeable gains and computation of the CGT liability are covered in Chapter 13, and private residence relief in Chapter 14. Business reliefs are the subject of Chapter 15.
>
> **Top Tips**
>
> Be careful to read all the information given in the scenario. In this case you were told that Grant had used his annual exempt amount, but that Alvita had not made any other disposals of assets during the year and so must still have her annual exempt amount available.
>
> **Easy Marks**
>
> There were easy marks in Question 16 for a basic gain computation leading to the calculation of CGT. Question 20 should have been quick and easy marks for identification of the correct statement.

16   The correct answer is: £43,000

	£
Ordinary shares in Dub Ltd	
Proceeds	240,000
Less cost	(25,000)
Gain	215,000
Less annual exempt amount (already used as stated in question)	(0)
Taxable gain	215,000
CGT: £215,000 × 20%	43,000

- The effect of the gift holdover relief election is that Grant effectively took over Delroy's original cost of £25,000.
- The disposal does not qualify for business asset disposal relief as Grant was neither an officer nor an employee of Dub Ltd and, in any case, had only owned the shares for just over two months (the minimum period for the conditions for the relief to be satisfied is two years).

The answer £21,500 assumes that business asset disposal relief applies to the disposal so the rate of tax is 10%. The answer £0 assumes this is an exempt disposal. The answer £42,400 deducts the annual exempt amount – read the question carefully!

17   The correct answers are:

- Business asset disposal relief would have been available.
- The cash gift would not have been a chargeable disposal.

Delroy's disposal would have qualified for business asset disposal relief because for at least two years prior to the disposal:

- Dub Ltd was Delroy's personal company as he owned at least 5% of the ordinary share capital.
- Dub Ltd was a trading company.
- Delroy was an officer or employee of Dub Ltd.

There are no capital gains tax implications of a gift of cash.

18 The correct answer is: £114,800

	£
Residential property	
Proceeds	497,000
Less cost	(152,600)
Gain before PRR	344,400
Less PRR (W)	(229,600)
Gain after PRR	114,800

Working

One-third of the residential property was always used exclusively for business purposes, so the private residence relief exemption is restricted to £(344,400 × 2/3) = £229,600.

The answer £229,600 is the PRR. The answer £0 assumes this is an exempt disposal. The answer £344,400 is the gain before PRR.

19 The correct answer is: £2,982

		£
Annual exempt amount	£3,000 × 24%	720
Basic rate band	£37,700 × (24 – 18)%	2,262
Total tax saving		2,982

The 50% ownership of the house would have been transferred from Marlon to Alvita on a no gain, no loss basis. The effect of this is that 50% of the gain on disposal would accrue to Marlon and 50% to Alvita.

Transferring 50% ownership of the house to Alvita prior to its disposal would have enabled her annual exempt amount and basic rate tax band for 2024/25 to be utilised.

The answer £720 is just the annual exempt amount saving. The answer £2,262 is just the basic rate band saving. The answer £9,768 is the annual exempt amount and the basic rate band, all at 24%.

20 27 May 2025

The CGT on disposal of a residential property is due within 60 days of the disposal.

Opal

> **Course Book references**
>
> Inheritance tax is covered in Chapter 18.
>
> **Top tips**
>
> Try drawing a timeline and mark on it the date of Opal's death and the lifetime transfers. Then mark the date which is seven years before Opal's death. It will be clear that the lifetime transfer in 2015 falls more than seven years before Opal's death and is therefore exempt.
>
> **Easy marks**
>
> There were some easy marks for working out the IHT on the death estate in Question 23.

21 The correct answer is: £656,000

£374,000 − £160,000 + £442,000 = £656,000

22 The correct answers are:
- Personal loan from a bank of £22,400
- Funeral cost of £5,200

The promise to pay the nephew's legal fees is not deductible as it is not legally enforceable.

23 The correct answer is: £338,000

	£
Chargeable estate	950,000
105,000 (W) × 0%	0
845,000 × 40%	338,000
950,000	
IHT on death estate	338,000

Working

	£
Nil rate band at death	325,000
Less:	
– PET 14 August 2015	(0)
– PET 7 November 2024	(220,000)
Available nil rate band	105,000

The potentially exempt transfer on 14 August 2015 is exempt from inheritance tax as it was made more than seven years before 20 March 2025.

The answer £250,000 has an unrestricted nil rate band. The answer £378,000 assumes that the PET in 2015 becomes chargeable on Opal's death. The answer £335,600 deducts two annual exemptions from the gift in 2024.

24 £88,000

If Opal were to live for another seven years, the potentially exempt transfer on 7 November 2024 would become exempt.

The inheritance tax payable in respect of her estate would therefore decrease by £(220,000 × 40%) = £88,000.

25 The correct answers are:
- The gifts must be habitual.
- Opal must have enough remaining income to maintain her normal standard of living.

Glacier Ltd

> **Course Book references**
> Value added tax is covered in Chapters 24 and 25.
>
> **Top tips**
> The tax point is frequently examined and is relevant in Question 26. The basic tax point for a supply of services is the date when they are completed, but if a VAT invoice is issued or payment received before the basic tax point, then this becomes the actual tax point.
>
> **Easy marks**
> There were easy marks in Questions 28 and 29 concerning the late payment and late filing penalties.

26   £3,480

	£
Sales	
VAT registered customers £(44,600 − 35,200) = £9,400 × 20%	1,880
Additional contract (1 March 2025)	1,600
Output VAT	3,480

The tax point for the contract is when the VAT invoice was issued on 1 March 2025, which is earlier than both the basic tax point of 15 April and the receipt of cash on 31 March.

27   Glacier Ltd will include:

Output VAT of £ 82

Input VAT of £ 120

On its VAT return for the quarter ended 31 March 2025 in respect of the managing director's company car.

	£
Output VAT £490 × 20/120	82
Input VAT £720 × 20/120	120

28   The correct answer is: 2% of the VAT liability and late payment interest

The late payment of VAT will result in a penalty of 2% of the VAT liability for that period since the liability was paid within 16 and 30 days of the due date, and late payment interest from the due date until the date that the VAT liability is paid.

29   The correct answers are:
- Once the threshold is reached, four quarterly returns must be submitted on time to reset penalty points to zero.
- Penalty points expire after two years unless the threshold of four points has been reached.

30   Glacier Ltd will be required to issue a VAT invoice when a standard rated supply is made to a VAT registered customer .

Section C

ALL three questions are compulsory and MUST be attempted.

31 Sarah

> **Course Book references**
>
> Employment income is covered in Chapter 3; the income tax computation in Chapter 2; and NICs are dealt with in Chapter 12. Corporation tax is covered in Chapter 19.
>
> **Top tips**
>
> Note 1 outlines the steps that you need to take to complete the question.
>
> **Easy marks**
>
> There were some easy marks for basic income tax and corporation tax computations.

Marking guide

		Marks
(a)	**Income tax liability**	
	Director's remuneration	0.5
	Dividends	0.5
	Personal allowance	0.5
	Basic rate on earnings	0.5
	Nil rate on dividends	0.5
	Basic rate on dividends	0.5
	National insurance contributions	
	Class 1 employee	1
	Class 1 employer	1
	Corporation tax	
	Trading profit	0.5
	Director's remuneration	0.5
	Employer's Class 1 NIC	0.5
	Corporation tax	0.5
	Total tax cost if incorporates	0.5
	Additional tax	0.5
		8
(b)	Salary attracting NICs	1
	Restrict salary, take more dividends	1
		2
Total		**10**

(a) **Sarah – Income tax liability 2024/25**

	Non-savings income	Dividend income	Total income
	£	£	£
Director's remuneration	30,000		
Dividends		10,000	
Net income	30,000	10,000	40,000
Less personal allowance	(12,570)		
Taxable income	17,430	10,000	27,430

Tax

Non-savings income

£17,430 @ 20%	3,486

Dividend income

£500 @ 0%	0
£9,500 (10,000 – 500) @ 8.75%	831
Income tax liability	4,317

Sarah – National insurance contributions 2024/25

	£
Employee Class 1 £(30,000 – 12,570) = 17,430 @ 8%	1,394
Employer Class 1 £(30,000 – 9,100) = 20,900 @ 13.8%	2,884

Corporation tax liability of the new limited company for the year ended 5 April 2025

	£
Trading profit	50,000
Less:	
– Director's remuneration	(30,000)
– Employer's Class 1 NIC	(2,884)
Taxable trading profit	17,116
Corporation tax £17,116 @ 19%	3,252

The total tax and NIC cost if Sarah incorporates her business is £11,847 (4,317 + 1,394 + 2,884 + 3,252).

Therefore, if Sarah incorporated her business, there would be additional tax and NIC payable as there would be an increase of £2,115 (11,847 – 9,732) compared to continuing on a self-employed basis.

Using the spreadsheet software in your CBE exam, your answer might look like this:

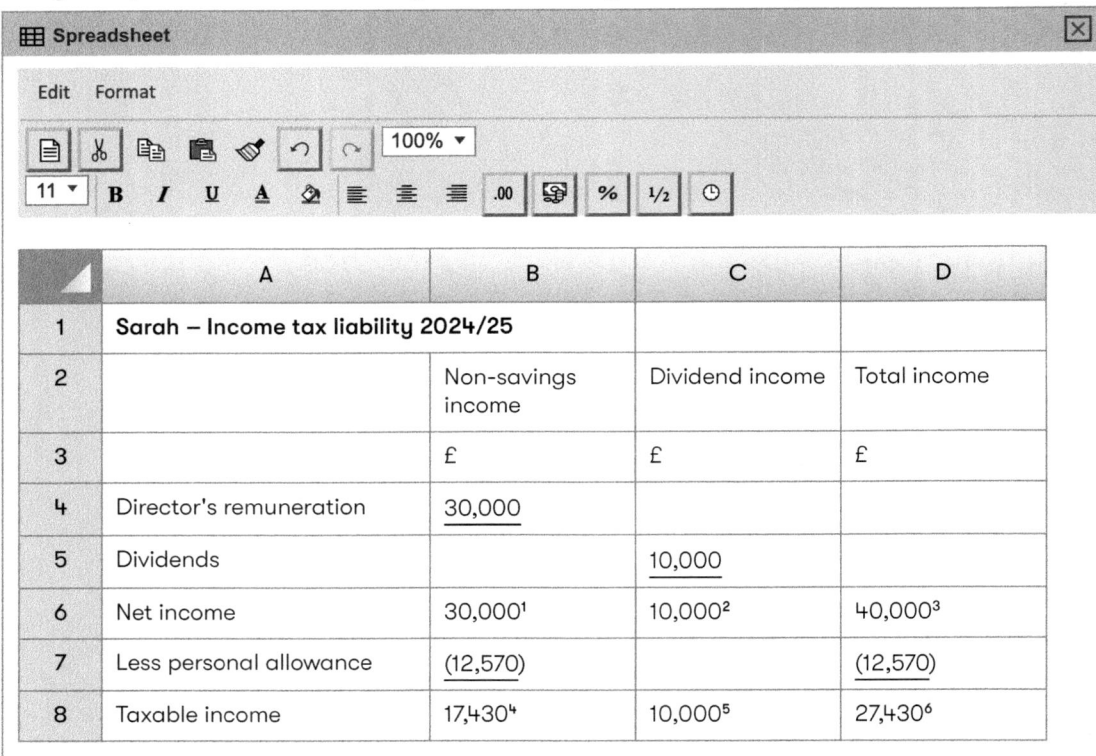

	A	B	C	D
1	Sarah – Income tax liability 2024/25			
2		Non-savings income	Dividend income	Total income
3		£	£	£
4	Director's remuneration	30,000		
5	Dividends		10,000	
6	Net income	30,000[1]	10,000[2]	40,000[3]
7	Less personal allowance	(12,570)		(12,570)
8	Taxable income	17,430[4]	10,000[5]	27,430[6]

[1] =SUM(B4:B5)
[2] =SUM(C4:C5)
[3] =SUM(B6:C6)
[4] =SUM(B6:B7)
[5] =SUM(C6:C7)
[6] =SUM(D6:D7)

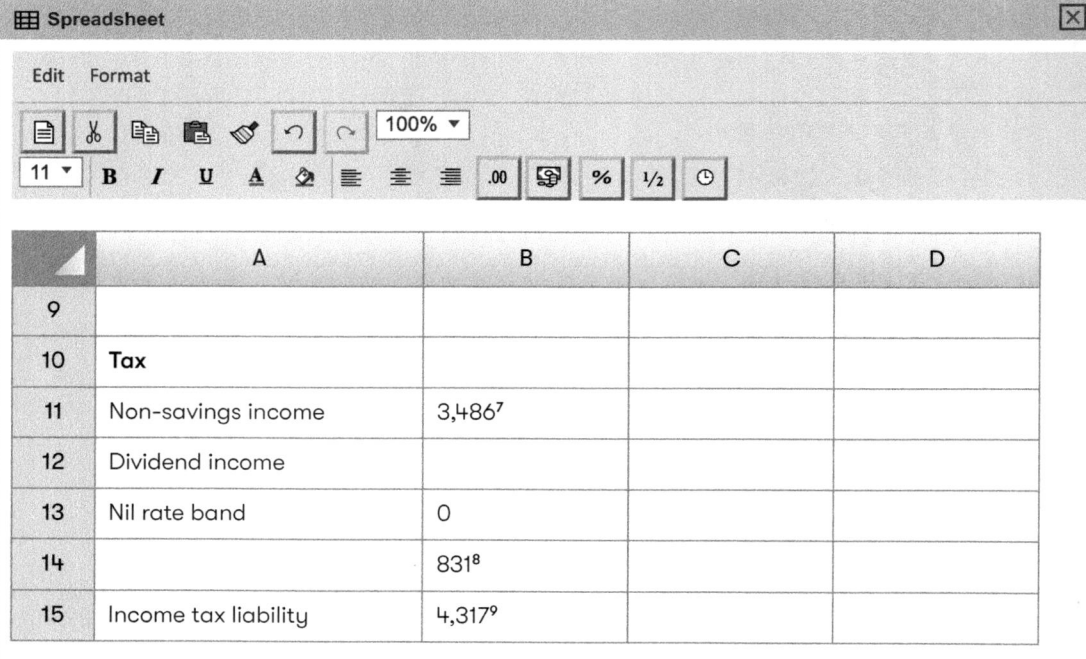

	A	B	C	D
9				
10	**Tax**			
11	Non-savings income	3,486[7]		
12	Dividend income			
13	Nil rate band	0		
14		831[8]		
15	Income tax liability	4,317[9]		

[7] =B8*20%

[8] =(C8-500)*8.75%

[9] =SUM(B11:B14)

	A	B	C	D
16				
17	Sarah – National insurance contributions 2024/25			
18	Employee Class 1	1,394[10]		
19	Employee Class 1	2,884[11]		

[10] =(30000-12570)*8%

[11] =(30000-9100)*13.8%

	A	B	C	D
20				
21	Corporation tax liability of the new ltd company for the year ended 5 April 2025			
22			£	
23	Trading profit		50,000	
24	Less	Director's remuneration	(30,000)	
25		Employer's Class 1 NIC	(2,884)[12]	
26	Taxable trading profit		17,116[13]	
27	Corporation tax		3,252[14]	
28			11,847[15]	
29	Therefore, if Sarah incorporated her business there would be additional tax and NIC payable as there would be an increase of £2,115 (11,847 – 9,732) compared to continuing on a self-employed basis.			

[12] =-B19

[13] =SUM(C23:C25)

[14] =C26*19%

[15] =B15+B18+B19+C27

(b)

The relatively high tax cost of Sarah incorporating her business arises because of her salary attracting both employee and employer NICs.

Restricting the salary to around £8,000 and taxing a correspondingly higher amount of dividends, would significantly reduce her overall tax cost.

32 Simon

Course Book references

Employment income is dealt with in Chapters 3 and 4.

Trading income is covered in Chapter 7 and capital allowances in Chapter 8.

Property income is the subject of Chapter 6.

The computation of taxable income is covered in Chapter 2.

Top tips

You should use the proforma taxable income computation and deal with more complicated computations in workings linked to the main computation.

Easy marks

There were some easy marks for computing employment benefits in part (a).

Marking guide		Marks
(a)	Employment income	0.5
	Salary	0.5
	Living accommodation	
	Annual value	1
	Additional benefit – market value	0.5
	Additional benefit – limit	0.5
	Additional benefit – benefit	0.5
	Furniture	1
	Loan benefit	1
	Trading income	
	Accounts profit	0.5
	Capital allowances – addition	0.5
	Capital allowances – WDA	1.5
	Salary paid to Art	1
	Profit share	1
	Property business income	
	Rent receivable	1

Marking guide	Marks	
Council tax	0.5	
Furniture	1.5	
Personal allowance	0.5	
		13
(b) 12 months of actual filing date	1	
Suspicion of undeclared income (or deductions incorrectly claimed)	1	
		2
Total		**15**

(a) Simon – Taxable income 2024/25

	£
Employment income	
Salary	24,010
Living accommodation – annual value	4,600
Living accommodation – additional benefit (W1)	1,530
Living accommodation – furniture £9,400 × 20%	1,880
Loan benefit £84,000 × 2.25% × 4/12	630
	32,650
Trading income (W2)	10,960
Property business income (W4)	5,940
Net income	49,550
Less personal allowance	(12,570)
Taxable income	36,980

Workings

1 *Market value*

	£
Market value when first provided to Simon	143,000
Less limit	(75,000)
	68,000
Additional benefit £68,000 × 2.25%	1,530

Tutorial note. Where the property was acquired by the employer more than six years before first being provided to the employee, the market value when first provided is used as the cost of providing the living accommodation.

2 Simon's share of the partnership's trading profit for the year ended 5 April 2025 is calculated as follows:

	£
Trading profit	29,700
Less capital allowances (W3)	(300)
	29,400
Less salary paid to Art	(2,000)
	27,400
Profit share £27,400 × 40%	10,960

3 **Capital allowances. Year to 5 April 2025**

	Car		Allowances
	£		£
Addition	8,333		
WDA @ 6%	(500)	× 60%	300
WDA c/f	7,833		

> **Tutorial note.** The partnership's car has CO_2 emissions over 50 grams per kilometre and therefore qualifies for writing down allowances at the rate of 6%.

4 **Property business income**

	£	£
Rent received £660 × 12		7,920
Council tax and water rates	1,320	
Replacement furniture relief		
Washing machine £(730 – 70)	660	
		(1,980)
Property business income		5,940

> **Tutorial note.** No relief is given for that part of the cost of the washer-dryer which represents an improvement over the original washing machine. Relief is therefore restricted to the cost of a similar washing machine. This figure is then reduced by the proceeds from the sale of the original washing machine.

Using the spreadsheet software in your CBE exam, your answer might look like this:

	A	B	C
1	**Simon – Taxable income 2024/25**		£
2	*Employment income*		
3	Salary		24,010
4	Living accommodation	– annual value	4,600
5		– additional benefit	1,530[1]
6		– furniture	1,880[2]
7	Loan benefit		630[3]
8			32,650[4]
9	*Trading income*		10,960[5]
10	*Property business income*		5,940[6]
11	Net income		49,550[7]
12	Less personal allowance		(12,570)
13	Taxable income		36,980[8]

[1] =(143000-75000)*2.25%

[2] =9400*20%

[3] =84000*2.25%*(4/12)

[4] =SUM(C3:C7)

[5] =C20

[6] =C27

[7] =SUM(C8:C10)

[8] =SUM(C11:C12)

Answers

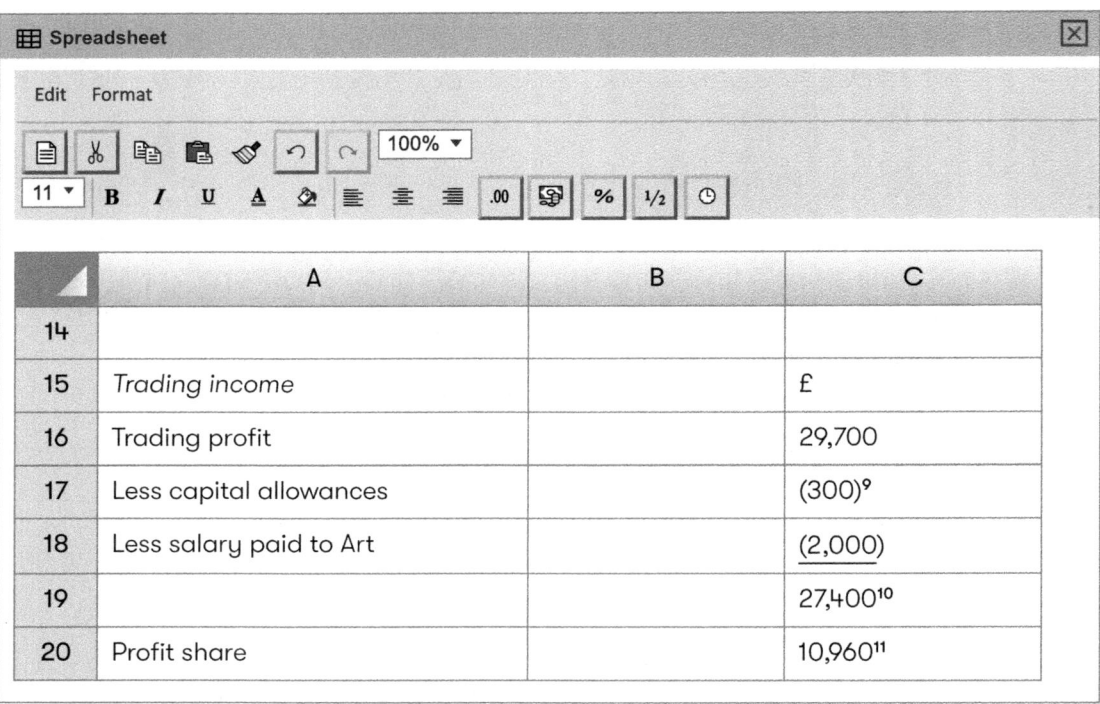

	A	B	C
14			
15	*Trading income*		£
16	Trading profit		29,700
17	Less capital allowances		(300)[9]
18	Less salary paid to Art		(2,000)
19			27,400[10]
20	Profit share		10,960[11]

[9] =25000*6%*(4/12)*60%
[10] =SUM(C16:C18)
[11] =C19*40%

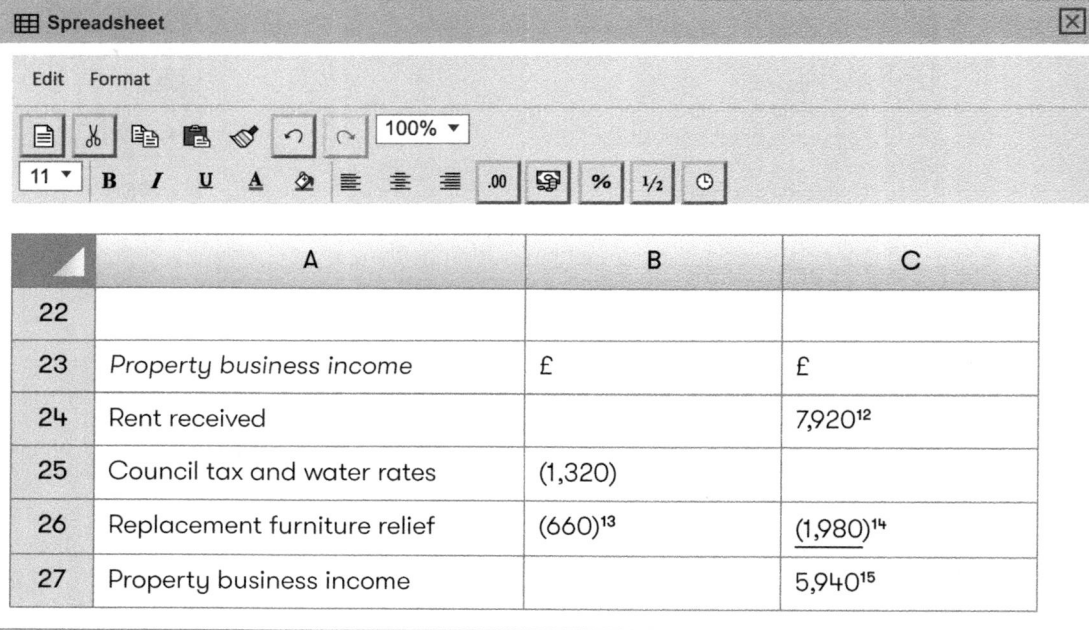

	A	B	C
22			
23	*Property business income*	£	£
24	Rent received		7,920[12]
25	Council tax and water rates	(1,320)	
26	Replacement furniture relief	(660)[13]	(1,980)[14]
27	Property business income		5,940[15]

[12] =660*12
[13] =-(730-70)
[14] =SUM(B25:B26)
[15] =SUM(C24:C26)

(b) Two advantages:

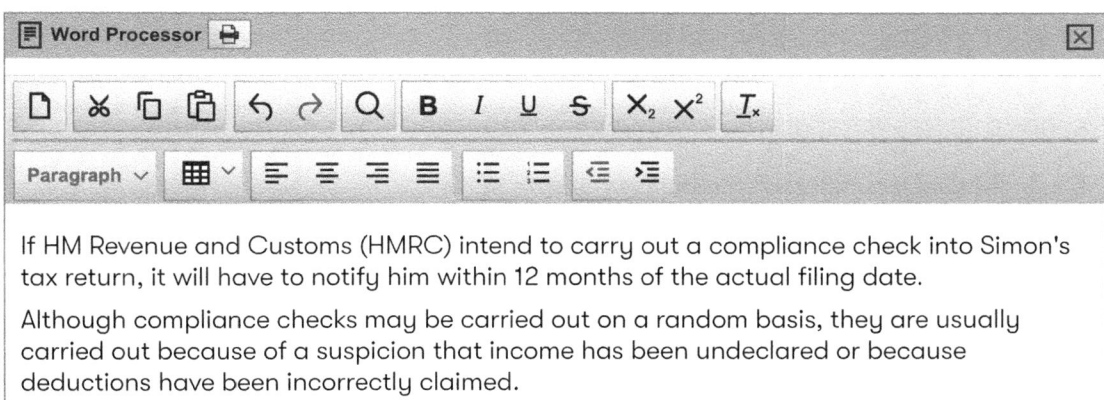

If HM Revenue and Customs (HMRC) intend to carry out a compliance check into Simon's tax return, it will have to notify him within 12 months of the actual filing date.

Although compliance checks may be carried out on a random basis, they are usually carried out because of a suspicion that income has been undeclared or because deductions have been incorrectly claimed.

33 Naive Ltd

Course Book references

The computation of taxable total profits and the computation of the corporation tax liability are covered in Chapter 19. The adjustment to trading profits is dealt with in Chapter 7 and capital allowances in Chapter 8.

Top tips

The best approach to this style of question is to start new computations using the information given in the question, rather than trying to correct the wrong computations.

Easy marks

There were some easy marks for the adjustment to trading profit and computation of corporation tax in part (a).

Marking guide	Marks
(a) Trading profit	
Depreciation	0.5
Donations to political parties	0.5
Qualifying charitable donations	0.5
Accountancy	0.5
Legal fees	0.5
Entertaining suppliers	0.5
Entertaining employees	0.5
Gift to customers – pens	0.5
Gift to customers – food hampers	0.5
Capital allowances brought from working	0.5
Capital allowances	
WDV brought forward	1
Annual investment allowance	1
Addition – car [1]	0.5
Addition – car [2]	0.5
Disposal	0.5

Marking guide	Marks	
WDA @ 18%	0.5	
WDA @ 6%	1	
Loan interest	1	
Qualifying charitable donations	0.5	
Corporation tax	0.5	
		12
(b) HMRC software automatically to produce in iXBRL	1	
Other software automatically to produce in iXBRL	1	
Tagging services and software used by Naive Ltd to tag	1	
		3
Total		**15**

(a) **Naive Ltd – Corporation tax computation for the year ended 31 March 2025**

	£
Trading profit (W1)	248,706
Loan interest	32,800
Total profits	281,506
Less qualifying charitable donations	(900)
Taxable total profits	280,606
Corporation tax	
£280,606 × 25%	70,152

Workings

1 *Trading profit for the year ended 31 March 2025*

	£
Operating profit before interest and taxation	274,530
Add:	
– Depreciation	15,740
– Donations to political parties	400
– Qualifying charitable donations	900
– Accountancy	0
– Legal fees	0
– Entertaining suppliers	3,600
– Entertaining employees	0
– Gifts to customers – pens	0
– Gifts to customers – food hampers	1,650
	296,820

	£
Less capital allowances (W2)	(48,114)
Adjusted trading profit	248,706

	AIA	Main pool	Special rate pool	Allowances
	£	£	£	£
WDV brought forward		12,400	13,600	
AIA additions				
Machinery	42,300			
AIA	(42,300)			42,300
Transfer to pool	0	0		
Non-AIA additions				
Car [1]		13,800		
Car [2]			14,000	
Disposal				
Special rate pool items			(9,300)	
		26,200	18,300	
WDA @ 18%		(4,716)		4,716
WDA @ 6%			(1,098)	1,098
WDV carried forward		21,484	17,202	
Allowances				48,114

> **Tutorial note.** Car [1] has CO_2 emissions between 1 and 50 grams per kilometre and therefore qualifies for writing down allowances at the rate of 18%. Cars do not qualify for the AIA.
>
> Car [2] has CO_2 emissions over 50 grams per kilometre and therefore qualifies for writing down allowances at the rate of 6%. The private use of the car is irrelevant since such usage will be assessed on the employee as a benefit.

Using the spreadsheet software in your CBE exam, your answer might look like this:

	A	B	C
1	Naïve Ltd – Corporation tax computation for the year ended 31 March 2025		
2			£
3	Trading profit		248,706[1]
4	Loan interest		32,800
5	Total profits		281,506[2]
6	Less qualifying charitable donations		(900)
7	Taxable total profits		280,606[3]
8	Corporation tax		70,152[4]

[1] =C24

[2] =SUM(C3:C4)

[3] =SUM(C5:C6)

[4] =C7*25%

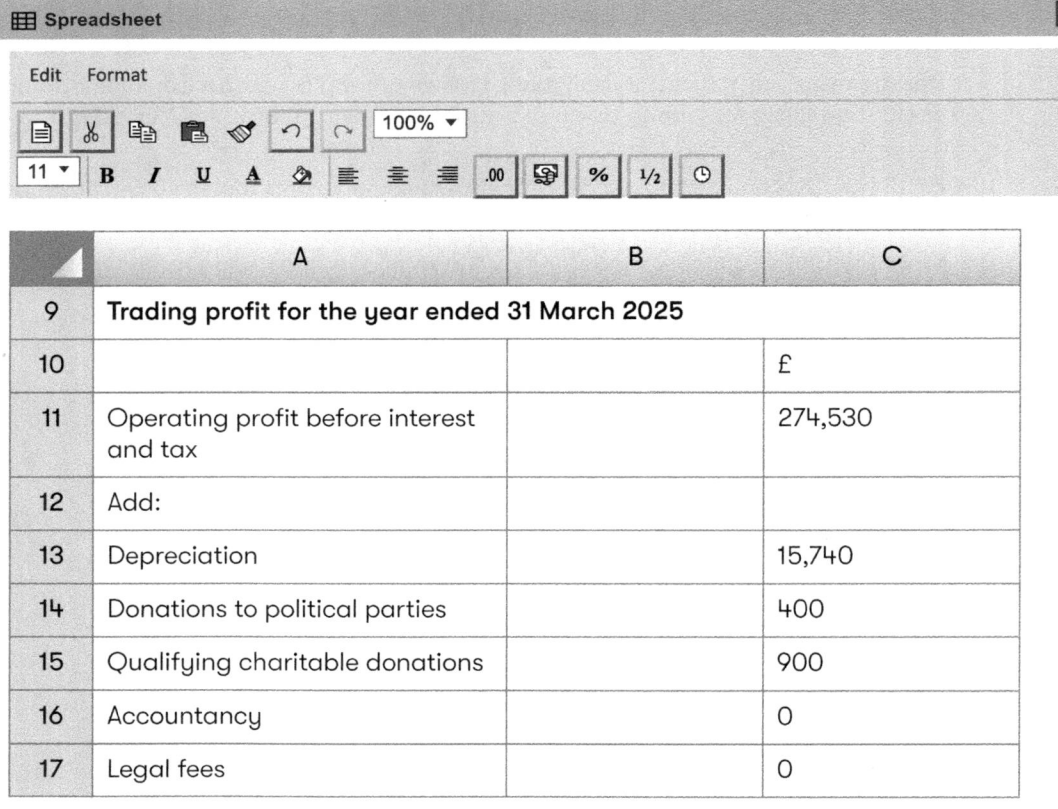

	A	B	C
9	Trading profit for the year ended 31 March 2025		
10			£
11	Operating profit before interest and tax		274,530
12	Add:		
13	Depreciation		15,740
14	Donations to political parties		400
15	Qualifying charitable donations		900
16	Accountancy		0
17	Legal fees		0

	A	B	C
18	Entertaining suppliers		3,600
19	Entertaining employees		0
20	Gifts to customers – pens		0
21	Gifts to customers – food hampers		1,650
22			296,820[5]
23	Less capital allowances		(48,114)[6]
24	Adjusted trading profit		248,706[7]

[5] =SUM(C11:C21)

[6] =E41

[7] =SUM(C22:C23)

	A	B	C	D	E
25	**Capital allowances**				
26		AIA (£)	Main pool (£)	Special rate pool (£)	Allowances (£)
27	WDV b/f		12,400	13,600	
28	**AIA additions**				
29	Machinery	42,300[8]			
30	AIA	(42,300)			(42,300)[9]
31	Transfer to pool	0	0		
32	**Non-AIA additions**				
33	Car (1)		13,800		
34	Car (2)			14,000	
35	Disposal				
36	Special rate pool items			(9,300)	
37			26,200[10]	18,300[11]	
38	WDA@18%		(4,716)[12]		(4,716)[13]
39	WDA@6%			(1,098)[14]	(1,098)[15]

Answers **441**

	A	B	C	D	E
40	WDV c/f		21,484[16]	17,202[17]	
41	Allowances				(48,114)[18]

[8] =42300*100%
[9] =SUM(B30:D30)
[10] =SUM(C27:C36)
[11] =SUM(D27:D36)
[12] =-C37*18%
[13] =C38
[14] =-D37*6%
[15] =D39
[16] =SUM(C37:C39)
[17] =SUM(D37:D39)
[18] =SUM(E27:E40)

(b)

If Naive Ltd has straightforward accounts, it could use the software provided by HM Revenue & Customs. This automatically produces accounts and tax computations in the iXBRL format.

Alternatively, other software which automatically produces iXBRL accounts and computations could be used.

A tagging service could be used to apply the appropriate tags to the accounts and tax computations, or Naive Ltd could use software to tag documents itself.

ACCA

Taxation (TX – UK) FA 2024

Mock Exam 3

December 2016 (amended to FA 2024)

Questions	
Time allowed	3 hours
ALL questions are compulsory and MUST be attempted	

DO NOT OPEN THIS EXAM UNTIL YOU ARE READY TO START UNDER EXAMINATION CONDITIONS

Section A

ALL 15 questions are compulsory and MUST be attempted.

1. Emil is registered for value added tax (VAT). For the quarter ended 31 March 2025, the input VAT incurred on his purchases and expenses included the following:

	£
Entertaining overseas customers	320
Purchase of new office equipment	1,250
Purchase of a new car for business and private use by one of Emil's employees	3,000

   What is the amount of input VAT recoverable by Emil in the quarter ended 31 March 2025 in respect of the entertaining, office equipment and car?

   £ ☐ (2 marks)

2. Acasta Ltd owns 75% of the ordinary share capital of Barge Ltd and 100% of the ordinary share capital of Coracle Ltd. Barge Ltd owns 75% of the ordinary share capital of Dhow Ltd. Coracle Ltd owns 51% of the ordinary share capital of Eight Ltd.

   Which companies, along with Coracle Ltd, are within Acasta Ltd's chargeable gains group?
   - ○ Barge Ltd, Dhow Ltd and Eight Ltd
   - ○ Barge Ltd only
   - ○ Barge Ltd and Dhow Ltd only
   - ○ None of the other companies

   (2 marks)

3. Nadia died on 13 February 2004, leaving an estate valued at £275,400 for inheritance tax purposes. Nadia left 50% of her estate to her son and 50% to her husband, Tareq.

   Tareq subsequently died on 17 January 2025. Tareq did not own a main residence at the date of his death.

   Neither Nadia nor Tareq made any lifetime gifts.

   The inheritance nil rate band for the tax year 2003/04 was £255,000.

   What is the maximum available nil rate band which can be used when calculating the inheritance tax payable in respect of Tareq's estate?
   - ○ £500,500
   - ○ £474,500
   - ○ £442,300
   - ○ £462,700

   (2 marks)

4   Habib purchased a copyright on 30 April 2008 for £31,320. The remaining life of the copyright at the date of purchase was 30 years. On 30 April 2024, Habib sold the copyright for £27,900.

What is Habib's chargeable gain or allowable loss for the tax year 2024/25 in respect of the disposal of the copyright?

○ (£3,420)
○ £11,196
○ £0
○ £13,284   (2 marks)

5   **Which of the following is the correct definition of an extra-statutory concession?**
○ A provision for the relaxation of the strict application of the law where it would lead to anomalies or cause hardship
○ Supplementary information providing additional detail in relation to the general principles set out in legislation
○ HM Revenue & Customs' interpretation of tax legislation
○ Guidance provided to HM Revenue & Customs' staff in interpreting and applying tax legislation   (2 marks)

6   **Complete the following sentence relating to the length of time a sole trader is required to keep their accounting records after the end of a tax year in which a self-assessment tax return has been completed.**

A sole trader is required to keep their accounting records for ▢ (1) ▼ months after the ▢ (2) ▼

Pull down list 1
- 12
- 60

Pull down list 2
- 31 January that follows the end of the tax year
- End of the tax year

(2 marks)

7   Red Dolphin Ltd provided the following benefits to its employee, Alonso, for the tax year 2024/25:

	Cost £
Cash vouchers	3,000
A gift of a new television	2,000

Red Dolphin Ltd always pays its tax liabilities and national insurance contributions (NIC) electronically. The benefits provided to Alonso were not payrolled.

Match the correct amount of class 1A NIC payable by Red Dolphin Ltd in respect of Alonso's benefits for the tax year 2024/25 and the due date.

£276		Class 1A
£414		Due date

£690

22 April 2025

31 January 2026

22 July 2025

(2 marks)

---

8 Modal Ltd lets out an unfurnished investment property.

During the year ended 31 December 2024, the company received rental income of £3,000 per month and paid electricity (relating to the rental property) of £200 per month. The electricity payment for December 2024 was not paid until 30 January 2025. Modal Ltd also paid interest of £1,200 per month on a loan taken out to finance the purchase of the rental property.

What amount of property business income will be included in Modal Ltd's corporation tax computation for the year ended 31 December 2024?

○ £33,600
○ £19,200
○ £33,800
○ £19,400

(2 marks)

---

9 **Which of the following will NOT cause Harper to be treated as automatically UK resident for the tax year 2024/25?**

○ Harper spending 192 days in the UK during the tax year 2024/25
○ Harper renting a house in the UK to live in and then occupying it (as her only home) throughout the tax year 2024/25
○ Harper accepting a 15-month contract for a full-time job in the UK on 6 April 2024
○ Harper's husband living in the UK throughout the tax year 2024/25 and Harper staying with him when she visits the UK

(2 marks)

10 Somily Ltd filed its self-assessment corporation tax return for the year ended 31 December 2024 on 15 March 2026.

What is the deadline for HM Revenue & Customs (HMRC) to start a compliance check enquiry into Somily Ltd's corporation tax return for the year ended 31 December 2024?

- ○ 31 December 2026
- ○ 31 January 2027
- ○ 15 March 2027
- ○ 30 April 2027

(2 marks)

11 On 6 April 2024, Melinda rented out a furnished room in her house to Jenny at a rent of £720 a month. Jenny continued to rent the room on the same terms until 5 July 2025.

Melinda continued to live in the house and paid for all of the living expenses, of which £175 a month related to the room rented out to Jenny.

What is Melinda's property income for the tax year 2024/25, assuming that any beneficial elections are made?

- ○ £1,140
- ○ £0
- ○ £6,540
- ○ £2,760

(2 marks)

12 Three unconnected companies have the following results for corporation tax purposes:

Company	Current accounting period	No. of associated companies	Taxable total profits (TTP) £	TTP for previous 12-month period £
Asher Ltd	y/e 31 March 2025	3	700,000	600,000
Barton Ltd	Four-month p/e 31 December 2024	0	600,000	1,600,000
Chelfry Ltd	y/e 30 November 2024	0	1,600,000	1,400,000

All the companies have had the same number of associated companies for many years. None of the companies have received any dividends.

Which of the three companies will NOT have to pay corporation tax by quarterly instalments for the current accounting period?

- ○ Asher Ltd only
- ○ Barton Ltd only
- ○ Chelfry Ltd only
- ○ Barton Ltd and Chelfry Ltd only

(2 marks)

13   David had the following taxable income (after deduction of his personal allowance) for the tax year 2024/25:

	£
Non-savings income	8,500
Savings income	2,400
Dividend income	2,750

What is David's total income tax liability for the tax year 2024/25?

Pull down list
- £2,177
- £2,221
- £2,377
- £2,421

(2 marks)

---

14   Gita died on 17 May 2024. On the date of her death, she owned the following assets:

	£
Investment property	390,000
Chattels and cash	70,000
Shares held in an individual savings account (ISA)	60,000

At the date of her death, Gita owed income tax of £25,000 in respect of the tax year 2024/25. Gita left £100,000 of her estate to her husband, with the remainder left to her daughter.

What is Gita's chargeable estate for inheritance tax purposes?

Pull down list
- £335,000
- £395,000
- £420,000
- £495,000

(2 marks)

15 Anika sold her 3,000 £1 ordinary shares in Distribo Ltd, a trading company, to her son, Hemi, for £53,000 on 14 July 2024. The market value of the shares on that date was £98,000. Anika had purchased the 3,000 shares on 28 October 2007 for £41,500. She has never worked for Distribo.

Identify, by clicking on the relevant boxes in the table below, the amount of gift holdover relief (if any) that could be claimed in respect of the disposal of these shares, and Anika's chargeable gain for the tax year 2024/25 after taking account of any available relief.

Option		
£0	£45,000	Gift holdover relief
£11,500	£11,500	Gain
£45,000		
£56,500		

(2 marks)

Section B

ALL 15 questions are compulsory and MUST be attempted.

Zoyla

Zoyla's capital gains tax (CGT) liability for the tax year 2024/25 is calculated as follows:

	Gain
	£
Ordinary shares in Minor Ltd	98,800
Ordinary shares in Major plc	44,400
Annual exempt amount	(3,000)
	140,200
CGT:	
– 10,600 at 10%	1,060
– 129,600 at 20%	25,920
	26,980

Minor Ltd is an unquoted trading company with an issued share capital of 200,000 £1 ordinary shares. Zoyla has been a director of this company since 1 April 2017. On 20 June 2024, Zoyla sold 20,000 of her holding of 45,000 ordinary shares in Minor Ltd. She had originally purchased 22,500 shares on 15 August 2023 for £117,000. On 12 December 2023, Minor Ltd made a 1 for 1 rights issue. Zoyla took up her allocation under the rights issue in full, paying £7.40 for each new share issued.

Major plc is a quoted trading company with an issued share capital of 2,000,000 £1 ordinary shares. Zoyla has been an employee of Major plc since 1 November 2022 when she acquired 16,000 ordinary shares in the company. On 6 March 2025, Zoyla sold her entire holding of ordinary shares in Major plc to her son for £152,000. On that date, shares in Major plc were quoted on the stock exchange at £9.62–£9.74.

Zoyla will not make any other disposals in the foreseeable future, and her taxable income will remain unchanged.

16 **Complete the following sentences to explain why neither of Zoyla's share disposals during the tax year 2024/25 qualified for business asset disposal relief.**

The disposal of shares in Minor Ltd did not qualifying for business asset disposal relief in the tax year 2024/25 due to:

The disposal of shares in Major plc did not qualifying for business asset disposal relief in the tax year 2024/25 due to:

Pull down list
- Holding period
- Size of shareholding

(2 marks)

17 What cost figure will have been used in calculating the chargeable gain on Zoyla's disposal of 20,000 ordinary shares in Minor Ltd?
- ○ £126,000
- ○ £104,000
- ○ £148,000
- ○ £252,000

(2 marks)

18 What proceeds figure will have been used in calculating the chargeable gain on Zoyla's disposal of 16,000 ordinary shares in Major plc?
- ○ £152,000
- ○ £154,400
- ○ £153,920
- ○ £154,880

(2 marks)

19 If Zoyla had delayed the sale of her 16,000 ordinary shares in Major plc until 6 April 2025, by how long would the related CGT liability have been deferred?

[Pull down list]

Pull down list
- 1 month
- 11 months
- 12 months
- 6 months

(2 marks)

20 Assuming that the tax rates and allowances for the tax year 2024/25 continue to apply, how much CGT would Zoyla have saved if she had delayed the sale of her 16,000 ordinary shares in Major plc until the following tax year?
- ○ £1,060
- ○ £2,720
- ○ £1,660
- ○ £600

(2 marks)

(Total = 10 marks)

Roman and Paris

Roman died on 7 August 2024, and his wife, Paris, died on 18 February 2025.

The couple had attempted to mitigate their inheritance tax (IHT) liabilities when they both made substantial gifts during 2022. These gifts made full use of their respective nil rate bands of £325,000, but unfortunately neither Roman nor Paris then survived long enough for any of the gifts to benefit from taper relief. Neither Roman nor Paris had made any previous lifetime gifts.

Roman

On 4 March 2022, Roman made a cash gift of £210,000 to his daughter. On 26 August 2022, he made a cash gift of £190,000 to a trust. No lifetime IHT arose in respect of the gift to the trust.

Roman's estate for IHT purposes was valued at £560,000. He did not own a main residence at the date of his death. Under the terms of his will, Roman left £300,000 to Paris (his wife) and the residue of his estate to his daughter.

Paris

On 12 December 2022, Paris made a gift of 75,000 £1 ordinary shares in Capital Ltd, an unquoted investment company, to her son. Before the transfer, Paris owned 100,000 of Capital Ltd's 250,000 ordinary shares. The market value of Capital Ltd's ordinary shares on 12 December 2022 was as follows:

Holding	Market value per share
	£
10%	5
30%	6
40%	8

Paris also made cash gifts of £80, £210, £195 and £460 to various friends during February 2023. The gifts of £80 and £195 were to the same friend.

Paris's estate for IHT purposes was valued at £840,000, including the inheritance from Roman (her husband). She did not own a main residence at the date of her death.

Under the terms of her will, Paris left a specific legacy of £20,000 to a friend and the residue of her estate to her grandchildren.

21 **How much IHT will be payable in respect of the gift made to the trust by Roman as a result of his death?**

- ○ £26,400
- ○ £30,000
- ○ £27,600
- ○ £13,200

(2 marks)

22 **Who will be responsible for paying the IHT arising from Roman's gift to the trust as a result of his death, and when will the tax be due?**

- ○ The personal representatives of Roman's estate on 30 April 2025
- ○ The personal representatives of Roman's estate on 28 February 2025
- ○ The trustees of the trust on 30 April 2025
- ○ The trustees of the trust on 28 February 2025

(2 marks)

23 **For IHT purposes, what was the amount of the transfer of value as a result of Paris's gift of 75,000 ordinary shares in Capital Ltd?**

- ○ £450,000
- ○ £600,000
- ○ £675,000
- ○ £425,000

(2 marks)

24 What is the amount of the cash gifts made by Paris to her friends during February 2023 NOT covered by the small gifts exemption?
- ○ £735
- ○ £460
- ○ £670
- ○ £0

(2 marks)

---

25 What is the amount of IHT payable in respect of Roman's and Paris's estates on death?

	Roman's estate	Paris's estate
○	£224,000	£336,000
○	£104,000	£336,000
○	£104,000	£328,000
○	£224,000	£328,000

(2 marks)

(Total = 10 marks)

Ardent Ltd

Ardent Ltd was incorporated on 1 April 2024 and commenced trading on 1 January 2025. The company voluntarily registered for valued added tax (VAT) on 1 January 2025, preparing its first VAT return for the quarter ended 31 March 2025.

Ardent Ltd's sales have been as follows:

2025	Standard rated	Zero-rated
	£	£
January	24,800	30,100
February	42,600	28,700
March	58,300	22,700
	125,700	81,500

Where applicable, the above figures are stated exclusive of VAT.

During the period 1 April to 31 December 2024, Ardent Ltd incurred input VAT of £120 each month in respect of payments made for advertising services. The company also incurred input VAT totalling £400 (£200 each) in respect of the purchase of two laptop computers on 10 July 2024. One of the laptop computers was scrapped on 30 November 2024 at a nil value, and the other laptop was not used until Ardent Ltd commenced trading on 1 January 2025.

During the quarter ended 31 March 2025, Ardent Ltd received standard rated invoices totalling £56,400 (inclusive of VAT) in respect of purchases and expenses. As at 31 March 2025, £11,400 (inclusive of VAT) of the purchases were unsold and therefore included in inventory.

Ardent Ltd was late in submitting its VAT return for the quarter ended 31 March 2025, and in paying the related VAT liability. The company currently does not use either the VAT cash accounting scheme or the annual accounting scheme.

26 From what date would Ardent Ltd have been required to be compulsorily registered for VAT?

[dropdown]

Pull down list
- 1 April 2025
- 1 February 2025
- 1 March 2025
- 1 May 2025

(2 marks)

27 What amount of pre-registration input VAT was Ardent Ltd able to recover in respect of the inputs incurred prior to it registering for VAT on 1 January 2025?
- ○ £920
- ○ £1,120
- ○ £1,480
- ○ £1,280

(2 marks)

28 Ignoring pre-registration input VAT, what amount of VAT should Ardent Ltd have paid to HM Revenue & Customs in respect of the quarter ended 31 March 2025?
- ○ £17,640
- ○ £32,040
- ○ £13,860
- ○ £15,740

(2 marks)

29 How and by when should Ardent Ltd have filed its VAT return for the quarter ended 31 March 2025?
- ○ Either on the HMRC website or by using Making Tax Digital software by 30 April 2025
- ○ Using Making Tax Digital software by 7 May 2025
- ○ Using Making Tax Digital software by 30 April 2025
- ○ Either on the HMRC website or by using Making Tax Digital software by 7 May 2025

(2 marks)

30 Ardent Ltd has one penalty point for the late submission of the March 2025 return.

Drag and drop the correct period and VAT scheme from the options below to correctly identify how long after 31 March 2025 Ardent Ltd will need to remain below the penalty threshold in order for the penalty point to expire, and which VAT scheme may help in avoiding such further defaults.

Options		Answer
6 months		Period after 31 March 2025
24 months		VAT scheme
Cash accounting scheme		
Annual accounting scheme		

(2 marks)

(Total = 10 marks)

Section C

ALL three questions are compulsory and MUST be attempted.

31 Jack

You should assume that today's date is 15 March 2025 and that the tax rates and allowances for the tax year 2024/25 continue to apply.

Jack, aged 44, is a widower following the recent death of his wife. He has just cashed in a substantial share portfolio and is now considering what to do with the proceeds.

Gift to a trust

The value of Jack's estate is in excess of £1,000,000, and he is worried about the amount of inheritance tax which will be payable should he die. His wife's nil rate band was fully used when she died.

Jack is therefore planning to make an immediate lifetime cash gift of £300,000 to a trust with the funds then being held for the benefit of his two children aged 10 and 12. Jack has not made any previous lifetime gifts.

Personal pension contribution

The only pension contributions which Jack has made previously is the gross amount of £500 per month which he saves into a personal pension scheme. Jack has continued to make these contributions throughout the tax year 2024/25. Although Jack has been saving into this scheme for the previous 15 years, he is concerned that he is not saving enough for his retirement. Jack therefore wants to make the maximum possible amount of additional gross personal pension contribution for the tax year 2024/25, but only to the extent that the contribution will attract tax relief at the higher rate of income tax.

Jack is self-employed, and his trading profit for the tax year 2024/25 is £100,000. He does not have any other income and expects to make the same level of profit in future years.

Individual savings account (ISA)

Jack has never invested any amounts in ISAs. During the next 30 days, he would like to invest the maximum possible amounts into stocks and shares ISAs.

Required

(a) Explain, with supporting calculations where necessary, why it is good inheritance tax planning for Jack to make the immediate lifetime cash gift of £300,000 to a trust.

Note. You are not expected to consider taper relief. **(3 marks)**

(b) (i) Advise Jack of the amount of additional gross personal pension contribution he can make for the tax year 2024/25 which will benefit from tax relief at the higher rate of income tax, and explain why this is a tax efficient approach to pension saving. The annual allowance was £40,000 per year for 2021/22 and 2022/23. **(4 marks)**

(ii) Calculate the amount of unused pension annual allowances which Jack will be able to carry forward to the tax year 2025/26 if the contribution in (i) above is made. **(1 mark)**

(c) Advise Jack as to the maximum possible amount which he can invest into stocks and shares ISAs during the next 30 days. **(2 marks)**

(Total = 10 marks)

32 Array Ltd

Array Ltd provides its employees with various benefits. It does not payroll benefits.

The benefits were all provided throughout the tax year 2024/25 unless otherwise stated.

Alice

Alice was provided with a petrol-powered car which has a list price of £24,600. The car has an official CO_2 emissions rate of 102 grams per kilometre. Alice made a capital contribution of £5,600 towards the cost of the car when it was first provided to her by Array Ltd.

Alice was also provided with fuel for her private journeys. The total cost to Array Ltd of fuel for the car during the tax year 2024/25 was £1,500.

During the tax year 2024/25, Alice drove a total of 12,000 miles, of which 8,000 were for business journeys.

Buma

Buma was provided with a loan of £48,000 on 1 October 2022, which she used to renovate her main residence. Buma repays £1,000 of the capital of the loan to Array Ltd each month, and by 6 April 2024 the amount of the loan outstanding had been reduced to £30,000. In addition, Buma paid loan interest of £180 to Array Ltd during the tax year 2024/25.

The taxable benefit in respect of this loan is calculated using the average method.

Claude

On 6 July 2024, Claude was provided with a mobile telephone. The telephone is a smartphone which is mainly used by Claude for personal internet access. It was purchased by Array Ltd on 6 July 2024 for £600.

On 6 January 2025, Claude was provided with a home entertainment system for his personal use. This was purchased by Array Ltd on 6 January 2025 for £3,200. The market value of the home entertainment system on 5 April 2025 was £2,400.

Denise

During May 2024, Array Ltd paid £10,400 towards the cost of Denise's removal expenses when she permanently moved to take up her new employment with Array Ltd, as she did not live within a reasonable commuting distance. The £10,400 covered both her removal expenses and the legal costs of acquiring a new main residence.

During February 2025, Array Ltd paid for £340 of Denise's medical costs. She had been away from work for three months due to an injury, and the medical treatment (as recommended by a doctor) was to assist her return to work.

Required

(a) State how employers are required to report details of employees' taxable benefits to HM Revenue & Customs following the end of the tax year, and the deadline for submitting this information for the tax year 2024/25. **(2 marks)**

(b) Calculate the taxable benefits which Array Ltd will have to report to HM Revenue & Customs in respect of each of its employees for the tax year 2024/25.

Note. Your answer should include an explanation for any benefits which are exempt or partially exempt. **(11 marks)**

(c) Calculate the class 1A national insurance contributions which Array Ltd would have had to pay in respect of its employees' taxable benefits for the tax year 2024/25, and state when this would have been due if paid electronically. **(2 marks)**

(Total = 15 marks)

33 Wretched Ltd

Wretched Ltd commenced trading on 1 August 2024, preparing its first accounts for the eight-month period ended 31 March 2025.

Wretched Ltd is incorporated in the United Kingdom, but its three directors are all non-resident in the UK. Board meetings are always held overseas.

The following information is available:

Trading loss

The trading loss based on the draft accounts for the eight-month period ended 31 March 2025 is £141,200.

This figure is before making any adjustments required for:

(1) Advertising expenditure of £7,990 incurred during April 2024

   This expenditure has not been deducted in arriving at the trading loss for the eight-month period ended 31 March 2025 of £141,200.

(2) The premium which was paid to acquire a leasehold office building on a ten-year lease

(3) Capital allowances

Premium paid to acquire a leasehold office building

On 1 August 2024, Wretched Ltd paid a premium to acquire a leasehold office building on a ten-year lease. The amount of premium assessed on the landlord as income was £34,440.

The office building was used for business purposes by Wretched Ltd throughout the eight-month period ended 31 March 2025.

Plant and machinery

On 1 August 2024, Wretched Ltd purchased three new laptop computers at a discounted cost of £400 per laptop. The original price of each laptop was £850, but they were sold at the discounted price because they were ex-display. Wretched Ltd also purchased three second-hand cars on 1 August 2024.

Details are:

	Cost	CO_2 emissions rate
	£	
Car [1]	8,300	0 grams per kilometre
Car [2]	12,300	40 grams per kilometre
Car [3]	18,800	125 grams per kilometre

Property business income

Wretched Ltd lets out a warehouse which is surplus to requirements. The warehouse was let out from 1 August to 31 October 2024 at a rent of £1,400 per month. The tenant left on 31 October 2024, and the warehouse was not re-let before 31 March 2025.

During the eight-month period ended 31 March 2025, Wretched Ltd spent £2,100 on advertising for tenants.

Due to a serious flood, Wretched Ltd spent £5,900 on repairs during January 2025. The damage was not covered by insurance.

Loss on the disposal of shares

On 20 March 2025, Wretched Ltd sold its entire 1% shareholding of £1 ordinary shares in Worthless plc for £21,400. Wretched Ltd had purchased these shares on 5 August 2016 for £26,200.

The indexation factor from August 2016 to December 2017 is 0.052.

Other information

Wretched Ltd does not have any associated companies.

Wretched Ltd will continue to trade for the foreseeable future.

Required

(a) State, giving reasons, whether Wretched Ltd is resident or not resident in the United Kingdom for corporation tax purposes. **(1 mark)**

(b) Assuming that Wretched Ltd is resident in the United Kingdom, calculate the company's trading loss, property business loss and capital loss for the eight-month period ended 31 March 2025.

Note. You should assume that the company claims the maximum available capital allowances. **(11 marks)**

(c) Explain how Wretched Ltd will be able to relieve its trading loss, property business loss and capital loss for the eight-month period ended 31 March 2025. **(3 marks)**

(Total = 15 marks)

Answers

DO NOT TURN THIS PAGE UNTIL YOU HAVE COMPLETED THE MOCK EXAM

A plan of attack

If this were the real Taxation (TX – UK) exam and you had been told to turn over and begin, what would be going through your mind?

Perhaps you're having a panic. You've spent most of your study time on income tax and corporation tax computations (because that's what your tutor/BPP Course Book told you to do), plus a selection of other topics, and you're really not sure that you know enough. So calm down. Spend the first few moments or so **looking at the exam** and develop a **plan of attack**.

Looking through the exam.

Section A contains **15 Objective Test (OT) questions** each worth **2 marks**. These will cover all sections of the syllabus. Some you may find easy and some more difficult. For Question 5, make sure you carefully consider each statement about extra-statutory concessions before making your choice. Don't spend a lot of time on anything you really don't know. For multiple choice questions you are not penalised for wrong answers, so you should answer all of them. If all else fails – guess!

Section B contains **three OT Case** scenarios. These each have **five questions** each worth **2 marks**. Make sure you read the scenario carefully before you start to answer the OTQs.

- **Questions 16 to 20** are about chargeable gains for an individual. In Question 18, do you know how quoted shares are valued if there is an element of a gift?
- **Questions 21 to 25** tests your knowledge of inheritance tax (IHT). Don't forget to double check your calculations especially in Question 21.
- **Questions 26 to 30** concerns value added tax (VAT). Question 29 should be easy marks about payment of VAT.

In **Section C** you have **three constructed response (long) questions**:

- **Question 31** for **10 marks** covers a number of areas of tax planning. These are inheritance tax lifetime gifts, pensions and individual savings accounts.
- **Question 32** for **15 marks** is an income tax computation which also tests national insurance contributions. The scenario involves the provision of employment benefits.
- **Question 33** for **15 marks** is a corporation tax question. The test for UK residence is examined, the calculation of losses for companies and the use of those losses.

All of these questions are compulsory.

This means that you do not have to waste time wondering which questions to answer.

Allocating your time

BPP's advice is always allocate your time **according to the marks for the question** in total and for the parts of the question. But **use common sense**. If you're confronted by an OTQ on a topic of which you know nothing, pick an answer and move on. Use the time to pick up marks elsewhere.

After the exam... **Forget about it**!

And don't worry if you found the exam difficult. More than likely other candidates will too. If this were the real thing you would need to **forget** the exam the minute you left the exam hall and **think about the next one**. Or, if it's the last one, **celebrate**!

Section A

1   £ 1,570

	£
Entertaining overseas customers	320
Purchase of new office equipment	1,250
Input tax recoverable	1,570

Note the difference between entertaining overseas customers (input tax recoverable) and UK customers (input tax not recoverable). Input tax is not usually recoverable on cars with any private use – this could be by the owner of the business or an employee.

2   The correct answer is: Barge Ltd and Dhow Ltd only

Companies are in a chargeable gains group if at each level there is a 75% holding and the top company has an effective interest of over 50% in the group companies.

There is a 75% holding of Barge Ltd by the top company Acasta Ltd so this is in Acasta Ltd's chargeable gains group.

There is a 75% holding of Dhow Ltd by Barge Ltd and an effective interest of over 50% (75% × 75% = 56.25%) by Acasta Ltd in Dhow Ltd so Dhow Ltd is also in Acasta Ltd's chargeable gains group.

Coracle Ltd is in Acasta Ltd's chargeable gains group (given in question). However, there is no 75% holding between Coracle Ltd and Eight Ltd so Eight Ltd cannot be in Acasta Ltd's chargeable gains group.

> **ACCA Examining Team's Comments**
>
> This question tested candidates' knowledge of the group relationship which is necessary for chargeable gains purposes. The most popular answer was the second option, with candidates appreciating that Barge Ltd was included because of the 75% group relationship with Acasta Ltd (and that Eight Ltd was correspondingly excluded). However, Dhow Ltd is also included in the chargeable gains group because the 75% group relationship need only be met at each level, subject to Acasta Ltd having an effective interest of over 50% (and 75% of 75% is 56.25%). So the correct answer was the third option.
>
> This demonstrates the need to carefully consider each alternative – not just quickly jumping to the most obvious one.

3   The correct answer is: £474,500

	£
Nil rate band (NRB) at Nadia's death in 2003/04	255,000
NRB used at Nadia's death	(137,700)
Unused NRB available for transfer	117,300
Tareq's NRB 2024/25	325,000
Nadia's transferred NRB adjusted for 2024/25 rate	
$£117,300 \times \dfrac{325,000}{255,000}$	149,500
Total NRB available for Tareq's estate	474,500

4   The correct answer is: £13,284

	£
Proceeds	27,900
Less cost $£31,320 \times \dfrac{14}{30}$	(14,616)
Gain	13,284

5   The correct answer is: A provision for the relaxation of the strict application of the law where it would lead to anomalies or cause hardship

6   A sole trader is required to keep their accounting records for 60 months after the 31 January that follows the end of the tax year

7   The correct answers are:

£276	Class 1A
22 July 2025	Due date

Class 1A: £2,000 × 13.8% = £276

The cash vouchers are treated as earnings and are subject to class 1 NIC, not class 1A.

Class 1A: £414 being NIC on the cash vouchers (3,000 × 13.8%) and £690 being NIC on both vouchers and television ((3,000 + 2,000) × 13.8%)

Due dates: 22 April 2025 (the month of the end of the tax year) and 31 January 2026 (the date for self-assessment return for tax year 2024/25)

8   The correct answer is: £33,600

	£
Rent receivable £3,000 × 12	36,000
Less electricity payable £200 × 12	(2,400)
Property business income	33,600

The electricity expense is deductible on an accruals basis (companies always use this basis), so the late payment for December 2024 does not affect the deduction. Finance costs for a company are a loan relationship and so not deducted in computing the property business income. They are also not subject to the finance cost restriction which only applies to individuals.

9   The correct answer is: Harper's husband living in the UK throughout the tax year 2024/25 and Harper staying with him when she visits the UK

The first three answers are automatic UK residency tests. The last answer is a combination of two of the sufficient ties tests and so is not an automatic UK residency test.

10 The correct answer is: 30 April 2027

The corporation tax return should have been filed by 31 December 2025. It was therefore filed late. The deadline for HM Revenue & Customs (HMRC) to start a compliance check enquiry is therefore the quarter day following the first anniversary of the actual filing date of 15 March 2026 so is 30 April 2027.

11 The correct answer is: £1,140

	£
Rent receivable £720 × 12	8,640
Less rent a room limit	(7,500)
Property business income	1,140

This is less than the normal basis of assessment which would be £8,640 × (175 × 12) = £6,540.

12 The correct answer is: Chelfry Ltd only

Asher Ltd was a large company in the current period and the previous period as its TTP exceeded the limit of £1,500,000/(3 + 1) = £375,000 in both periods and so will have to pay corporation tax by quarterly instalments for the current period.

Barton Ltd was a large company in the current period and the previous period as its TTP exceeded the limit of £1,500,000 in the previous period and £1,500,000 × 4/12 = £500,000 in the current period and so will have to pay corporation tax by quarterly instalments for the current period.

Chelfry Ltd was a large company in the current period as its TTP exceeded the limit of £1,500,000 but was not a large company in the previous period as its TTP did not exceed the limit. It is therefore not required to pay corporation tax by quarterly instalments for the current period.

13   £2,177

	£
Non-savings income	
£8,500 @ 20%	1,700
Savings income	
£1,000 @ 0%	0
£1,400 (2,400 – 1,000) @ 20%	280
Dividend income	
£500 @ 0%	0
£2,250 (2,750 – 500) @ 8.75%	197
Income tax liability	2,177

The answer £2,221 omits the dividend nil rate band. The answer £2,377 omits the savings income nil rate band. The answer £2,421 omits both the savings income nil rate band and the dividend nil rate band.

14   £395,000

	£
Investment property	390,000
Chattels and cash	70,000
Shares in an ISA	60,000
Income tax owed	(25,000)
Total estate	495,000
Less spouse exemption	(100,000)
Chargeable estate	395,000

Remember that the ISA exemptions only apply for income tax and capital gains tax.

15   The correct answers are:

£45,000	Gift holdover relief
£11,500	Gain

	£
Proceeds (MV)	98,000
Less cost	(41,500)
Gain before relief	56,500
Gift holdover relief (balancing figure)	(45,000)
Gain = actual proceeds minus original cost £(53,000 × 41,500)	11,500

Section B

Zoyla

> **Course Book references**
>
> CGT business reliefs are covered in Chapter 15. Shares and securities are the subject of Chapter 16. The calculation of CGT liability and the payment date are dealt with in Chapter 13.
>
> **Top Tips**
>
> The conditions for business asset disposal relief are often tested so make sure that you know them!
>
> **Easy Marks**
>
> There were easy marks in Question 19 for identifying the deferral period for the capital gains tax (CGT) liability based on the payment dates for each tax year.

16 The disposal of shares in Minor Ltd did not qualifying for business asset disposal relief in the tax year 2024/25 due to:

  Holding period

The disposal of shares in Major plc did not qualifying for business asset disposal relief in the tax year 2024/25 due to:

  Size of shareholding

A disposal of shares in a company qualifies for business asset disposal relief if the company is the individual's personal company, which is one where the shareholder owns at least 5% of the ordinary share capital of the company, the company is a trading company and the shareholder is an officer or employee of the company. These conditions must be satisfied for at least two years prior to the disposal of the shares.

The shares in Minor Ltd were acquired on 15 August 2023 and disposed of on 20 June 2024 and so the conditions were not satisfied for at least two years.

The shares in Major Ltd were a shareholding of (16,000/2,000,000 × 100) = 0.8% and so Major Ltd was not Zoyla's personal company due to the size of the shareholding.

17 The correct answer is: £126,000

Date	Transaction	No. of shares	Cost £
15 August 2023	Acquisition	22,500	117,000
12 Dec 2023	Rights issue 1 new share for every 1 original held @ £7.40	22,500	166,500
		45,000	283,500
20 June 2024	Sale	(20,000)	(126,000)
c/f		25,000	157,500

18 The correct answer is: £154,880

The actual proceeds are £152,000 but this must be compared with the market value of the shares to see if this is a sale at an undervalue. The market value per share is £9.62 + 1/2(9.74 × 9.62) = £9.68. The total market value is therefore £9.68 × 16,000 = £154,880 which is used as the proceeds for capital gains tax purposes.

19   12 months

The date of the CGT liability on the sale of Major Ltd shares on 6 March 2025 (tax year 2024/25) was 31 January 2026. If Zoyla had delayed the sale until 6 April 2025, the disposal would have been in the tax year 2025/26 and so the CGT liability would have been due on 31 January 2027 thus deferring the payment by 12 months.

20   The correct answer is: £1,660

	£
Tax saved due to availability of another annual exempt amount: £3,000 × 20%	600
Tax saved due to part of the gain being taxed at basic rate instead of higher rate: £10,600 × (20% -10%)	1,060
Total CGT saving	1,660

The answer £1,060 is just the higher rate tax saving. The answer £2,720 uses 20% for both calculations. The answer £600 is just the annual exempt amount saving.

Roman and Paris

Course Book references
Inheritance tax is the subject of Chapter 18.

Top Tips
A gift of shares in an unquoted company will usually involve a computation of the amount by which the donor's estate decreases as in Question 23. You need to compare the value of the shareholding before the gift and after the gift.

Easy marks
There were easy marks in Question 22 for identifying the persons responsible for paying the inheritance tax on death on the chargeable lifetime transfer and the date of payment.

21   The correct answer is: £26,400

	£	£
4 March 2022		
Gift	210,000	
Less:		
– Annual exemption 2021/22	(3,000)	
– Annual exemption 2020/21 b/f	(3,000)	
– Potentially exempt transfer		204,000
26 August 2022		
Gift	190,000	
Less:		
– Annual exemption 2022/23	(3,000)	
– Annual exemption 2021/22 b/f	(0)	
– Chargeable lifetime transfer		187,000

	£	£
7 August 2024		
Nil rate band at death	325,000	
Less PET now chargeable and within seven years of CLT	(204,000)	
Available nil rate band for CLT	121,000	
IHT on CLT:		
– £121,000 @ 0%		0
– £66,000 @ 40%		26,400
– £187,000		26,400

The calculation above is for teaching purposes to show in detail how the computation works. In the exam you could simplify it to:

£((190,000 – 3,000) – (325,000 – (210,000 – 3,000 – 3,000))) @ 40% = £26,400

> **ACCA Examining Team's Comments**
>
> This question caused particular problems. The requirement was to establish how much inheritance tax was payable in respect of a chargeable lifetime transfer as a result of the donor's death. The chargeable lifetime transfer had been preceded by a potentially exempt transfer.
>
> In selecting the most popular alternative, candidates failed to take account of the £3,000 annual exemptions which were available. In selecting the second most popular alternative, candidates did not appreciate that the two gifts were made in consecutive tax years, meaning that three annual exemptions were available rather than the two used in this option.
>
> This demonstrates just how careful candidates need to be in using each piece of information given, be it a date, number or fact.

22 The correct answer is: The trustees of the trust on 28 February 2025

23 The correct answer is: £675,000

	£
Before: 100,000 @ £8	800,000
After: 25,000 @ £5	(125,000)
Transfer of value	675,000

Before the transfer, Paris owned a 100,000/250,000 × 100 = 40% shareholding and after the transfer she owned a 25,000/250,000 × 100 = 10% shareholding.

24 The correct answer is: £735

	£
Gifts to same friend exceeding £250 in tax year £(80 + 195)	275
Gift exceeding £250	460
Gifts not covered by small gifts exemption	735

25 The correct answer is:

Roman's estate	Paris's estate
£104,000	£336,000

Roman's estate

	£
Death estate	560,000
Less spouse exemption	(300,000)
Chargeable death estate	260,000
Nil rate band used by lifetime transfers	
£260,000 @ 40%	104,000

Paris's estate

	£
Chargeable death estate	840,000
Nil rate band used by lifetime transfer	
£840,000 @ 40%	336,000

There is no exemption for legacies on death to another person other than a spouse or civil partner.

Ardent Ltd

> **Course Book references**
> Value added tax is covered in Chapters 24 and 25.
>
> **Top tips**
> In Question 27, note the different time limits for pre-registration input tax to be recovered. The time limit for services is six months before registration but for goods it is four years before registration.
>
> **Easy marks**
> There were easy marks in Question 29 for the filing requirement and date.

26 1 April 2025

	£
January 2025 £(24,800 + 30,100)	54,900
February 2025 £(42,600 + 28,700)	71,300
	126,200

Note that all taxable supplies (here standard rated and zero rated) are taken into account when working out whether the registration threshold has been exceeded.

The registration threshold of £90,000 is exceeded by 28 February 2025. Ardent Ltd should therefore have notified HMRC by 30 March 2025, with registration effective from 1 April 2025.

27 The correct answer is: £920

	£
Advertising: £120 × 6 months (max) before registration	720
Computer acquired in four years before registration and still held at registration	200
Input tax reclaimable	920

28 The correct answer is: £15,740

	£
Output tax £125,700 @ 20%	25,140
Less input tax £56,400 × 1/6	(9,400)
VAT payable to HMRC	15,740

It is not relevant whether the purchases are still held in inventory.

29 The correct answer is: Using Making Tax Digital software by 7 May 2025

30 The correct answers are:

24 months	Period after 31 March 2025
Annual accounting scheme	VAT scheme

Individual penalty points expire after two years where the trader remains below the penalty threshold (of four points for a trader that submits quarterly returns). However, they do not automatically expire once the penalty threshold has been reached. A business then has to submit four quarterly returns on time for their penalty points total to be reset to zero.

The annual accounting scheme may help because only one VAT return is required each year so there are fewer occasions to trigger points.

Section C

31 Jack

> **Course Book references**
>
> Inheritance tax is the subject of Chapter 18. Pension contributions are covered in Chapter 5. The ISA limits are dealt with in Chapter 2.
>
> **Top tips**
>
> There are three marks for part (a) so you should be making three relevant points to obtain these marks. It is important to attempt all three parts of the question to gain a reasonable overall mark.
>
> **Easy marks**
>
> There were some easy marks in part (b)(i) for working out the available annual allowances and in part (c) for identifying the ISA limits. The basic information required is in the tax rates and allowances provided in the examination.
>
> **ACCA Examining Team's Comments**
>
> This question proved difficult for many candidates, with some aspects consistently causing problems:
>
> (1) As regards part (a), long, detailed, computations were often provided when the answer was quite straightforward. For example, the gift would have reduced the taxpayer's death estate by £300,000, so the inheritance tax saving was simply £120,000 (£300,000 at 40%). There was no need for before and after computations.
>
> (2) As regards part (b), few candidates appreciated that restricting the amount of personal pension contributions to the amount qualifying for tax relief at the higher rate minimises the cost of pension saving because each £100 saved effectively only costs £60 (£100 less 40% tax relief).
>
> (3) As regards part (c), very few candidates realised that the 30-day period fell into two tax years, so the taxpayer could invest £20,000 by 5 April 2025, and then another £20,000 (using the tax year 2025/26 limit) on or after 6 April 2025.

Marking guide | **Marks**

(a)	Chargeable lifetime transfer	1	
	No inheritance tax	1	
	Inheritance tax saving	1	
			3
(b) (i)	Higher rate income	1	
	Available annual allowances	2	
	Minimising cost of pension saving	1	
			4
(ii)	Unused annual allowances	1	
			1
(c)	ISA limits	1	
	Maximum investments	1	
			2
Total			**10**

Answers 473

(a) The gift will be a chargeable lifetime transfer of £294,000 (£300,000 less annual exemptions of £3,000 for 2024/25 and 2023/24).

No lifetime inheritance tax will be payable because this is less than the nil rate band, and if Jack survives for seven years, there will be no additional inheritance tax liability either.

The value of Jack's estate will therefore be reduced by £300,000, which will mean an eventual inheritance tax saving of £120,000 (£300,000 at 40%).

> **Tutorial note.** Although it might itself be fully exempt, the chargeable lifetime transfer will have to be taken into account when calculating any inheritance tax liability arising on any further lifetime transfers which may be made within the following seven years. After seven years, a further gift can be made to a trust.

(b) (i) For 2024/25, £(100,000 – 12,570 – (37,700 + (500 × 12))) = £43,730 of Jack's income is currently taxable at the higher rate of income tax.

This is less than the available annual allowances of £(40,000 × 2 + 60,000 × 2 – (500 × 12 × 4)) = £176,000 for 2024/25.

Restricting the amount of personal pension contributions to the amount qualifying for tax relief at the higher rate will minimise the cost of pension saving because each £100 saved will effectively only cost £60 (£100 less 40% tax relief).

> **Tutorial note.** Unused annual allowances can be carried forward for up to three years.
>
> Although Jack's approach to pension saving will maximise the available tax relief, it will mean that some carried forward annual allowances are wasted.

(ii) Jack will have unused allowances of £98,270 being £(60,000 – 6,000 – 43,730) = £10,270 from 2024/25, £(60,000 – 6,000) = £54,000 for 2023/24 and £(40,000 – 6,000) = £34,000 from 2022/23 to carry forward to 2025/26.

Where an annual allowance is exceeded with contributions made in a tax year the current year AA is used first and then the unused AA from the previous three years can be used on a first-in, first out basis.

Tax year	Annual allowance £	Already used (£500 × 12) £	Additional contribution in 2024/25 £	Carry forward to 2025/26 £
2021/22	40,000	(6,000)		0
2022/23	40,000	(6,000)		34,000
2023/24	60,000	(6,000)		54,000
2024/25	60,000	(6,000)	(43,730)	10,270

There is nothing to carry forward from 2021/22 to 2025/26 because only the previous three years' unused allowance can be carried forward (ie 2022/23, 2023/24, 2024/25). The allowance in 2022/23 is £40,000 and £6,000 is used so £34,000 can be carried forward to 2025/26. The allowance in 2023/24 is £60,000 and £6,000 is used so £54,000 can be carried forward to 2025/26. The allowance in 2024/25 is £60,000 and £6,000 is used as well as the £43,730 calculated in (b)(i) so £10,270 £(60,000 – 6,000 – 43,730) can be carried forward to 2025/26.

(c) Jack can invest in an ISA for 2024/25 by 5 April 2025, and another ISA for 2025/26 between 6 April 2025 and 5 April 2026. The maximum possible amount which he can invest into stocks and shares ISAs during the next 30 days is therefore £20,000 × 2 = £40,000.

32 Array Ltd

> **Course Book references**
>
> Employment income is dealt with in Chapter 3 and 4.
>
> **Top tips**
>
> Make sure you know the filing dates for the main forms that need to be submitted to HMRC and the payment dates for payments that need to be made to HMRC.
>
> **Easy marks**
>
> There were easy marks in part (b) for standard benefit computations. However, you must be very accurate in your computations to obtain all the marks available.
>
> **ACCA Examining Team's Comments**
>
> This was the income tax question. It was well answered. In part (a), many candidates appreciated that reporting is done using form P11D, but the submission deadline was often not known.
>
> Less well-prepared candidates often discussed (at length) submission details for self-assessment tax-returns.
>
> There were many exceptional answers to part (b). Common mistakes included:
>
> - For the car and fuel benefits, not ignoring the fuel cost and the mileage figures – both of which were irrelevant to the benefit calculations.
> - For the beneficial loan, not commencing calculations with the amount of the loan outstanding at the start of the tax year – this figure was given – but instead trying to work from the original loan amount.
> - For the home entertainment system, using the value at the start of tax year rather than the original purchase price.
>
> Part (c) was reasonably well answered, although a few candidates included employee salaries when calculating the class 1A national insurance contributions.

Marking guide

		Marks	
(a)	Form P11D	1	
	Submission deadline	1	
			2
(b)	**Alice**		
	Car benefit percentage	1	
	Car use taxable benefit	2	
	Fuel taxable benefit	1	
	Buma		
	Interest benefit	2	
	Deduction for interest paid by employee	0.5	
	Claude		
	Mobile phone	1	
	Home entertainment system	1.5	
	Denise		
	Relocation costs	1	
	Medical costs	1	
			11

Marking guide	Marks
(c) Class 1A NIC	1
Payment date	1
	2
Total	**15**

(a) Details of employees' taxable benefits are reported to HM Revenue & Customs (HMRC) using a form P11D for each employee.

The P11D submission deadline for 2024/25 is 6 July 2025.

(b) **Alice**

The relevant percentage for the car benefit is 16% + 9% ((100 – 55)/5) = 25%.

The car was available throughout 2024/25, so the taxable benefit is £(24,600 – 5,000) × 25% = £4,900.

The fuel benefit is £(27,800 × 25%) = £6,950.

> **Tutorial note.** The amount of capital contribution which can be used to reduce the list price when calculating a car benefit is restricted to £5,000.
>
> The proportion of business mileage is not relevant to the calculation of the car benefit.

Buma

	£
$\dfrac{30{,}000 + (30{,}000 - (1{,}000 \times 12))}{2} \times 2.25\%$	540
Less: Interest paid	(180)
Taxable benefit	360

Claude

The provision of one mobile telephone does not give rise to a taxable benefit even if the telephone is a smartphone.

The taxable benefit for the use of the home entertainment system is £(3,200 × 20% × 3/12) = £160.

> **Tutorial note.** The home entertainment system has not been given to Claude, so the market value on 5 April 2025 is irrelevant.

Denise

Only £8,000 of the relocation costs is exempt, so the taxable benefit is £(10,400 – 8,000) = £2,400.

The payment of medical costs of up to £500 does not result in a taxable benefit provided the medical treatment is recommended in writing by a medical professional to assist an employee to return to work following a period of absence due to ill-health or injury lasting at least 28 days.

(c) The employer's Class 1A NIC payable by Array Ltd for 2024/25 is £(4,900 + 6,950 + 360 + 160 + 2,400) = 14,770 @ 13.8%) = £2,038.

If paid electronically, this would have been payable by 22 July 2025.

33 Wretched Ltd

> **Course Book references**
>
> Company residence is covered in Chapter 19. The calculation of losses is also covered in Chapter 19 and the use of losses is dealt with in Chapter 21.
>
> **Top tips**
>
> All companies which are UK incorporated are UK resident for corporation tax purposes.
>
> If a company is not incorporated in the UK, it is resident in the UK only if its central control and management are exercised in the UK.
>
> **Easy marks**
>
> The capital allowances computation in part (b) should have produced easy marks provided that you used the standard layout.
>
> **Examiner's comments**
>
> For part (a), candidates were required to state whether the company was resident or not resident in the UK for corporation tax purposes.
>
> This requirement resulted in a very surprising number of incorrect answers, with at least half the candidates deciding that the company was not resident because of its central management and control being exercised overseas.
>
> Part (b) was generally very well answered, although there were a couple of consistent problems. Firstly, it was often not appreciated that a second-hand car does not qualify for the 100% first year allowance. And secondly, indexation allowance was often used to increase the capital loss.
>
> Part (c), provided candidates appreciated that it was the company's first period of trading, was then well answered. However, candidates who overlooked this basic fact spent a lot of time discussing all the various (irrelevant) loss reliefs, with a few candidates discussing the income tax relief for a loss incurred in the early years of a trade.

Marking guide

		Marks	
(a)	Company residence	1	
			1
(b)	**Trading loss**		
	Pre-trading expenditure	1	
	Deduction for lease premium	1.5	
	Capital allowances		
	Additions qualifying for AIA	1	
	AIA	0.5	
	Car [1]	1	
	Car [2]	0.5	
	Car [3]	0.5	
	WDA main pool	1	
	WDA special rate pool	1	
	Property business loss		
	Rent receivable	0.5	
	Advertising	0.5	
	Repairs	0.5	

Marking guide	Marks
Capital loss	
Proceeds	0.5
Cost	0.5
Indexation allowance	0.5
	11
(c) Trading loss relief	1
Property business loss relief	1
Capital loss relief	1
	3
Total	**15**

(a) Companies which are incorporated in the UK such as Wretched Ltd are resident in the UK regardless of where their central management and control is exercised.

(b) **Wretched Ltd – period ended 31 March 2025**

Trading loss

	£
Trading loss	(141,200)
Advertising expenditure	(7,990)
Deduction for lease premium £(34,440/10) × 8/12	(2,296)
Capital allowances (W)	(4,424)
Revised trading loss	(155,910)

Tutorial note. The advertising expenditure incurred during April 2024 is pre-trading and is treated as incurred on 1 August 2024. It is therefore deductible, and an adjustment is required.

Working

Capital allowances

	AIA	Main pool	Special rate pool	Allowances
	£	£	£	£
Additions qualifying for AIA				
Laptops ((£400 × 3))	1,200			
AIA @ 100%	(1,200)			1,200
Transfer to pool	0	0		
Additions not qualifying for AIA				
Car [1]		8,300		
Car [2]		12,300		
Car [3]			18,800	

Taxation (TX – UK) FA 2024

	AIA	Main pool	Special rate pool	Allowances
	£	£	£	£
		20,600		
WDA @ 18 × 8/12		(2,472)		2,472
WDA @ 6% × 8/12			(752)	752
TWDVs carried forward		18,128	18,048	
Allowances				4,424

> **Tutorial note.** The original cost of the laptops is irrelevant.
>
> Although car [1] has zero CO_2 emissions, it is second hand and therefore does not qualify for the 100% first year allowance. It instead qualifies for writing down allowances at the rate of 18%.
>
> Car [2] has CO_2 emissions between 1 and 50 grams per kilometre and therefore qualifies for writing down allowances at the rate of 18%.
>
> Car [3] has CO_2 emissions over 50 grams per kilometre and therefore qualifies for writing down allowances at the rate of 6%.

Property business loss

	£
Rent receivable £1,400 × 3	4,200
Less:	
– Advertising	(2,100)
– Repairs	(5,900)
Property business loss	(3,800)

Capital loss

	£
Disposal proceeds	21,400
Less:	
– Cost	(26,200)
– Indexation allowance	(0)
Capital loss	(4,800)

> **Tutorial note.** Where a company makes a capital loss, then no indexation allowance is available because it cannot be used to increase a loss.

(c) The trading loss of £155,910 will be carried forward and relieved against the total profits of the next accounting period (and then subsequent accounting periods if there is any unrelieved loss). The company can decide how much of the loss is to be relieved in each accounting period.

The property business loss of £3,800 will be carried forward and relieved against total profits in the same way as the trading loss.

The capital loss of £4,800 will be carried forward and relieved against the first available chargeable gains.

ACCA

Taxation (TX – UK) FA 2024

Mock Exam 4

(Section C from March/June 2024)

Questions	
Time allowed	3 hours
ALL questions are compulsory and MUST be attempted	

DO NOT OPEN THIS EXAM UNTIL YOU ARE READY TO START UNDER EXAMINATION CONDITIONS

Section A

ALL 15 questions are compulsory and MUST be attempted.

1   Simon has been a sole trader since 2012, preparing accounts to 31 May each year. In the year to 31 May 2024, he had trading profits of £60,000 and in the year to 31 May 2025 he had trading profits of £66,000. There were no transitional profits.

    What is the amount of Class 4 national insurance contributions (NIC) that Simon will have to pay for the tax year 2024/25?

    £ [ ]   **(2 marks)**

---

2   **Which TWO of the following statements about tax appeals are correct?**
    - ☐ The First Tier Tribunal deals with straightforward cases such as the imposition of fixed filing penalties.
    - ☐ The Crown Prosecution Service (CPS) conducts tax appeals against taxpayers.
    - ☐ The taxpayer must apply for an internal review by HM Revenue and Customs (HMRC) before making an appeal to the Tax Tribunal.
    - ☐ The Upper Tribunal hears appeals against decisions of the First Tier Tribunal.   **(2 marks)**

---

3   Kate sold a flat in November 2024, realising a gain of £22,500. The flat had always been rented out to tenants and was the only chargeable asset that Kate owned. Kate had taxable income of £31,500 in the tax year 2024/25. She made a gross gift aid donation of £800 in December 2024.

    What is Kate's capital gains tax liability for the tax year 2024/25?
    - ○ £4,308
    - ○ £4,980
    - ○ £3,200
    - ○ £4,260   **(2 marks)**

4   Melton plc prepared accounts for the 12-month period to 31 July 2024. There will not be a compliance check into this accounting period.

Complete the following sentence about the retention of records for Melton plc by matching the date of retention and the maximum penalty into the relevant target area.

Melton plc will be liable for a penalty of up to [(1) ▼] if it does not retain its records until [(2) ▼].

Pull down list 1
- £1,000
- £3,000

Pull down list 2
- 31 July 2026
- 31 July 2030

(2 marks)

---

5   Nicola bought a residential property on 6 April 2024. She let it out immediately at an annual rent of £2,000 per month, all of which was received in the tax year 2024/25.

Nicola had bought the property using an interest-only mortgage. The interest paid in the tax year 2024/25 was £9,500. She paid £2,400 in the year to a managing agent.

For many years, Nicola's only income has been employment income of £60,000.

What is Nicola's additional income tax liability in respect of her property business income in the tax year 2024/25?

- ○ £8,640
- ○ £7,700
- ○ £6,740
- ○ £4,840

(2 marks)

6   Shona had always been resident in the UK before the tax year 2024/25. She spent more than 90 days in the UK in every tax year up to 2024/25.

Shona's only relative is her father who is UK resident in 2024/25.

Shona owns a house in the UK which is available to her for the whole of 2024/25. On 6 April 2024, Shona bought an overseas house where she spent 260 days during 2024/25. She lived in her UK house for the remaining 105 days. Shona is neither employed nor self-employed.

How many ties does Shona have with the UK for the tax year 2024/25 for the purposes of the sufficient ties test for UK residence?

[▼]

Pull down list
- Four
- One
- Three
- Two

(2 marks)

---

7   Ronald is self-employed.

He purchased a house and lived in it for two years. The house was then unoccupied for five years because Ronald went to work outside the UK. He then lived in the house for three years. Ronald then went to live with his mother and the house was unoccupied for six and a half years. Finally, Ronald lived in the house for the last six months of his ownership.

How many months of Ronald's 17-year period of ownership of the house will be exempt for the purposes of private residence relief?

○ 66 months
○ 150 months
○ 153 months
○ 165 months

(2 marks)

---

8   Charlotte's tax payable for the tax years 2023/24 and 2024/25 is as follows:

	2023/24	2024/25
	£	£
Income tax on trading income	9,000	10,600
Class 4 NIC	1,350	1,800
Capital gains tax	1,750	4,970

Charlotte made the appropriate payments on account on 31 January 2025 and 31 July 2025.

What is the amount payable due on 31 January 2026 in respect of the tax year 2024/25?

- ○ £2,050
- ○ £7,020
- ○ £6,570
- ○ £5,270

(2 marks)

---

9 On 1 December 2025, Devonte was issued by HM Revenue & Customs (HMRC) with a notice to file his tax return for the tax year 2024/25. Devonte submitted his return online on 20 February 2026. HMRC wishes to conduct a compliance check into this return.

Complete the following sentence about the submission of the online return and the date by which HMRC will have to notify Devonte of a compliance check into the return by matching the date of submission of the tax return and the date of notification of the compliance check into the relevant target area.

The due date for the submission of the return was [▼] and HMRC must notify Devonte by [▼] of a compliance check into the return.

Pull down list
- 20 February 2027
- 28 February 2026
- 28 February 2027
- 30 April 2026
- 31 January 2026
- 31 January 2027

(2 marks)

---

10 Caster plc sold the whole of its 4% shareholding in Antics Ltd on 15 November 2024. Caster plc had purchased 10,000 shares in Antics Ltd on 16 July 2010 for £20,000. There was a 1-for-2 rights issue at £2.50 per share in December 2017 and Caster plc took up all its rights.

The indexation factor between July 2010 and December 2017 was 0.190.

What is the indexed cost of the shares sold in November 2024?

£ [   ]

(2 marks)

11   On 12 August 2020, Patience made a gross chargeable transfer (after all exemptions) of £175,000.

On 24 November 2024, she gave £180,000 to a trust.

Patience agreed to pay any lifetime inheritance tax (IHT) due.

How much IHT will be payable by Patience on the November 2024 transfer of value?

○ £6,000
○ £4,800
○ £7,500
○ £4,500

(2 marks)

12   Alberto died on 3 September 2024. His only asset was his main residence valued at £525,000 which he left to his daughter. Alberto had made a potentially exempt transfer (after all exemptions) of £40,000 in July 2022. He had been divorced for several years.

What is the inheritance tax (IHT) liability on Alberto's death estate?

○ £26,000
○ £10,000
○ £96,000
○ £0

(2 marks)

13   Rebecca started trading on 1 January 2023 and her taxable turnover for the first 12 months of trading was £5,500 a month.

For the first seven months of 2024 her taxable turnover was as follows:

	£
January 2024	8,100
February 2024	8,300
March 2024	9,400
April 2024	10,200
May 2024	10,500
June 2024	11,300
July 2024	11,600

What was the date by which Rebecca must have notified HM Revenue & Customs (HMRC) that she was liable to be registered for value added tax (VAT)?

Pull down list
- 30 August 2024
- 30 July 2024
- 30 June 2024
- 30 September 2024

(2 marks)

14 Which TWO of the following are required for a full value added tax (VAT) invoice to be valid?
- ☐ Customer's VAT registration number
- ☐ Supplier's email address
- ☐ Date of invoice
- ☐ Total invoice price excluding VAT

(2 marks)

15 Wogan Ltd started trading on 1 April 2023 and made a trading loss of £700,000 in the year ended 31 March 2024. It had no other income or gains in the accounting period and made no qualifying charitable donations.

In the year ended 31 March 2025, Wogan Ltd had the following taxable total profits:

	£
Trading profits	500,000
Chargeable gain	18,000
Total profits	518,000
Less: qualifying charitable donation	(15,000)
Taxable total profits	503,000

Assuming that Wogan Ltd uses its trading loss in the most tax efficient manner, what is the company's unused trading loss carried forward at 1 April 2025?
- ○ £197,000
- ○ £200,000
- ○ £215,000
- ○ £182,000

(2 marks)

Section B

ALL 15 questions are compulsory and MUST be attempted.

Avery and Baylor (Sep/Dec 2022)

Avery and Baylor are a married couple.

Avery

Avery disposed of various assets during the tax year 2024/25, with these disposals resulting in chargeable gains of £98,600 qualifying for business asset disposal relief and other chargeable gains of £73,800. None of the gains are in respect of disposals of residential property.

Avery is an additional rate taxpayer and has unused capital losses of £24,400 brought forward from the tax year 2020/21.

Investment property

On 19 July 2024, Baylor transferred an investment property to Avery. On that date, the property was valued at £340,000.

Baylor's mother had originally purchased the property on 25 August 2010 for £156,000. Baylor's mother died on 6 October 2019 and the property was inherited by Baylor. On that date, the property was valued at £213,000. Baylor added a basement extension to the property during March 2021 at a cost of £51,000.

Ordinary shares in Sala plc

On 18 August 2024, Baylor sold her entire shareholding of £1 ordinary shares in Sala plc. Prior to the disposal, she had the following transactions in the ordinary shares of Sala plc:

		Cost/(proceeds) £
12 April 2013	Purchased 38,000 shares	98,800
23 October 2016	Sold 6,000 shares	(19,200)
1 November 2016	Purchased 8,000 shares	24,800

Ordinary shares in Alas Ltd

On 11 November 2024, Baylor sold her entire holding of £1 ordinary shares in Alas Ltd, an unquoted trading company, to her son for £180,000. The market value of the shares on that date was £220,000. The shares had been purchased on 1 August 2009 for £55,000. Baylor's son sold the entire shareholding on 28 March 2025 for £210,000.

An election will be made to hold over as much as possible of the gain as a gift of a business asset.

16 What is Avery's capital gains tax liability for the tax year 2024/25 assuming that this is calculated on the most favourable basis?

○ £19,740
○ £19,140
○ £29,000
○ £21,880

(2 marks)

17 What is Avery's base cost for the investment property which was transferred from Baylor on 19 July 2024?
- ○ £340,000
- ○ £264,000
- ○ £207,000
- ○ £213,000

(2 marks)

18 What cost figure will have been used by Baylor when calculating the chargeable gain on her disposal of ordinary shares in Sala plc on 18 August 2024?
- ○ £104,400
- ○ £108,000
- ○ £107,478
- ○ £105,000

(2 marks)

19 How much of the gain arising on Baylor's sale of the ordinary shares in Alas Ltd to her son can be held over by making a gift holdover relief claim?
- ○ £40,000
- ○ £165,000
- ○ £125,000
- ○ £30,000

(2 marks)

20 By what date will an election have to be made in order to hold over Baylor's gain on the sale of the ordinary shares in Alas Ltd to her son, and who must make the claim?

	Date	Claimant
○	By 5 April 2029	Either Baylor or her son
○	By 31 January 2026	Baylor and her son
○	By 5 April 2029	Baylor and her son
○	By 31 January 2026	Either Baylor or her son

(2 marks)

(Total = 10 marks)

Diggory Ltd

Diggory Ltd is a manufacturing company which owns 78% of another manufacturing company, Chang Ltd. Both companies have been registered for value added tax (VAT) for many years. The companies do not currently have a group registration. Both only make standard-rated supplies.

The following information is available in respect of Diggory Ltd's value added tax (VAT) for the quarter ended 31 December 2024:

(1) Output VAT of £36,500 has been charged in respect of sales. This figure includes output VAT of £700 where an invoice was issued on 2 January 2025 for goods supplied on 29 December 2024 and output VAT of £500 where an invoice was issued on 24 December 2024 for goods supplied on 5 January 2025.

(2) In addition to the above, Diggory Ltd also charged output VAT of £460 on sales to Chang Ltd.

(3) Input VAT included the following:

	£
Entertaining UK customers	210
Entertaining overseas customers	330
Redecorating a room in the managing director's house	500
Building a wall around Diggory Ltd's car park	2,300

In the quarter to 31 March 2025, Diggory Ltd supplied goods to a customer in another country which operates a valued added tax on certain goods. The goods had a VAT-exclusive price of £1,200. The rate of VAT in the other country on the goods supplied is 15%.

Diggory Ltd has evidence of the export in the form required by HM Revenue and Customs.

Diggory Ltd is considering expanding its business. It will either acquire part of the business of a sole trader, John, or will acquire 100% of the shares in Downs Ltd. Both John and Downs Ltd are registered for VAT. Downs Ltd makes largely zero-rated supplies.

If Diggory Ltd acquires part of the business of John, this will satisfy the requirements to be a transfer of a going concern. John will continue to run the remainder of his business. Diggory Ltd is considering entering into a group registration.

21   What is the amount of output VAT should be charged on the sales in (1) and (2) for the quarter to 31 December 2024?

   ○ £36,960
   ○ £36,260
   ○ £35,300
   ○ £35,760   (2 marks)

22   What is the amount of input VAT recoverable on the expenses in (3) for the quarter to 31 December 2024?

   ○ £2,300
   ○ £330
   ○ £2,630
   ○ £3,130   (2 marks)

23   What is the amount of VAT that Diggory Ltd will charge on the sale of the goods to the customer in another country?

   ○ £180
   ○ £0
   ○ £240
   ○ £200   (2 marks)

24 Which TWO of the following statements about Diggory Ltd's acquisition of part of the business of John as a transfer of a going concern are correct?

☐ Diggory Ltd will automatically be liable for any outstanding VAT penalties incurred by John in respect of the part of the business acquired.

☐ The acquisition of the part of the business of John is outside the scope of VAT.

☐ If the VAT chargeable on the acquisition is less than £1,000 it need not be paid.

☐ John will not need to register again for VAT.

(2 marks)

25 Which TWO of the following statements about Diggory Ltd group's possible VAT group registration are correct?

☐ The Diggory Ltd group must appoint one of the group companies to be a representative member which is solely liable for paying the group VAT liability.

☐ Downs Ltd should not be included in the group registration because it is largely making zero-rated supplies.

☐ Supplies of services by Diggory Ltd to Chang Ltd will be disregarded for VAT purposes if they are both within the group registration.

☐ Each of the companies in the Diggory Ltd group will have to make separate VAT returns.

(2 marks)

(Total = 10 marks)

Christophe

You should assume that the current date is 22 April 2025.

On 10 December 2021, Christophe was appointed as a director of an investment company, Custard Ltd, and he acquired a 3% shareholding of the company at a cost of £10 per share. On 5 April 2024, he acquired a further 48% shareholding in Custard Ltd at a cost of £80 per share.

Due to unexpected ill-health, Christophe wished to reduce his involvement in Custard Ltd and on 1 April 2025, he resigned his directorship and gave a 49% shareholding in Custard Ltd to his son, Dexter. The values of the shares on 1 April 2025 were as follows:

Shareholding %	Value per share £
51–75	120
26–50	90
1–25	30

Custard Ltd has always had 10,000 shares in issue. Christophe has no other chargeable assets.

Christophe has been told by a friend that he ought to have waited until 6 April 2025 to make the gift of the Custard Ltd shares to Dexter as this would have been beneficial for capital gains tax (CGT). If Christophe had delayed the gift until 6 April 2025, the values of the shares in Custard Ltd would have been the same as on 1 April 2025.

Christophe is considering making regular payments of £250 to his granddaughter each month, starting on 30 April 2025, to cover some of her living costs while she is at university. He will not make any other gifts in the tax year 2025/26. You have advised Christophe that the gifts to his granddaughter will be exempt from inheritance tax (IHT).

The following information is available about the income and expenses of Christophe:

Tax year	Gross income	Expenses
	£	£
2024/25	60,000	25,000
2025/26	20,000	18,000

Christophe was married to Leah for many years. Leah died in March 2009 and in her will she left her estate of £250,000 to Christophe. The IHT nil rate band in 2008/09 was £312,000. Leah had made a potentially exempt transfer of £20,000 (after all exemptions) to her sister in August 2005.

Assume the tax rates and allowances in 2024/25 also apply in future years.

26 **What is the IHT transfer of value made by Christophe on 1 April 2025?**

£ ☐ (2 marks)

27 **What is Christophe's gain chargeable to CGT on 1 April 2025?**
- ○ £216,176
- ○ £56,000
- ○ £70,000
- ○ £69,176 (2 marks)

28 **Which TWO of the following statements about the CGT advantages of Christophe delaying his gift until 6 April 2025 are correct?**
- ☐ He would have been able to set the annual exempt amounts for both 2024/25 and 2025/26 against the chargeable gain.
- ☐ Payment of the CGT liability would have been postponed for 12 months.
- ☐ He would have been chargeable to CGT at 10% instead of 20% on some of the taxable gain.
- ☐ He would have been entitled to business asset disposal relief on the disposal. (2 marks)

29 **Which of the following IHT exemptions applies to the gifts made by Christophe to his granddaughter?**
- ○ Normal expenditure out of income exemption
- ○ Small gifts exemption
- ○ Annual exemption 2025/26
- ○ Annual exemption 2024/25 (2 marks)

30 What amount of Leah's unused nil rate band can Christophe's personal representatives claim to reduce the IHT payable on his death?
   ○ £260,417
   ○ £292,000
   ○ £304,167
   ○ £308,333 (2 marks)

(Total = 10 marks)

Section C

ALL three questions are compulsory and MUST be attempted.

31 Triple A Ltd (Mar/Jun 2024)

You should assume that today's date is 15 March 2024.

You are a trainee Chartered Certified Accountant dealing with the tax affairs of Afia, Afua and Akua who have been in partnership since 6 April 2010. The partnership's profits have recently increased, so the partners are considering incorporating the partnership's business on 6 April 2024. The new limited company would be called Triple A Ltd.

Your assistant has correctly calculated some of the relevant tax figures.

Partnership

If the partners continue to trade as a partnership, their total income tax liabilities and national insurance contributions (NIC) (for all three partners) for the tax year 2024/25 will be:

	£
Income tax	55,896
Class 4 NICs	9,051
	64,947

This is based on Afia, Afua and Akua sharing profits equally. The figures are after taking account of the personal pension scheme contributions made by each partner. None of the partners has any other income except for their partnership share.

Triple A Ltd

If the partners incorporate the partnership's business, Triple A Ltd's taxable total profits for the year ended 5 April 2025, **before** taking account of director's remuneration and company pension scheme contributions, will be £264,000.

(1) The directors will be paid gross director's remuneration of £50,270 for 2024/25.

(2) The total class 1 employee NICs payable (for all directors) in respect of this director's remuneration will be £9,048. The total amount of class 1 employer NICs will be £17,044.

(3) During the tax year 2024/25, Triple A Ltd will make a pension contribution of £20,000 into the company's occupational pension scheme for each of the three directors. The directors will then not personally make any pension contributions.

(4) During the tax year 2024/25, Triple A Ltd will pay dividends of £8,500 to each director.

Required

Assuming the business is run as a company from 6 April 2024:

(a) Calculate the tax payable by the three individuals; and **(5 marks)**

(b) Calculate the tax payable by Triple A Ltd; and **(3.5 marks)**

(c) Compare the total tax and national insurance contributions (NIC) liabilities for the partners (as shown in the scenario) and the tax as calculated at (a)(i) and (ii) plus the NIC (as shown in the scenario for Triple A Ltd) and state if there is any saving.

Notes.

1 You should indicate by the use of zero (0) any items which are not taxable or deductible.

2 You should assume that the rate of corporation tax remains unchanged. **(1.5 marks)**

(Total = 10 marks)

32 Dada (Mar/Jun 2023, amended)

Dada ceased employment with Curly plc on 31 December 2024, having been employed since 1 January 2018. Dada is also self-employed and prepares accounts for his business to 31 March each year using the accruals basis.

The following information is available for the tax year 2024/25:

Self-employment

Dada's tax adjusted trading profit based on his draft accounts for the year ended 31 March 2025 is £29,800. This figure is **before** making any adjustments required for:

- Advertising expenditure of £1,300 incurred during November 2024 to promote Dada's business
- Expenditure incurred on client entertaining of £560
- The cost of Dada's office (see note (1) below)
- Capital allowances (see note (2) below)

Notes.

1 Dada runs his business using one of the six rooms in his private house as an office. The total running costs of the house for the year ended 31 March 2025 were £2,400. No deduction has been made for the cost of the office in calculating the profit of £29,800.

2 **Capital allowances**

The tax written down value of both the main pool and the special rate pool as at 1 April 2024 is nil.

On 1 January 2025, Dada purchased a laptop computer for £1,200.

This laptop computer was sold on 20 March 2025 for £400. Dada had elected for this laptop computer to be treated as a short-life asset. A replacement laptop computer was purchased on the same day for £2,700.

On 1 May 2024, Dada brought his private car into his business at its market value of £14,000.

The car has a CO_2 emission rate of 39 grams per kilometre. The car is used 80% for business journeys in his self-employment.

Employment

During the period from 6 April to 31 December 2024, Dada was paid a gross monthly salary of £5,400.

During the period from 6 April to 31 December 2024, Dada contributed a total of £2,340 into Curly plc's occupational pension scheme.

Dada used his private car for business purposes. During the period from 6 April to 31 December 2024, he drove 16,400 miles in the performance of his duties for Curly plc, for which the company paid an allowance of 30 pence per mile.

On 10 May 2024, Dada spent £460 on a replacement suit which he only wore when meeting clients of Curly plc. The suit was scrapped, with nil proceeds, on 31 December 2024.

Other income

On 31 May 2024, Dada received a premium bond prize of £500.

During the tax year 2024/25, Dada received interest of £270 from UK Government securities (gilts).

On 30 November 2024, Dada received interest of £1,030 on the maturity of savings certificates from NS&I (National Savings and Investments).

Required

(a) Calculate Dada's revised tax adjusted trading profit for the year ended 31 March 2025.

Note. Your computation should commence with the draft profit per accounts of £29,800, indicating by the use of zero (0) any item which does not require adjustment. **(6 marks)**

(b) Calculate Dada's taxable income for the tax year 2024/25.

Note. Note: You should indicate by the use of zero (0) any items which are not taxable or deductible. (7 marks)

(c) State TWO advantages for an employee if their employer had payrolled the taxable benefits provided to the employee. (2 marks)

(Total = 15 marks)

33 Deimos Ltd, Elara Ltd and Fenrir Ltd (Mar/Jun 2024)

You should assume that today's date is 5 March 2025.

You are a trainee Chartered Certified Accountant assisting your manager with the tax affairs of three unrelated limited companies, Deimos Ltd, Elara Ltd and Fenrir Ltd.

Deimos Ltd

Deimos Ltd ceased trading on 30 September 2024, preparing its final financial statements for the 17-month period 1 May 2023 to 30 September 2024. On 1 October 2024, the company's shareholders passed a resolution to commence winding up procedures. The winding up of Deimos Ltd was completed on 28 February 2025, with the company ceasing to exist on that date.

Elara Ltd

Elara Ltd's summarised statement of profit or loss for the year ended 31 December 2024 is as follows:

	Note	£
Operating profit	1	612,900
Other income:		
Loan interest receivable	2	1,100
Profit on disposal of freehold warehouse	3	99,300
Finance costs:		
Interest payable	4	(900)
Profit before taxation		712,400

Notes.

1. **Operating profit**

    Depreciation of £8,820, qualifying charitable donations of £2,300 and leasing costs of £4,200 have been deducted in arriving at the operating profit of £612,900. The leasing costs relate to a car with an official CO_2 emissions rate of 124 grams per kilometre which was leased from 1 June 2024.

    Elara Ltd incurred £2,576 on entertaining clients and £75 on gifts of calendars to customers (each calendar costing £7.50 each and bearing the company's name). These costs have also been deducted in arriving at the operating profit of £612,900.

2. **Loan interest receivable**

    The loan was made for non-trading purposes on 1 October 2024. The loan interest of £1,100 was accrued at 31 December 2024.

3. **Profit on disposal of freehold warehouse**

    On 21 December 2024, Elara Ltd sold a freehold warehouse for £204,000. The warehouse had been purchased for £104,700 in 2016, and its indexed cost on 21 December 2024 was £108,800.

Elara Ltd has made a claim to rollover the gain on the warehouse against the replacement cost of a new freehold warehouse which was purchased on 6 January 2025 for £168,000.

The freehold warehouse and the replacement warehouse have been, and are, used entirely for business purposes by Elara Ltd.

4   **Interest payable**

The interest payable is in respect of Elara Ltd's 4.5% loan notes which were repaid on 31 January 2024. Interest of £5,400 was paid on 31 January 2024, and an accrual of £4,500 had been provided for at 1 January 2024. The loan notes were issued in order for Elara Ltd to purchase plant and machinery.

Capital allowances

The tax written down value of both the main pool and the special rate pool as at 1 January 2024 is nil.

On 10 February 2024, Elara Ltd purchased an overhead crane for £220,000. The crane is a long-life asset.

On 1 March 2024, Elara Ltd purchased a new car with CO_2 emissions of 25 grams per kilometre for £30,000.

Fenrir Ltd

Fenrir Ltd's forecast corporation tax liability for the year ending 31 March 2025 is £132,500. This is based on forecast taxable total profits of £530,000. Because these figures are relatively high compared to previous years, Fenrir Ltd plans to take three measures prior to the end of the company's accounting period on 31 March 2025:

(1) Four new cars will be purchased for a total cost of £64,000. All four cars will have zero CO_2 emissions.

(2) A dividend of £60,000 will be paid to the company's shareholders.

(3) Rent of £18,000 covering the six-month period 1 April to 30 September 2025 will be paid in advance.

Required

(a) Identify Deimos Ltd's accounting periods throughout the period 1 May 2023 to 28 February 2025. **(2 marks)**

(b) Calculate Elara Ltd's taxable total profits for the year ended 31 December 2024.

Note. Your computation should commence with the operating profit figure of £612,900, and should also list all of the items referred to in the scenario, indicating by the use of zero (0) any items which do not require adjustment. **(9 marks)**

(c) Calculate the amount of corporation tax which Fenrir Ltd will save for the year ending 31 March 2025 by taking the three measures prior to 31 March 2025.

Note. Your answer should be supported by appropriate explanations. **(4 marks)**

(Total = 15 marks)

Answers

DO NOT TURN THIS PAGE UNTIL YOU HAVE
COMPLETED THE MOCK EXAM

A plan of attack

If this were the real Taxation (TX – UK) exam and you had been told to turn over and begin, what would be going through your mind?

Perhaps you're having a panic. You've spent most of your study time on income tax and corporation tax computations (because that's what your tutor/BPP Course Book told you to do), plus a selection of other topics, and you're really not sure that you know enough. So, calm down. Spend the first few moments or so **looking at the exam** and develop a **plan of attack**.

Looking through the exam.

Section A contains **15 Objective Test (OT) questions** each worth **2 marks**. These will cover all sections of the syllabus. Some you may find easy and some more difficult. In Question 2, where you are asked to identify the true statement, read the possible answers at least twice before you decide which one to select. Don't spend a lot of time on anything you really don't know. For multiple choice questions you are not penalised for wrong answers, so you should answer all of them. If all else fails – guess!

Section B contains **three OT Case** scenarios. These each have **five questions** each worth **2 marks**. Make sure you read the scenario carefully before you start to answer the OTQs.

- **Questions 16 to 20** test your knowledge of CGT, transfers between spouses, pooling provisions and gift holdover relief. Question 20 is a relatively quick question as you don't need to do any calculations.

- **Questions 21 to 25** concern VAT for companies in a small group. Make sure to double check your calculations to avoid losing marks for simple mistakes. A couple of knowledge questions with no calculations should save you some time here.

- **Questions 26 to 30** are about inheritance tax (IHT). Read the questions carefully to make sure you answer the question set. For example, in Question 26 you are considering IHT and in Q27 CGT on the same gift.

In Section C, you have three constructed response (long) questions:

- **Question 31** is worth **10 marks** and covers alternative ways of extracting profits.
- **Question 32** is worth **15 marks** and is an income tax question with trading losses.
- **Question 33** is worth **15 marks** and is a corporation tax question.

Allocating your time

BPP's advice is always allocate your time **according to the marks for the question** in total and for the parts of the question. But **use common sense**. If you're confronted by an OTQ on a topic of which you know nothing, pick an answer and move on. Use the time to pick up marks elsewhere.

After the exam...**Forget about it!**

And don't worry if you found the exam difficult. More than likely other candidates will too. If this were the real thing you would need to **forget** the exam the minute you left the exam hall and **think about the next one**. Or, if it's the last one, **celebrate**!

Section A

1   £ 2,557

First calculate the assessable profit for 2024/25.

£60,000 × 2/12 + £66,000 × 10/12 = £65,000

	£
£(65,000 – 50,270) = 14,730 × 2%	295
£(50,270 – 12,570) = 37,700 × 6%	2,262
Class 4 contributions	2,557

Class 4 NICs are based on the assessable profits on a tax year basis.

2   The correct answers are:
- The First Tier Tribunal deals with straightforward cases such as the imposition of fixed filing penalties.
- The Upper Tribunal hears appeals against decisions of the First Tier Tribunal.

HMRC conducts tax appeals against taxpayers. The CPS provides legal advice and institutes and conducts criminal prosecutions in England and Wales where there has been an investigation by HMRC. The taxpayer does not have to use the internal review procedure before making an appeal to the Tax Tribunal.

3   The correct answer is: £4,260

	£
Chargeable gain	22,500
Less annual exempt amount	(3,000)
Taxable gains	19,500
Tax	
£((37,700 + 800) – 31,500) = 7,000 × 18%	1,260
£(19,500 – 7,000) = 12,500 × 24%	3,000
Total capital gains tax	4,260

The residential property rates apply.

The answer £4,308 does not adjust for Gift Aid. The answer £4,980 does not deduct the annual exempt amount. The answer £3,200 uses the rates of 10% and 20% which apply to other assets.

4   Melton plc will be liable for a penalty of up to £3,000 if it does not retain its records until 31 July 2030 .

5   The correct answer is: £6,740

	£
Rent received	24,000
Less: Agent's fees	(2,400)

	£
Property business income	21,600
£21,600 × 40%	8,640
Less	
Finance costs tax reducer £9,500 × 20%	(1,900)
Income tax liability on property business income	6,740

The answer £8,640 does not make any adjustment for the finance costs. The answer £7,700 does not deduct the agent's fees in the computation of property business income. The answer £4,840 allows full deduction of the finance costs in the property business income computation.

6 Two

The two ties are: available accommodation in the UK, in which she spends at least one night in the tax year, and more than 90 days spent in the UK in either or both of the previous two tax years.

Shona's father is not treated as close family (not a spouse/civil partner or child under the age of 18) so that tie does not apply. She does not have substantive UK work. She is not present in the UK at midnight for at least an equal number of days in the tax year as in any other country.

7 The correct answer is: 153 months

	Exempt months	Chargeable months	Total months
Actual occupation	24		24
Deemed occupation – up to 4 years self-employed overseas, plus 1 year any reason	60		60
Actual occupation	36		36
Deemed occupation – remaining 2 years up to 3 years any reason	24		24
Unoccupied		51	51
Last 9 months of ownership	9	—	9
Totals	153	51	204

The answer 66 months is the actual occupation. The answer 150 months ignores the last nine months of ownership rule and only gives six months of actual occupation. The answer 165 months treats the overseas period as fully exempt – this only applies if the taxpayer is employed (rather than self-employed) outside the UK.

8   The correct answer is: £7,020

	£
Income tax £(10,600 – 9,000 payments on account)	1,600
Class 4 NIC £(1,800 – 1,350 payments on account)	450
Capital gains tax	4,970
Amount payable on 31 January 2026 for 2024/25	7,020

There are no payments on account for capital gains tax.

The answer £2,050 is just the income tax and the Class 4 NIC. The answer £6,570 ignores the Class 4 NIC. The answer £5,270 treats the capital gains tax as having payments on account.

9   The due date for the submission of the return was ⬚28 February 2026⬚ and HMRC must notify Devonte by ⬚20 February 2027⬚ of a compliance check into the return.

The notice to file a return was issued after 31 October 2025 so the due filing date was the last day of the three-month period starting with the issue. Because the return was made on or before the due date, the date for notification of the compliance check is the first anniversary of the actual filing date.

10   £ ⬚36,300⬚

	£
July 2010 shares	20,000
Add:	
– Indexation to December 2017	
– 0.190 × £20,000	3,800
December 2017 shares (10,000/2 × £2.50)	12,500
Total indexed cost	36,300

Indexation is frozen at December 2017, so there is no further indexation allowance on either the original shares or the rights issue shares.

11   The correct answer is: £6,000

	£
Gift	180,000
Less AE × 2 (2024/25 and 2023/24 b/f)	(6,000)
	174,000
Less nil rate band available £(325,000 – 175,000)	(150,000)
	24,000
IHT @ $^{20}/_{80}$	6,000

The answer £4,800 uses the rate of 20%. The answer £7,500 does not deduct the annual exemptions. The answer £4,500 deducts annual exemptions again from the brought forward transfer.

12 The correct answer is: £26,000

	£
£175,000 @ 0% (residence nil rate band)	0
£285,000 @ 0% (£(325,000 – 40,000) nil rate band)	0
£65,000 @ 40%	26,000
£525,000	26,000

The residence nil rate band is the lower of the maximum (2024/25) of £175,000 and the value of the main residence.

The answer £10,000 applies the full nil rate band. The answer £96,000 does not apply the residence nil rate band. The answer £0 assumes that the residence nil rate band is £525,000 and so there is no liability on the estate.

Since Alberto was divorced there can be no transfer of the residence nil rate band nor the nil rate band between spouses.

13 30 July 2024

Rebecca was required to notify HMRC within 30 days of exceeding the £90,000 registration threshold ie 30 July 2024 (30 days after the year to 30 June 2024 when her cumulative 12-month turnover was £90,800).

14 The correct answers are:
- Date of invoice
- Total invoice price excluding VAT

The customer's VAT registration number is not required, only the supplier's VAT registration number. The supplier must give a business name and address but is not required to give an email address.

15 The correct answer is: £197,000

	£
Loss brought forward	700,000
Used in y/e 31.3.25	(503,000)
Loss carried forward at 1.4.25	197,000

The loss brought forward is set against total profits but the claim can be restricted to leave total profits of £15,000 in charge to preserve tax relief on the qualifying charitable donation.

The answer £200,000 sets the brought forward loss against trading profits only. The answer £215,000 sets the brought forward loss against trading profits only but restricts the loss used to leave trading profits in charge to cover the qualifying charitable donation. The answer £182,000 does not restrict the claim to leave total profits in charge to cover the qualifying charitable donation.

Section B

Avery and Baylor

16 The correct answer is: £19,140

Avery will want to make the best use of the capital losses brought forward and the annual exempt amount (AEA). The gain qualifying for business asset disposal relief (BADR) will be taxed at 10% and the other gains will be taxed at 20% (because Avery is an additional rate taxpayer). Therefore, the losses and AEA will be best used against the other chargeable gains ((73,800 − 24,400 − 3,000 = 46,400 at 20% = 9,280) + (98,600 at 10% = 9,860) totalling capital gains tax of 19,140).

The incorrect options are:

- £19,740 forgetting to deduct the AEA ((98,600 at 10%) + ((73,800 − 24,400) at 20%) = 19,740)
- £29,000 no BADR given ((98,600 + 73,800 − 24,400 − 3,000) at 20% = 29,000)
- £21,880 losses and AEA set against the gain chargeable to BADR ((98,600 − 24,400 − 3,000) at 10% + (73,800 at 20%) = 21,880)

17 The correct answer is: £264,000

As Avery and Baylor are married, the transfer of the property will be made on a no gain no loss basis, so that Avery (the transferee) will take over the property at the cost to Baylor (the transferor). The cost to Baylor is the probate value (the market value of the property at the date of death) of £213,000 plus the enhancement expenditure on the basement extension of £51,000 totalling £264,000.

The incorrect options are:

- £340,000 being market value at the date of transfer
- £207,000 the original cost to Baylor's mother plus the enhancement expenditure (156,000 + 51,000 = 207,000)
- £213,000 being just the probate value

18 The correct answer is: £105,000

The shares were all sold in August 2024 and the base cost will be established by reviewing the earlier transactions in these ordinary shares. The 6,000 shares sold on 23 October 2016 will have been matched with the shares purchased within 30 days of the sale meaning that of the 8,000 shares purchased on 1 November 2016, 6,000 will be matched with the 23 October 2016 disposal. Therefore, the amount to be included as cost in the share pool in respect of the November purchase will be 2,000/8,000 × £24,800 = £6,200. This will be added to the cost of original purchase in April 2013 of £98,800 giving a total cost remaining in the pool of £105,000.

The incorrect options are:

- £104,400 no matching of the disposal in October 2016 (98,800 − 19,200 + 24,800 = 104,400)
- £108,000 taking the 6,000 disposal in October 2016 from the original pool ((98,800 × 32,000/38,000) + 24,800 = 108,000)
- £107,478 taking the 6,000 disposal as a proportion of the total original cost and cost in November 2016 ((98,800 + 24,800) × 40,000/46,000 = 107,478)

19 The correct answer is: 40,000

The sale will be deemed to take place at market value of £220,000 because it is not an arms-length transaction. The cost of the shares was £55,000 therefore the gain before any gift holdover relief is £165,000. The amount which qualifies for gift holdover relief will be restricted by the excess of proceeds received by Baylor over the original cost of the shares (180,000 − 55,000 = 125,000, this amount will be chargeable immediately). Thus, the total gain of £165,000 which is not so restricted is £40,000 (165,000 −125,000 = 40,000) and can be deferred/held over.

The other incorrect options are:

- £165,000 being the gain without any relief
- £125,000 being the part of the gain which cannot be held over/deferred and which is immediately chargeable
- £30,000 this uses the proceeds received by Baylor's son to calculate the amount of gift holdover relief ((210,000 − 55,000) − (180,000 − 55,000) = 30,000)

20 The correct answer is:

Date	Claimant
By 5 April 2029	Baylor and her son

The transferor (Baylor) and the transferee (Baylor's son) can jointly claim within four years of the end of the tax year of the transfer.

Diggory Ltd

21 The correct answer is: £36,260

	£
Sales £(36,500 − 700)	35,800
Sale to Chang Ltd (no group registration)	460
Output VAT	36,260

The tax point for the goods supplied on 29 December 2024 is 2 January 2025 (invoice within 14 days) and so the output tax is not due for payment in the 31 December 2024 quarter. However, the tax point for the goods supplied on 5 January 2025 is the issue of the invoice on 24 December 2024 and so no adjustment is needed for this supply.

The answer £36,960 does not adjust for the 29 December 2024 supply. The answer £35,300 omits the sales to Chang Ltd and adjusts for both the 24 and 29 December 2024 supplies. The answer £35,760 adjusts for the 24 and 29 December 2024 supplies.

22 The correct answer is: £2,630

	£
Entertaining UK customers	0
Entertaining overseas customers	330
Redecoration	0
Wall	2,300
	2,630

Input VAT on business entertaining is only recoverable if it relates to the cost of entertaining overseas customers. No input tax is recoverable on expenditure on domestic accommodation for directors. There is no distinction between capital and revenue expenditure for VAT so input tax is recoverable on the building of the new wall (capital).

The answer £2,300 disallows all the input VAT except on the wall. The answer £330 disallows all the input VAT except on the overseas entertaining. The answer £3,130 disallows UK customer entertaining only.

23 The correct answer is: £0

Diggory Ltd will charge VAT at zero rate because there is general zero-rating where a UK VAT registered trader exports goods.

The answer £180 charges VAT at the rate in the other country – this is not relevant for UK VAT. The answer £240 charges the supply at the UK standard rate. The answer £200 treats the supply as VAT-inclusive and charges the supply at the UK standard rate.

24 The correct answers are:
- The acquisition of the part of the business of John is outside the scope of VAT.
- John will not need to register again for VAT.

Diggory Ltd is not taking over the registration of John and so is not liable for his VAT penalties and John will not have to re-register for VAT.

The rule that if the VAT chargeable is less than £1,000 it need not be paid applies on deregistration.

25 The correct answers are:
- Downs Ltd should not be included in the group registration because it is largely making zero-rated supplies.
- Supplies of services by Diggory Ltd to Chang Ltd will be disregarded for VAT purposes if they are both within the group registration.

This is because Downs Ltd is in a repayment position and will continue to benefit from cash flow repayments by completing monthly VAT returns.

All members of the Diggory Ltd group will be jointly and severally liable for any VAT due from the representative member.

The Diggory Ltd group will make one VAT return.

Christophe

26 £ 606,000

	£
Before: (3% + 48%) = 51% 5,100 shares @ £120	612,000
After: (51% – 47%) = 2% 200 shares @ £30	(6,000)
Transfer of value	606,000

27 The correct answer is: £69,176

	£
Proceeds (49%) 4,900 shares @ £90 per share	441,000
Less: Cost (W)	(371,824)
Gain	69,176

Working

Cost of shares

	No. of shares	Cost £
10 December 2021 @ £10 per share	300	3,000
5 April 2024 @ £80 per share	4,800	384,000
	5,100	387,000
	(4,900)	(371,824)
1 April 2025 disposal	200	15,176

The answer £216,176 uses £120 per share as the proceeds. The answer £56,000 does not pool the shares and treats the 5 April 2024 shares as sold first. The answer £70,000 does not pool the shares and treats the 10 December 2021 shares as sold first.

28 The correct answers are:
- Payment of the CGT liability would have been postponed for 12 months.
- He would have been chargeable to CGT at 10% instead of 20% on some of the taxable gain.

The payment date for the disposal on 1 April 2025 (2024/25) is 31 January 2026 and, on a disposal on 6 April 2025 (2025/26), would be 31 January 2027.

Christophe is a higher rate taxpayer in 2024/25 since his income exceeds the total of the personal allowance and the basic rate band £(12,570 + 37,700) = £50,270. In 2025/26 (assuming 2024/25 rates and allowances), his income is within that total, so some of the taxable gain would have been chargeable at 10% instead of 20%.

Christophe would only have been able to set the annual exempt amount for 2025/26 against the chargeable gain on 6 April 2025. It is not possible to carry forward CGT unused annual exempt amounts, unlike IHT annual exemptions.

He would not have been entitled to business asset disposal relief on the disposal because Custard Ltd is an investment company. Business asset disposal relief for shares only applies to those in trading companies.

29 The correct answer is: Annual exemption 2025/26

The normal expenditure out of income exemption cannot apply because Christophe only has excess income of £(20,000 – 18,000) = £2,000 which is insufficient to cover the gifts of £(250 × 12) = £3,000. The small gifts exemption only applies to gifts up to £250 per donee in a tax year; once exceeded all of the gifts to the same donee are chargeable. The annual exemption for 2024/25 has been used against the gift on 1 April 2025 and, in any case, the current year exemption is used first.

30 The correct answer is: £304,167

$$\frac{£(312,000-20,000)}{312,000} \times £325,000 = £304,167$$

The answer £260,417 treats the exempt estate passing to Christophe as the unused nil rate band. The answer £292,000 does not deal with the increase in the nil rate band. The answer £308,333 treats the PET as being reduced by 20% taper relief. Remember that taper relief reduces death tax on a lifetime transfer, not the transfer itself.

Section C

31 Triple A Ltd

(a) Total income tax liability 2024/25

	A	B
1		£
2	Director's remuneration	50,270
3	Pension contribution	0
4	Dividend income	8,500
5		58,770
6	Personal allowance	(12,570)
7	Taxable income	46,200
8		
9	Income tax	
10	37,700 (50,270 – 12,570) at 20%	7,540
11	500 at 0%	0
12	8,000 (8,500 – 500) at 33.75%	2,700
13	Income tax liability	10,240
14	Three directors (10,240 × 3)	30,720

(b) Corporation tax liability of Triple A Ltd for the year ended 5 April 2025

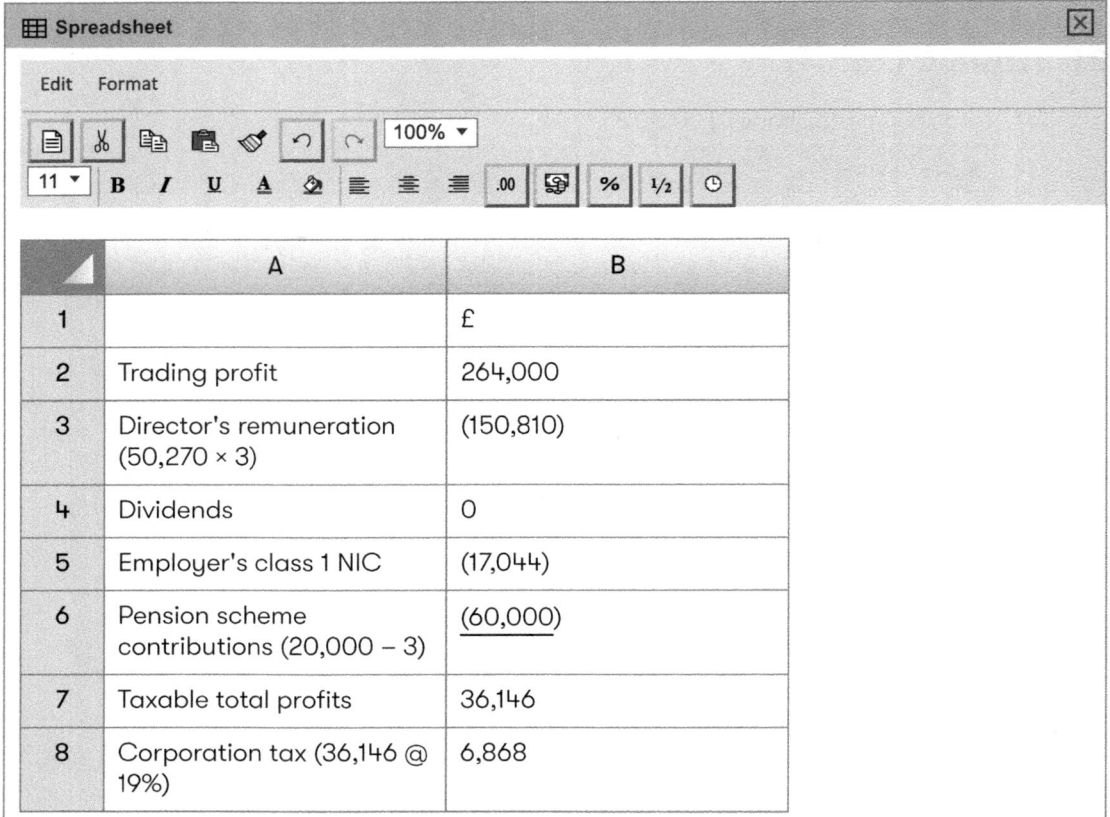

	A	B
1		£
2	Trading profit	264,000
3	Director's remuneration (50,270 × 3)	(150,810)
4	Dividends	0
5	Employer's class 1 NIC	(17,044)
6	Pension scheme contributions (20,000 – 3)	(60,000)
7	Taxable total profits	36,146
8	Corporation tax (36,146 @ 19%)	6,868

(c)

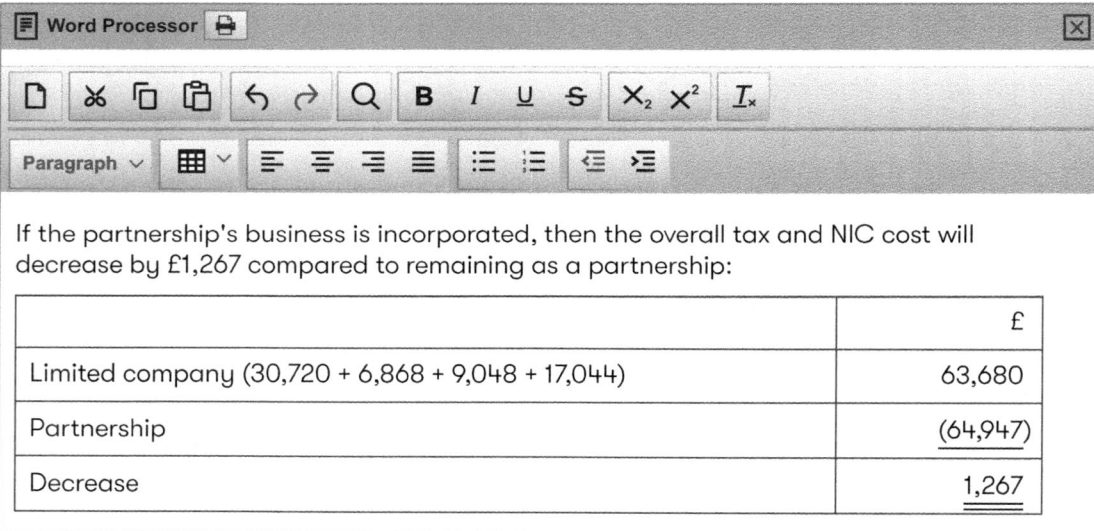

If the partnership's business is incorporated, then the overall tax and NIC cost will decrease by £1,267 compared to remaining as a partnership:

	£
Limited company (30,720 + 6,868 + 9,048 + 17,044)	63,680
Partnership	(64,947)
Decrease	1,267

32 Dada

(a) Dada – Trading profit for the year ended 31 March 2025

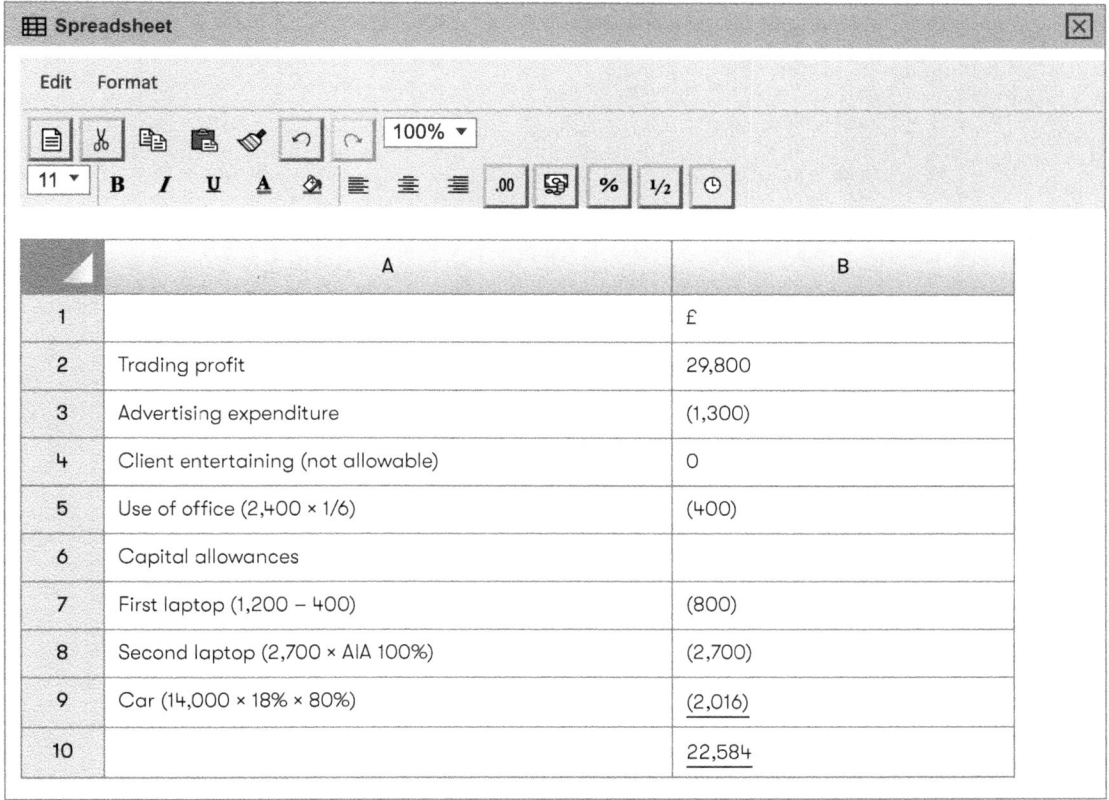

	A	B
1		£
2	Trading profit	29,800
3	Advertising expenditure	(1,300)
4	Client entertaining (not allowable)	0
5	Use of office (2,400 × 1/6)	(400)
6	Capital allowances	
7	First laptop (1,200 – 400)	(800)
8	Second laptop (2,700 × AIA 100%)	(2,700)
9	Car (14,000 × 18% × 80%)	(2,016)
10		22,584

Tutorial note. Short-life assets are kept in single asset pools, so the disposal of the first laptop will result in a balancing allowance.

Tutorial note. Dada's car has CO_2 emissions between 1 and 50 grams per kilometre and therefore qualifies for writing down allowances at the rate of 18%.

(b) Dada – Taxable income computation 2024/25.

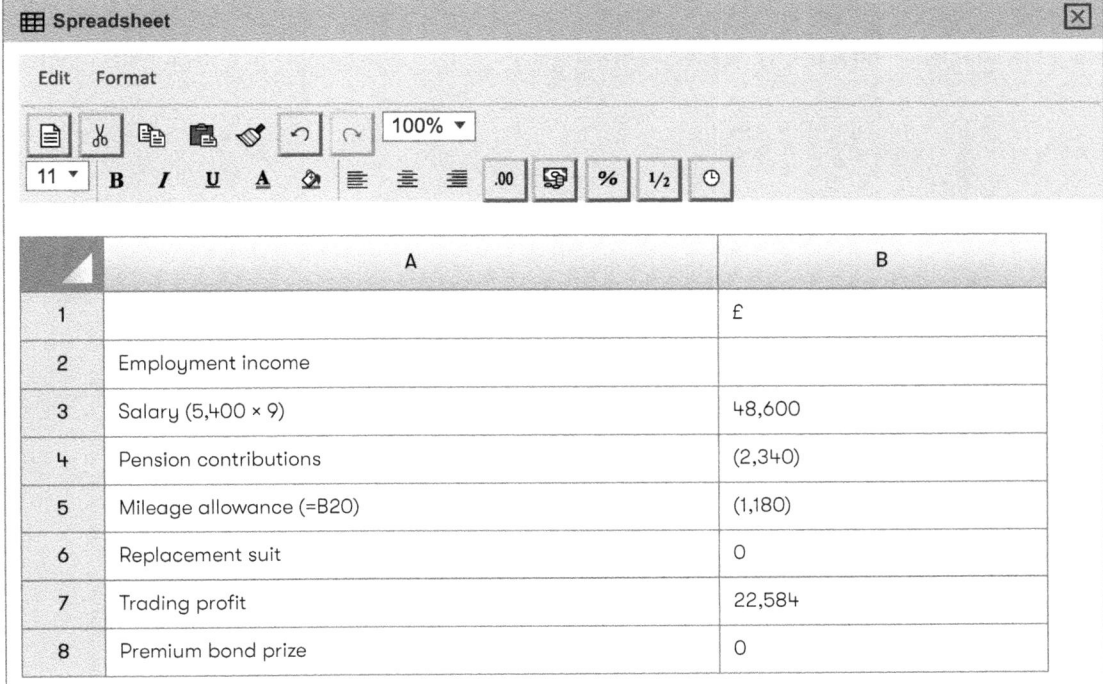

	A	B
1		£
2	Employment income	
3	Salary (5,400 × 9)	48,600
4	Pension contributions	(2,340)
5	Mileage allowance (=B20)	(1,180)
6	Replacement suit	0
7	Trading profit	22,584
8	Premium bond prize	0

	A	B
9	Interest from UK Government securities	270
10	Interest from savings certificate	0
11		67,934
12	Personal allowance	(12,570)
13	Taxable income	55,364

	A	B
14	Mileage allowance	
15		£
16	10,000 miles @ 45p	4,500
17	6,400 miles @ 25p	1,600
18		6,100
19	Mileage allowance 16,400 @ 30p	(4,920)
20		1,180

Tutorial note. The cost of clothing for work (with the exception of a uniform or protective clothing) is not an allowable deduction.

(c)

1. As the tax on benefits is collected through the payroll, on a real time basis, income tax should not be underpaid, and the employee will not have any unexpected tax liabilities in respect of the taxable benefits which have been payrolled.
2. There is no need to declare payrolled benefits on the employee's self-assessment tax return.

33 Deimos Ltd, Elara Ltd and Fenrir Ltd

(a)

Deimos Ltd

Accounting periods

1 May 2023 to 30 April 2024

1 May 2024 to 30 September 2024

1 October 2024 to 28 February 2025

> **Tutorial note.** An accounting period cannot be longer than 12 months, so the period of account ended 30 September 2024 must be split into two accounting periods.
>
> **Tutorial note.** The resolution to commence winding up procedures is irrelevant here because it happens immediately following the end of Deimos Ltd's period of account to 30 September 2024.

(b) **Taxable total profits for the year ended 31 December 2024**

	A	B
1		£
2	Operating profit	612,900
3	Depreciation	8,820
4	Qualifying charitable donations	2,300
5	Lease of car (4,200 × 15%)	630
6	Entertaining clients	2,576
7	Gifts of calendars	0
8	Interest payable (5,400 – 4,500)	(900)
9	Capital allowances:	
10	(AIA 100% × 220,000)	(220,000)
11	(WDA 18% × 30,000)	(5,400)
12	Trading profit	400,926
13	Interest receivable	1,100
14	Chargeable gain (204,000 – 168,000)	36,000

	A	B
15		438,026
16	Qualifying charitable donation	(2,300)
17	Taxable total profits	435,726

Tutorial note. Sale proceeds of £36,000 are not reinvested from the sale of the freehold warehouse. This amount of the gain remains chargeable.

(c)

Fenrir Ltd

Cars

This expenditure will reduce Fenrir Ltd's corporation tax liability by £16,000 (64,000 at 25%). The new cars will have zero CO_2 emissions and will therefore qualify for the 100% first year allowance.

Dividend

The payment of a dividend will not affect Fenrir Ltd's corporation tax liability because dividends are paid out of post-tax profits.

Rent paid in advance

This expenditure will not affect the company's corporation tax liability for that year. Fenrir Ltd's financial statements must be prepared on the accruals basis, so the rent paid in advance will not be deductible for the year ended 31 March 2025.

Tax Tables

Supplementary information

(a) Calculations and workings need only be made to the nearest £.
(b) All apportionments should be made to the nearest month.
(c) All workings should be shown in Section C.

Tax rates and allowances

The following tax rates and allowances are to be used in answering the questions.

Income tax

		Normal rates	Dividend rates
Basic rate	£1 – £37,700	20%	8.75%
Higher rate	£37,701 – £125,140	40%	33.75%
Additional rate	£125,141 and over	45%	39.35%
Savings income nil rate band	Basic rate taxpayers		£1,000
	Higher rate taxpayers		£500
Dividend nil rate band			£500

A starting rate of 0% applies to savings income where it falls within the first £5,000 of taxable income.

Personal allowance

	£
Personal allowance	12,570
Transferable amount	1,260
Income limit	100,000

Where adjusted net income is £125,140 or more, the personal allowance is reduced to zero.

Residence status

Days in UK	Previously resident	Not previously resident
Less than 16	Automatically not resident	Automatically not resident
16 to 45	Resident if 4 UK ties (or more)	Automatically not resident
46 to 90	Resident if 3 UK ties (or more)	Resident if 4 UK ties
91 to 120	Resident if 2 UK ties (or more)	Resident if 3 UK ties (or more)
121 to 182	Resident if 1 UK tie (or more)	Resident if 2 UK ties (or more)
183 or more	Automatically resident	Automatically resident

Child benefit income tax charge

Where income is between £60,000 and £80,000, the charge is 1% of the amount of child benefit received for every £200 of income over £60,000.

Car benefit percentage

The relevant base level of CO_2 emissions is 55 grams per kilometre.

The percentage rates applying to petrol cars (and diesel cars meeting the RDE2 standard) with CO_2 emissions up to this level are:

51 grams to 54 grams per kilometre	15%
55 grams per kilometre	16%

The percentage for electric cars with zero CO_2 emissions is 2%.

For hybrid-electric cars with CO_2 emissions between 1 and 50 grams per kilometre, the electric range of the car is relevant:

Electric range	
130 miles or more	2%
70 to 129 miles	5%
40 to 69 miles	8%
30 to 39 miles	12%
Less than 30 miles	14%

Car fuel benefit

The base figure for calculating the car fuel benefit is £27,800.

Company van benefits

The company van benefit scale charge is £3,960, and the van fuel benefit is £757.

Vans producing zero emissions have a 0% benefit.

Individual savings accounts (ISAs)

The overall investment limit is £20,000.

Rent-a-room relief

The rent-a-room limit is £7,500.

Pension scheme limits

Annual allowance – 2021–22 and 2022–23	£40,000
Annual allowance – 2023–24 and 2024–25	£60,000
Minimum allowance	£10,000
Income limit	£260,000

The maximum contribution that can qualify for tax relief without any earnings is £3,600.

Approved mileage allowances: cars

Up to 10,000 miles	45p
Over 10,000 miles	25p

Capital allowances: rates of allowance

Plant and machinery

Main pool	18%
Special rate pool	6%

Cars

New cars with zero CO_2 emissions	100%
Second-hand cars with zero CO_2 emissions	18%
CO_2 emissions between 1 and 50 grams per kilometre	18%
CO_2 emissions over 50 grams per kilometre	6%

Annual investment allowance

Rate of allowance	100%
Expenditure limit	£1,000,000

Enhanced capital allowances for companies

Main pool first year allowance (full expensing)	100%
Special rate pool first year allowance	50%

Structures and buildings allowance

Straight-line allowance	3%

Cap on income tax reliefs

Unless otherwise restricted, reliefs are capped at the higher of £50,000 or 25% of income.

Corporation tax

Financial year	2022	2023	2024
Small profits rate	N/A	19%	19%
Main rate	19%	25%	25%
Lower limit	N/A	£50,000	£50,000
Upper limit	N/A	£250,000	£250,000
Standard fraction	N/A	3/200	3/200

Marginal relief

(Upper limit − Augmented profits) × Standard fraction × $\dfrac{\text{Taxable total profits}}{\text{Augmented profits}}$

Quarterly instalments

| Profit threshold | £1,500,000 |

Value added tax (VAT)

Standard rate	20%
Registration limit	£90,000
Deregistration limit	£88,000

Penalties for late VAT payments

Days late	Penalty
Up to 15 days	None
16 to 30 days	2%
More than 30 days	4% plus a 4% daily penalty

Inheritance tax: Tax rates

	£
Nil rate band	325,000
Residence nil rate band	175,000
Rate of tax on excess	
− Lifetime rate	20%
− Death rate	40%

Inheritance tax: taper relief

Years before death	Percentage reduction
More than 3 but less than 4 years	20%
More than 4 but less than 5 years	40%
More than 5 but less than 6 years	60%
More than 6 but less than 7 years	80%

Capital gains tax: Tax rates

	Normal rates	Residential property
Rates of tax:		
– Lower rate	10%	18%
– Higher rate	20%	24%
Annual exempt amount		£3,000

Capital gains tax: business asset disposal relief and investors' relief

Lifetime limit	
– business asset disposal relief	£1,000,000
– investors' relief	£10,000,000
Rate of tax	10%

National insurance contributions

Class 1 Employee	£1 – £12,570 per year	Nil
	£12,571 – £50,270 per year	8%
	£50,271 and above per year	2%
Class 1 Employer	£1 – £9,100 per year	Nil
	£9,101 and above per year	13.8%
	Employment allowance	£5,000
Class 1A		13.8%
Class 4	£1 – £12,570 per year	Nil
	£12,571 – £50,270 per year	6%
	£50,271 and above per year	2%

Rates of interest (assumed)

Official rate of interest	2.25%
Rate of interest on underpaid tax	7.75%
Rate of interest on overpaid tax	4.25%

Standard penalties for errors

Taxpayer behaviour	Maximum penalty	Minimum penalty – unprompted disclosure	Minimum penalty – prompted disclosure
Deliberate and concealed	100%	30%	50%
Deliberate but not concealed	70%	20%	35%
Careless	30%	0%	15%

Additional CBE Mock Exam

Please find below information and a link relating to an additional CBE Mock Exam. This Mock Exam has been written by the BPP team and built in the ACCA exam software. Please sit this exam at home at a time convenient to you and self-review using the model answers available at the end of the assessment.

It is extremely important to follow the below guidelines when attempting this Mock Exam:

- Please make sure that you launch the exams using **Google Chrome** in order to enjoy the full functionality of the Software.
- Only launch the exam once you are ready to fully complete it.
- Remember to retain a copy of the pdf output of your script as this will be useful for you to self-review and self-mark the script.
- The Mock Exam is set to time out after 4 hours. There will be a timer on the top right of the screen. You will be warned if the 4 hours is about to expire.
- We recommend that you use a wired internet connection wherever possible to reduce the likelihood of any internet outage during the Mock Exam.
- In the same way as the real exam environment, this Mock Exam must be sat in one attempt. Once you close out of the exam it will save your output to pdf. You will not be able to re-enter the exam or pick it up where you left off.

Link here:

https://ondemand.questionmark.eu/delivery/open.php?session=0445026000445026&customerid=612294&NAME=x&GROUP=x

Tell us what you think

Got comments or feedback on this book? Let us know.
Use your QR code reader:

Or, visit:
https://www.smartsurvey.co.uk/s/BFO4OC/

Need to get in touch with customer service?

www.bpp.com/request-support

Spotted an error?

https://learningmedia.bpp.com/pages/errata